Women and Culture Series

The Women and Culture Series is dedicated to books that illuminate the lives, roles, achievements, and status of women, past or present.

Fran Leeper Buss
Dignity: Lower Income Women Tell of Their Lives and Struggles
La Partera: Story of a Midwife

Valerie Kossew Pichanick
Harriet Martineau: The Woman and Her Work, 1802–76

Sandra Baxter and Marjorie Lansing
Women and Politics: The Visible Majority

Estelle B. Freedman
Their Sisters' Keepers: Women's Prison Reform in America, 1830–1930

Susan C. Bourque and Kay Barbara Warren
Women of the Andes: Patriarchy and Social Change in Two Peruvian Towns

Marion S. Goldman
Gold Diggers and Silver Miners: Prostitution and Social Life on the Comstock Lode

Page duBois
Centaurs and Amazons: Women and the Pre-History of the Great Chain of Being

Mary Kinnear
Daughters of Time: Women in the Western Tradition

Lynda K. Bundtzen
Plath's Incarnations: Woman and the Creative Process

Violet B. Haas and Carolyn C. Perrucci, editors
Women in Scientific and Engineering Professions

Sally Price
Co-wives and Calabashes

Patricia R. Hill
The World Their Household: The American Woman's Foreign Mission Movement and Cultural Transformation 1870–1920

Diane Wood Middlebrook and Marilyn Yalom, editors
Coming to Light: American Women Poets in the Twentieth Century

Leslie W. Rabine
Reading the Romantic Heroine: Text, History, Ideology

Joanne S. Frye
Living Stories, Telling Lives: Women and the Novel in Contemporary Experience

E. Frances White
Sierra Leone's Settler Women Traders: Women on the Afro-European Frontier

Catherine Parsons Smith and Cynthia S. Richardson
Mary Carr Moore, American Composer

Barbara Drygulski Wright, editor
Women, Work, and Technology: Transformations

Lynda Hart, editor
Making a Spectacle: Feminist Essays on Contemporary Women's Theatre

Verena Martinez-Alier
Marriage, Class and Colour in Nineteenth-Century Cuba: A Study of Racial Attitudes and Sexual Values in a Slave Society

Kathryn Strother Ratcliff et al., editors
Healing Technology: Feminist Perspectives

Mary S. Gossy
The Untold Story: Women and Theory in Golden Age Texts

Jocelyn Linnekin
Sacred Queens and Women of Consequence: Rank, Gender, and Colonialism in the Hawaiian Islands

Glenda McLeod
Virtue and Venom: Catalogs of Women from Antiquity to the Renaissance

Making a Spectacle

M A K I N G

CONTRIBUTORS

Stephanie Arnold

Gayle Austin

Nancy Backes

Jan Breslauer

Susan Carlson

Sue-Ellen Case

Rosemary Curb

Mary K. DeShazer

Elin Diamond

Jill Dolan

Yolanda Broyles González

Jonnie Guerra

Lynda Hart

Anita Plath Helle

Helene Keyssar

Vivian M. Patraka

Janelle Reinelt

Jenny S. Spencer

Margaret B. Wilkerson

EDITED AND WITH AN INTRODUCTION
BY LYNDA HART

A

SPECTACLE

FEMINIST ESSAYS ON CONTEMPORARY WOMEN'S THEATRE

THE UNIVERSITY OF MICHIGAN PRESS   ANN ARBOR

1992 1991   4 3

Library of Congress Cataloging-in-Publication Data

Making a spectacle : feminist essays on contemporary women's theatre /
Lynda Hart, editor
    p. cm. — (Women and culture series)
    Includes bibliographies.
    ISBN 0-472-09389-4 (alk. paper) ISBN 0-472-06389-8
(pbk. : alk. paper)
    1. American drama—Women authors—History and criticism.
2. American drama—20th century—History and criticism. 3. English
drama—Women authors—History and criticism. 4. English drama—20th
century—History and criticism. 5. Women in literature.
6. Feminist theater. I. Hart, Lynda, 1953- . II. Series.
PS338.W6M3 1989   88–28831
812'.54'099287—dc19   CIP

Acknowledgments

I would like to thank all the contributors for their collaboration with me on this
book. Special thanks to Mary DeShazer, Susan Carlson, and Anita Helle who read
drafts of my introduction and gave me very useful suggestions; Elin Diamond, Sue-
Ellen Case, Jill Dolan, and Vivian Patraka whose advice and encouragement are much
appreciated. I am grateful to all the photographers who donated their work for this
collection, Salli Lovelarkin for inspirational dialogue about feminism and theatre, Leslie Thrope for support and encouragement throughout the process, LeAnn Fields for
her commitment and enthusiasm, and Eunice Staples for her careful preparation of
parts of the manuscript.

Page v epigraph from "Enclave Esclave" by Catherine Clément, translated by Marilyn
Schuster, from *New French Feminisms,* ed. by Elaine Marks and Isabelle de Courtivon
(Amherst: University of Massachusetts Press, 1980), copyright © 1980 by The Uni-
versity of Massachusetts Press.

Foreseen, unforeseen spectacle. The setting up of a debate at the podium constructs, on the fringe of this particular spectacle, a counter-spectacle, from which certain characters begin to emerge. A hall where public meetings are usually held, a hall peopled with political echoes, the ghosts of banners, leaves little room for an exchange of theoretical discourses. It is an untenable structure, a performance straining the limits of the possible: a theoretical debate presented and set forth among intellectuals and for intellectuals on the sexuality of women. Between the audience and the stage, Italian footlights made of lights and wood: the too numerous audience, by convention, cannot intervene. It is on this point that the other spectacle will emerge: implicated yet meant to be mute, "the audience," essential character, will nevertheless intervene. It will speak and cause things to happen: with its own bodies and voices, by moving, shouting, upsetting the order of the other spectacle. It will cause and speak disorder in relation to the order of the debate: but as a character it plays its role in the complex ensemble formed by the podium and its listeners; and that ensemble is no longer a spectacle for anyone. And then the audience splits apart: anything but unanimous, divided, multiple.

—Catherine Clément

Contents

LYNDA HART

Introduction: Performing Feminism

> She is providing words, emotions, and an imaginative structure for others
> to inhabit and create anew onstage. A playwright—in this theoretical
> sense—thus makes other people speak and act—. . . . No wonder, then,
> that even the woman playwright with the mildest of messages is bound
> to be seen as an anomaly, if not an actual threat. Who knows what she
> will say once she gives voice?
>
> —Michelene Wandor

The above quotation is from Michelene Wandor's valuable study of British
women's theatre which bears the telling title *Carry On, Understudies.*[1] An
understudy is one who learns the part of another and waits prepared to appear as a substitute. It thus evokes the voices of women who are suppressed,
heard only when unforeseen circumstances make it necessary for them to speak
onstage, and then only as ventriloquists for the "real" actors. But in its nega-
tivity it announces their existence, creating knowledge of their presence and
urging them out of the shadows.

It also points to the critical neglect of women's theatre, clearly the genre
that has received the least scholarly attention. In 1975, Elaine Showalter said
that "feminist criticism has allowed us to see meaning in what previously has
been empty space."[2] But over a decade later, an abundance of books are now
available about women poets and prose writers, while feminist critics still
have much ground to break in our explorations of women's theatre. This
book's contribution to filling the still sparsely occupied critical space is "making a spectacle," in defiance of the warning generally given to women to
avoid having attention drawn to themselves, a prohibition against being publicly seen and heard. This collection of essays celebrates the intersection of
feminism and theatre; we write to disregard that injunction, appropriating
the stage to assert our own images and dismantle what seems to be the last
bastion of male hegemony in the literary arts.

Spectacle derives from the Latin *spectare,* "to behold." The power of the spectator, and of those who create the spectacles, is discovered in the dormant meaning of *see,* "a seat of authority, especially a throne." Seeing is also the root of *theatre,* from *theoria,* "a looking at," a speculation. The *theatron,* the place of viewing, has rendered the woman playwright anomalistic, deviant when visible. As a form, the drama is more public and social than the other literary arts. The woman playwright's voice reaches a community of spectators in a public place that has historically been regarded as a highly subversive, politicized environment. The theatre is the sphere most removed from the confines of domesticity, thus the woman who ventures to be heard in this space takes a greater risk than the woman poet or novelist, but it may also offer her greater potential for effecting social change. Wandor sees in the theatre an "extraordinary range of potential voice and subject matter which makes the advent of women writers into theatre both so necessary and so exciting."[3] The latter half of the twentieth century has seen an emergence of women playwrights in numbers equal to the entire history of their dramatic foremothers. The power inherent in this collective confrontation challenges the very structures of "reality" that have kept women behind the scenes.

With a subversive twist, Marilyn Frye playfully appropriates the Ur-metaphor for the drama, *theatrum mundi,* the world as stage, refocusing our attention on the power of the background and implicitly calling the woman as "stagehand" to emerge center stage:

> All eyes, all attention, all attachment must be focused on the play, which is Phallocratic Reality. Any notice of the stagehands must be oblique and filtered through interest in the play. Anything which threatens the fixation of attention on the play threatens a cataclysmic dissolution of Reality into Chaos. Even the thought of the possibility of distraction is a distraction. The ever-present potential for cosmological disaster lies with the background. . . . There is nothing in the nature of the background that disposes it to be appropriately tame.[4]

In Frye's analogy, Reality is shaped and fixed, like stage realism's *mise en scène.* The unified foreground is constructed to pass for what is essential, objective, actual. Feminist adjustment of the lens to the background reveals the singular perspective that has placed women outside of representation — hidden, offstage, invisible — while representation has nonetheless been grounded in women. Frye's stagehands and Wandor's understudies metonymically capture the paradoxical positioning of women in dramatic discourse that Teresa de Lauretis articulates: ". . . while culture originates from woman and is founded on the dream of her captivity, women are all but absent from history and cultural process."[5]

Feminist theory of dramatic respresentation simultaneously addresses the absence of women from conventional theatre while it struggles to construct alternative ways of seeing. In a genre laden with famous male-created female heroines, from Antigone, to Portia, to Nora, the feminist seer nonetheless recognizes the absence of women's experience in the tradition. Playwright and theorist Hélène Cixous tells us that she stopped going to the theatre because "it was like going to [her] own funeral." In the theatre she found "the horror of the murder scene repeated and intensified with more violence even than fiction," and declared that "a woman must die before the play can begin."[6]

Jeannette Savona points out that Cixous's "murder scene," which confronts the minimalization or depletion of women "by all historical, anthropological, or psychological theories of humankind and by all philosophical or linguistic systems of thought," was written shortly after Cixous's own debut as a playwright.[7] After producing five plays herself, Cixous's profound skepticism shifted into a recognition of the power inherent in feminist theatrical articulations. According to Savona, Cixous began to see "the playwright's miraculous power to unite and disturb her audience, and perhaps even change them."[8] Such a transformation in attitude signals the emergence of strategies for foregrounding women's reality on the stage. By appropriating certain dramatic conventions and methods, subverting their customary usage and turning the lens of "objectivity" to re-present women through their own looking glasses, the women playwrights discussed in this book and the authors who call attention to their disruptions are canceling and deforming the structures that have held women framed, stilled, embedded, revoking the forms that have misrepresented women and "killed them into art."[9]

If the feminist writer's first efforts were investigations of the male-inscribed literary tradition, a second and ongoing effort has been to document women's realities as constructed by women writers. A shift in the last decade has been toward rigorous exploration of the language of representation itself. The constitutive dramatic aesthetic, the "mirror held up to nature," is a particularly pernicious concept for the feminist critic of the theatre, firmly entrenched as it has been by the Aristotelian directive which has had a powerful and lasting hold on the drama, dictating a linear structure that "imitates an action" embedded in conflict, climaxes, recognitions, and resolutions.[10] As feminist criticism has taught us, Woman and Nature have been equated in patriarchal discourses, thus woman becomes the screen onto which men project their fantasies of women, or rather of Woman—the monolithic Other. This aesthetic

of mimesis has maintained the hegemony of realism in the drama which effectively masks the *re-creational* power of mimesis. The drama then must be challenged not only on the basis of what it represents but how it reproduces meaning through representation.

The assumption of objectivity which informs mimetic theory presup-
poses a division of experience, encoding differences as Difference grounded
in gender polarity. The supposed objectivity of the artist must have something
to look at, something that is Other than itself. As the subject/author records
nature, eschewing selectively structured representations that are shaped by the
personal experience and historical specificity of the perceiver, there is the
persistent denial that "objectivity" is simply one lens among many. The feminist critic must seek ways out of this discourse to bring about change, for
this is the master's way of seeing, and as Toril Moi reminds us "as long as
the master's scopophilia, love of looking, remains satisfied, his domination is
secure."[11]

The shift in feminist perspective from discovering and creating positive
images of women in the content of the drama to analyzing and disrupting
the ideological codes embedded in the inherited structures of dramatic representation is documented in the articles contained in this collection. Feminist
readers will remember Gubar and Gilbert's well-known perception of the
woman writer's dilemma as they discuss it in the context of the evil stepmother in *Snow White*. Remembering that the evil stepmother trusts the wisdom of the mirror and dies dancing frenetically in a pair of red-hot shoes,
Gilbert and Gubar point out that the "Queen's looking glass speaks with the
King's voice," and they ask: "Does the Queen try to sound like the King . . .
or does she 'talk back' to him in her own vocabulary, her own timbre, insisting on her own viewpoint?"[12]

But when the feminist critic shifts her perspective from the plight of the
Queen within the narrative to the structure of the frame that contains her,
then the Queen has neither of these options. She must move outside of the
frame, for the voice of the patriarchy speaks not only to the Queen but through
her. When we recognize that there are no evil stepmothers, the image in the
mirror becomes a chimera in both of its meanings—a fabulous monster en-
gendered by the fears of its author and an imaginary projected illusion created
and maintained by focusing on the foreground. When the understudies seize
the stage, when the stagehands come out from the wings and address the audience, Reality is exposed as illusionism and the woman playwright can begin
to be heard.

In contemporary women's plays we continue to see women experiencing what Elizabeth Lenk describes as "those terrible moments when woman searches for herself in the mirror and cannot find herself. The mirror image has got lost somewhere, the gaze of men does not reflect it back to women."[13] In one of the most important articles in feminist film theory, Laura Mulvey holds that the gaze is itself male in the mainstream cinematic tradition in which the woman's "to-be-looked-at-ness" is actually built "into the spectacle itself." Mulvey's argument that "cinematic codes create a gaze, a world, and an object, thereby producing an illusion cut to the measure of desire," does not transfer simply to the construction of the dramatic apparatus, but nonetheless has significant implications for the feminist theatre critic.[14] The forms and structures of patriarchal discourse are, in Adrienne Rich's words, a "game of mirrors," and the woman who looks into the tradition for self-reflection often experiences "psychic disequilibrium," sensations that may feel like brushes with madness.[15]

In Sue Townsend's *The Great Celestial Cow*, Sita is accused of madness when she insists that her image is not contained within the glass. As she sits alone in front of the mirror she addresses her absence: "Sita, where are you? I don't know where you are. Come back to me. You've been away so long I'm afraid I won't know you when you come back." Sita searches for herself in her body, pinching her arm, pulling her hair, punching her belly. When her husband, Raj, intrudes on this scene, he wrenches her violently in front of the mirror and screams at her: "You are there, you mad woman, you are there. You want proof?" For "proof" he slaps her, knocking her to the floor.[16]

The women in Caryl Churchill's *Light Shining in Buckinghamshire* steal a mirror from a house they pillage, an unbroken mirror, one in which "you see your whole body at once." "They must know what they look like all the time," one woman realizes, "and now we do."[17] By stealing the mirror, the women anticipate seeing themselves, the privilege formerly reserved for the ruling class, the royalty, the real.

The exits out of this framing mirror will be both escapes and attacks—Cixous's "sorties."[18] One possible site of escape is through the body. Alone among all literary productions, the theatre's medium is the physical body—the virtual corporality of the text makes the drama unique. Since it is primarily women's bodies that have been politicized in systems of exchange, the textualization of the female body poses special problems and potential for the woman playwright. David Cole argues that the theatre alone "provides the opportunity of experiencing imaginative truth as present truth. In theatre imaginative events take on for a moment the presentness of physical event. . . . All the arts, to some extent, make *present;* theatre alone makes *presence*."[19] This "making presence" can for the woman playwright be both the power and danger of the drama. Cixous sees the theatre's ability "to get across the living, breathing, speaking body" as a "fortunate position" and the theatre's raison d'être.[20]

If the female body is at the root of male fear, the blank space that he must master, then it also has great power for the woman playwright as a medium for articulation. As Susan Gubar reminds us, "the female body has always been feared for its power to articulate *itself*."[21] Only in the theatre is the word made flesh, and thus holds the potential to become, in Adrienne Rich's words, "a resource rather than a destiny."[22] With a cautious awareness of the threat inherent in a reaffirmation of essentialism, the woman dramatist can delicately play with the body. In this genre where it is *sine qua non,* she cannot overlook its power for transformation.

Joanna Russ challenges an audience to confront the way in which women's bodies have been laden with signs that directly affect their material reality and conflict with their sense of self as subject in her one-act play, *Window Dressing.* In the opening image a woman is seen on the stage standing silent and still, posed. She does not make an entrance; she is simply there for the spectators to hold in their gaze for a few suspended moments. She is enclosed in a glass case that is both window and mirror. The glass case is of course held within a larger frame, the playing space, so she is doubly on display. Russ creates an ambiguous and resistant moment in the theatre by exploiting the theatre's unique ability to cause a disequilibrium in the audience that relies on the fact of the female body. We do not know, in these first few moments, if Marcia is a mannequin or a "real woman." When she begins to speak, her entry into the symbolic world of discourse may lead an audience to infer that she is a subject unto herself. But the verbal discourse and the visual image are disjunctive. For when Marcia does speak she identifies herself as an object, a mannequin. Her identity is determined by the clothing she wears that changes from scene to scene as she is manipulated by a male dresser's hands. On the stage, the fact of the actress's body is a striking reminder of the way in which women's bodies are used to facilitate systems of exchange. The "living doll" assumes whatever life is given to her by unseen hands.

Marcia's nascent emergence into personhood is signaled by her acquisition of language. Russ's bold presentation of a woman's body as politicized space confronts the spectators with an image of woman in the object position, and insists that we witness her difficult recognition of herself as subject and object simultaneously. In the first scene Marcia denies any discomfort with her objectification. But her words belie this claim when the lights in her show-case begin to dim:

> When they turn the lights out in the evening, you can hear a little sigh-ing sound, like a hundred leaves all falling, drifting and circling down. That's all of us. We die each time the lights are turned out.[23]

These words on the printed page become corporeal in performance, a visceral manifestation of a woman's alienation from even the most fundamental space that she might own—her body.

The female body and its costumes are manipulated by Pam Gems to dis-arm the dominant culture's expectations in *Queen Christina*. An audience pre-pared to meet the Queen may find themselves enchanted along with the suitor-Prince as "a beautiful young woman . . . wearing a simple but beautiful riding habit" walks onto the stage.[24] Gems invites her audience to enter the play from the male suitor's perspective so that we are affronted and baffled by the rude and slovenly "man" who is overly intimate with the "Queen." When the battered man in hunting clothes turns out to be Christina herself, and the mis-recognized woman in riding clothes is recognized as Ebba, Christina's lover, Gems effectively confronts her audience with received ideas about mascu-line and feminine appearance. Christina's entrance is a set-up that reveals the politicization of the body and its costumes and disrupts the dominant order's assumption of heterosexuality.

Gems's subtle subversion depends primarily on crossdressing, a strategy for the playwright to foreground the cultural imposition of gender through costume. In most conventional definitions of acting, the assumption that a "real self" exists beneath the persona, or mask, is fundamental. Thus, as An-nette Kuhn points out, crossdressing allows for a "vision of fluidity of gender options . . . a utopian prospect of release from the ties of sexual difference that bind us into meaning, discourse, culture."[25] Caryl Churchill takes the threat of disrupting fixed gender identity one step further by *crossgendering* characters in *Cloud 9*. Whereas crossdressing is usually sexual disguise—an audience either knows that the characters' costumes and traditional gender identities are disjunctive or they seek to discover this information in the play's narrative—Churchill's crossgendering suggests a deeper level of gender con-struction and imposition. Churchill appropriates a convention of classical the-atre and subverts it into social commentary. We are not meant to see behind the mask of the man who plays Betty, for example, in *Cloud 9*. Instead, we are confronted with a recognizably male actor playing a woman's part. Thus Betty's words, her first speech for example, establish multiple ambiguities:

> I live for Clive. The whole aim of my life
> Is to be what he looks for in a wife.
> I am a man's creation as you see,
> And what men want is what I want to be.[26]

Here the gap between the dialogue and the visual image of the actor creates a disjunction that on one level highlights the feminist distinction between gender and biological sexuality. On the one hand, Betty is the subservient wife whose absence of self is revealed through her internalized male identification. On another level, the image of the male actor raises the question of the constitution of male desire. Since "Betty" is a man, then "what men want" is not only a male-created image of woman, but also a homoerotic vision displaced where it can be mastered and controlled at a safe distance.

By seizing the body and subverting its customary representations, these playwrights create a theatrical discourse that highlights the politicization of feminine appearance, foregrounding the categorization, containment and misrecognition of women's diversity. The presence of the living, speaking body in the theatre maximizes the potential for such startling reconceptualizations. The feminist playwright's collection of subversive exits from the dominant discourse multiplies in power when the physical stage space is restructured and acknowledged as a political arena.

As Nancy Reinhardt points out, historical evidence attests to the relationship between the male-defined *polis* and the politics of stage space: "The dominant *public* action both on the stage and in the audience stresses a male world in which women are either kept to the sides, in recesses, or are placed on display for the male viewer."[27] In ancient, medieval, and Renaissance drama, especially in the tragedy and serious drama, "stage-center [the open neutral acting space] is reserved for men . . . the 'doers' of the main action. The sides, background, niches and balconies function as the inner domestic space where women are usually kept."[28]

Feminist critiques of capitalist patriarchy have demonstrated how social spaces have been colonized by men, relegating women and other marginalized people to minimal spaces cordoned off by the privileged classes. This colonization of space occurs materially and metaphorically, and the theatrical acting space, which is material more exactly than in any of the other literary genres, can be manipulated to disclose and critique women's confinement while suggesting liberating strategies from the patriarchal order. In *Mollie Bailey's Traveling Family Circus: Featuring Scenes from the Life of Mother Jones,* Megan Terry constructs a play with a prologue that addresses women's spatial dilemma through visual representation. Two Celtic queens are suspended over the audience on a trapeze as they cross the Irish Sea on a raft. This simple opening image suggests the precarious equilibrium of women who venture out of the domestic space; it is a dangerous balance that these women must maintain in a patriarchal world.

Terry's women are on journeys out of their confinement. But many women playwrights continue to use stage space in conventional ways, particularly writers who have received a significant amount of critical acclaim, like Marsha Norman and Beth Henley. The anxiety of women who are limited to the hearth is evident in the grotesque distortions of Henley's female characters. In *Crimes of the Heart,* for example, the MaGrath sisters' action takes place exclusively in the kitchen. Although they exit that space, we are never shown any alternative area for them to inhabit. Norman's *'night, Mother* is probably the most powerful statement of a woman's confinement in contemporary drama. Jessie has only one place to go—behind the door where she commits suicide. Her lack of mobility is neatly captured metaphorically in the shoebox that contains the items she bequeaths; Jessie's possibilities in the world encompass a space no larger than that shoebox.

The absence of opportunity and choice that these interior spaces symbolize can lead to bitterness, anxiety, hysteria, and violence, as Maureen Duffy's play, *Rites,* powerfully demonstrates. *Rites* is set in a "ladies room," a set that is ironically chosen as a space that commonly excludes men. Duffy's play is a contemporary revision of *The Bacchae*—Agave's story rather than Pentheus's. Like the women in Clare Boothe Luce's *The Women,* who are trapped in spaces that have conventionally been defined as women's rooms—bedrooms, kitchens, beauty parlors—Duffy's all-woman cast is enclosed in a conventional woman's space. Luce's and Duffy's characters cannot form communities with other women and their actions range from petty bickering and husband stealing in Luce's play to life-denial and murder in Duffy's play. Although the women in *Rites* are united in their felt oppressions and hatred of men, their feelings are not politically articulated. At the end of the play the women kill an androgynous character who enters the washroom whom they mistake for a male but turns out to be a female. Duffy describes the concept that informs her finale: "In the very moment when the women have got their own back on men for their type-casting in an orgasm of violence, they find they have destroyed themselves and in death there is no difference."[29]

The play's action criticizes the women for their separatist desires and their transformation of oppression into violence on the level of the plot. However, in the wider context of the play, Duffy makes an important comment on the women's behavior through the play's scenic design. She appropriates the dumb-show convention as a crucial frame for the play's action. Before an audience meets the cast of characters, we witness the construction of the set in a slow and deliberate pantomime as a procession of workmen, gender specific but de-individualized by their white uniforms, silently construct the set. In a solemn ritual they carry on the pieces of the lavatory and build it as the spectators watch them; then they disappear as the women take the stage.

The dumb-show device attacks the formal conventions of realism and establishes a frame of reference from which the remainder of the play must be observed. The device crucially reminds us that the space within which the all-woman cast act out their vulgarity and violence is male-created. The ladies room is far from being a liberated space; on the contrary, it is a privilege designed to distort women's action.

Maria Irene Fornes also uses stage space and audience movement to critique women's social oppression. In part two of *Fefu and Her Friends,* the action occurs in four different spaces simultaneously. Audience members are required to move from space to space in order to follow the action. Fornes innovatively uses the set to draw the audience physically into the environment that her women characters occupy so that the spectators must viscerally experience its limitations and confinement. Once again we see the unique ability of theatre to insist on spectators' immediate, felt confrontation with these women's experience. While I could cite numerous examples of women's plays that represent confinement and enclosure, there are feminist playwrights who are creating alternative visions in which time and space are held open, collapsed, or suspended, and women characters experience liberation.

For example, in Caryl Churchill's *Top Girls,* the time/space continuum is disrupted when she brings both real and imaginary women from diverse cultures and historical periods into a contemporary setting. Marlene, a twentieth-century white career executive, has lunch with a cast of characters that includes the ninth-century Pope Joan, disguised as a man; Patient Griselda, the obedient wife of Chaucer's *The Clerk's Tale*; Lady Nijo, a Japanese emperor's courtesan; Isabella Bird, a nineteenth-century Scot; and Dull Gret, the woman in Brueghel's painting who leads an army of women through hell fighting devils. Eve Merriam's precursive play, *Out of Our Fathers' House,* similarly brings together women from various communities to transcend time and space. These groupings challenge the realistic theatre's adherence to linearity and spatial contiguity. The reality they mirror is multiple, diverse, transformative, relational, and associative, not fixed and isolated.

In the New York–based lesbian-feminist company WOW café, the boundaries are further broken. This company uses a modified platform stage with a curtained area, but this separation is disrupted by the spectators' free-mingling among the performers who sometimes invite audience participation. Lois Weaver, one of the founding members of the troupe, often arrives in full costume and remains in character before, during, and after the performance for a party where it is difficult to distinguish among performers, characters, and spectators.[30] These and other women playwrights and women-centered troupes are seeking new relationships between the performing space and the audience that challenge the hierarchical structures of mainstream theatre. Communal creation replaces the "anxiety of influence" that forces a singular thinker to attempt an overthrow of his precursors.[31]

As a cultural and literary construct, the theatre's advantage is in its multiple methods of conveying meaning. In no other genre does the writer have access to the power and challenge of working with the body and material space. Nonetheless, language remains a primary tool for the dramatist. Feminist analysis of the essentially masculinist structure of language poses the problem of dis-covering and de-forming linguistic patterns for the feminist playwright. Megan Terry has attacked the assumption that "words alone make great drama," while at the same time foregrounding the oppressive power of naming.[32] In her play, *American King's English for Queens,* Terry insisted upon the meaningfulness of language in the midst of the absurdist movement in drama that devalued language.[33] In this play, Silver Morgan is captured by the Connell family in their "snipe hunt," and she accepts her definition because she is so named. Feminists can appreciate Terry's snipe hunt as a metaphorical search for the monolithic Woman, an elusive and oppressive expression of male fantasy that denies the multiplicity of women's experience.

An important stage in the disruption of language is clearing a space for new questions to be asked. Teresa de Lauretis refers to the "spaces of contradiction" where the woman writer can "turn back the question upon itself and re-make stories . . . destabili[zing] and finally alter[ing] the meaning of representations."[34] Such a language of contradiction is incipient, though incompletely realized, even in women's plays that are relatively conventional in their structures.

Marsha Norman's first play, *Getting Out,* draws upon the playwright's personal relationship with a young woman who had followed a familiar "deviant" social path—from prostitution to robbery to murder—and an institutionalized route to "recovery"—from reform schools for girls to the state penitentiary. In the dominant discourse, the formulated questions about Norman's character, Arlie, might have been "where did she go wrong and how was she, or wasn't she, reformed?" Instead, Norman's play asks how the dominant order *deformed* Arlie and how Arlene (Arlie after getting out) can exist with integrity in a society that has marked her as damaged goods. By using the divided self characterization Arlie/Arlene, Norman deviously critiques the culture that blames and punishes the victim. Significantly, Arlie demands that she be called Arlene, renaming herself in an effort toward liberation.

Other women playwrights experiment more boldly with linguistic patterns as they seek to express their characters' experience. In *for colored girls who have considered suicide/when the rainbow is enuf,* Ntozake Shange seeks a way to "learn our common symbols, / preen them / and share them with the world."[35] Shange's women are born out of silence and invisibility into voice and community. The language of her choreopoems splits open syntax, interrupts linearity, deforms and fragments sentences as she captures the sound and rhythm of the voices that emerge from women's bodies, touching, creating meanings from the depth of their absence. From the "spook house" of her confinement, the lady in brown hears

> another song with no singers
> lyrics / no voices
> & interrupted solos
> unseen performances[36]

Shange's women of color begin as fragmented voices, but their isolation diminishes as the play progresses; their choreopoems overlap and conjoin in theme and repetition. Their movements bring them closer to each other where they weave together and hear each other's speech. Movement alone in this play creates a language, a dance of difference and diversity that nonetheless reveals shared experience. Shange rejects the white male master's discourse, choosing instead a language that highlights her character's eccentricity and marginality.

Josette Féral describes feminine discourse as an effort to "express the porous, uncentered nature of women; it is a policy favoring the fragment rather than the whole, the point rather than the line, dispersion rather than concentration, heterogeneity rather than homogeneity."[37] Diversity and simultaneity of voices is a strong feature of this language. In *Letters Home,* a play based on the relationship of Aurelia and Sylvia Plath, Rose Leiman Goldemburg creates two voices, mother's and daughter's, that are at times simultaneous and yet diverse, exploring the possibilities for oneness and difference. Her characters "range in and out of each other's space" physically and linguistically as their bodies and voices cross, overlap, intersect, and change places, creating a duet that explodes the myths surrounding these two particular women while also confronting the institutionalization of mother/daughter bonds. By listening to their own and each other's speech, these characters insist through their dialogue that spectators question convenient assumptions about women's lives.

Language, space, and the body are loci for the woman playwright to dramatically challenge the images of women determined in dominant discourses. Not one, but all of these sites must be re-visioned for the feminist enterprise to succeed onstage. As more and more women begin to choose the stage as an arena for their visions, we, as critics, are called upon to discuss, analyze, and demonstrate their efforts. Our efforts combined are clearing public spaces for the foregrounding of women's realities.

Maria Irene Fornes looks forward to a time "when we start respecting imagery and sensibility which are unique," a time when "the gender of the writer will be the last thing we will think of."[38] The theatre at present is a long way from such a time. The writers in this volume share the energy of creating and revealing meaning in what previously has been empty space. As feminist critics of the theatre, we are collectively engaged in bringing back what playwright Joan Schenkar has called "news from the end of the nerves . . . feelings that are otherwise forbidden, forms that are as yet unimagined."[39]

The eighteen articles in this collection are divided into four conceptual categories that point to the methodologies employed by the writers. None of the categories, however, is exclusive of each other; many if not most of the articles cross categories in some ways since feminist perspectives are rarely singular. For the readers' convenience I have grouped the articles in ways that I hope will be useful.

A word about the politics and design of this book: it is not an attempt to form a female canon of playwrights. The playwrights chosen for discussion were not prescribed by the editor. The idea for this book occurred to me when, in 1984, I was teaching a course on contemporary women playwrights and found that no single collection existed that brought together a wide-ranging group of scholarly articles in English on contemporary women's theatre. I began to seek out those writers whose work in the field was familiar to me through journal articles, conference presentations, and word of mouth. Hence these articles were all in some stage of process although only one had been previously published.

These are then the ideas and the playwrights that critics were interested in pursuing. Out of their interests this book has evolved. Obviously there are many women playwrights whose work is not discussed in this book. Diversity was a goal for the collection, not comprehensiveness. The advantage in planning a book without a prescriptive ordering of the parts is in the excitement of discovering the multiple threads of analysis by individual writers that weave together into some startling webs of meaning and understanding. As editor of the volume I have followed a feminist process to the best of my ability; it is indeed a collective undertaking. All of the contributors have graciously offered me advice and we have exchanged and criticized each other's work during the process.

In Part 1 I have grouped five essays that analyze the uses of metaphor in women's plays. Vivian Patraka's essay, "Mass Culture and Metaphors of Menace," opens the section with an analysis of metaphors drawn from cannibalism and cooking, pathology and freakishness, performance and ritual in four plays by Joan Schenkar. Together these metaphors form what Patraka calls "an intertextual system of tropes" that track obsession and what it represses. Unlike the conventional use of metaphor, to make the strange familiar, Schenkar's tropes are estranging conceptualizations that menace an audience's psychological defenses. This obsessional use of metaphor extends to the way Schenkar frames each play with a form of mass culture and so reveals the repressed of each form's content and convention.

Nancy Backes's essay examines the revisioning of metaphors drawn from the preparation and consumption of food in Tina Howe's plays. Feminist analysis of the "intimate relationship between food and women," and its often destructive social and psychological consequences manifested in eating disorders, serves as a ground for Backes's analysis. Is it possible, she asks, "for women to take a bite of an unknown fruit, one plucked from their own fantastic orchards?" In Tina Howe, Backes finds a writer who is one of "the *new* nouvelle cuisine's top chefs" in her representations of women characters who "control their bodies without starving them."

In "Music as Metaphor: New Plays of Black Women," Margaret Wilkerson shows how contemporary plays by women of color use musical metaphors in ways that exceed the traditional mood music or special numbers of a musical. The centrality of music in the works of many women of color is represented in these plays by black women through metaphors that express "the deepest, unspoken feelings and experiences of human existence."

Gayle Austin's "The Madwoman in the Spotlight: Plays of Maria Irene Fornes" draws on Gilbert and Gubar's concept of the palimpsestic madwoman as the author's double (*Madwoman in the Attic*) and shows how Fornes recreates and extends this concept in plays that dramatically render women's confinement and sometimes escape. In Fornes's stagings, the madwoman becomes social and actual. By bringing her into the spotlight, the metaphor takes shape viscerally and Fornes's plays become radical movements "into the attic" where the madwoman "can no longer be seen as a mere metaphorical disturbance."

The final essay in Part 1 is Mary DeShazer's "Rejecting Necrophilia: Ntozake Shange and the Warrior Re-Visioned" which explores the possibilities of women as metaphorical warriors in three of Shange's plays as well as in the playwright's self-definition. An image steeped in pejorative connotations for many feminists, the woman as warrior nonetheless figures prominently in the writings of radical feminists and particularly women of color like Shange who defines herself as a "war correspondent . . . in a war of cultural and aesthetic aggression." DeShazer begins with an overview of the image as it has been claimed or disclaimed by feminists, then discusses its evolution in Shange's drama.

In Part 2, "Reformulating the Question," four writers undertake the difficult work of exposing assumptions that are deeply entrenched in traditional critical discourses. Through these writers' feminist lenses, new questions can be asked about old forms. Susan Carlson's essay, "Revisionary Endings: Pam Gems's *Aunt Mary* and *Camille*," analyzes the way in which Gems's plays take on and revise traditional assumptions about comedic and tragic endings. The "revised and revisionary" endings in these plays represent social and sexual changes through transformed resolutions in novel relationships among the characters. Carlson argues that Gems's endings insistently "re-interpret theatre structures so that the disproportionate power of conclusions works for, not against, women and others on the margins of society."

Jonnie Guerra's contribution, "Beth Henley: Female Quest and the Family Play Tradition," addresses Henley's persistently negative images of women and seeks an explanation for Henley's aborted female quests in her adoption of the dominant male structure—the American family play. Henley's attempt to chart quests for female autonomy is undermined by the family play's structural limitations in presenting female subjectivity. Guerra argues that ultimately this structure is "an inhospitable context for portrayals of women's journeys toward autonomy."

Lynda Hart's essay, "'They Don't Even Look Like Maids Anymore,'" reconsiders questions about the infamous Papin murderers whose motives have been explored by historians and psychologists, and whose story has been dramatically retold by Jean Genet and Wendy Kesselman. Unlike Genet's more psychoanalytic approach, Kesselman seeks in large part to position the sisters historically. In the historical records the Papin sisters' sexual identity was the subject of much speculation. Kesselman does not, however, choose to leave the sisters' sexual lives ambiguous. In her play, their sexual preference is clearly for each other. My essay reopens this material for exploration of the relationship between Kesselman's uses of history, violence, and lesbian identity.

The final article in this part is Jenny Spencer's "Marsha Norman's *She-tragedies.*" Spencer reconsiders the eighteenth-century form denoted *she-tragedies* by the critical establishment as an apt and revealing description of Norman's plays, *Getting Out, 'night, Mother,* and *The Laundromat.* From this unusual angle Spencer analyzes Norman's female characters in "painfully contradictory" dilemmas, called upon as they are to "assume and maintain their sexual identity" under conditions that they cannot control. If little or no "real" action occurs in Norman's plays, Spencer argues that the dialogue between women *is* the action, but that finally it is a language that offers the women limited access to autonomy, caught as they are in social circumstances that dictate male misrecognition of women as shaping and determining female subjectivity.

The writers in Part 3 are engaged in what Helene Keyssar calls "doing dangerous history—historical explorations [that] seek not only to discover the forgotten achievements of women but to examine the conditions under which gender conflicts have repeatedly arisen and repeatedly been resolved such that women have remained subordinate to men." In collaboration with Jan Breslauer, Keyssar's essay begins Part 3 with "Making Magic Public: Megan Terry's Traveling Family Circus." Terry's 1983 collaboration with JoAnne Metcalf, *Mollie Bailey's Traveling Family Circus: Featuring Scenes from the Life of Mother Jones,* brings together the historical political activist, Mother Jones, and the fictive ringmistress of a circus, Mollie Bailey. Terry's play "orients the spectator towards alternative ways of viewing the present and the past." Breslauer and Keyssar argue that the unconventional spatial and temporal configurations in this play challenge an audience to consider history as "as much a human [and usually male] construct as any other enterprise." At the same time, the play frees an audience to imagine a world authored and transformed so that "differences among women as well as between women and men [are] a source of strength rather than weakness."

Stephanie Arnold's contribution, "Dissolving the Half Shadows: Japanese American Women Playwrights," offers a historical perspective on the emergence of playwrights Momoko Iko, Wakako Yamauchi, Karen Yamashita, and Velina Houston. Arnold discusses their Issei (first-generation immigrant) plays, which document their mothers' histories and dramatize modes of survival, and the Nisei plays, which examine "the uneasy relationships between women and men whose reliance on traditional roles has been shattered by war." Arnold's essay is rich in information obtained through interviews with Japanese American producers, playwrights and performers. She brings these writers out of the shadows into a spotlight where they can be recognized as "part of a vibrant diversity of theatre throughout the West."

Anita Plath Helle's article, "Re-Presenting Women Writers Onstage: A Retrospective to the Present," argues that "the creation of a new literary history remains at issue in a number of biographical dramas about women writers." Helle analyzes recent plays that recreate the experience of women writers, including Gertrude Stein and Sylvia Plath, and political activists like Susan B. Anthony and Maud Gonne. Helle considers whether or not these women become subjects of their own discourse when they are recreated onstage. These plays are important not simply because they present images of women, but when and if they "document and examine the ways in which the anomalous woman writer is created and maintained."

In "Toward a Re-Vision of Chicano Theatre History: The Women of El Teatro Campesino," Yolanda Broyles González focuses on the lost legacy of women in El Teatro and begins to map the contours of this cultural erasure. Broyles González describes the struggles and contributions of Chicana women which significantly alter established versions of Chicano theater history. She finds in the women's roles "the most enduring contradictions within the company," and she charts the accomplishments of Chicana women who have opened up new territory for subsequent generations. Broyles González's feminist excavation and reclamation shifts our attention to the women's creative process, destabilizing the male-centered heroic, monolithic image of the troupe. Her essay is a pioneering work in reconstructing women's participation in the over two hundred years of Mexican history in what is today the southwestern U.S.

Janelle Reinelt's "Michelene Wandor: Artist and Ideologue" finishes this part. As critic, historian, activist, and playwright, Michelene Wandor's work has offered us extensive analysis of the relationship between the Women's and Gay Movements in Britain and British fringe theatre. Reinelt's essay demonstrates that Wandor, "although possessing her own specific, personal history . . . provides a prototype for the experiences of many women who began to work seriously in the British theatre during the ferment of the sixties." Reinelt gives us an overview of Wandor's crucial work which ensures "that the history [of feminist and gay theatre in Britain] is publicly acknowledged and recorded for the future." In the second part of her essay, Reinelt discusses Wandor's diversity in subject matter, staging experiments, and working conditions, in three very different plays—*Whores D'Oeuvres, AID Thy Neighbor,* and *The Wandering Jew.*

The writers in Part 4 are concerned with the relationship between theatre and ideology. Their essays analyze the success or failure of women playwrights to exceed, disturb, or disrupt the limitations of dramatic representation. Elin Diamond's essay, "(In)Visible Bodies in Churchill's Theater," begins with an analysis of a double strain in Churchill's plays: "on the one hand, a commitment to the apparatus of representation . . . on the other hand, a consistent though less obvious attention to the powers of theatrical illusion. . . ." Diamond focuses on the body as a "kind of limit-text of representational information, a special site of inquiry and struggle." After examining a range of selective Churchill plays, she concentrates on *Fen* and *A Mouthful of Birds,* arguing that the inability of the "orificial body"—"the polymorphous, drive-ridden, repressed, instinctual" body—to appear in representational frames takes on specific political resonance in these plays.

In "Toward a Butch-Femme Aesthetic," Sue-Ellen Case considers the problematics of women inhabiting the traditional subject position and explores the difficulty in articulating possibilities for a new heterogeneous, heteronomous position. Case argues that heterosexual contexts for the female subject are sites of continuing entrapment for women. She offers an alternative—the butch-femme couple as a "dynamic duo" presented in performance by the lesbian-feminist company Split Britches. Within this "space of seduction" Case finds a place where the female subject can be recuperated and playfully cohabit, "free from biological determinism, elitist essentialism, and the heterosexist cleavage of sexual difference."

Rosemary Curb's "Mirrors Moving Beyond Frames: Sandra Shotlander's *Framework* and *Blind Salome*" finds in this Australian playwright's works female characters who seek centers for themselves on the peripheries or altogether outside traditional frames of reference. Shotlander's experiments with stage design permit characters and spectators some escape from the confinement of conventional representation. In *Framework,* for instance, one technique "reverses the specular process by making objects ordinarily seen be the seers of action." Curb defines the women's action in *Framework* as a "lesbian quest," a reality outside the frame of phallocentrism. In *Blind Salome,* the quest is not specifically lesbian, but in this play the female characters also search for, and find, ways to shed "the confining and blinding veils created by the male gaze." In both plays, art and history serve as mirrors that the female characters appropriate to their own visions.

The final essay in the collection is Jill Dolan's "Bending Gender to Fit the Canon: The Politics of Production." Dolan's essay uses Norman's *'night, Mother* as an exemplary case study to show how a woman playwright's intentions can be deformed through the process of production and by critical reception. Dolan exposes the political agenda at work in canon formation and warns against the creation of a new monolithic subject position for women's plays that would merely replicate the universal, exclusionary subject position that has dominated theatre history. By examining *'night, Mother* against the context of traditional texts, Dolan heightens awareness of the ideology expressed in the theatre as cultural discourse.

NOTES

Since this introduction was written, two major books in the field have been published: Sue-Ellen Case, *Feminism and Theatre* (New York: Methuen, 1988), and Jill Dolan, *The Feminist Spectator as Critic* (Ann Arbor: UMI Research Press, 1988).

1. Michelene Wandor, *Carry On, Understudies: Theatre and Sexual Politics* (London and New York: Routledge and Kegan Paul, 1986), p. 128.

2. Elaine Showalter, "Review Essay," *Signs* 1, no. 2 (Winter 1975): 435.

3. *Understudies*, p. 128.

4. Marilyn Frye, *The Politics of Reality: Essays in Feminist Theory* (New York: The Crossing Press, 1983), p. 170.

5. Teresa de Lauretis, *Alice Doesn't: Feminism, Semiotics, Cinema* (Bloomington, Ind.: Indiana University Press, 1984), p. 13.

6. Hélène Cixous, "Aller à la mer," trans. Barbara Kerslake, *Modern Drama* 27, no. 4 (December 1984): 546.

7. Jeannette Laillou Savona, "French Feminism and Theatre: An Introduction," *Modern Drama* 27, no. 4 (December 1984): 541–42.

8. Ibid., p. 542.

9. Sandra Gilbert and Susan Gubar, *The Madwoman in the Attic* (New Haven: Yale University Press, 1979), p. 17.

10. For further discussion of the significance of Aristotle's *Poetics* and its implications for the feminist theatre critic, see Nancy S. Reinhardt, "New Directions for Feminist Criticism in the Theatre and the Related Arts," in *A Feminist Perspective in the Academy: The Difference It Makes,* ed. Elizabeth Langland and Walter Gove, pp. 25–51 (Chicago: University of Chicago Press, 1981). See also Sue-Ellen Case, *Feminism and Theatre* (New York: Methuen, 1988) for a more extended analysis.

11. Toril Moi, *Sexual/Textual Politics: Feminist Literary Criticism* (New York: Methuen, 1985), p. 132.

12. Sandra M. Gilbert and Susan Gubar, *The Madwoman in the Attic,* p. 46.

13. Elizabeth Lenk, "The Self-Reflecting Woman," in *Feminist Aesthetics,* ed. Gisela Ecker, trans. Harriet Anderson, p. 57 (Boston: Beacon Press, 1985).

14. Laura Mulvey, "Visual Pleasure and Narrative Cinema," *Screen* 16, no. 3 (Autumn 1975): 11.

15. Adrienne Rich, "Invisibility in Academe," *Blood, Bread, and Poetry: Selected Prose 1979–1985* (New York: W. W. Norton, 1986), p. 199. Rich is speaking specifically of lesbian experience in this essay, but she points out that "lesbians are not the only people to know it" (invisibility), and of course academe is only one example of a context in which such erasure occurs.

16. Sue Townsend, *The Great Celestial Cow* (London: Methuen, 1984), p. 22.

17. Caryl Churchill, *Light Shining in Buckinghamshire,* in *Plays: One* (London: Methuen, 1985), p. 207.

18. Hélène Cixous and Catherine Clément, *The Newly Born Woman,* trans. Betsy Wing, *Theory and History of Literature,* vol. 24 (Minneapolis: University of Minnesota Press, 1986). See "Sorties: Out and Out: Attacks/Ways Out/Forays," p. 63.

19. David Cole, *The Theatrical Event: A Mythos, A Vocabulary, A Perspective* (Middletown, Conn.: Wesleyan University Press, 1975), p. 5.

20. Cixous, "Aller à la mer," p. 547.

21. Susan Gubar, "'The Blank Page' and the Issues of Female Creativity," in *Writing and Sexual Difference,* ed. Elizabeth Abel, p. 76 (Chicago: The University of Chicago Press, 1982).

22. Adrienne Rich, *Of Woman Born: Motherhood as Experience and Institution* (New York: Bantam Books, 1977), p. 21.

23. Joanna Russ, *Window Dressing* in *The "New" Women's Theatre,* ed. Honor Moore (New York: Vintage Books, 1977), p. 65.

24. Pam Gems, *Queen Christina,* in *Plays by Women,* vol. 5, ed. Mary Remnant, p. 18 (London: Methuen, 1986).

25. Annette Kuhn, *The Power of the Image: Essays on Representation and Sexuality* (London: Routledge and Kegan Paul, 1985), p. 50.

26. Caryl Churchill, *Cloud 9* (New York: Methuen, 1984), p. 4.

27. Reinhardt, p. 29.

28. Ibid, p. 42.

29. Maureen Duffy, *Rites,* in *Plays By and About Women,* ed. Victoria Sullivan and James Hatch, p. 351 (New York: Vintage Books, 1974).

30. For further discussion of the WOW café, see Jill Dolan, "An Evening in the East Village," and Alisa Solomon, "The WOW Café," in *The Drama Review: Thirty Years of Commentary on the Avant-Garde,* ed. Brooks McNamara and Jill Dolan (Ann Arbor, Mich.: UMI Research Press, 1986).

31. I refer here to Harold Bloom's well-known and influential conception of the male poet's desire to overthrow or destroy his predecessors in order to create. Harold Bloom, *The Anxiety of Influence: A Theory of Poetry* (New York: Oxford University Press, 1973).

32. Megan Terry, "Who Says Only Words Make Great Drama," *New York Times,* 10 November 1968, sec. 2.

33. For further discussion of Megan Terry's use of language see Kathleen Gregory Klein, "Language and Meaning in Megan Terry's 1970s 'Musicals,'" *Modern Drama* 27 (1984): 574–83.

34. Teresa de Lauretis, p. 7.

35. Ntozake Shange, *for colored girls who have considered suicide/when the rainbow is enuf* (New York: Bantam Books, 1980), preface.

36. Shange, p. 2.

37. Josette Féral, "Writing and Displacement: Women in Theatre," trans. Barbara Kerslake, *Modern Drama* 27, no. 4 (December 1984): 559.

38. Maria Irene Fornes, "The 'Woman' Playwright Issue," *Performing Arts Journal* 21, no. 3 (1983): 91.

39. Joan Schenkar, "The 'Woman' Playwright Issue," *Performing Arts Journal* 21, no. 3 (1983): 97.

PART I

Re-creational Metaphors

VIVIAN M. PATRAKA

Mass Culture and Metaphors of Menace in Joan Schenkar's Plays

Contemporary playwright Joan Schenkar's "comedies of menace for the mental stage"—*Signs of Life* (1979), *The Last of Hitler* (1982), *Fulfilling Koch's Postulate* (1985), and *Family Pride in the Fifties* (1986)[1]—all function as disturbing, surreal landscapes of collective mind. A central strategy in the plays to achieve this is the use of unusual linguistic tropes that extend into visual figuration on stage. By *trope* I mean a figurative mode of analogizing, i.e., the displacing and distorting in language of an experience by means of comparison or assimilation to other experience. If tropes structure experience and are often the linguistic equivalent of a psychological defense mechanism against problematical domains of experience, then Schenkar instead uses tropes, especially metaphor, to break down our psychological defenses.[2]

Her metaphors menace our received conceptions because they do not assimilate what is unfamiliar or strange to the more familiar, but the reverse, thereby making the familiar strange by its connection to an equivalence so disturbing or peculiar that it is destructive to the acquired meanings and sensations associated with the original image or idea. In *The Last of Hitler*, for example, cooked chicken as oven food is conflated with the victims of the Holocaust in a macabre envisioning of the routineness of genocide and in *Signs of Life*, female sexual organs are imaged as anarchic gardens, creating a horrific, metaphoric rationale for gynecological surgery. Thus Schenkar's metaphors defamiliarize us to the original "normal" context, clarifying the constructedness, the artificiality of even the most familiar situations and images. This technique explodes the usual tropes by which we structure experience, especially those clichéd encodings based on convention, authority, or custom which gain their power by seeming natural and inevitable by overuse and which create the oblivion of sustained association. Imbedded in a language that is skewed, altered, repetitive, Schenkar's metaphors are performed by and on the bodies of the actors who serve as carriers of them, most often infecting spectators by the use of insinuating comedy. In engaging us in this way, the plays make us look at how we assimilate, recreate, and extend dominant discourse through metaphor.

If menace means defamiliarizing the conventional and its conventions, it also means refamiliarizing us, with "a shudder of recognition," to what we've repressed. Schenkar told me her intention is to "invade people's dreams," that her metaphors serve as "an ax of urgency, cutting through, breaking down the door of consciousness." So if dreams are symbolic fulfillments of our unconscious wishes, her metaphors become a condensed, symbolic language for repressed desires. If, in the words of *Fulfilling Koch's Postulate,* the unconscious is "something you cannot see, from which grows something you cannot cure" this suggests a pathology only the symptoms of which are readable. Thus Schenkar's metaphors, always repetitive, track obsessions—ways of simultaneously protecting against unconscious desire and expressing it. The obsessional quality of both metaphor and the characters who express them lulls, irritates, and transfixes spectators, undercutting any notion of progress in the plays as illusion.

Schenkar's metaphors emphasize the ideological weight of what has been repressed by suggesting a collaboration between the unconscious, the "raw stuff of terror," and whatever ideas and structures are socially dominant. For example, germ theory, prominent in the 1940s, becomes in *The Last of Hitler* the metaphoric structure for expressing a murderous paranoia directed at Jews, and the celebration of the new technologies of plastic in the fifties of *Family Pride* metaphorizes the polymorphous drives beneath the fixed identities of the nuclear family. The insistence in the plays on a community of obsessions, motives, and nightmares conveys the unconscious as a complex, entangling web between the characters created in collaboration with the culture they inhabit. In each of the four plays, the two-halved brain is a template for the stage set, as if all of what we see is being staged inside a giant brain. Within this brain, every character is an aspect of a different set of emotions and thoughts that make up the entire consciousness of the play and of the culture this consciousness represents. They all have nerves into this central ganglion so that if one feels something, there is reaction in all the others. That the universe on stage is a closed system also manifests itself in the repetition among the characters of the same, obsessional metaphors. Moreover, an intertextual system of tropes within all four plays, drawn from cannibalism and cooking, from pathology and freakishness, and from performance and ritual creates a continuing analysis of gender politics and sexuality, fascism and violence, language and invention, and memory and history in relation to our psychic lives.

As exemplified by the depiction of nintenth-century gender politics in *Signs of Life,* Schenkar's work conveys the way the larger social structures in which we live are in themselves obsessional. Thus they contain what has been repressed in both senses of the word *contain.* And they do not prevent (are perhaps constructed to allow) certain members of society to express themselves in word and deed beyond acceptable limits. In the patriarchal culture depicted in *Signs of Life, The Last of Hitler,* and *Fulfilling Koch's Postulate* this overweening, dangerous imagination attaches especially to the male characters, making them both fascinating and repellent. By implication, Schenkar's vision does not celebrate the liberation of the unconscious. For her, "everything is down there" and it can be dangerous, menacing, murderous. It has always struck her as indicative that "biologically, humans are the only animals in the world that will eat anything that won't eat them first" and cannibalism is a recurring motif in her works.

With Schenkar's plays all framed within a proscenium arch, their tropes spew out of the mouth of the theatre onto the audience, spreading the contamination of metaphorizing into the audience. As spectators, we too are "framed" by the playwright, "set-up" with rigged evidence to incriminate us into her vision. And if the proscenium is one frame for the language of metaphor, the playwright's framing of each play by a particular form of mass culture serves as another. Schenkar chooses the form of mass culture popular at the time in which the play is set: for *Signs of Life,* it is the carnival sideshow; for *Last of Hitler,* the radio; for *Fulfilling Koch's Postulate,* the comic strip; and for *Family Pride in the Fifties,* the television.

As transmitters of information and entertainment, these forms of mass culture spread (as in the transmission over the radio airwaves of the pathology of fascism), shape (as in the certification of normality the carnival sideshow bestows on what is not in it) and contribute to (as in the television equation of familial coherency with eating as a group) the discourse of metaphor. By using dominant forms of mass culture, then, Schenkar historicizes how this discourse, especially that of dominant culture, is conveyed. This historicizing gives context and particularity to what might otherwise be viewed as either archetypal or as evanescent and deserving of nostalgia. It also creates distance between the spectator and what appears on stage, although unlike Brecht's distancing effect, Schenkar's invented distance between our world and the world on stage collapses under the weight of the obsessions her characters express, annulling much of the possibility of social change while reminding us of how historically determined our present is by our past.

If in Schenkar's works, mass culture operates as a frame, a kind of conceptual proscenium, it is also visually represented on stage: in *Signs of Life,* the multiple stage locations are the multiple acts of a sideshow, a visual punning on the marginalized, "side" spaces women inhabit; the frame of the giant radio brain in *The Last of Hitler* is simultaneously that of the radio listener and the radio; in *Fulfilling Koch's Postulate,* the double framed playing space simulates a double frame of a comic strip; and the set of *Family Pride in the Fifties* is encased in a windowless television screen, with windows shaped like television screens at the back of the set. As a result, we as audience for the play are also resituated as the audience of the mass culture form. This double position of audience forces us to reexamine our own familiarity with and pleasure in the conventions of each form. When P. T. Barnum in *Signs of Life* beckons to the audience to see his freaks, it is we who are his suckers.

The obsessional use of metaphor is extended by the way Schenkar depicts each form of mass culture—freakshow, comic strip, radio (news, cooking show, variety show) or television (family situation comedy)—as in itself obsessional both in its form and in the content it produces or conceals. Each continuing show (or strip) produced within a mass culture form contains the same set-up, the same premises, the same motives repeated over and over—an exercise in how many changes can be wrung on that situation by altering the particulars. What Schenkar uncovers in her treatment of mass culture in all four plays is the unconscious, the repressed of that form's content and conventions. For example, in *Family Pride in the Fifties,* the underside of the conventions of the family situation comedy and the underside of the family shaping itself within the content and ideology of that form is murderousness, vacuity, and claustrophobia.

In *Signs of Life* each character suggests "an aspect of a *shared* consciousness" (p. 313), a communal dream in the first-person plural that expresses an incestuous, horrible inbreeding of pain. Schenkar creates an exaggerated distance between the nineteenth-century America in which the play is set and the present that collapses as the play progresses. Her embroidered tapestry of the real and the invented embeds enough factual material and recognizable people (e.g., Henry James, his sister Alice, her companion, Kathryn Loring, and P. T. Barnum) in the text so that her own version of history supplants the "real" one. Some of her characters might never have met (e.g., Henry James and P. T. Barnum); some don't even meet in the play (e.g., Jane Merritt, the Elephant Woman of Barnum's freakshow, and Alice James) despite connections set up between them by repeating motifs; and some resonate for the audience in multiple ways (e.g., Dr. Sloper is a character from James's *Washington Square,* as well as a version of Dr. Marion Sims, the "father" of American gynecology and inventor of the "Uterine Guillotine," an instrument for its removal).

Signs of Life is framed by Barnum's urging to the audience at the outset to view a freakshow from his American Museum, so the audience becomes a performing or self-conscious one for the freakshow. Performance in a freakshow serves as metaphor for what the whole play depicts: the self-conscious performing by women and men within the narrative of nineteenth-century American gender ideology. Early in the play, a scene in a workhouse containing idiots, spasmodics, and various disabled people depicts a female warden giving a class in "lookin' and seein' and bein' a freak" (p. 322). Thus freakishness as performance has its own aesthetic conventions regardless of the physical particulars. The abnormal must be constructed and performed and always in relationship to a constructed normality that is equally performed. Freakishness is contextualized by the expectations of a voyeuristic audience for a performance that privileges vision over the other senses in the spectator's act of ascertaining the separation, the distance between himself and the freak. Looking at freaks is then an epistemology, a way of knowing based on difference. It is terrifying to look, but consoling as it confirms one's standardness and hence authority.

The fantasy world of the freakshow is also a visual reflection of the psychic obsessions of the culture that produced it. The instructions given to freaks to smile, laugh, and look to the side suggest patterns of female socialization in nineteenth-century America. In discussing the rise of gynecology, G. J. Barker-Benfield describes how a "defensive . . . ideology" for financial gain from and social control over women after the Civil War escalated the notion of women as pathological or deformed by virtue of their genitalia: "The assumption of women's special liability to mental sickness by way of her characteristic menstrual and reproductive functions pushed all women close to the criminal category. . . . If women were only sex organs, and female sex organs were by nature a menace to health unless run to earth by pregnancy, then women were by nature sick; and . . . woman's sickness was construed as intolerable social disorder."[3] With their sexual organs the locus of their abnormality, to be a woman was to be a freak. Indeed, all the women in the play *are* deformed—from living within their constructed abnormality which like the set of the play, is "vacant [they are invisible as persons], clearly confining and entirely out of the light" (p. 319).

If, in an inversion of the actual freakshow, "woman as deformed" extends what can't be seen in public to what can, then the metonymy of sexual organs standing for the entire woman is inverted in the character Jane Merritt, the Elephant Woman: her entire body is deformed with the exception of her genitalia. That P. T. Barnum later constructs another such freak, in the Rhinoceros Woman, another conflating of the bestial and the female, emphasizes the general applicability of the freakshow to women just as does his claim that "I have to show one half of the world to the other" (p. 327). In film theorist Laura Mulvey's discussion of scopophilia, she refers to how, in certain films, "the power to subject another person to the will sadistically or to the gaze voyeuristically is turned onto the woman as the object of both."[4] This applies to Schenkar's freakshow as well except that in the freakshow the objects of the gaze may be unwilling (tears leak out of Merritt's eyes) but are not unknowing. Locked into an economy of sexual difference, of historical, material, and psychological complicities, Alice James resists by staging her own spectacle, her own public performing of freakdom, in fits that include her saying her shocking sentence.

That freaks are not only produced but managed for gain is represented in *Signs of Life* as the actions of a cultural, entrepreneurial, and medical ruling caste. Just so, Dr. Sloper performs his butcherous sexual surgery in an operating theater to advance his reputation and his profits. Film theorist Annette Kuhn identifies the way "the annulment of the threat posed by the feminine tends to be brought about in Hitchcock's films by a specific form of fetishisation in which the woman's body is cut up" including "at the level of narrative itself."[5] This is certainly Sloper's narrative, who must cut women with a knife in order to satisfy his need to look: "With these hands I have opened all the organs of the female pelvis. . . . Scooped up ovaries without question, extracted uteri without number. Ahh, Mr. James, the signs of life are closer to the bone than you imagine. And when you find them, there's no stopping until you're covered with blood. . . . When you find them you must cut and cut" (pp. 344–45). The "attractions of such repulsiveness" for Sloper reveal his obsessional need to investigate and demystify that which is resistant to control. And his epistemology is based on mutilation and death. Henry James manifests a similar parasitism and deadly desire to know. To get material for his novel, he metaphorically performs surgery on his sister, plunging his "pen deep into her bosom" to produce "life with her heart's blood" (p. 345).

If a freakshow tells spectators where to look, it also tells them where not to look. Schenkar redirects our eyes to the rage, pain, and wit of her female freaks. And she reveals the menace of the historically revered males,

Sloper and James, through her metamorphosing of the tea ritual, the sign of civility, into a recurring, freakish event. Both men are cannibalistically nostalgic about the women they've exploited, since in stage-apron time where tea occurs, both Alice James and Jane Merritt are dead, one from cancer and the other by her own hand. James panics over finding "blood in my cup" and "bone in my biscuit," to which Sloper merely responds, "*Just desserts,* Mr. James" (p. 319). Since we are constituted as the freakshow audience for *Signs of Life* and since the freakshow is as "live" as theatre is, our own voyeurism as theatergoers is implicated, just as we also are implicated in the construction of normality and what it represses. The play does not ask us to equate ourselves with Barnum's "American Museum" of nineteenth-century grotesqueries, but to see it as exhibits of what has produced us and to examine what it has led to in our own culture.

If the freakshow of *Signs of Life* stages the obsessions of the visual imagination, then *The Last of Hitler,* a surreal work staged in a collective radio brain, centers on those of the auditory imagination. The huge radio console on stage is framed by a radio proscenium; embedded in the radio are the two miked broadcasters who are contemporary and so self-consciously present "The Last of Hitler" radio show. The radio speaker hangs over the top of the stage like an immense, malignant mushroom or toothless mouth and the giant radio tubes glow with fluorescent pink light as if organic and growing. The radio show is organized around a group of escalating metaphors. These are shifted from character to character in order to reveal the process by which we project onto the Other that which is most feared, identify it as contagious, and image ourselves as its victims. Schenkar stages radio, the dominant form of entertainment in the 1940s, as sending waves of bigotry, paranoia, and hatred over the airwaves to radiate in our brains.

In a Kosy Kabin near an unnamed Jewish resort town in Florida, Hitler and Eva Braun drink endless cups of tea as they gradually sink into stereotypic images of Jews. Somewhere in a laboratory in Vermont, Dr. Reich takes care of the Dionne quintuplets with the help of two Russian nurses straight out of vaudeville. Reich is in search of a cure for the disease of "Hitler," but fascistically orders the nurses to feed the children nothing but tea since "germs breed in milk." A Hassidic Jew, symbolically seen but never heard, keeps turning the radio dial in search of a representation of his culture. That he never finds it (and furiously pulls out the giant radio plug at the end of the play) metaphorizes the genocide of a people and their disappearance from the American airwaves. What he hears instead is "The Mary Lee Taylor Cooking Show" where Mary Lee and her announcer, John Cole, perform inaccurate narratives

A scene from Joan Schenkar's *Family Pride in the Fifties*. (Photo by Sylvia Plachy.)

about Jewish dietary laws, competing for who can give the most bizarre account. By implication, how a culture's customs are presented within mass culture is a stand-in for the treatment of those who perform them. The strategy of staging the Hassid implicates many Jewish spectators as well, getting them to examine their own responses to a more traditional, less "assimilated" version of Jewishness.

In describing writing for radio, Angela Carter states that radio facilitates "tricks with time—and also with place, for radio can move from location to location with effortless speed, using aural hallucinations."[6] Schenkar's many-layered pastiche of allusions keeps shifting time and space as a way to relocate her portrayal of the spread of anti-Semitism and of fascism out of Germany and into both the America of the late forties and the contemporary one. Investigating radio's potential to become "a vast circulatory system transmitting poisons to infected cells," Schenkar emphasizes the power of broadcasting, of the voice in the dark, to convey language undiluted by visual imagery penetrating within our domestic spaces. Since we need not stop our everyday activities to hear it, what is heard insinuates itself into the fabric of our lives. Throughout the play, characters who obsessively listen to radio repeat the phrase "I heard it on the radio" as a kind of validation of any popular sentiment they express — a direct transmission from the cultural brain to theirs. It is as if the voices on radio become a single, coherent, authoritative Voice: outside the Voice lurks the terrifying landscape of infectious difference, "the impure" of fascist ideology.

Schenkar uses incongruities and the "tension between black comedy and bizarre pathos" (p. 10) which Carter thinks radio sustains best in order to undercut the authority of the Voice and dramatize without melodramatizing its victims. In her heightened version of patronizing or joking anti-Semitic remarks, for example, on "The Mary Lee Taylor Cooking Show" (the radio as test kitchen for ideas cooked up for public consumption), or in the other characters' endless, formulaic conversations about who heard what person is Jewish or who heard what is caused or run by Jews, Schenkar uncovers an "emotional plague" that leads to abuse and death, literally envisioned at the end of the play when the radio turns into a giant crematoria. The radio commercials, which the play reveals continue the discourse of a show rather than interrupt it, both pander to and create an American fascination with eugenics (in the promises of "better babies") and perfect cleanliness. This obsessive rejection of difference leaks out in the conception of children as filthy, infectious, incorrect, and untouchable and there are ten abused children mentioned in the play — either victims of fascism or fascists in the making.

The Last of Hitler plays with the trope of projection to clarify the conventions of radio. Projection as exemplified by ventriloquism becomes a paradigm of radio itself. The point of ventriloquism is to mislead, to throw the voice so that its source is obliterated as, to take it a step further, is the ideology of its own making. On radio, there is no way to "read lips," to observe the slips that give away the constructedness of the voice or its content. Interruptions in the continuous flow of voice are static (and Schenkar puts in a lot of radio static, signifying all that has become invisible).

A riveting visual image of ventriloquism is that of Dr. Reich and the six-year-old skeleton Edmond in a tableau recalling an Edgar Bergen–Charlie McCarthy routine. The cynical, accusing, and rumor-mongering dummy spews forth a repertoire of tasteless jokes. On one level his performance suggests the perils of the communication of ventriloquism: he is an innocent skeleton held by a crafty actor who speaks for him. But the impressions derived from this exchange are more ambiguous: Is Edmond dead, alive, or ghost; child or adult; dummy, autonomous, or even ventriloquist; performer or performed upon? One way to regard this is as an imaging of how the repressed elements of a people are projected onto a leader who speaks for them. But this ambiguous performance also highlights a shifting space between the two, a kind of reciprocal projection that suggests the multidirectional web of trans-actions among an authoritarian leader and his followers. *The Last of Hitler*'s portrayal of Hitler constructs a performer, a theatricalizer of those followers' desires, implicating the desires of the audience in the process. Thus the remark of Dr. Reich about "the throbbing of Hitler's will sending electric impulses through the black air" with "all the endings of my nerves stiffen[ing] like antennae to receive his transmissions" must be juxtaposed with the parodic characterization of Hitler as under a permanent headset, the biggest radio ad-dict of the play. This juxtaposition suggests that radio itself does not simply impose ideas on listeners: as a form of popular consumption it is situated by their continuing responses.

Creating her own structure of pathology, Schenkar conveys that the con-dition we metaphorize as Hitler is our problem on a cellular level—bred so deeply within us that it is hard to envision what kind of eugenics would root it out. The horror of the Final Solution is wedded to the horror that there is no final solution to eradicate fascism. The challenge of the play is directed at the audience to imagine its own voice in the dark, its own mental radio show, its own latent narrative of prejudice. And if, as pointed out in the play, emotional plague is the most deadly disease because its symptoms are invis-ible, then the auditory imagination that collaborates with radio might be the best way to track it.

If the cook in *The Last of Hitler* is cooked in her own oven, the cook in *Fulfilling Koch's Postulate* is "a real killer." Within a proscenium designed as a giant mouth that extends into the stage as an infected throat (hanging with pustules of infection), two playing spaces are sculpted out by a large uvula at the back of set. These two "separate spheres" are the domains, respec-tively, of the cook (as in Mary Mallon, known as "Typhoid Mary") and the master of the house (as in Dr. Robert Koch, the Berlin bacteriologist who first identified bacterial transmission of disease). Mary in the kitchen and Koch in the lab, each with a devoted if sly and tricky assistant, "are fat, flat, crude" and "very Katzenjammer." In forty-four scenes in forty-four minutes, the highly choreographed, broad, vulgar movements of the actors become a comic strip in motion.

Like "The Katzenjammer Kids," *Fulfilling Koch's Postulate* is full of pranks and mischief. But, usually, comics that focus obsessively on violence portray either children (as less civilized, more primitive than adults) or animals (per-petually injuring or recovering from injury). Schenkar keeps the violent an-tics, but uncovers what is repressed by the focus of most comics: the violence of adults, of adults acting within their professional identities. There are no children in *Fulfilling Koch's Postulate* on whom to displace the violence and the animals in kitchen and lab are permanently killed.

Deelevating the status of scientist, the play equates the scientist experimenting with the cook (*Koch* is German for cook) testing and manipulating food. The laboratory, scalpel, and outsized, phallic test tubes match the kitchen, butcher knife, and big cooking pots. In both kitchen and lab, they "cut and cut and peel and peel" to produce dead animals. The Cook's opening aria begins "I hacked a duck to death today, I beat an egg to froth today" and throughout the play she chops, boils, chews, and tastes. Thus the way Schenkar arranges the language of cooking exposes the violent underside of this activity. In the play's deliberately limited vocabulary, especially the Cook's speeches weight the stress of sentences on the verbs. The stark centrality of these verbs embeds in the language of the play itself the comic strip's unrelenting focus on action. In *Fulfilling Koch's Postulate,* this translates into the ferociously obsessive focus on the doings of profession which both scientist (pedantically) and cook (possessively) manifest and transfer to their assistants. And the more the assistants learn, the more infected and the less sexually active they become.

In comics like "The Katzenjammer Kids," confusions that facilitate mischief abound. In *Fulfilling Koch's Postulate,* the confusions, the "jokes," the slips and accidents do mischief to the stability of some of the most rigidly maintained oppositions. In fact, typhoid fever, caused by taking into the body food or water that has been contaminated by feces of a person carrying the disease, is itself a confusion of taking in and putting out. In the play this leads to a metaphoric equating of food and fecal matter, of what the cook cooks and what she excretes. Moreover, the signs of disease and of sexual arousal (being hot, wet, sweaty, burning up) get confused so that sexuality becomes a pathology. And sex and cooking (as in "doing the necessary") overlap as do genitalia and the professional accoutrements of cookbook and test tube. The cook as carrier of disease conflates with the cook's body, with its two mouths, as the carrier of female desire (and she "won't stop" "cooking" despite Koch's warnings). That the oven equates to the womb, and carrying germs becomes "mothering" disease, conveys a collapse of the metaphors of cooking, mothering, sexuality, and disease into an incoherence reflective of the simultaneous reductive dichotomizing and equating that dominant gender ideology imposes on women. By overheating these metaphoric equivalences, Schenkar causes the "Kaboom!" of comic strip explosions.

Furthermore, in *Fulfilling Koch's Postulate,* the confusion of what we take into our stomachs and what we take into our heads overlaps in the imaging of the mouth as taker in of food and the mouth as maker of speech, as maker of infectious letters—rendered in dialogue and in the scientific writings of Koch and the cook's written recipes—like the balloons emerging from the mouths of comic strip characters. The mouth emerges as the point of consciousness, as the point of circulation for food, disease, sex and ideas, as postulator and pustulator. Finally, by skewing history (Koch never left Germany and died before Mary Mallon was ever identified as a carrier of typhoid), Schenkar undermines the traditional responses of revulsion for Mary as contaminating pariah and idealization of Koch as hero of medicine by suggesting how interconnected the structuring of medical and social pathologies really is.

In its division into "grotesquely illuminated vignettes," *Fulfilling Koch's Postulate* parallels the discontinuous, segmented form of the comic strip in which each strip has the same set-up but is not worked into a continuous, causal narrative. It is, then, the comic form itself that undercuts Koch's postulate and his etiology or causal narrative of disease, his ascendancy as logical reader of the invisible. Instead the form supports recurring action, such as cooking, so that ultimately the cook's postulate, her menacing, axiomatic "I am the Cook!" triumphs. But the play also undercuts this form: the neat, square frames of comics that control and contain the chaos turn into "very thin walls" that metaphorically dissolve as words, letters, germs, food, and desires travel back and forth across the stage. Perhaps the postulate offered for examination to the audience is one that both Koch and the Cook repeat: "There is nothing funnier than death." The two-dimensionality of the comic strip is imaged in the two-dimensional characters, in the "forced perspective" furniture, and in the flat wooden props (Velcroed in back) of pigs, rabbits, and fish that are slammed with maniacal cheerfulness onto the furniture. Perhaps in implicating the spectator's pleasure in the anarchy, the mechanically raw sex, and the violence, *Fulfilling Koch's Postulate* conveys the way "there is nothing funnier than death" only when we two-dimensionalize, flatten, and frame, and so distance the victim of it.

If *Fulfilling Koch's Postulate* was saturated in infected food, *Family Pride in the Fifties* depicts a foodless television supper. At the outset of Patricia Mellencamp's essay "Situation Comedy, Feminism, and Freud: Discourses of Gracie and Lucy," she states that "During the late 1940s and the 1950s, linked to or owned by the major radio networks, television recycled radio's stars, formats, and times through little proscenium screens, filling up the day. . . . Television was then (and continues to be) both an ecology—a repetition and recycling through the years—and a family affair, in the 1950s conducted collectively. . . ." Coincident with this, she goes on to note, "women were being urged to leave the city, work force, and salaries; move to the suburbs, leisure and tranquillity; raise children; and placate commuting, overworked husbands for free."[7] *Family Pride in the Fifties,* set within the theatrical proscenium of an oversized television, portrays the dehistoricized television version of what Mellencamp delineates.

To heighten the claustrophobic nature of the post-war invention of the nuclear family, Schenkar has two connected tables in a V-shape extending out toward the audience at which two families are locked into an eternal present of dinnertime. One family is crude, and has two sons, one is fake refined, and has two daughters; the wives are sisters, the husbands are brothers — complementary clones. The dehistoricizing of the family on television is repeated in miniature by the way the children know no one in their extended family, and are amazed to learn grandparents exist.

If Schenkar shows the vacuity of 1950s family life in her heightened version of television (the deadpan leadenness of "Ozzie and Harriet" and "Father Knows Best"), she also uncovers the murderous underside ("pride" is, after all, the numerical classifier for lions) of the "family show." A production decision was made never to have any food eaten at table because, in Schenkar's words, "What they're eating is each other. Every time you sit down to a dinner table, you sit down to potential death. Every instrument around you, except the plate, which is neutral, is an instrument of murder — forks, knives [these are outsized in the production]. And given what happens in the internal structure of families, it's remarkable that so many families leave the dinner table alive." For all their savagery, false tolerance, and inanity, the families before us seem shell-shocked and only an insubstantial reflection. Indeed, one family has no television and watches the reflection of the other family's television in their window, so they get only a reflection of a reflection. The reflection Schenkar stages for us is the family dinner as continually repeated spectacle in which the family watches itself performing the television version of family and becomes a simulacrum of itself. The whole family show — the competition between families based on the supposed talents and intelligence of their children, the placating gestures, the pretentious, meaningless sayings, the eruptions of violence, the worries over the masculinity and femininity of the children, and the children's rebellion or defeat — is obsessively reproduced in this somnambulistic display. This defamiliarizes, makes strange and unnatural, this particular familial configuration.

The 1950s familial ideal is also given a cultural context by the way the play metaphorizes the characters' absence or presence on stage as a relationship to television's historical moment. Grandparents are invisible because they are too old to have been influenced deeply by the coming of television. The parents are young enough to have internalized its values and simulated its content. They are present for the first two parts but disappear from the last when only the children, whose cognitive structures were molded by television's form and conventions, remain. To metaphorize this transformation, they are presented as four headshots on four television sets facing out at the audience. Dana Polan's essay "Brief Encounters: Mass Culture and the Evacuation of Sense" describes the "substituting for the older American dream of earthly conquest a new dream of America as an endless performance," a "merging of self into the vastness of a mass spectacle."[8] In *Family Pride in the Fifties,* the children are consumed by the spectacle of television and reproduce its performative model of reality.

In an eerie, elegiac sequence [it is the faces of the child actors who appear before us but "everything happened already" in their lives], the girl Joan constructs a television cosmology: ". . . when you're ready to be born, they turn on the set with your name on it and . . . all the TV angels hold their breath and . . . suddenly! the reception is perfect, there you are on the picture tube, and then you live on TV and grow up on TV and if you're lucky you get your own show on TV. And your show keeps on playing until you get older and kind of stale and people get tired of it and the ratings go down and then they cancel it and they turn your set off. And *that's life.*" In this extended metaphor, success means enough people want to watch you perform (or at least are willing to cue into the sound of you while otherwise engaged and so not flick the channel) and immortality equates with being recycled from show to show. The Subject becomes an internal approximation of television's conventions of personality and the one child who steps out of these conventions to express her pain loses her show and so dies. In the nebulous, unreal space between television and materiality that these characters inhabit (it's as if, when the set is shut off, it's the viewer who disappears, whose world unravels), they can speak, they can cry, but their vision is limited by the containment of their screens and they can't touch each other. The claustrophobic togetherness of the first two parts is replaced in part three with isolation as if containment within television were an escape from the fifties family itself. At the end of *Family Pride in the Fifties,* all four sets wink out and only "the old 1950s test pattern" remains, a kind of punning visual reminder in abstracted television terms of what the whole play explored.

Dana Polan describes the way "mass culture has become one of culture studies' most recurrent Others—a repository and a stereotypic cause of all the social ills of life under capitalism" (p. 169). Schenkar's work avoids this reductiveness by emphasizing the collaborative relationship between mass culture and its consumers and between mass culture and dominant ideology in general, exposing the way mass culture shapes ideas and metaphors already extant within a culture. Polan also notes the way many forms of mass art (unlike the stereotypical equating of these forms with linear, realistic narrative) "employ . . . nonrealist, nonnarrative rhetoric" although he cautions against the presumption that "anything non-narrative must necessarily challenge the operation of ideology" (pp. 170–71). The discontinuous segments that associatively structure Schenkar's plays parallel the way she conceives the mass culture form within each play. It is her own postmodern aesthetic, then, that makes these forms subversive instead of simply disruptive, challenging of received ideas, even as her plays delineate a major way in which these ideas are transmitted. She achieves this by her use of metaphor to uncover what is repressed in the form's content and conventions and, also, by revealing what is literally present in a mass culture show or image that the viewer must suppress in order to consume the work easily.

And, after all, Schenkar writes plays, only "serial" if all her plays are thought of as a continuous show. In fact, the form of the one-time theater event itself operates as a subverting of the obsessive repetitiveness of the mass culture form staged within it. Furthermore, a sense of winding down pervades the endings of all four plays. The tea ritual has begun to disintegrate along with the language and characters at the end of *Signs of Life*. The characters in, what is after all, the *last* of Hitler, decline into their fates, into obscurity and death. Koch's Postulate is *fulfilled* in the performance of it on stage and three of the characters grow sicker and sicker. And in *Family Pride in the Fifties,* the family is gone. If this creates an aura of loss for the spectator, it is in part based on what Schenkar presents as having been exploited, ruined, or destroyed by the characters and by a culture's ruling obsessions. But it is also the loss that comes from being infected with the sense of how addictive these obsessions are. Schenkar undercuts both the way metaphor continually reinscribes itself and the conserving structure of metaphoric equivalences, and hence its addictiveness. She accomplishes this by hollowing out her metaphors from the inside, decentering them by slightly altering and skewing them in the course of their repetitions. Having broken down the spectator's resistance to what has been repressed, Schenkar's plays leave us with an empty space, a gap that is menacing, dangerous to us but that vibrates with possibilities.

NOTES

1. Joan Schenkar, *Signs of Life,* in *The Women's Project: Seven New Plays by Women,* ed. Julia Miles (New York: Performing Arts Publications and American Place Theatre, 1980; also in New York: Samuel French, 1982). *The Last of Hitler, Fulfilling Koch's Postu-*

late, and *Family Pride in the Fifties* are in unpublished manuscript form. For a discussion of another Schenkar play, *Cabin Fever* (New York: Samuel French, 1980), see Vivian M. Patraka, "Foodtalk in the Plays of Caryl Churchill and Joan Schenkar," *Theatre Annual* 40 (1985): 137–57.

2. My understanding of tropes is based on my reading of Hayden White, *Tropics of Discourse: Essays in Cultural Criticism* (Baltimore: Johns Hopkins University Press, 1978).

3. G. J. Barker-Benfield, *The Horrors of the Half-Known Life: Male Attitudes Toward Women and Sexuality in Nineteenth-Century America* (New York: Harper Colophon, 1977), 84, 123.

4. Laura Mulvey, "Visual Pleasure and Narrative Cinema," in *Art After Modernism: Rethinking Representation,* ed. Brian Wallis, 371 (New York: New Museum of Contemporary Art/David R. Godine, 1984).

5. Annette Kuhn, *Women's Pictures, Feminism and Cinema* (London: Routledge and Kegan Paul, 1982), 105.

6. Angela Carter, *Come unto These Yellow Sands* (Newcastle upon Tyne: Bloodaxe Books, 1985), 7.

7. Patricia Mellencamp, "Situation Comedy, Feminism, and Freud: Discourses of Gracie and Lucy," in *Studies in Entertainment: Critical Approaches to Mass Culture,* ed. Tania Modleski, 80–81 (Bloomington and Indianapolis: Indiana University Press, 1986).

8. Dana Polan, "Brief Encounters: Mass Culture and the Evacuation of Sense," in *Studies in Entertainment,* 179–80.

NANCY BACKES

Body Art:
Hunger and Satiation in the
Plays of Tina Howe

To male critics, such as E. M. Forster, food is sustenance, period; the only aesthetic consideration Forster allows is gustatory: does the food taste good or bad?[1] Virginia Woolf, on the other hand, complained of the writer's "convention not to mention soup and salmon and ducklings, as if soup and salmon and ducklings were of no importance whatsoever. . . ."[2]

However, even female critics can misapprehend food. Blanche Gelfant, for example, proposes a "hungry heroine"[3] devoted to "dignified survival," a heroine who "points to a way out of the impasse reached by oppressed heroines who become self-starving, suicidal, or mad"[4] — in other words, a heroine with an appetite voracious as any man's who recognizes that men control the food supply and demands her fair share of it. Such a woman, however, is in quest of men's food, and as Sandra M. Gilbert and Susan Gubar say in *The Madwoman in the Attic*, "the foods and fictions that sustain men are precisely those that have contributed to the sickening of women."[5] Worse, Gelfant's "hungry heroine" is a destructive creature. Anzia Yezierska's autobiographical persona that Gelfant admires, is, after all, a masculine, social Darwinian who does not hesitate to take the oatmeal and bread from her sister's nine starving children so that she might continue to write.

For many women food is the symbol of unequal status. In *A Room of One's Own*, Woolf showed how power of one sex meant denial to the other, how plenitude — food, books, talk, thought — at a men's college meant impoverishment at the female counterpart. "One cannot think well, love well, sleep well, if one has not dined well,"[6] Woolf insisted, yet thin soup, prunes, and water were the fare at the women's college, while the men not only ate well but also enjoyed the intellectual progeny of a satisfied appetite: the after-dinner consideration of higher things, which are the "offspring of luxury and privacy and space."[7] Such differentiation has a long history. For example, food for Milton's Eve in *Paradise Lost* was the means toward the ends of love, power, and equality;[8] since Eve was condemned for eating,[9] she was implicitly told not to seek those things. And so it is that women are taught to suppress their appetites. Girls are instructed to repress their own needs for self-satisfaction and self-assertion and are taught instead to be submissive and docile[10]—to be the bearers of nourishment rather than the partakers of it (except, of course, when dining in restaurants, which usually feature fare created by men, reinforcing male control of the public realm; in public places women must eat this foreign food—do things the male way—or starve).

For women, food has been encoded into the idioms of restraint and defiance. Susie Orbach, who has written extensively on the intimate relationship between food and women, recognizes that there is a "cultural insistence" on food as women's "especial domain." "Food," Orbach continues, "is the medium through which women are addressed; in turn, food has become the language of women's response."[11] Food, then, is a medium of expression. Seeking acknowledgment, many women sculpt their bodies, explicitly exceeding the Pygmalion-like ideal in order to enter their own distinctive realm.

But to force females to squeeze into a constrictively narrow definition of beauty, is to force them to the realization that to fit comfortably within it they must almost disappear. Thus their extreme acquiescence to male dicta becomes their means of escape from those very standards. This is Eve's story rewritten: in it, she rejects the apple, and along with it, male standards, male power, male knowledge. Unfortunately, such integrity can be had only at the dark price of reality: the females who imitate this new Eve can starve to illness or death. Gilbert and Gubar say that "to be trained in renunciation is almost necessarily to be trained in ill health."[12] To reject the "poisoned apples"[13] that their culture gives them often means that young women have no apple to eat at all. Their responses are not inactive, as Gelfant avers, but rather, truculently active; indeed, these are private actions. An anorexic woman "is not the passive victim of the diet doctor," Orbach insists. ". . . [S]*he* remains supremely in charge and *active* in relation to the suppression of her bodily needs."[14] These women are pale rebels acceding in the extreme to the patriarchy's notions of beauty and intellectual conformity until they almost will themselves out of existence.

Where is the simple sustenance that a male critic like E. M. Forster once promised, and where is the freedom through hunger that Blanche Gelfant assures the sisters to Faust? In Forster's *Passage to India* a character sings a song so mysterious and beautiful that the narrator describes it as the song of an unknown bird. Is it possible for women to take a bite of an unknown fruit, one plucked from their own fantastic orchards? Many of the most talented, and often underrated, women writers long have been plying audiences with a version of nouvelle cuisine, magically transforming calories on their own comparable worth scale into energetic rebellion, intellectual satisfaction, emotional gratification, and unimpeded progress. A good place to begin an examination of the ingredients of these tasty repasts is in the plays of Tina Howe, one of the *new* nouvelle cuisine's top chefs.

Howe uses the outrageous and the absurd to make her dramatic truths more acceptable. Often these truths are feminist in nature. "I'm not identified as a feminist writer," she wrote in *American Theatre*, "yet I'm convinced I *am* one—and one of the fiercer ones, to boot."[15] Howe has said that she wants to "reach new heights of comic pathos."[16] Indeed, while her comedy is wildly exuberant and her characters vividly eccentric, the plays are infused with a subterranean sense of desperation.

Howe's works display a wide range of approaches, but one of their common characteristics is their ability to give concrete representation to inner states of mind; Howe's ideas come alive and take up actual space. Consider Howe's first full-length work. It concerns a father who invents wings and spends a great deal of time running uphill to test them, and a mother who likes to play a game of who can stay in the closet the longest.[17] Although Howe keeps the manuscript hidden, it is clear from her description of it that the play is about space: space as it is registered with the claustrophobe, who feels she is overwhelming a narrow confinement, and space as it is known by the agoraphobiac, who feels overwhelmed by boundless area, conditions that correspond to those existing in bulimic and anorexic women. Indeed, the emaciation associated with anorexia nervosa has been described by Orbach as "an expression of a woman's confusion about how much space she may take up in the world."[18]

In *Birth and After Birth* Howe metaphorically used binging and purging to illuminate the paradox of impulsive anarchy and suffocating control inherent within the family unit and to illustrate the simultaneous compulsions for overindulgence and restraint that uneasily coexist in an individual woman. Her original, daring treatment caused Howe's agent to release her and brought vitriolic rejections—"often with accompanying threats and spittle"[19]—from every major theatre in the country. To this day, the play has not been professionally performed outside of drama workshops.

Howe insists that the four-year-old celebrating his birthday in *Birth and After Birth* be played by an adult man. This peculiarity emphasizes the point that in literature created by women, as Gilbert and Gubar point out, bulimia is represented by huge, powerful monsters,[20] which are the antithetical doubles for impotent selves. Sandy, Nicky's mother, has great difficulty reconciling the myth of motherhood with the demanding reality of this overpowering, unmanageable child; Sandy, has, she realizes, created a monster.

In recoil, Sandy tries to reestablish control over her own body, and she accomplishes this with the methods of anorexia. She starves. There is no food at Nicky's birthday party, except for a birthday cake, which is brought out but never eaten. Sandy loses a front tooth at the end of the play, and her other one is loose; without the proper human implements, it will soon be impossible to eat even if she would will herself to food, an action that seems unlikely. Equal to her physical starvation is Sandy's intellectual impoverishment. Forced by the motherhood trap to devote all of her attentions to the boy, Sandy has lost all of her intellectual curiosity; she is either indifferent to or disgusted by the stories that Mia and Jeffrey, the childfree career anthropologists, tell of birth and after birth in other cultures.

Sandy's conscious mind remains tightly connected to the utopian publicity attached to motherhood; she is profoundly ashamed that she cannot conceive another child. Yet it is no real surprise that she cannot, for intellectually and emotionally starved by her society, she retaliates by starving her body of another pregnancy. "[S]elf-starvation," say Gilbert and Gubar, "returns . . . girls to the physical state of small children, just as it interrupts the menstrual cycle which has been defined for them as a 'curse'"[21]—but, one hastens to add, not as big a curse as the child that might result from conception, which is, of course, the other means to stop menstruation. Sandy's retaliation with her body, then, is also—ironically—her salvation, her only chance to preserve a sense of selfhood. "Since eating maintains the self, in a discredited world it is a compromise implying acquiescence"[22] is how Gilbert and Gubar say it. Sandy's desire is to stop life: her own and that of future generations.

Yet having thrown her own biological system into an uproar, Sandy at least wants to experience vicariously giving birth. Although Mia does not wish to have children, she is not without ambivalence regarding the decision. As a result, Sandy can manipulate her into a false birth ritual; this suggests that control of the body is a fragile thing, easily overtaken by any social pressure. Nevertheless, this particular false birth that Mia enacts onstage is significant because it has been made possible through the imaginations of the two women, who, without the aid of men, have managed to conceive a child.

Mia's and Sandy's ritual is like the female-dominated birth ritual of the Whan See women once witnessed in the field by Jeffrey and Mia. That birth ceremony reverses the psychoanalytic model which holds that anorexia nervosa is rooted in an oral impregnation fantasy: the fear that pregnancy results from eating. The Whan See women stuff the newborn baby back into the birth canal sixteen times in a primitive effort to control their bodies' products. As the Whan See women exercise this cannibalistic rite in their desire to force the womb to take back its product, their babies usually die. Their fierce hunger for control has given them an appetite for their own bodies. Is this not in some sense like the anorexic woman, who, denied society's food, denies herself ordinary food and thereby causes her body to feed off of itself?

Self-abnegation can take other forms. Both Sandy and Bill, Nicky's father, starve themselves of adulthood, and regress into the more pleasant fare of their own childhoods. In fact, the bigger, more demanding, and adult-like Nicky gets, the weaker and more childlike his parents become. They recall their own childhood birthday parties. Sandy eventually regresses as far as it is possible to go. She imagines water, can even smell it; she is retreating to the sea, the great womb of all humankind.

Sandy's encounters with dark realities that are the nether sides of golden dreams and pretty images have put her, in fact, on an anorexic-bulimic binge-purge cycle. Metaphorically speaking, it was the overindulgence in the motherhood myth fostered by society that caused her to have this monster. A nourisher—Sandy has been up all night preparing for Nicky's party—she denies herself nourishment. She is haggard. "When I looked in the mirror this morning," Sandy says, "I saw an old lady. Not *old* old, just used up. (*She scratches her head; a shower of sand falls out*) It's the weirdest thing, it doesn't look like dandruff or eczema, but more like . . . I don't know, like my head is drying up and leaking. . . ."[23] "Drying up" is an anorexic metaphor for shriveling to fit an already tight space; "leaking" is a metaphor for purging bulimic bloat.

Birth and After Birth, through its fantastic-absurd elements, represents the reality faced by hundreds of thousands of women each day: the consuming need to control their lives and their destinies, and the resented discovery that they can control only their own bodies. For the woman who feels suffocated by mounds of child and responds by ingesting mounds of food, who feels trapped by the burden that has been expelled from her womb, much the way a bulimic feels trapped by her own flesh, and who, in the manner of the Whan See, is torn by conflicting impulses to expel the excess and simultaneously to resist that life-giving expulsion—for all these women Howe provides awareness, understanding, and catharsis.

This time the vehemence of the rejections to the play stunned Howe. What had gone wrong? What did she need to do to succeed as a playwright? She concluded that she had been approaching the theatre from an isolated, if youthfully exuberant, sight line. She began to believe that the core of *Birth and After Birth* had forced potential producers to look at realities too familiar yet too secret. Therefore, in 1974, she made a calculated study of current, successful plays. She found that all were set in unlikely places. Howe reasoned that her unusual ideas would not be rejected if they could be contained in an equally unusual setting.

Always driven to be original, Howe decided to create a drama in a setting never before seen on a stage. She tried a library and a department store before settling upon a museum. It took Howe just six months to complete *Museum,* even though her first version had forty-four characters; the New York run in 1977–78 was trimmed to eighteen characters. The play dramatizes a day of museum life from the viewpoint of the art objects, a vantage point that enabled Howe to exploit a unique dynamic tension: the heightened hostility between viewers of art and the art works, and between art and audience.

What is really going on? Is this another Howe reversal of a societal norm? In Western culture, in celluloid, art, and life, women are objects; they receive the gaze of men who are the "bearer of the look," to borrow Laura Mulvey's phrase.[24] Orbach, too, acknowledges that women's bodies are "to both women and men, objects of alienation, fascination and desire."[25] Suppose an objet d'art managed to look back? What, for instance, does one make of the brazen, open-faced gaze of the four identical huge white canvases painted by Zachery Moe? One response is to deface the work, which is exactly what one gallery patron surreptitiously does. Objects, after all, must know their place.

The interactive nature of the art exhibit entitled "The Broken Silence" inspires passionate responses. A variety of art viewers—from the lonely to the enthusiastic to the superficial to the indifferent—makes a pilgrimage to the show on its last day. On this sort of Judgement Day, the omnipotent and omniscient Guard manages his domain with firm but dispassionate detachment. When the Guard steps out, however, so does decorum. The art works are savagely attacked. Silence and noise become analogous to order and chaos, respectively.

The gallery is the temporary center of the universe, a conjunction of opposites where anything goes, where good takes on the form of evil, and vice versa, where silence takes on the form of sound—Mr. Moe, who is mute, recalls how his son's early sketches were *"noisy* with life!"[26]—where foreboding becomes deep beauty, and where conformity becomes chaos. The gallery encourages the transcendence of limitations. In such a world the color white is not blank. Rather, it is fulfilled, pregnant with possibility. It is, as Chloe

Trapp, the Curator, says, "the one color carrying in it the potential for all other colors."[27]

The conformity-rebellion motif in particular suggests an alliance with those who contort their bodies, manipulating them as an artist might manipulate media: to adhere to an aesthetic, while also rebeling against it by creating a grotesque representation of its twisted dictates. A modern woman constantly edits, redesigns, or recomposes; in short, she devotes much attention to worrying about her body and getting it right.[28] Similar to culinary art and home decorating, this effort becomes an expression of creativity, as though the woman were manipulating so many pounds of clay. Orbach notes that women think of their bodies as "arenas for constant improvement and resculpting."[29] Yet Howe pushes for the exceptions, for the deviations from the ideal; Chloe Trapp, the Curator, again speaking of one of the artists in the show, illuminates the feasibility of individuality: "Rather than imposing his will upon materials in order to force them into a preordained form, Williams obeys the inherent capabilities of a given material and follows the suggestions offered by its particular qualities."[30]

This play can be experienced as an imaginary reshaping of the body, of the so-called female aesthetic. Tink Solheim, who hugs one of her friend Agnes Vaag's "menacing" sculptures "made of animal teeth, feathers, fur, claws, bone, shell, wings, horn, scales, sponge, and antennae,"[31] makes an important discovery. She thinks of each figure as a masterpiece, a "SMALL MIRACLE."[32] "There's a secret. . . .," Tink explains.[33] "Aggie told me that she hid a special surprise inside each piece. . . . It's not visible to the naked eye. You can only find it through vibrations of sound or touch. . . ."[34] Because Agnes Vaag, as Tink puts it, "only reveals the surface,"[35] the inner beauty must be discovered by a daring explorer. As Tink caresses a statue, a forbidden activity in an art gallery, she *"suddenly releases the miracle buried in* [the piece entitled] The Holy Wars of Babylon Rage Through the Night. *The lights dim. A floodlight pours down on the statue and Bach's* Dorian Toccata and Fugue in D minor, BWV 538 *for organ swells from a speaker concealed in the pedestal."*[36] Everyone is moved and *"slowly draws near the statue to worship."*[37] When the Guard, the authority, the enforcer of a competing set of standards, gets too close, *"he breathes on it in a certain way and the music stops; the lights go back to normal."*[38] The world is not quite ready for a woman-centered aesthetic, let alone a goddess-centered theology.

Howe has said that there is a "grisly female aria . . . at the core of the play."[39] This is suggested by Agnes Vaag, an artist who scrounges the woods of state parks looking for the "found objects" of bones, beaks, and feathers for her figures. Moreover, according to Tink, on one outing Agnes Vaag nibbled, licked, and sucked on the skeletons she found. These bones, which she transformed into art, not only nourished her need to create but also were in need of the transformational nourishment from a caring hand. To Vaag, the fragile white bones have a kind of perfection. But the mystical qualities are inside the figures she designs; revolting grotesque collages of cast-off fragments on the outside, the statues are as spontaneously beautiful and expressive as Bach on the inside. Similarly, regardless of whatever superficial body art women display, inside there are the fundamental linkages, an undeniable shared femininity, a medley of the hidden that makes them women. Although mysterious, it is the song, unlike Forster's, of a *known* bird.

Howe admits to a preoccupation with food and its concomitants. In a 1983 interview for *New York,* Howe told Ross Wetzsteon: "I have a fear of eating. Food was of absolutely no value in our house; meals were a time to talk. And dining out is *terrifying* to me. . . .What I wanted to do in both *Museum* and *The Art of Dining* was to present a lovely exterior, then seduce the audience into the dark and mysterious places inside."[40] *The Art of Dining,* produced in 1979, was the result of Howe's "alternatingly terrifying and hilarious"[41] reaction to food. In the play Ellen is the co-owner and sole chef of The Golden Carrousel. Floating Island, Pears and Cointreau with Frozen Cream, Hollandaise Sauce, Sauce Veloute, Mornay Sauce, Sole Bonne Femme, Poulet Farci, Billi Bi, Belgian Oxtail Soup, Roast Duckling in Wine with Green Grapes (which are replaced with sliced peaches because Ellen's husband, Cal, an unreconstructed binge eater, has devoured the grapes), and Veal Prince Orloff are the elaborate culinary staples.

How could an anorexic woman find pleasure here? The answer is simple: the food is made safe, made "un-foreign" — domesticated, if you will — because it is prepared by a woman. Here the witch's cauldron yields unique, but very unsinister, fare. None of the diners throughout the unfolding of the play gets precisely the dish that he or she ordered, but because this is a female fantasy, the woman chef is not chastised; indeed, no one seems to notice. The entrées are exquisite. Ellen, afflicted with a female detail-oriented perfectionism, wants only a few diners nightly so that she can prepare perfect meals for them. However, Cal's appetite for money (he books too many diners) and food (he eats every item she prepares) makes that impossible. Ellen learns that she can use her own ingenuity to make dishes that are tasty and satisfying. The dishes, like the operation of The Golden Carrousel, attain their beauty in a nontraditional way. Gone, figuratively and literally, are the men's foods.

All of the feasters on Ellen's kitchen arts at The Golden Carrousel have been tyrannized and tantalized by food in various ways, and are described by the playwright in terms of their appetites: Hannah Galt is "hungry"; Paul Galt is "hungrier";[42] Elizabeth Barrow Colt, Howe's persona,[43] is "afraid of food";[44] Herrick Simmons is a "hearty eater"; Nessa Vox is a "guilty eater"; Tony Stassio, chronically anorexic/bulimic, is "a sneaky eater";[45] David Osslow, who links food with art, is "a man with a glowing appetite and glowing literary taste."[46] Osslow's binding of art and imagination to food is usually the exclusive domain of female characters. Howe's Cal adds another twist: he is the bulimic person, and because of that threatens to undermine the restaurant's business because he is unable to resist eating the tasty dishes as fast as they are prepared. Cal is also the headwaiter; he therefore assumes the traditional female role of bearer of food.

By reversing the roles in this feminine fantasy, Howe shows us that it is the political inequality, and not the predispositions of gender, that creates eating disorders. The shifting expectations also point out a keen difference between Howe and the nineteenth-century eating disorders described by Gilbert and Gubar: nineteenth-century women were writing about the limitations in their experience, while Howe writes about the possibility of freedom. This insistence on transcendence is at the core of Howe's nouvelle cuisine.

Howe wants her audience to bring a healthy appetite to this woman's table. Thus, she has Herrick Simmons, Nessa Vox, and Tony Stassio satirize classic cases of anorexia and bulimia. First these women argue elaborately over which wine to order; the discussion becomes a scheme to avoid the confrontation with food. However, once the dishes arrive, instead of an anorexic competition to see who can eat the least, the women have a rather shrill fight over who has ordered which entrée, since each dish that Cal brings out is more beguiling than the previous one. The scene becomes not only a reversal of our expectations regarding the classic female skimpy eater, but also a satire of the determined, competitive "hungry heroine" who will battle her own gender to obtain what she insists is hers.

At one point, however, Tony Stassio, the chronic dieter, rebels against this masculine competition, and pushes her bass away after only a few mouthfuls, saying that she has had enough. Undoubtedly she is full—full of and disgusted by the patriarchal grab for power she witnesses. The other two continue to savor the dishes arrayed before them, and become pointedly irritated at Stassio who refuses to eat and who pronounces herself to be fat. Nessa Vox, in anger, accuses her: Stassio, Vox humiliatingly insists, has hidden stores of food in her house, just as an alcoholic has hidden bottles. Her rage building, Vox declares that as soon as Stassio arrives home she will secretly devour third-rate snacks extracted from the frozen depths of her refrigerator.

Later, the women have a frank discussion about breasts. A woman, it seems, proudly flashed a round breast at Herrick Simmons on Fifth Avenue in New York; the action pleased Simmons, and her description of it pleases Vox. In this reversal, in which Howe again has a woman assume a traditional male role, that of flasher, Howe shows us another difference between men and women. Men flash to threaten and shock; they are using their physical bodies to symbolize their power over women. The woman, in contrast, flashed her breast in proud defiance of female restriction, and, moreover, flashed to someone of her own sex in a gesture that affirmed their sisterhood. Furthermore, her breast was round, which suggests that to be round is to be feminine; there is no need to fear the calories that enhance this roundness.

It becomes clear from the women's discussion of the flashing incident and the ensuing discussion of their own breasts that their ideal body types have been male-defined. Tony Stassio confesses that she has "shitty breasts" and that when she gains weight they get "*really* pendulous! 'Old bananas,' [her] brother used to call [her]!" Herrick Simmons, outraged, believes that all breasts are beautiful and life-giving.[47] Simmons's position reinforces the idea that when a woman bears the food it is safe to eat. She also angrily defies the male standards that insist women see their bodies in certain ways, indeed, that the very breasts that suckled males as babies be shaped in a certain way. Suddenly aware of the real issues involving food and their implications, the women eat with bitter avidity.

The wacky misadventures and sad comedy of the socially inept Elizabeth Barrow Colt also are central to the play's themes. Colt is a writer whose presumably insightful literary glimpses are not related to her ability to see literally, for she is horribly nearsighted. "Eye 'troubles,'" Gilbert and Gubar point out, ". . . seem to abound in the lives and works of literary women."[48] In *The Art of Dining*, however, disease is always the basis for salvation. Also, much of the comedy in Howe's play comes from Colt's blissful ignorance of the material world because she cannot see it. Nevertheless, Colt's eyes elicit favorable comment from her publisher (and the other diners); he finds them "extraordinary."[49]

Moreover, since Howe is a writer who consciously works with images and metaphors, an audience might begin to suspect that Howe is making a point about the connection between the invisible and the visible worlds. Elizabeth Barrow Colt is more at ease with the invisible world of her private

Anne Shropshire as Fanny Church and Lyn Greene as Mags Church
in a scene from the Cincinnati Playhouse in the Park's production of
Painting Churches by Tina Howe. (Photo © Sandy Underwood.)

imagination than she is with the visible society of the public restaurant. Shut up with her imagination for company, Colt creates art for public consumption, in much the same manner that Ellen, another hidden artist, creates gourmet dishes for her hungry customers. However, Colt's hidden existence is a lonely half-life. Colt is the agoraphobiac, the anorexic victim, who must be nurtured by women's food before she can feel safe and become part of the social world.

Nudging, nurturing, and nourishing this reclusive artist will take some doing. For example, in a comic sequence Colt spills her bowl of soup on her lap; upon being furnished a new one, she drowns her lipstick in it. In two neat gestures, Howe has shown the rebellious refusal of food (the spilled soup), and the rejection of beauty standards (the drowned lipstick). It later becomes clear that Colt, like most women, is hungry and desires a meal that will take her own needs into consideration. Where will she find it? When she seeks the women's room, she inevitably finds herself in Ellen's kitchen.

Other important issues coalesce in this character. Her monologues connect female art with female rebellion. Colt tells David Osslow, her publisher, that she grew up in a suffocatingly wealthy household; controlling her intake of food was the only control she could exercise during the oppressive mealtimes. The idiosyncrasies of her parents' mealtimes—which were indicative of their rigid, narrow philosophies—sickened her; she did not want to be like her mother and father. Ordered to clean her plate, she spit half-chewed bits of food into her napkin. Colt, however, managed to sublimate hunger and transform it into art. Her fiction is the product of that hunger, as well as a product of her extraordinarily clear, but nearly blind, eyes. Unlike male discovery of identity, which provokes, as Oedipus showed, a self-inflicted blindness, Howe's *The Art of Dining* suggests that female blindness frees the woman artist, as Elizabeth Barrow Colt shows, to discover the liberating potential in life and art.

In another monologue, Colt tells of her mother, an eccentric in outrageous hats adorned with plastic fruits, who did not understand the intricacies of cooking, nor the delicate nourishing properties of food, nor, by implication, the necessity of maternal nourishment for her child; in despair, Colt's mother once stuck her head into the oven—the symbolic hearth-center of the household—in a suicide attempt. The plastic fruits, however, caught on fire; she withdrew her head, and was thereafter condemned to life. In much the same way, Eve's successors have been given plastic fruits—mere tokens of the real thing—which burn and inflict pain rather than taste good and nourish; condemned to life, the necessary diet to be healthy in such a barren life remains a mystery for many women.

Colt and the other diners at The Golden Carrousel solve that mystery, however. At the end of the play, all the diners, male and female, are equalized by their common, primitive hunger. Elizabeth Barrow Colt makes a brief speech about sharing in the feast before a great communal fire. If we allow ourselves to imagine this fire glowing within a cave, then we are in familiar territory. Caves, as Gilbert and Gubar point out, are female places, metaphors for the womb.[50] Safe in a nourishing place, her uniqueness and potential for growth encouraged rather than suppressed, Colt joins the other feasters. She feels equal to them, no longer inadequate; the stage directions pointedly say: *"She helps herself to some crepe and for the first time all evening, she eats. She looks at ELLEN, who smiles at her."*[51] The Golden Carrousel, it turns out, is a matriarchal microcosm. The metaphor of the pretty carousel, pointlessly spinning, its parts moving up and down, representing binging and purging, is transformed by a woman into a place where no one need deny or be denied nourishment while enjoying the ride.

Howe's next full-length effort, *Painting Churches*, in the first twelve drafts was about a concert pianist who returned home to be fitted for a dress for her debut. After three years, Howe realized that her attempts to break new dramatic ground by putting a nonverbal character between two highly verbal characters simply was too flaccid. When Howe allowed her keen interest in the visual arts to surface, she was struck by the solution: a portrait painter (Margaret "Mags" Church) returns to Boston to do a canvas of her parents for her first one-woman show. The eccentric parents—the senile, aesthetic Gardner Church and the chattering, flamboyant Fanny Church—are presented to show their tenderness, humor, antagonism, deterioration, and pain as they move to the final bleakness of death. Their approval of their daughter's rendering of them is Tina Howe's way of reconstructing the final approval she wanted, but never asked for, from her own parents when they were alive.

This hunger for approval is central to the play, which was first produced in 1983. Although Mags is an accomplished artist and a distinguished person—she wears *"distinctive clothes"* and has *"very much her own look"*[52]—her mother in particular criticizes her deviation from the genteel Brahmin norm, her renderings in her portraits, and her choice of associates, as well as her presentation of herself. Mags responds by filling her wounds with food. Never particular about what she ingests, Mags throughout the play eats a variety of nonessential foods, including Saltines, Sara Lee banana cake, and tapioca. Mags admits that she eats like that only when she comes home.

On the surface, Mags seems to tolerate, if a bit ruefully, her narcissistic parents' nonacceptance of her. In this, she exhibits the classic pattern of the binge eater, who seemingly takes the hard knocks of life with ease, only to surrender frequently to them, seeking the balm of calories for her pain and rage. Orbach explains that the emotions involved—in Mags's case, the hurt of parental rejection—are too painful for acknowledgement: "[T]he woman cannot embrace them or examine them. They terrify her so that she goes towards food in an attempt to quell and bury them."[53] Food to Mags has always represented the artistic impulse; using it as a kind of medium, she, like Elizabeth Barrow Colt, is able to transform pain into beauty. Her great childhood masterpiece, like Agnes Vaag's sculpture in *Museum*, had rich texture and great tactile appeal. Like the Vaag piece, Mags's work had a lot to say about nurturing and form.

She designed this work in exile. When Mags was nine years old, she was banished from the dinner table for six months. At that table, food for her had become a tool for her creative purposes: she played with it, squirted it between her front teeth. Her father admired the intricate designs that resulted, but her mother, a stickler for table manners, had already constricted the child so that she feared the procedures of eating. The tyranny of the table triggered Mags's refusal to ingest food. Orbach reports that anorexic women recall their childhood mealtimes as situations of "rigid order or chaotic confusion."[54] Mags experienced the first and created the other.

Mags's response to rigidity was defiance of parental control and management of her self, a self that emerged in deviant ways, first as a food artist, and later as a painter. Mags's rage at the Churches' rules caused her hunger to seek satiation beyond food. In her room, she denied the nourishment that was sent to her; refusing to ingest repulsive worldly offerings and to excrete disgustingly their remains later, she simply flushed the food down the toilet. Her energy (hyperactivity is a symptom of anorexia nervosa), her desire to express herself, and her need for some sort of transcendental, liberating force, led her to more creative endeavors.

The refusal of food was an assertion of will. Mags could not reform her parents; indeed, she could not get them to acknowledge her as a distinct human being. Control of her own body was the only means of self-assertion available to Mags. Rudolph M. Bell in *Holy Anorexia,* which posits that many medieval Italian women saints had anorexia, argues that the disorder manifests itself because of "a need to establish a sense of oneself."[55] This "quest for autonomy"[56] is central to the condition. Hilde Bruch, a noted expert on the subject, wrote in *Eating Disorders: Obesity, Anorexia Nervosa, and the Person Within*:

> Anorexics struggle against feeling enslaved, exploited, and not permitted to lead a life of their own. They would rather starve than continue a life of accommodation. In this blind search for a sense of identity and selfhood they will not accept anything that their parents, or the world around them, has to offer. . . . [In] *genuine* or *primary anorexia nervosa,* the main theme is a struggle for control, for a sense of identity, competence, and effectiveness.[57]

An emblem of independence, food to the young Mags also was a sensuous medium that deserved a noble end. Exiled to her own creative cave, she listened to her parents eating as though she were hearing them engaged in sex: "[I] sat on my bed listening to you: clinkity-clink, clatter clatter, slurp, slurp." The noises unconsciously inspired her, and as she looked around for something to do, she noticed that her crayons had melted on the radiator "into these beautiful shimmering globs, like spilled jello, trembling and pulsating. . . ." She discovered that sex is creative, beautiful, magical; she took a red crayon and melted it on the "hissing lid. It oozed and bubbled like raspberry jam!"[58] She soon melted all of her crayons, transformed the phallic objects; her oral impregnation fantasy became a grand, colorful sculpture. However, the creation begins to "show" after the first trimester: "AFTER THREE MONTHS THAT RADIATOR WAS . . . SPECTACULAR! I MEAN, IT LOOKED LIKE SOME COLOSSAL FRUIT CAKE, FIVE FEET TALL! . . ."[59]

That it was food that impregnated her imagination is clear: "For every color," she says, "I imagined a taste." Yellow represented "lemon curls dipped in sugar"; red represented "glazed cherries laced with rum"; green represented "tiny peppermint leaves veined with chocolate."[60] In the manner of an expanding womb under skin and clothing, she kept the creation hidden under blankets during the day. She came to think of it as a growing part of her identity; not as the separate monster that Sandy created in *Birth and After Birth*, but as her "huge . . . looming . . . teetering sweet. . . ."[61] Here was a fanciful, exotic delight that was the antithesis of a powerless little girl.

The creation met an untimely end; it was aborted by Mags's parents, who appeared in her bedroom when Mags was having a nightmare. Her creation stood uncovered in all of its feminine glory, "like some . . . gigantic Viennese pastry! . . . Mummy screamed . . . 'IT'S FOOD!' she cried . . . 'IT'S ALL THE FOOD SHE'S BEEN SPITTING OUT! OH, GARDNER, IT'S A MOUNTAIN OF ROTTING GARBAGE!' "[62] Fanny, unable to cope with the sensuous creations of the cave, ordered the art work destroyed. In retelling the story as an adult, Mags acknowledges that the sculpture was indeed "a monument to my cast-off dinners," but its substance was not food. "I found my own materials,"[63] Mags says pointedly. She rejected the bitter offerings of an inhospitable environment to create a sweeter structure much closer to her own needs.

Now she has returned to her childhood environment on her own terms, as a portrait artist with recognized talent. She uses her own materials again, this time to transform her parents into art. Her obsession with food has not destroyed her; she is very much alive. She has chosen her future instead of thinness, and people instead of a diet.[64] Now her materials and her parents' materials, her imagination and their discipline, her art and their expectations, now she and they must confront one another and negotiate creation of an artwork that accurately represents the truest parts of each.

Howe's concerns for the body, for art, for food, and for pregnancy, co-alesce into a mature rendering of space in *Coastal Disturbances,* which opened at the Second Stage in 1986. These themes shift, are buried, then revealed again in the twenty tons of sand that cover the stage at Circle in the Square, the play's eventual home. The setting this time is a *"stretch of private beach on the North Shore of Massachusetts,"*[65] where near-naked bodies reveal truths about the human condition.

Howe once again chooses a visual artist as a protagonist. Holly Dancer, 24, is a beautiful photographer, who relies on Milky Way candy bars and m & m treats to calm her nerves. When Holly meets Leo Hart, 28, the life-guard and an astonishing physical specimen, she depends on a Milky Way to satisfy her arousal. Holly also consumes the calorie-laden chocolates while va-cantly staring at the horizon, as if in contemplation of the compelling pull of the future. For the time being, Holly trades food for that future.

This choice of neurosis over health is also evinced in her unlikely alliance with the pretentious André, who is twice her age, who pets her with a fa-therly indulgence, and who fills her with vague promises of a show in his gallery. She does not resist his paternal tenderness, but it is sex with Leo that provides fulfilling joy. Nevertheless, she remains aligned with André, and de-fends this choice by telling Leo that "[André] makes me crazy, but I'm just so alive with him. . . ." To which Leo responds: "And with me, you're only happy, right . . . ?"[66]

Fantasies of unusual pregnancies reminiscent of *Birth and After Birth* and *Painting Churches* abound in *Coastal Disturbances.* Faith Bigelow, 35, and her husband after years of trying have at last conceived a baby; their adopted seven-year-old daughter, Miranda, touchingly expresses the thought: "I feel as if all three of us made it."[67] Faith welcomes the insistent sturdiness that comes with fully using and taking up space. In contrast, Ariel, 36, believes that her "equipment has dried up. . . . After ten hours of hard labor," Ariel sadly jokes, "I'd push out this small grey . . . moth."[68] She, like Sandy in *Birth and After Birth,* reckons with images of shriveling to fit comfortably within confinement. Ariel's mental state is in unhappy tandem with her physical self; lost in space, she has attempted suicide numerous times.

In this play, though, Howe comes to terms with her preoccupation with space evident in the hidden manuscript of her first full-length play and in all succeeding plays. There is space registered by the unborn generation carried within the allegorically named Faith, who experiences the joyous crowding of the space within; in contrast, there is Ariel's moth fluttering in her dusty, useless expanses. But Ariel, like Agnes Vaag and Mags Church, will find her own materials and create a space for her and her son, Winston. This is symbolized by the ragg wool, hemp, mohair, and angora piece that she is weaving: "It started out as a shawl," she tells Faith, "but is turning into this gigantic . . . *house!*"[69] Unlike Mags's aborted, teetering sweet, it will be a fanciful, yet enduring space, because her most permanent creation, her son, is helping her make it. This illustrates the power belonging to a woman, who, like all the weavers of mythology, has the power to create not only her own motherhood, but also her own fate.

Other signs of a reckoning with space are present. There are the children, Miranda and Winston, bratty and exuberant, but also attempting to understand the vast, bewildering adult world. There are the young, vital single people, Holly and Leo, who might blend their explosive vitality and end up with happiness; their shared blanket marks a space of love. There is the middle-aged André, who with no talent of his own will simply slide across the shiny veneer of photographic talent provided by others. There are Hamilton and M. J. Adams, who are in their early seventies and late sixties, respectively, and who, having raised their family of nine, are now trying to make final sense of the world: in the pieces of coral that Hamilton finds on the beach, and in M. J.'s watercolors that attempt to capture the shifting changes of the world. The anniversary tent that they erect is a demarcation of their own space. It signifies the private endurance of a long life together despite such tribulations as philandering and frustration. In the end, they find themselves both closed off and enclosed; sealed from the expanse of beach and the endless horizon, they confront the other and the self.

Neurotic patterns may give way to happiness, which must be created by responsible people consciously seeking its beautiful, gauzy enclosure. Stripped of illusion, people face themselves and then one another. As Holly tells Leo when she explains that she took photographs of herself in the nude: "There's something about facing your own body that's . . . I don't know. . . . It's exhilarating."[70] In *Coastal Disturbances* once the prerequisite of accepting the body is met, the person clothes, houses, and shares that body, a citadel of life and art.

By focusing on food and the body, Howe's plays remind audiences of a woman's drive and a woman's need to control her own destiny. So many of Howe's female characters, like so many women in life, learn that they cannot control life-at-large, but that they can control their own bodies. But these are hungry women, and controlling their bodies is rarely enough: virtually all of Howe's protagonists manage to transform their hungers, cravings, and excess energies into art.

In *Birth and After Birth* Sandy's abject surrender to starvation was her means to control her life, her means of release from monsters; she also managed to create life imaginatively in a false pregnancy for Mia. Agnes Vaag in *Museum* transformed the detritus of life into enlightenment. In later plays — *The Art of Dining, Painting Churches,* and *Coastal Disturbances* — Howe introduces the possibility of love, a creative love that occurs through the same self-transcendence that makes personal art. Elizabeth Barrow Colt in *The Art of Dining* is nudged from her shell because of her brilliant art, an art that is fashioned from deep, sublimated cravings. Margaret Church in *Painting Churches* also transformed her hunger into art: not in a selfish Faustian quest for knowledge, as Blanche Gelfant urges upon "the sisters to Faust," but with the protective, embracing gossamers of love and forgiveness. In *Coastal Disturbances* there are hints that it is possible to move even beyond art, that one can, when one is ready, look at love full in the face without bracing oneself with food; love, like food, is something to be given, received, and enjoyed. If food in the early stages of Howe's career was either symbol or allegory, only to evolve into a weapon for self-assertion and shield for the self, then it finally became the addiction that induced a transformation of the highest order: from solipsistic rebellion to full, mature love.

Howe approaches her theatrical tasks in unusual ways. Her passion for unlikely places breathes life into ostensibly lifeless settings. She also insists on a double focus. Once the setting is established, she urges people to laugh at the superficial situation until they are plunged into the deeper level of self-recognition. She endeavors to show the frailty in success, the darkness beyond the light, the decay in the elegance, and the desperation in the humor. She relies on the theatricality of the visible to hint at the invisible. Howe has the courage to appear silly in order to show comedy's dark wisdom.

Howe offers her audiences a new restaurant not likely to appear in a Mobil travel guide. Its menu needs some translation, but the food is distinctive and healthy; hearty and delicate, it has been exquisitely prepared. There are just a few rules of the house. Howe insists that women have the right to control their bodies without starving them, to choose intellectual and artistic satisfaction wthout losing love, and to ensure that their private rebellions have public consequences.

NOTES

1. E. M. Forster, *Aspects of the Novel* (New York: Harvest/Harcourt Brace Jovanovich, 1955), 49, 53.

2. Virginia Woolf, *A Room of One's Own* (San Diego: Harvest/Harcourt Brace Jovanovich, 1929), 10.

3. Blanche Gelfant, "Sister to Faust: The City's 'Hungry' Woman as Heroine," in *Women Writers and the City: Essays in Feminist Literary Criticism,* ed. Susan Merrill Squier, 270 (Knoxville: University of Tennessee Press, 1984).

4. Gelfant, 268.

5. Sandra M. Gilbert and Susan Gubar, *The Madwoman in the Attic: The Woman Writer and the Nineteenth-Century Literary Imagination* (New Haven: Yale University Press, 1979), 374.

6. Woolf, 18.

7. Woolf, 24.

8. Gilbert and Gubar hint at this, 196.

9. Gilbert and Gubar discuss the misogyny inherent in the "myth of origins," 391.

10. Gilbert and Gubar, 54.

11. Susie Orbach, *Hunger Strike: The Anorectic's Struggle as a Metaphor for Our Age* (New York: Norton, 1986), 23.

12. Gilbert and Gubar, 54.

13. Gilbert and Gubar, 57.

14. Orbach, 30.

15. Tina Howe, "Antic Vision," *American Theatre*, September 1985, 14.

16. Tina Howe, personal telephone interview, 27 September 1985.

17. The characters are fantastic versions of Howe's parents: Quincy Howe, the noted radio commentator, journalist, editor, and author; and Mary Post Howe, a painter and colorful socialite. Howe later refined the characters for *Painting Churches.*

18. Orbach, 14.

19. Howe, "Antic Vision," 12.

20. Gilbert and Gubar, 86.

21. Gilbert and Gubar, 391.

22. Gilbert and Gubar, 391.

23. Tina Howe, *Birth and After Birth,* in *The New Women's Theatre: Ten Plays by Contemporary American Women,* ed. and with an intro. by Honor Moore, 110 (New York: Vintage, 1977).

24. Laura Mulvey, "Visual Pleasure and Narrative Cinema," *Screen* 16.3 (1975): 11, quoted in Judith Mayne, "Feminist Film Theory and Women at the Movies," *Profession 87* (New York: Modern Language Association, 1987), 15.

25. Orbach, 35.

26. Tina Howe, *Museum,* in *Three Plays by Tina Howe* (New York: Avon, 1984), 68.

27. Howe, *Museum,* 40.

28. Orbach, 23.

29. Orbach, 36.

30. Howe, *Museum,* 47.

31. Howe, *Museum,* 10.

32. Howe, *Museum,* 54.

33. Howe, *Museum,* 54.

34. Howe, *Museum,* 55.

35. Howe, *Museum,* 55.

36. Howe, *Museum,* 58.

37. Howe, *Museum,* 59.

38. Howe, *Museum,* 60.

39. Howe, "Antic Vision," 12.

40. Ross Wetzsteon, "The Mad, Mad World of Tina Howe," *New York,* 28 November 1983, 66.

41. Howe, "Antic Vision," 14.

42. Tina Howe, *The Art of Dining,* in *Three Plays by Tina Howe* (New York: Avon, 1984), 72.

43. Howe, "Antic Vision," 14.

44. Howe, *Dining,* 72.

45. Howe, *Dining,* 105.

46. Howe, *Dining,* 107.

47. Howe, *Dining,* 143.

48. Gilbert and Gubar, 58.

49. Howe, *Dining,* 135.

50. Gilbert and Gubar, 93–96, passim.

51. Howe, *Dining,* 149.

52. Tina Howe, *Painting Churches,* in *Three Plays by Tina Howe* (New York: Avon, 1984), 163.

53. Orbach, 16.

54. Orbach, 64.

55. Rudolph M. Bell, *Holy Anorexia,* epilogue William N. Davis (Chicago: University of Chicago Press, 1985), 8.

56. Bell, 8.

57. Hilde Bruch, *Eating Disorders: Obesity, Anorexia Nervosa, and the Person Within* (New York: Basic Books, 1973), 250–51, quoted in Bell, 17.

58. Howe, *Churches,* 193.

59. Howe, *Churches,* 194.

60. Howe, *Churches,* 194.

61. Howe, *Churches,* 194.

62. Howe, *Churches,* 195.

63. Howe, *Churches,* 195.

64. William N. Davis, in the epilogue to Bell's *Holy Anorexia,* discussed the goals of intervention: "Treating anorexia . . . necessitates taking action. . . . At the least it means making an effort to dramatically and significantly engage the patient so that her powerful need to choose thinness instead of a future and a diet instead of people can be reversed," 189.

65. Tina Howe, *Coastal Disturbances* (New York: Samuel French, 1987), 9.

66. Howe, *Disturbances,* 85.

67. Howe, *Disturbances,* 31.

68. Howe, *Disturbances,* 33.

69. Howe, *Disturbances,* 82.

70. Howe, *Disturbances,* 23–24.

MARGARET B. WILKERSON

Music as Metaphor:
New Plays of Black Women

When I told a colleague a couple of years ago that I was working on an anthology of plays by black American women, she looked surprised and exclaimed, "Oh, I didn't know that you could narrow plays down to such a minute group." She spoke as if I were writing about left-handed polo players who had been born in New Jersey or curly-haired women with short legs, as if black women playwrights had nothing in common. It was, I found, a fairly typical response for academics, for the black woman artist remains largely invisible in dramatic literature and art. Except for the "occasional" achievement of a Lorraine Hansberry or an Ntozake Shange, the black woman playwright goes unnoticed. Even Hansberry and Shange are often ignored in contemporary American drama courses or in season schedules of major theatres.

Yet the black woman's experience in this America is unparalleled. Social, political, and economic forces have long demeaned and distorted her life, beginning with her enslavement in America. Not only was she a slave, but her children were defined as slaves as well, regardless of their paternity. The enormity of this fact is almost incomprehensible, for it made the black woman the legal instrument of her people's slavery. She was an anomaly of the slave system — suffering the same brutality as her male counterpart, yet enduring as well those forms of oppression peculiar to her gender — rape and forced childbearing. Her plight caused white women to take a second look at their own oppression, while her own survival forced her to fight for her people's liberation. Thus the women's movement was born out of the black movement for liberation with the black woman as midwife. She is but one hundred and twenty-one all-too-human years from the ending of slavery — a short span by human generations. And the years between have been one long, torturous struggle to gain full human and civil rights. Injustice has intruded into her most private moments as she has continued to define herself beyond the stereotypes of mammy and whore that have pervaded the canon of American literature and drama.[1]

In recreating and redefining herself, the black woman has found in music a powerful metaphor for her experience. The grunts and moans of the work songs and the blues, the veiled messages of the spirituals, the sassy truths of rhythm and blues tell her story with urgency and passion. Black music, born out of the need for an expressive as well as a coded and private language, is as implicitly political as the lives these writers depict. And writers from Langston Hughes to Alice Walker, from Richard Wright to Lorraine Hansberry to Ntozake Shange, have attempted to emulate the efficiency and evocative qualities of that form. Langston Hughes rarely traveled without his record player and attempted through several works to capture in poetry the sound and sense of music. LeRoi Jones in *Blues People* traced the Negro's pathway to American citizenship through the analogy of the slave's music. Many artists consider black music to be America's most sophisticated and expressive art form.

Ma Rainey, in Broadway playwright August Wilson's *Ma Rainey's Black Bottom,* captures one of the fundamental qualities of black music that distinguishes it from Euro-American music: Music is "life's way of talking. You don't sing to feel better. You sing because that's a way of understanding life."[2] Jazz and blues and other forms of black music are inseparable from the attitudes and experiences that shaped them. The changes in pitch and time, the shifts in stress, the texture of timbre and vibrato negate European regularity and stability of tone, and deliver a music whose emphasis is as much an *expression* as the artifact itself. This music "speaks" the rage, the irony, the profundity of Black-American life in tonalities and colorations absent from conventional western speech. The source of instrumentation, whether it be voice or saxophone, is unimportant as the horns of jazz musicians emulate the human voice. And the voice of the blues singer co-opts the timbre of the saxophone or the grunt and holler of the "speaking voice." Ethnomusicologists now widely accept the influence of African music on the development of Black-American music. African drumming set the foundation through its complex, phonetic reproduction of words and its polyphonic and contrapuntal rhythmic structures.

For the playwright, this rich musical background stimulates new ways of conceptualizing music as an element of drama. Thus contemporary black women playwrights find in music a second language that gives expression to the profound anguish and joy of their vision and experience. They are mining this rich vein in innovative ways, finding in the dissonant tones of black music a powerful expressive mode. They have responded to Ntozake Shange's call for a radical new approach to black theatre that recaptures and creates anew black art traditions.

In the preface to her anthology of plays, *Three Pieces,* Shange writes: "As a poet in american theater / I find most activity that takes place on our stages overwhelmingly shallow / stilted and imitative."[3] While recognizing the popularity of Broadway plays about the lives of black musicians and singers (*Eubie, Bubbling Brown Sugar, Ain't Misbehavin', Mahalia*), she criticizes the form, the musical, that is used to portray these "black people who conquered their environments / or at least their pain with their art. . . ."[4] She goes on to ask:

> what is a writer to do to draw the most human & revealing moments from lives spent in nonverbal activity . . .[5]

Her answer is provocative and implicitly critical of American theatrical forms.

> if Fats Waller & Eubie Blake & Charlie Parker & Savilla Fort & Katherine Dunham moved the world outta their way / how did they do it / certainly not by mimicking the weakest area in american art / the american theater. we must move our theater into the drama of our lives / which is what the artists we keep resurrecting (or allowing others to resurrect) did in the first place / the music & dance of our renowned predecessors appeals to us because it directly related to lives of those then living & the lives of the art forms.[6]

If black writers are to capture the nascent primacy and vitality of theatre, then they must be bold in discarding useless theatrical forms derived from the expressive needs of Euro-Americans and pioneer in developing indigenous forms from black culture, according to Shange.

> i wd suggest that we demolish the notion of straight theater for a decade or so, refuse to allow playwrights to work without dancers & musicians. "coon shows" were someone else's idea. we have integrated the notion that a drama must be words / with no music & no dance / cuz that wd take away the seriousness of the event / cuz we all remember too well / the chuckles & scoffs at the notion that all niggers cd sing and dance / & most of us can sing & dance / & the reason that so many plays written to silence & stasis fail / is cuz most black people have some music & movement in our lives. we do sing & dance. this is a cultural reality. this is why I find the most inspiring theater among us to be in the realms of music & dance. . . .
>
> the fact that we are an interdisciplinary culture / that we under-

stand more than verbal communication / lays a weight on afro-american
writers that few others are lucky enough to have been born into.[7]

Shange herself willingly accepted this "weight" in her first version of *Boogie
Woogie Landscapes* in which she presented herself "with the problem of having . . . [her] person / body, voice & language / address the space as if . . .
[she] were a band / a dance company & a theater group all at once. Cuz a
poet shd do that / create an emotional environment / felt architecture."[8] And
who can forget the moving climax at the end of Shange's outstanding work,
for colored girls who have considered suicide / when the rainbow is enuf, which occurs
not through the spoken word, but through song, gesture, and finally the
dance of the women, as they sing, "i found god in myself. . . ."

In *Spell #7*, Shange evokes a potent symbol of the exploitation of black
music, the minstrel, in the form of a giant mask on stage, an opening cake
walk of black-face minstrels, and a wise-cracking magician whose speech is
filled with innuendoes. In nineteenth- and early twentieth-century American
theatre, the black-faced minstrel who sang and danced was the primary image
of blacks on stage. Initially the "music" of the minstrels, played by whites
in black face, was an imitation of jigs and songs created by southern slaves.
As blacks gradually replaced the white performers, the mask of black face remained for a time, but the "music" was gradually replaced by new and authentic black songs and dances. By using the minstrel concept to frame *Spell #7*,
Shange evokes the ambivalence of artists under political pressure and sets a
proper context for her black characters (who are artists) to gather at their favorite club to "act out" the frustrations of their lives. They cast away their minstrel masks, reclaiming their true visages and their song in this lyrical work.
Thus, the reconceptualization of music in theatrical form is not limited to
obvious insertions of "musical pieces" as in the typical American musical, but
as in the case of this Shange play, may lead to characterizing the artist's contemporary situation through the historical and pervasive musical stereotype,
the minstrel.

Hansberry, who wrote more than a decade before Shange, used music
to express the multiple dimensions of reality. Two of her works, *Les Blancs*
and *Toussaint,* both of which were unfinished at her death in 1965, illustrate
this approach. In *Les Blancs,* set in an African country in the midst of a violent revolution, Hansberry critiques the colonialists' mentality that assumes
a right to "settle" Africa and to impose upon it their "civilization." The
strains of European classical music are clearly anachronistic in the bush and
are soon overwhelmed by the African drums. In the only completed scene

from her play, *Toussaint,* which was intended to become an opera about the great Haitian liberator, she used music more directly, as subtext to express the contradictions in a "genteel civilization" that was built on the enslavement and brutalization of other human beings. The first scene of the unfinished play begins with "island music" characteristic of Haitian native culture.

The Great House of a sugar plantation on Santo Domingo in the 1780s — immediately before the outbreak of the Haitian Revolution. The massed voices of field slaves can be heard, welling up in the distance in a song of fatigue. Their music is an organ-toned plaint which yet awaits a Haitian Moussorgsky. It is, of course, punctuated by the now distinctive rhythms of the island.

> Oh, when will the sun go down!
> Oh, when will the shadows come?
> Shadow of night!
> Shadow of rest!
>
> Oh, when will the night hide the cane?
> Oh, when will the dark hide the sun?
> Night, the friend!
> Friend, the night!

As this strong music fades it is promptly replaced by the fragile tinkle of an eighteenth-century French minuet being played somewhere in the house on a delicate harpsicord.[9]

The minuet continues more or less throughout the scene, providing counterpoint and comment on the scene of muted violence played out on stage between Bayon de Bergier and his Creole wife, Lucie. Both are trapped in the oppressive system that keeps Bayon merely a petty bourgeois subject to a Parisian absentee owner, and Lucie, a "bought" Creole wife who shares his bed, his limited fortune, but not his heart. The gentle strains mock the horror of a slave being beaten outside their window. The final moments of the scene crystallize the meaning of the music: like its creators, the European colonialists, the music is indeed beautiful, but it is laced in human blood.

Lucie has angrily attacked Bayon for her lowly status as a wife: "A creature purchased is a creature purchased! To dress one in laces and sit her at the head of your dining board is no true index of value!"[10] Her words sharply remind that she is both wife and slave, that her "position" comes at the price of subordination — a kept though married woman. Then she speaks her venomous words to her bodyservant, Destine, whom she alternately slaps and

caresses—forcing herself sexually on her helpless slave. Destine is "stolid . . .
her face fixed like a mask." Here Hansberry cleverly introduces another element—silence—which forms yet another counterpoint to the angry, demanding words of Lucie, the cries of human pain outside the window, and the
strains of the minuet. In another sense, the cries of the male slave being beaten
outside contrast the visibility of his suffering to the private anguish of the
female slave in Lucie's room. Within this one scene, Hansberry depicts, largely
in nonverbal terms, the hierarchy of oppression with music as an ironic counterpoint. The lilting melody of the minuet, the white man's music, broken
by the cries of the slave without, the spoken rage of the wife/slave and the
tense silence of the servant within betray the casual, routine horrors that undergird this "civilization."

The use of a verbal rather than nonverbal contrapuntal form, adopted
from musical counterpoint, appears in Alice Childress's *Wedding Band,* a play
set in South Carolina about a ten-year relationship between a white man and
a black woman. At the emotional climax of this play, the language of the
lovers explodes with their racial baggage as each accuses the other of failing
to understand each other's feelings. Here Childress uses a verbal form of musical counterpoint to capture the frustration of the couple:

> *Julia.* Get out. Get your things and get out of my life. (*The remarks be-
> come counterpoint. Each rides through the other's speech. . . .* [emphasis
> mine] Must be fine to own somethin'—even if it's four walls and a
> sack-a-flour.
> *Herman.* . . . My father labored in the street . . . liftin' and layin' down
> cobblestone . . . liftin' and layin' down stone 'till there was enough
> money to open a shop. . . .
> *Julia.* My people . . . relatives, friends and strangers . . . they worked
> and slaved free for nothin' for some-a the biggest name families down
> here . . . Elliots, Lawrences, Ravenals. . . .
> *Herman.* Great honor, working for the biggest name families. That's
> who you slaved for. Not me. The big names.
> *Julia.* . . . the rich and the poor . . . we know you . . . all of you . . .
> Who you are . . . where you came from . . . where you goin'. . . .
> *Herman.* What's my privilege . . . Good mornin', good afternoon . . .
> pies are ten cents today . . . and you can get 'em from Schumann for
> eight. . . .
> *Julia.* "She's different" . . . I'm no different. . . .
> *Herman.* I'm white . . . did it give me favors and friends?[11]

The scene continues as the mood gradually shifts and the lovers finally reconcile their differences. Like jazz musicians, Herman and Julia play from a common melody, their love, but each out of his and her own need, own racial history and pain. The two independent but related themes subtly influence each other, even in their dissonance, and form a single harmonic texture. Childress's use of conterpoint is a brilliant choice at this moment in the play. The contrast between Herman and Julia has been made evident throughout the play. He, a white baker and of the working class, comes from a family with pretensions of superiority. She, a black woman domestic, comes from a legacy of slavery. Even visually, they present contrast and separateness. And Childress has not ignored the racial antipathy and stereotyping that each has inherited. Reconciliation is impossible without full recognition of their strong and potentially destructive differences. Counterpoint provides the perfect means for capturing their dissonance as well as the new music that this interracial couple must create.

Newer plays, by Alexis DeVeaux, the poetry editor of *Essence,* Aishah Rahman, and P. J. Gibson place the identity of the musician at the center of the work. In these plays, the musician (often male) is the lover or the bearer of love. Although there have been several notable black women musicians over time, the image of the jazz instrumentalist is essentially masculine. That masculine image, however, is softened and defined by the music itself that encompasses and expresses qualities associated with both women and men. Because the music is sensual, beautiful, and in touch with the intangible and the instinctive, it seems reasonable to assume a higher level of consciousness for its creator.

Alexis DeVeaux's *The Tapestry* depicts the struggle of a young black woman, Jet, to master self and lover's needs during the time when she must study for her law exams. Axis, her lover, is a musician who demands her attention and cannot understand the personal sacrifice that she must make in order to achieve this step in her hoped-for career. So he must be "serviced" sexually by her closest friend, Lavender, who is more than willing to accommodate him. While Axis is only one of several personal issues that she must resolve, his betrayal is potentially the most devastating to Jet. When Jet confronts him with his infidelity, he erupts into an angry tirade, claiming his right to sexual freedom.

> *Axis.* yeah thats right   thats just what
> i tell her and you know why?
> because all she wants is somebody to love her

a minute of a night   an hour
she dont care   she knows a man needs a woman
to let him be
if hes going to survive balls intact
in this country
somewhere down the line a man in my family
was lynched   did they use a rope?
it dont matter he was the first eunuch
with a snapped neck
he gets to carry the dead weight of all the family
men before me   as far as im concerned
my father was the last one
. . . .
im a whole man you hear me?
i don't take nothing from nobody
i love whoever i goddamn feel like it!
[*He exits.*][12]

In this instance, the musician is less than his music. DeVeaux strikes a sharp contrast between the beauty of Axis's music, his creative talent, and his insensitivity to Jet's needs. At the same time, his parting statement reminds us of his fallibility, indeed the pain that he carries as a black man. While the audience may condemn Axis for his actions, it is difficult to ignore the history that he cites. Jet, of course, has her own legacy of pain and struggle, which she attempts to transform into an asset for society as well as herself. At the end of the play, she literally pulls herself up and goes forth to take her law exams. Axis, however, remains the imperfect instrument of beautiful sounds. (It is worth noting that in 1987 Alexis DeVeaux wrote a play, *Elbow Rooms,* that was produced at Wabash College, an all-male college, in which the roles of Jet and Axis are reversed. That play, in which she intends to reflect the changes in the 1980s, focuses on a young man in the midst of exams whose girlfriend dates his best friend and claims for herself the sexual freedoms that Axis demands.)

P. J. Gibson takes the image of the musician a step further in *Brown Silk and Magenta Sunsets* as the "magic" (the music) that comes from the male musician's horn becomes a personal attribute. In this play, Lena Larsen Salvinoni is obsessed by the memory of her first lover, Roland Watts, whom she seduced while still a teenager. In a flashback to her youth, Lena is fascinated by this musician who lives in her building. His music makes love to her. The young Lena is speaking to Veeda, a woman who sings with Roland's band.

Veeda. Oh, Mr. Roland. You like Mr. Roland?

Lena. I like to listen to him play. Even watch him when he practices. How he holds that saxophone and closes his eyes.

Veeda. Guess I ain't been watchin' him the way you been watchin' him.

Lena. He got nice lips too. They're prettier than Mr. Mike's and Mr. Bob's.

Veeda. Oh yeah?

Lena. Umm humm. And you ever see how he puts it in his mouth, the saxophone. He wets his lips . . . (*She demonstrates.*) And then he . . . kinda sucks it in, like you do a straw. I think that's what makes his music sound so good.

Veeda. You do.

Lena. Umm humm. 'Cause that time yaw had that Mr. . . . . (*thinks*) Willis over . . . When he was playin' with Mr. Roland. He ain't wet his lips and he ain't suck on the mouthpiece and his music was flat. It ain't sound mood. It ain't make your innard feel like they been ridin' on the Ferris wheel out at Kennywood Park.

Veeda. Roland's music makes you feel all that?

Lena. (*Places her hand on her hip.*) It don't do that to you? Last Friday night. When he was practicin? It came down the stairs, crawled in my window, slipped up on my pillow and sang to me. His music sings to me.[13]

The delightful sensuality of this scene masks the serious implications of Lena's attitude. Lena is, in fact, seduced by the sensuousness of Roland's music, and spends the rest of her life trying to replicate the ecstasy of that magical union. Here music becomes the metaphor for the ideal and total relationship, something that proves to be unattainable for Lena. Later when Lena and Roland live and travel together with the band, the realities of motherhood, the hardships of traveling on the road, and the poverty of their relationship and circumstances distort that ideal. Lena, permanently seduced by Roland's music, becomes obsessive about Roland, choosing to lavish all of her attention on him, leaving none for their young daughter. The relationship ends in tragedy when the daughter commits suicide. Music comes from the soul and represents a triumph, however momentary, over human imperfection and frailty. Roland remains, in Lena's memory, as the idealized, magical musician, the closest that Lena can get to the pure and total union between self and "other." Lena tries desperately to make Roland into that "other," but, in fact, music is. Aishah Rahman's *Unfinished Women Cry in No Man's Land While a Bird*

Gina Scales, Liana Asim, Michelle Whitfield, Lori Reed, and
Anthony Bryan (background) in a scene from *Unfinished Women
Cry in No Man's Land While a Bird Dies in a Gilded Cage,* produced
by the St. Louis Black Repertory Company.

Dies in a Gilded Cage is more innovative than most in its handling of musician
and music. The play focuses on pregnant teenagers living at the Hide-A-Wee
Home for Unwed Mothers, who are at the point of deciding whether or not
to give their babies up for adoption. Placed alongside this setting on stage
is Pasha's boudoir where Charlie Parker ("The Bird"), the brilliant black saxophonist, lives out his final moments.

Framing the new and troubled lives of the babies is the death of Charlie
Parker. As with many other writers, the heightened existence of the black
musician claims Rahman's attention. Parker is one of the most important saxo-
phonists in the history of black music. An exciting instrumentalist who ranks
alongside Louis Armstrong, Parker was an innovator whom trumpet players,

piano players, guitar players, and others have continued to emulate. One of Parker's hallmarks was his ability to make his saxophone sound like the human voice. His music "spoke," almost literally. Rahman picks up this trait in *Unfinished Women* by requiring a saxophonist to provide the background sounds of the play. She insists that the music be live. During the course of the play, the wail of the saxophone often simulates the wail of a newborn baby.

What has Charlie Parker to do with these children bearing children? The answer comes at the very end of the play as one girl, Wilma, who is particularly stunned by Parker's death, describes the night when she became pregnant.

> I went down to Birdland one night and everybody was waiting for him [Charlie Parker] and when he finally showed he looked like he slept under the bandstand and hadn't shaved for weeks. I never saw anything like that and I never heard anything like his music. Charlie Parker played in tongues. . . .[14]

Wilma's thoughts seem to shift as she begins to ponder the baby inside her.

> I don't want to give up my baby, but . . . I know that it's a boy in here. S'funny what Bird meant to me. Secretly, I always wanted to be a man 'cause they can do things and go places. Bird is the man I wanted to be. Maybe my son will be like him. Dig that. Maybe I'm giving up a Charlie Parker. Maybe I'm thinking about giving up a Charlie Parker.[15]

Wilma, who is seriously contemplating giving her baby up for adoption, does not romanticize motherhood. In this passage, she begins to realize the significance of the baby's existence. She "knows" that it is a boy. The choice of gender by Rahman is deliberate, for it connects the innocent, new life and the human potential that the baby represents with the tragic life of Charlie Parker. It also places Wilma at the center of the universe as daughter and lover as well as mother and father (in her fatherless world) to creative genius.

As the soliloquy continues, Wilma remembers the baby's father as "someone I met at a dance. . . . He's just a man I gave myself to and I can't blame him for anything."[16] This passage underscores the casualness of their union and Wilma's failure to consider the likely consequences. Suddenly, she calls the pregnancy a curse that "got my mother and now it's got me . . . fatherless child, manless woman. . . ." Like typhoid, she watched it "pick . . . off" her friends one by one, while everyone wondered "who's next . . . who's next . . .

and now it's my turn. . . ."[17] There is a sense of helplessness in this passage imposed as much by racial restrictions as by gender constraints. Charlie Parker, whose masculine freedom she fantasized about, is shown in the play to be a frustrated black man whose creative genius was abused by a society that would not fully accept the implications of his talent; he died of drug abuse. Up to this point, scenes have alternated between the home for pregnant teenagers and the apartment where Parker pours out his wasting, waning life. Wilma's own legacy of fatherlessness and poverty has led her to this moment; she is, after all, a black female teenager, prey to the legacy of unemployment and social disorganization that distorts and devastates black relationships. Wilma's fantasy of freedom is a chimera in a racist and sexist society.

The tone of the monologue shifts as live saxophone music supports it. Here Wilma describes the moment and the meaning of conception.

> In Anthony's room, in his bed, lying there on my back, I could feel myself far below him, I was on the bottom of an ocean and he was the moon way up over me. A moon I could smell, a moon I could touch but whose face floated in and out of my mind. His body was spread all over, covering me like space. I crouched inside of myself, listening like an animal to our silence.[18]

In this second of silence, Bird's music floats in through an open window and takes her "back to a memory [she] . . . was born with."

> Following the music's heartbeat I took a journey I could no longer avoid and along the way I helped a woman toss her newborn baby overboard a slaveship. I joined hands with my mother as she took her mother's hand and I took my place in the circle of black women singing old blues. The man, spread high above me, worked over me, his sweat dripping down in my eyes and my voice screaming higher and higher along with Parker's sax . . . both sounds pouring over me, pulling me, pushing me to a point of passion, a point of pain and then . . . silence . . . and the smell of the rain falling outside as he breaks into my womb and bursts inside of me, overflowing on the sheets and bed and everything and I knew that the cycle of passion and pain, blood and birth, and aloneness had once again started, inside of me and I lay there wondering how many moons before i could become virgin again![19]

Rahman's frankly sensual language gives texture to sexual passion. Bird, the musician par excellence whose life wastes away before us on stage, is the real lover. Anthony, "the man," is almost incidental to the experience; he is merely the instrument who, led by Parker's music, brings Wilma to the point of conception. Bird's music embodies not only love, but the painful history of Wilma's forebears. Her sexual journey, charted by Bird's music, takes her back through the centuries to the Middle Passage when African mothers killed their babies rather than rear them in slavery. The expected pleasure of Wilma's orgasm is drowned in the ambivalence and uncertainty of conception—a child born into the twentieth-century legacy of slavery. She is awash in the passion and pain, the blood and birth, the bitter and the sweet—the eternal opposites that fuse into one being, one understanding. Like the women in DeVeaux's and Gibson's plays, the promise she anticipates of the music is not fulfilled. But perhaps she has not fully heard or understood this music born of the hope and disappointment that is the black experience, this music that "speaks" so eloquently and authoritatively the anger, passion, and ambivalence of the black voice. Only at this moment of existential commitment, at this moment when she enters the circle of her foremothers, does she begin to know the real meaning of the music and the musician that she idolizes. But it is Wilma who will bear and live with the responsibility of that moment. Even as she wonders how long before she can again become virgin, one unto herself, she senses that the answer may well be "never."

Later in the play, Wilma explains that the music is the unifier: "It's only in the head of a musician that I begin to understand. Only a musician can make sense for me. Only a musician knows how to connect shoes with cardboard to cover holes to P. S. 184 on 116th Street and Lenox Avenue to the red taste of watermelon and mocking white smiles to Anthony's smile and smell of Florida Water to late night loneliness and . . . this . . . [indicating her unborn baby]."[20] Although this passage is strikingly similar to a passage in Toni Morrison's *The Bluest Eye,* Rahman carries the idea further, basing her entire play around music and musician as embodiment of the passionate essence of life itself. Wilma, as characterized by Rahman, replaces the image of the baby-maker who seeks in motherhood a substitute for a relationship with a man or even the promiscuous girl whose immorality catches up with her. Although earlier in the play, Wilma has angrily shouted, "God! I HATE babies!"[21] when her roommate's baby continues to cry, Wilma now hesitates to give her baby away because she fears that she may be giving up another Charlie Parker. The death of this great musician, whose life embodies the personal and collective tragedy spawned by a cruel society that destroys its black creative geniuses, is a poignant reminder to Wilma what, in effect, her baby's life may really mean. Parker's music has brought her from a casual fling to the heart of life itself — creation and the ambivalence as well as the responsibility of bringing a black child into a racist world.

In *Unfinished Women* Rahman finds in music an extraordinary way of expressing the personal dilemma, the political reality, and the sensual dimension of women's lives. At the same time she challenges the stereotypes and simplistic thinking that would claim that the problem with teenage pregnancy is "in the crotch." Music becomes the means for "knowing" as well as an eloquent metaphor for the joy and anguish of black women's lives. In Rahman's world, there is no simplistic separation between "knowing" women and ignorant, insensitive men. Bird, for all his dissipation is a priest, a seer. He "knows" — or at least, he captures the meaning of his people's experience and knowledge in his music, despite his own fallibility. Like the African drummer, he initiates the ritual, in this case, of procreation, but it is up to the players, the dancers, to hear and understand the lessons of his music.

These and other black women playwrights are moving theatre into the drama of their lives, as Shange exhorts, shaping theatrical styles rather than distorting their experience to fit conventional modes. Music becomes a powerful instrument in their hands. Musical forms, particularly counterpoint, are adapted to enhance the effect of dialogue in Childress's work, while the historical and cultural significance of certain musical forms provide ironic commentary in Hansberry's and Shange's plays. But it has taken DeVeaux, Gibson, and Rahman to test the extent to which music itself can be integral to dramatic action and can enhance meaning. Rahman, in a recently produced three-character play *The Lady and the Tramp*, actually included a celloist as the third character who delivers musical commentary on the conversation between a black man and woman. This choice on the part of black women playwrights has serious implications for dramatic interpretation and criticism. When music, which exists in time and space like theatrical performance, becomes a primary dramatic element, the notion of "text" is permanently changed. And black music, with its complex rhythms and reliance on improvisation, makes musical notation (the equivalent of text) only marginally useful.

For these playwrights, music becomes metaphor for the deepest, unspoken (and often unspeakable) feelings and experiences of human existence; it becomes a nonverbal text with a life and significance of its own. Ironically, while it gives voice to human action, it may silence the conventional critic, forcing him or her to experience rather than simply read the text. In the hands of black women playwrights, the notion of theatre is changing because they know that music is as emotional, sensual, and political as the lives of black women.

NOTES

1. This paragraph is paraphrased from the introduction to my anthology, *9 Plays by Black Women* (New York: New American Library, 1986).

2. August Wilson, *Ma Rainey's Black Bottom* (New York: Samuel French, 1984).

3. Ntozake Shange, "black theater traditions," in *Three Pieces* (New York: St. Martin's Press, 1979).

4. Ibid.

5. Ibid.

6. Ibid.

7. Ibid.

8. Ibid.

9. Lorraine Hansberry, *Toussaint,* in *9 Plays by Black Women,* ed. Margaret B. Wilkerson, 55 (New York: New American Library, 1986).

10. Ibid., 62.

11. Wilkerson, 128–29.

12. Alexis DeVeaux, *The Tapestry,* in *9 Plays by Black Women,* 189.

13. P. J. Gibson, *Brown Silk and Magenta Sunsets,* in *9 Plays by Black Women,* 452.

14. Aishah Rahman, *Unfinished Women Cry in No Man's Land While a Bird Dies in a Gilded Cage,* in *9 Plays by Black Women,* 220.

15. Ibid.

16. Ibid.

17. Ibid., 221.

18. Ibid., 221.

19. Ibid.

20. Ibid., 235.

21. Ibid., 208.

GAYLE AUSTIN

The Madwoman in the Spotlight: Plays of Maria Irene Fornes

The madness of women has been a major concern in the work of feminist theorists such as Sandra M. Gilbert, Susan Gubar, Elaine Showalter, Hélène Cixous, and Catherine Clément. Female madness is also a rather common image in drama and has been used by male playwrights for centuries. As Showalter points out, Ophelia was *the* major image of female madness in Victorian England.[1] The madwoman's use by female playwrights has been far less frequent, however, reflecting their much smaller numbers. But in the last decade, Maria Irene Fornes has used the image to great advantage in three of her plays.

Fornes, a Cuban native who has been writing plays in New York City since the early 1960s, is a major figure in the off-off-Broadway scene and the winner of several Obie awards. Her work is notable for many reasons, one of which is its portrayal on stage of complex female characters and of the female unconscious. Three of her plays, *Fefu and Her Friends* (1977), *Sarita* (1984), and *The Conduct of Life* (1985), contain madwomen figures who are speaking, acting subjects. Examining these plays through a feminist lens focused on the madwoman figure shows Fornes to be a playwriting exemplar in both form and content.

Sandra M. Gilbert and Susan Gubar's *The Madwoman in the Attic*[2] develops work on a female tradition and traits of women's writing using nineteenth-century fiction and poetry only. In applying to women writers Harold Bloom's theory about the male writer's "anxiety of influence," they find that the woman writer experiences an "anxiety of authorship" or "a radical fear that she cannot create, that because she can never become a 'precursor' the act of writing will isolate or destroy her" (49). She seeks a precursor who "proves by example that a revolt against patriarchal literary authority is possible" (49). Contemporary women writers of fiction and poetry may feel less of this anxiety than women of earlier centuries because they have female precursors, but women playwrights are still in need of more such models than they presently have. Wider dissemination of criticism and production of Fornes's work would be one step in lessening some "anxiety of authorship." But for the nineteenth-century woman writer, this anxiety left a mark on her writing.

Women writers coped by *"revising* male genres, using them to record their own dreams and their own stories *in disguise."* Gilbert and Gubar call these works palimpsestic: "works whose surface designs conceal or obscure deeper, less accessible (and less socially acceptable) levels of meaning" (73). Very often the madwoman appeared in these palimpsestic works, "not merely, as she might be in male literature, an antagonist or foil to the heroine," but as "the *author's* double, an image of her own anxiety and rage" (78). The irony, of course, is that by "creating dark doubles for themselves and their heroines, women writers are both identifying with and revising the self-definitions patriarchal culture has imposed on them" (79).

One of the best examples of the use of the mad double is that of Bertha Mason Rochester in *Jane Eyre* (1847). In their detailed analysis of that novel, Gilbert and Gubar point out the many ways in which Bertha does what Jane wishes she might do, "is the angry aspect of the orphan child, the ferocious secret self Jane has been trying to repress" (360), and "not only acts *for* Jane, she also acts *like* Jane" (361). They conclude that "the literal and symbolic death of Bertha frees her [Jane] from the furies that torment her and makes possible . . . wholeness within herself" (362).

Another device used in these palimpsestic works is that of confinement (and sometimes escape). Very often female characters felt space anxiety in houses or rooms, and sometimes it was the madwoman who was so confined. (Bertha was not only mad but confined to the attic of her husband's house.) One paradigm of such imagery is "The Yellow Wallpaper" (1890) by Charlotte Perkins Gilman, in which a recent mother is confined to a garret room and forbidden to write as treatment for a nervous disorder. The woman worsens and eventually sees, locked behind the wallpaper of the room, a woman whom she helps escape by tearing off much of the wallpaper. Madness and confinement meet again in this story and together tell a powerful tale of female experience. This paradigm, however, is not one confined to the nineteenth century, or to women writers of prose.

Fornes's 1977 play *Fefu and Her Friends*[3] has a cast of eight women, has very little conventional plot, and takes place in five separate audience/stage spaces. The setting is described as follows:

New England, Spring 1935

Part I. Noon. The living room. The entire audience watches from the auditorium.

Part II. Afternoon. The lawn, the study, the bedroom, the kitchen. The audience is divided into four groups. Each group is guided to the spaces. These scenes are performed simultaneously. When the scenes are completed the audience moves to the next space and the scenes are performed again. This is repeated four times until each group has seen all four scenes.

Part III. Evening. The living room. The entire audience watches from the auditorium. (P. 6)

The house is Fefu's and the other characters are women who gather there to discuss a fundraising program for a vaguely defined cause related to education. The action of the play is the interactions of the women over the course of one afternoon and evening. It demonstrates the synapses between women when they are not with men. As Fefu says early in the play:

> Women are restless with each other. They are like live wires . . . either chattering to keep themselves from making contact, or else, if they don't chatter, they avert their eyes . . . like Orpheus . . . as if a god once said "and if they shall recognize each other, the world will be blown apart." They are always eager for the men to arrive. When they do, they can put themselves at rest, tranquilized and in a mild stupor. With the men they feel safe. The danger is gone. That's the closest they can be to feeling wholesome. Men are the muscle that cover the raw nerve. They are the insulators. The danger is gone, but the price is the mind and the spirit. . . . High price [author's ellipses]. (P. 13)

The play itself proceeds to dramatize a bit of that "danger" that occurs when female raw nerves are not insulated by men.

Part of the play's effect has to do with the close proximity of the audience to the performers in the smaller, enclosed spaces of the scenes in Part II. Audience members on two of the four sides of each room seem to "eavesdrop" on the conversations that take place there, more intimate than in the other two parts. The audience is split up, has to move around physically, must become active in order to see the entire performance. This unusual use of space has been remarked upon in criticism of the play, but has not seemed to have an influence on many other plays. It is one of many ideas this play presents that might profitably be explored by other writers, as well as critics. It is a play that must be experienced to be fully comprehended. Part of its effect comes from confining the audience in the same limited space the characters inhabit. The play also exhibits a feminist use of the madwoman.

The character of Julia enters Part I in a wheelchair and another character describes how Julia fell down at the same moment a hunter shot a deer, and from that moment has not been able to walk. While delirious, Julia said "That she was persecuted.—That they tortured her. . . . That they had tried her and that the shot was her execution. That she recanted because she wanted to live. . . ." (15). Fefu recalls that years ago Julia "was afraid of nothing," and that "she knew so much."

In Part II in the bedroom, as the stage direction says, "*Julia hallucinates. However, her behavior should not be the usual behavior attributed to a mad person*" (23). In her monologue, Julia relates persecution such as that which had been described in Part I. She was beaten, but never stopped smiling. She recites: "I'm not smart. I never was. Neither is Fefu smart. They are after her too. Well she's still walking!" She guards herself from a blow. Later she says, "Why do you have to kill Fefu, for she's only a joker? 'Not kill, cure. Cure her.' Will it hurt? (*She whimpers.*) Oh, dear, dear, my dear, they want your light" (24–25). She then recites a prayer that gives many of the reasons man has considered woman evil. Julia finally says, "They say when I believe the prayer I will forget the judges. And when I forget the judges I will believe the prayer. They say both happen at once. And all women have done it. Why can't I?" (25).

In Part III, after a rehearsal of the fundraising "show," Julia has a long speech in which she says, "Something rescues us from death every moment of our lives," and that she has been rescued by "guardians." However, she is afraid one day they will fail and "I will die . . . for no apparent reason" (35). Later on, Fefu, alone on stage, sees Julia walk, and seconds later she reenters in her wheelchair. Near the end, Fefu and Julia struggle, Fefu telling her to try to walk and to fight. Julia says she is afraid her madness is contagious and tries to keep away from Fefu. Fefu wants to put her own mind to rest and loses courage when Julia looks at her. She finally asks Julia to "Forgive me if you can," and Julia says, "I forgive you" (40). Fefu gets a shotgun used earlier in the play, goes out, a shot is heard, Julia's hand goes to her forehead and as it drops, blood is seen, and Julia's head drops. Fefu enters with a dead rabbit and all the women surround the dead Julia.

This series of scenes, interspersed among others, establishes the "madwoman" Julia as Fefu's double. The play itself, taking place less than ninety years after *Jane Eyre,* has a certain "feel" of the nineteenth century and there are striking similarities between Fefu/Julia and Jane/Bertha. Julia acts out the repressed, angry side of Fefu by struggling with the "guardians," and perhaps her death frees Fefu at the end of the play. But Fornes is a twentieth-century woman and the differences are also striking. The play is as if written by Jane and Bertha, with Rochester pushed offstage, his control lessened by his absence. Julia is not in the attic, but in the spotlight, speaking the truth for herself as subject alternately with speaking the text of male conventional attitudes about women in her "prayer." Fefu and Julia together, overtly bonded and overtly in conflict, make an open statement of women's predicament in the public forum of the theatre.

In the end, Fefu does what Julia cannot—acts. The madwoman is "killed" by her double. This action has many possible interpretations. For Helene Keyssar, ". . . Julia chooses not to fight but to yield. Fefu, however, will not let Julia go. Unable to reinvigorate her friend verbally, Fefu moves to Julia's symbolic terrain and shoots a rabbit." The meaning of this act for Keyssar is that, "Symbolically at least, and on stage where all things are possible, the woman-as-victim must be killed in her own terms in order to ignite the explosion of a community of women."[4] For Beverley Byers Pevitts, "if we recognize ourselves as women, 'the world will be blown apart.' When this does happen, the reflection that was made by others will be destroyed and we will be able to rebuild ourselves in our own image, created by woman." Julia, then, "is the one who is symbolically killed in the end of the play so that the new image of herself can emerge."[5]

In an interview with this writer in April, 1987, Fornes answered questions about the madwomen in her plays:

> Julia is really not mad at all. She's telling the truth. The only madness is, instead of saying her experience was "as if" there was a court that condemned her, she says that they did. I guess that's what makes her mad rather than just a person who is a visionary. The elements of her fantasy are visionary—they are completely within the range of clear thinking. Her fantasies are very organized.

The use of confinement in *Fefu* is also both like and unlike its use in nineteenth-century fiction. On the stage confinement is a visual, visceral reality. In Part II of *Fefu* the audience is confined, along with the actors, in the separate spaces of a woman's house. In the bedroom there is a particular sense of confinement because it is, *"A plain unpainted room. Perhaps a room that was used for storage and was set up as a sleeping place for Julia. There is a mattress on the floor"* (23). In its original production, this was the smallest space in the play and with the same number of audience members in the space as had been in larger spaces, there was a greater sense of confinement associated with Julia than with the other characters. As has been mentioned, there is a contrasting sense of escape or release for Julia at the end of the play, which is underlined by the audience's memory of her in that cramped bedroom. By making the audience experience crowding, the play shows the metaphor to be "social and actual," as Gilbert and Gubar say of women's use of the image, as opposed to men's "metaphysical and metaphorical" use of it. Julia does not possess the ability to leave the room. This fact is reinforced by the presence of Julia's wheelchair in the small bedroom, helping to further crowd the audience and to visually remind them that Julia possesses no means to leave this confinement.

Two other plays by Fornes, both included in a volume of her plays published in 1986,[6] also make good use of the madwoman figure and the image of confinement on stage. *Sarita* (1984) tells the story of a Hispanic girl of thirteen from the South Bronx, who passionately loves a boy who is habitually unfaithful to her. Over the course of the eight years of the play (1939–47) Sarita is loved by a young soldier, but is drawn back to her obsessive former love until she is driven to kill him and goes mad. The play takes place in twenty short scenes over two acts, with the inclusion of many songs whose lyrics are written by Fornes. While the story itself may seem familiar in outline, it becomes fresh because it is told from the point of view of the young woman involved. Rather than, as in so many plays in the standard canon, seeing how the madwoman affects the lives of those around her, we see how events and emotions make a lovely young woman go mad. Sarita is her own subject, speaking and acting for herself.

Fornes sees Sarita's madness as quite different from Julia's in *Fefu*:

> I think Sarita goes mad because when you are pushed to such a state of emotional upheaval as to murder the person that you loved, I think going mad is normal. If you don't go mad it's a coldness, callous. It's like having a fever. It's normal to have a fever when you have a bug in your system—it's part of the system protecting itself and I think to break down is inevitable.

Fornes's description of Sarita's "fever" echoes in many ways Catherine Clément's discussion of the hysteric in her book written with Hélène Cixous. In southern Italy women dance a tarantella to rid themselves of spider bites, though, as she states, "because tarantulas do not exist in this region, we have to conclude that these are psychical phenomena."[7] The hysteric speaks with her body and performs socially unacceptable acts because she has a "bug" in her system. Sarita also breaks her "fever" in this manner.

The scenes between Sarita and her lover take place in a narrow, box-like kitchen area above and behind the main stage area. The kitchen is the space in which Sarita is confined, waiting for the return of her lover, and suffering the pangs of sexual longing. She does not enter or leave this space in view of the audience, but is simply there when lights come up and go down. Her "social and actual" confinement is keenly portrayed.

The Conduct of Life (1985) also portrays the confinement of a young Hispanic woman, played in the original production by the same actress, Sheila Dabney, who won an Obie award for her performance as the original Sarita. *Conduct* concerns a trio of women who are in subservient positions in the house of a Latin American army officer, Orlando. The most confined of the trio is Nena, a young street girl Orlando picked up and brought first to a warehouse, then to his cellar, to sexually abuse and sometimes feed. The other two women are Olimpia, a servant in the house who sometimes works or plays with Nena, and Leticia, Orlando's wife, who thinks she is a mother figure to Orlando. Over the course of nineteen scenes, with no intermission, set in the present but visually presented as anytime from the 1940s onward, the audience sees Orlando brutalize Nena in the name of love and sexuality, and drive his wife to shoot him at the end. Again, Nena is confined in a box-like space above and behind the main stage area, and then is brought down into the cellar area. Again, her confinement is actual and cannot be escaped. But in this play the similarities among Nena, Leticia, and Olimpia present a view of women as subjects under subjugation that echoes Cixous and Clément in their discussion of Freud's patient, Dora.

From the beginning of the play, madness is discussed. In her first speech, to Orlando and his male friend, Alejo, Leticia says she would throw herself in front of a deer to prevent its being killed by "mad hunters," and Orlando responds with, "You don't think that is madness? She's mad. Tell her that— she'll think it's you who's mad." When Orlando leaves, Leticia confesses to Alejo:

> He told me that he didn't love me, and that his sole relationship to me was simply a marital one. What he means is that I am to keep this house, and he is to provide for it. That's what he said. That explains why he treats me the way he treats me. I never understood why he did, but now it's clear. He doesn't love me. (P. 69)

In the next scene Orlando brings Nena into the warehouse room. The scene is brief—a few words and then:

(He grabs her and pushes her against the wall. He pushes his pelvis against her. He moves to the chair dragging her with him. She crawls to the left, pushes the table aside and stands behind it. He walks around the table. She goes under it. He grabs her foot and pulls her out toward the downstage side. He opens his fly and pushes his pelvis against her. Lights fade to black.) (P. 70)

In the next scene Olimpia is introduced through a long monologue in which she tells Leticia, in detail, what she does in order to prepare breakfast for the family in the morning. The accumulation of detail is comical, but the link between the two women is established clearly, as both women must "keep this house," while Orlando is oblivious to what either is doing or thinking. The two women bicker over what is to be served for lunch and dinner, Olimpia asserting her will point for point with Leticia. Though Olimpia is the servant, Leticia's only action as the "boss's wife" is to hand money to Olimpia to go shopping at the end of the scene.

Orlando forces sex on Nena two more times, the second time reaching orgasm, and then giving her food and milk. The lines of similarity among the three women become clearer as the scenes progress. When Leticia goes away on a trip, Orlando slips Nena into the house and down to the cellar. Orlando and Alejo talk about a man Orlando interrogated and who is dead. Orlando insists he just stopped him from screaming and then the man died. He does not see himself as being the cause. The connection between political torture and subjugation of women is made by the juxtaposed, rapidly intercut scenes.

Leticia senses there is a woman in the house to whom Orlando is making love, and she feels there is nothing she can do. Orlando tells Nena that "What I do to you is out of love. Out of want. It's not what you think. I wish you didn't have to be hurt" (82). Leticia pleads with Orlando, "Don't make her scream," and Orlando responds, "You're crazy" (82). Then he says, "She's going to be a servant here," and in the next scene Nena is cleaning beans with Olimpia and speaking, for the first time at length, about her grandfather and how Orlando found her and "did things" to her (83–84). Nena sounds like Julia in *Fefu* when she says he beats her "Because I'm dirty," and "The dirt won't go away from inside me" (84). Leticia feels he is becoming more violent because of his job. She does not appear to perceive the fact that his violence at work and home come from a common root. The three women finally sit together at a table as the lights come down on scene seventeen.

In the final scene, Orlando forces Leticia to say she has a lover and to make up details of their meeting. When Orlando physically hurts Leticia, she screams and then, "*She goes to the telephone table, opens the drawer, takes a gun and shoots Orlando. Orlando falls dead. . . . Leticia . . . puts the revolver in Nena's hand and steps away from her.*" Leticia asks, "Please . . . " and Nena "*looks at the gun. Then, up. The lights fade*" (88).

The play is over. The doubled madwomen figures have come together, one acting for the other as well as herself, then (possibly) asking help of her double in ending her own torment. The release here is different from that at the end of *Fefu*. The killing of the intolerable lover is more complex than that in *Sarita*. Women are linked by their subjugated roles. The actions of the man make them mad, but they manage both to act and to connect despite their madness and confinement. And the man's self-deception about what he is doing to the women around him is linked to the wider political realm.

When asked to comment on the madwoman in *Conduct* compared to *Sarita*, Fornes explained:

> Certainly, if you think of Leticia after the murder she would probably go through something similar, but I think Leticia would be able to cope a little better. She would have to go through a period of understanding everything. But I thought you meant the person who goes mad in *The Conduct of Life* was Nena. . . . Nena is much more vulnerable; Leticia is a strong person. She's older and more in possession of herself. But Nena is ill, she's been battered, she's abused. I think she's closer to madness than Leticia.

Fornes touches on a central point here; both Leticia and Nena are different aspects of the "madwomen" figure. Nena in her near-mute state when in the presence of a male and Leticia in "speaking" with a gun are similar to Hélène Cixous's description of Freud's patient, Dora: "like all hysterics, deprived of the possibility of saying directly what she perceived . . . still had the strength to make it known." And the role of love in the women characters' "conduct of life" is echoed in Cixous's statement: "The source of Dora's strength is, in spite of everything, her desire."[8]

Clément, in disagreeing with Cixous, finds that the hysteric's eccentricity is tolerated because she is not really threatening to the basic social structure. Fornes makes her hysterics have a clear effect and balances them with a third figure, the "maid." Unlike the "maid" in Freud's writing, Olimpia is not a seductress. She represents housework, the nonsexual side of the wife's duties, while Nena is the merely sexual, though the husband does bring her into the house and make her play the role of a "maid." As Cixous quotes Freud, "'the servant-girl is the boss's wife repressed,' but in Dora's case, Dora is in the place of the boss's wife: the mother is set aside."[9] But in Fornes's case not too far aside, for the mother appears in the form of the wife, Leticia. The play illuminates both Cixous's ideas about the hysteric and Clément's social concerns: "The family does not exist in isolation, rather it truly supports and reflects the class struggle running through it. The servant-girl, the prostitute, the mother, the boss's wife, the woman: that is all an ideological scene."[10]

Taken together, these three plays give a broad picture of the effects of confinement and madness on women in the twentieth century. In both *Fefu* and *Conduct* Fornes shows us a multiple female character, composed of individuals but, as seen on the stage, a whole that is more than its parts. She shows us what Showalter considers "the best hope for the future. . . . In the 1970s, for the first time, women came together," to challenge the dominant ideology and propose their own alternative, including political activism.[11]

By taking an audience *into* the attic the madwoman there can no longer be seen as a mere "metaphorical" disturbance. By letting the madwoman speak for herself, Fornes has performed a radical act. On the stage we *see* her, and other women, escape confinement in various ways. And by placing her women in the spotlight, Fornes helps the audience, as well as future women playwrights, escape restriction by form, society, and themselves.

NOTES

1. Elaine Showalter, *The Female Malady: Women, Madness, and English Culture, 1830–1980* (New York: Pantheon Books, 1985; reprint ed., New York: Penguin Books, 1987), 10–11.

2. (New Haven: Yale University Press, 1979). Subsequent page numbers in parentheses.

3. In *Wordplays* (New York: Performing Arts Journal Publications, 1980). Subsequent page numbers in parentheses.

4. *Feminist Theatre* (New York: Grove Press, 1985), 125.

5. "Fefu and Her Friends," in *Women in American Theatre: Revised and Expanded Edition,* ed. Chinoy and Jenkins (New York: Theatre Communications Group, 1987), 316.

6. *Maria Irene Fornes: Plays* (New York: Performing Arts Journal Publications, 1986). Subsequent page numbers in parentheses.

7. Hélène Cixous and Catherine Clément, *The Newly Born Woman,* trans. Betsy Wing (Minneapolis: University of Minnesota, 1986), 19.

8. Ibid., 154.

9. Ibid., 151.

10. Ibid., 152.

11. Showalter, 249–50.

MARY K. DeSHAZER

Rejecting Necrophilia: Ntozake Shange and the Warrior Re-Visioned

"Necrophilia: the most fundamental characteristic and first principle of patriarchy: hatred for and envy of Life"

— Mary Daly

In *Webster's First New Intergalactic Wickedary of the English Language*, feminist theorist Mary Daly further defines *necrophilia* as "death worship," the destructive desire of those already dead inside. The Necrophilic State is upheld by rape, genocide, and war, "the logical expression of phallocentric power." In contrast to these violent manifestations of phallic lust, she posits a woman-centered *biophilia*: "the Original Lust for Life that is at the core of all Elemental E-motion; Pure Lust, which is the Nemesis of patriarchy." I have found it both instructive and entertaining to peruse Daly's metadictionary and discover which of her characters and coinages are necrophilic and which are biophilic. On the one hand, I found in Word Web Three a slew of patriarchal mummies and dummies, Androcratic Assumers, deadfellows, and wasters: "the celebrated conquerors, missionaries, and heroes of civilization/snivelization." Her preferred population is housed in Word Webs One and Two as "inhabitors of the background": those Amazons, Witches, Spinsters, Hags, and Crones who weave a new language and "crone-ology" on the boundaries of patriarchal space.[1]

Although Daly presumably intends to include all radical women in her crone-ological vision, she at times falls into the trap of simplistic polarization: dystopian patriarchal space is countered by utopian Amazonian boundaries. In fact, boundaries are themselves complex territories comprised of hilly terrain, outer banks, and unacknowledged ravines. As Gloria Anzaldúa explains, such borderlands are places of contradiction where "keeping intact one's shifting and multiple identity and integrity, is like trying to swim in a new element, an 'alien' element" — an effort both exhilarating and exhausting.[2] In examining Daly's discourse, therefore, I wonder who exactly are the crones who inhabit her boundaries? Specifically, where in her spatial dichotomy do women of color live? Doubly displaced by institutionalized racism as well as sexism, women of color have traditionally been marginalized on the border-lands of the boundaries. There they have too often had to fight not only white patriarchs but Black men and white women as well to proclaim their centrality in any struggle for liberation, indeed to assert their very presence. There they have become warriors raging against their own invisibility.

Nowhere in the *Wickedary*, however, does Daly gloss the word *warrior*, perhaps because it is a problematic term for many feminists.[3] At first glance it would seem clearly necrophilic, an "anti-biotic" concept, to use Daly's phrase, that embodies the destructive powers of patriarchy. Men love war, Viet-nam veteran William Broyles tells readers of *Esquire*, because they intuit deep within them the intense and inevitable union "between sex and destruction, beauty and horror, love and death." War, he continues with frighteningly necrophilic illogic, allows men to touch the mythic domain in their souls, much as childbirth initiates women into the power of life.[4] Or as J. Glenn Gray explained in *The Warriors*, his analysis of soldier-psychology in World War II, thousands of young men who had never been conscious of their violent im-pulses learned through military life "the mad excitement of destroying."[5]

Given such masculinist analyses, many women have had good reason to view with ambivalence or reject outright the term *warrior* as metaphor and/or theoretical construct. In *Gyn/ecology*, for instance, Daly explores the problem she finds in using the warrior image to express the complexity of women's rage and resistance. Furious women prefer to resist fighting, to focus instead on "breaking boundaries, bounding free," she asserts. Such women therefore reject male war ecstasy yet are ever vigilant, aware that patriarchs will under-mine our efforts to free ourselves. "Besieged Furies *do* fight back," Daly con-cludes, "and thus there is a warrior element in Sisterhood." Yet women must not underestimate the dangers inherent in forging our own version of any masculinist concept, she argues. "Crones know that this warrior aspect of Amazon bonding becomes truly dreadless daring only when it is focused be-yond fighting."[6] Furthermore, many international women realistically fear that embracing a warrior identity will make them vulnerable to military/imperialist censors and torturers in their countries. Hence the editor's dis-claimer in a recent "Woman as Warrior" issue of *woman of power*:

Throughout this issue, the word *warrior* is used as a metaphor. It is not intended to mean that the women profiled or pictured are involved in military activity of any kind, or in the bearing or transporting of arms, or in armed resistance, insurrection or attempts to overthrow any government. This material should not be understood to mean such things or used against these women for purposes of persecution, interrogation, incarceration or further oppression.[7]

Other women simply dismiss the term *warrior* because they equate it with patriarchal violence. *A Feminist Dictionary,* for example, glosses it only in the pejorative: "the warrior-woman, using sexuality as a weapon, is a masculinist construct, the true counterpart of the macho male."[8]

Until recently I too have been suspicious of the word *warrior.* As a white southern girl from a working-class family, I was protected from the battles my electrician-father and homemaker-mother undertook on my behalf—battles to stave off the landlord a few more days, to convince the insurance collector not to drop the overdue policy, to persuade military personnel in the army hospital where my dad worked that his arthritis really had kept him from work that day. I thought no one in my family had ever fought. As a college student in the 1960s I, like many, embraced the antiwar movement and its favorite slogan, "give peace a chance." As a graduate student in the 1970s and a teacher in the 1980s, I joined the feminist antinuclear movement and named myself pacifist. These choices I made with good intentions and careful reasoning, and I continue to endorse a philosophy of nonviolence, to argue that pacifism need not equal passivity.

Yet during the past five years, as I have read extensively women writers of color from many nations and have grown more radical in my own feminist politics and vision, the metaphor and identity of the woman warrior have taken on new meaning. I have begun to realize that for many women, especially those who lack class or color or heterosexual privilege, the warrior image reflects a profound commitment to combatting not just sexism, the sole focus of too many white liberal feminists, but racist, elitist, and heterosexist oppressions as well. As women warriors living in the borderlands, radical feminists emphasize the pervasive links among all forms of denial and dehumanization, refusing to rank oppressions and thereby employ mainstream, hierarchical thinking. The Combahee River Collective's statement of Black feminist purpose sums up this stance:

> We are actively committed to struggling against racial, sexual, heterosexual, and class oppression and see as our particular task the development of an integrated analysis and practice based upon the fact that the

major systems of oppression are interlocking. The synthesis of these oppressions creates the conditions of our lives. As Black women we see
Black feminism as the logical political movement to combat the manifold
and simultaneous oppressions that all women of color face.[9]

As a white feminist I have learned much from the Combahee women's vision
and others like it, and I have come to agree with Barbara Smith that "the
concept of simultaneity of oppression is . . . one of the most significant ideological contributions of Black feminist thought."[10] I now believe that anyone
committed to fighting against these insidious and interwoven oppressions
must at times name herself warrior.

It no longer surprises me, therefore, that women writers who rage
against their own and their sisters' marginalization and subordination frequently claim a warrior identity, revisioned not as a necrophilic zest for destruction but as a biophilic source of life-preservation and enhancement. Thus
Maxine Hong Kingston defines herself as a woman warrior, on whose back
words of vengeance are carved; she will fail her family if she becomes but wife
or slave when they need her protection from an evil king's thugs. "My mother
taught me the song of the warrior woman, Fa Mu Lan. I would have to
grow up a woman warrior." Alice Walker, in turn, names her mother a
"sister-warrior," who knew what her writer-daughter needed to know. Toni
Cade Bambara calls herself and other writers of color "creative combatants."
Cherríe Moraga wars with words, "to clarify my resistance to the literate."
As a "Black lesbian feminist warrior poet," Audre Lorde celebrates her warrior
sisters who rode in defense of the African goddess Seboulisa's queendom. Adrienne Rich offers painstaking insight into the stresses of biophilic resistance:
"there must be those among whom we can sit down and weep, and still be
counted as warriors." And Chilean-born poet Marjorie Agosin describes the
woman warrior as silence-breaker and storyteller:

> . . . Our own history obliges us to speak, to loose words of fire. Thus
> we come out of the silence and darkness to show ourselves as we are:
> free women, warrior women. We are washers of clothes, teachers, law-
> yers, journalists, poets. We are mothers, sister, wives, daughters. . . . We
> wage our war every day in the country called Chile or Guatemala or the
> United States. We are new women with new stories to tell.[11]

Of all the women quoted above, Audre Lorde in particular has helped
me understand the warrior woman's commitment to telling new stories and

waging multiple battles. Her poems are replete with images of warring women: "warrior queens"; "like a warrior woman"; "like my warrior sisters"; "Assata my sister warrior." At times the epithet "warrior" becomes an emblem of hope for the future generations of Black women: "I bless your child with the mother she has/with a future of warriors and growing fire." In celebrating the women warriors of Dan, Lorde enacts a strong re-visionist impulse, for she insists that these warriors be not secret but open, vulnerable. "I come as a woman," she proclaims, no longer "a secret warrior with an unsheathed sword in my mouth / hidden behind my tongue / slicing my throat to ribbons."[12] Instead, her weapons are erotic heat and poetic language, a combination vital for continued growth and vision.

While Lorde clearly rejects war in its masculinist guise — stealthy, vindictive — she does not reject it altogether; she refuses to be silenced or become a mirror to the male warrior. As long as unjust wars continue — in the United States, the Third World, and elsewhere — radical women must join the resistance. Thus Lorde supports the revolutionary forces of U.S.-invaded Grenada, her mother's birthplace, in their slogan "Forward Ever, Backward Never."[13] She implores all Black people — women and men, gay and straight — to lay aside their disagreements and undertake a collective battle against global injustice:

> We are Black people living in a time when the consciousness of our intended slaughter is all around us. People of Color are increasingly expendable, our government's policy both here and abroad. We are functioning under a government ready to repeat in El Salvador and Nicaragua the tragedy of Vietnam, a government which stands on the wrong side of every single battle for liberation taking place upon this globe. . . . Can any one of us here still afford to believe that efforts to reclaim the future can be private or individual? Can anyone here still afford to believe that the pursuit of liberation can be the sole and particular province of any one particular race, or sex, or age, or religion, or sexuality, or class?[14]

Feminists cannot afford such divisions, Lorde eloquently reminds us. Just as we lack the luxury to be pacifists, neither can we let ourselves fight one another rather than our common enemies. Yet in joining forces we must not overlook the pressing issue of difference.

> As women, we have been taught to either ignore our differences or to view them as causes for separation and suspicion rather than as forces

for change. Without community, there is no liberation, only the most vulnerable and temporary armistice between an individual and her oppressor. But community must not mean a shedding of our differences, nor the pathetic pretense that these differences do not exist."[15]

We must continue to confront and explore our common differences, Lorde concludes, to enable ourselves to fight battles as sisters.

What, then, will happen when radical women and men, many of them people of color, rename the background of patriarchy as the foreground of a new order? How do we shift from inhabitants of the borderlands to combatants on the front lines of global battles against oppression? And what *are* the front lines?

The front lines aren't always what you think they are.

— Ntozake Shange

How do we re-imagine ourselves as women, as writers, as warriors who resist and revolt and yet stake out as our final destination a territory beyond history, perhaps beyond war? These questions have led me to the feminist choreopoems and theory of Ntozake Shange, who offers a profound vision of how to reject necrophilia — to name the warrior within, taking courage from her struggle and that of her comrades. Like many other radical women of color, Shange portrays herself as writer and her speakers/characters both as warriors, angry and rebellious figures who fight against racism, sexism, capitalist imperialism; and as mothers, nurturers who must birth strong selves and communities, care for the world's children, and resist the necrophilic state. For Shange, drama is fueled by "combat breath," a term she borrows from Franz Fanon's studies of colonialism and defines as "the living response / the drive to reconcile the irreconcilable / the black n white of what we live and where." The women and, more rarely, men who speak in *for colored girls who have considered suicide/when the rainbow is enuf* (1976), *Spell #7* (1979), and *Bocas: A Daughter's Geography* (1981) describe the anger and pain they feel in such attempts at reconciliation.[16] Their voices respond to what the playwright calls "the involuntary restrictions n amputations of their humanity / in the context of combat breathing."[17] Some of Shange's character/combatants fail to overcome their oppressors: Crystal in the "Beau Willie Brown" segment of *for colored girls,* who loses her children through her victimized husband's desperate act of violence; or the manic magician in *Spell #7,* who expresses what Margaret Wilkerson calls "the perceptual and psychological limitations which

a racist and sexist society seeks to impose on women and men."[18] Others
emerge from combat victorious: the speaker in *Bocas: A Daughter's Geography*
drives the offending patriarchs, those "flat old men," right off the face of the
earth, Pied-piper-like (pp. 21–23).

In all three plays Shange struggles to define the war zone from the perspective of people of color, to chart new territory inhabited by a population
under siege. Yet these three works reveal a movement in her conceptualization
of the war effort. In *for colored girls,* her combatants are young Black women
concerned primarily with assessing the damage done by sexism. They cross
the boundary from silence to speech, naming their exploitation at the hands
of Black and white men and staking out a new country beyond this war,
defined by nurturant female community. *Spell #7* differs from *for colored girls*
in that its speakers are Black American men as well as women, unemployed
actors and musicians who locate themselves in the trenches, where they examine the impact of racist, sexist, and economic oppression on their lives.
They are not actually engaged in physical battle but instead fight verbally, plot-
ting their revenge against the prevailing system, at times assaulting their audience or one another. *Bocas: A Daughter's Geography* catapults its speakers, who
are global warrior-mothers, into active combat and, finally, to victory over
the oppressors whom they vanquish by banishing. The powerful white western men who once inhabited and ruled the foreground are driven not into
the background, which continues to be sacred Third World space, but off
the globe altogether.

A brief examination of these three plays will better illustrate the ways
in which Shange identifies her combatants and defines their enemies. *For colored girls* begins with a segment spoken by the lady in brown, who defines
a Black girl's world as one of broken promises, male violence, her own en-
forced silence: "she's been dead so long / closed in silence so long / she doesn't
know the sound of her own voice" (p. 3). Black women from all cities, classes,
and cultural milieux have experienced sexual oppression; and Shange's speakers
reveal the commonality of women's experiences. Even when they appear to
be sexual actors, women are victimized. Giving up her virginity is at first seen
by the lady in yellow as an act of empowerment—"you gave it up in a buick?
yeh, and honey, it was wonderful"—but in the context of contemporary sexual violence, it becomes a poignant loss: "I never did like to grind" (pp. 9–
10). Sexuality as a trap for women is especially well illustrated in the "i usedta
live in the world" segment, in which Shange's ladies describe their outrage
at being harassed on the streets of Harlem by twelve-year-old strangers. Although her narrative implicitly reveals racial and economic oppressions as fac-

tors in Harlem's decline, her primary emphasis is on the violations of women that occur there:

> i usedta live in the world
> really be in the world
> free & sweet talkin
> good mornin & thank you & nice day
> uh huh
> i cant now
> i cant be nice to nobody
> nice is such a rip-off
> reglar beauty & a smile in the street
> is just a set-up
> (p. 41)

Spell #7, in contrast, focuses partly on sexist oppression but mainly on issues of color and class. The grotesque minstrel-show parody that begins the play jolts the audience with that familiar, insidious brand of racism once labeled comedy; and the magician's opening speech reveals the impact of internalized oppression on Black children who wanted desperately to be made white. "What cd any self-respectin colored american magician / do wit such an outlandish request," lou wonders as he recounts this story, besides put away his magic tools altogether, for "colored chirren believin in magic / waz becomin politically dangerous for the race." But now lou is back with his magic, he tells us, and "it's very colored/very now you see it/now you / dont mess wit me" (pp. 7–8). The play quickly becomes an angry reclamation of those physical and psychic territories appropriated from Black Americans by racist terrorists: school kids, police, lynch mobs. "This is the borderline," one character, alec, claims in identifying himself and his dreams, "this is our space / we are not movin" (p. 11). The only safe territory, the characters reveal, is segregated space where magic rules and masks come off. But even a protected haven from which to speak cannot offset the daily horrors these unemployed performers face. Lily wishes for just one decent part, like lady macbeth or mother courage, only to be reminded by eli that she can't play lady macbeth when "macbeth's a white dude" (pp. 13–14). Bettina's show remains open, "but if that director asks me to play it any blacker / i'm gonna have to do it in a mammy dress" (p. 14). What white audiences want is what they get, the actors bitterly remind us, and even selling out to racist taste doesn't pay the bills. Near the end of the play, alec offers one powerful suggestion that would make him less tired. A gong would sound for three minutes, all over the world, while "all the white people / immigrants & invaders / conquistadors

& relatives of london debtors from georgia / kneel & apologize to us" (p. 46). This is not impossible, he insists; this is Black magic.

In *Bocas: A Daughter's Geography,* first performed in New York City as *Mouths,* the embattled speaker-mother embraces a fluid identity global in its concerns. Like Virginia Woolf's, Shange's country is the whole world:

> i have a daughter/mozambique
> i have a son/angola
> our twins
> salvador & johannesburg/cannot speak
> the same language
> but we fight the same old men/in the new world
> (p. 21)

Her litany of places in which poor people of color are rising up continues, haunting and incantatory: habana, guyana, santiago, managua. The necrophiliacs who dominate the world's peoples remain ensconced in their tunnel visions, "unaware of . . . all the dark urchins / rounding out the globe / primitively whispering / the earth is not flat old men" (p. 22). Here the playwright juxtaposes ironically the men's flatness, their one-dimensionality, with the round, wholesome humanity of the embattled daughters and sons, with their multiple tongues. People of color have power in both their numbers and the justice of their cause, Shange implies; if they but persevere, "the same men who thought the earth was flat"—who lack empathy and vision—will "go on over the edge." This victory for the oppressed will then result in mass and massive revolutionary nurture, "rounding out the morning," as warriors become mothers, "feeding our children the sun" (p. 22–23).

The woman writer's role in a culture under siege is intense and subversive, Shange claims; she thus describes herself as "a war correspondent . . . in a war of cultural and esthetic aggression."[19] A war correspondent, of course, is traditionally neither the initiator of battles nor an enlisted military person, but instead a reporter-critic who surveys and monitors the fighting. Yet as a poet-correspondent who is Black and female, Shange suffers under attack as bitterly as any foot soldier. From her observations at the front she rejects a dispassionate stance in favor, ultimately, of a furious rage "about oppression of women and children, racism, imperialism in Latin America and Africa, apartheid."[20] And so she wars with her words.

Like other feminist writers, one word Shange insists upon using as a weapon is *power*—not power over others, domination, the hallmark of patriarchy; but the power of breaking silence, saving lives of those in occupied territory. The forces of necrophilia don't understand, Shange explains, that women "see the world in a way that allows us to care more about people than about military power. The power we see is the power to feed, the power to nourish and to educate. But these kinds of powers are not respected, and so it's part of our responsibility as writers to make these things important."[21] As Adrienne Rich has said, even common words must be reconsidered, laid aside, recast with new meanings.[22] At the head of this list of re-visioned words, for Shange as for Rich, is power.

This view of the warrior's word-power can be further seen in Shange's self-identification as a linguistic writer/righter of wrongs. When *Spell #7* was first produced in 1979, one New York reviewer accused her of destroying the English language. "The man who thought i wrote with intentions of out-doing the white man in the acrobatic distortions of english waz absolutely correct," Shange retorted. "i can't count the number of times i have viscerally wanted to attack deform n maim the language that i was taught to hate myself in."[23] *Spell #7* was excruciating to write, she explained, because it demanded that she confront her murderous impulses over the constrictions of racism. Her primary spokesperson in that choreopoem, the magician/narrator, asserts belligerently the goal at hand: "Crackers are born with the right to be alive / i'm making ours up right here in yr face" (p. 52). The magician, whom Shange describes as "powerful in his deformities," defiantly names his subversive goal; his claim echoes Shange's own as she concludes her response to the white reviewer: "i haveta fix my tool to my needs / i haveta take it apart to the bone / so that the malignancies / fall away / leaving us space to literally create our own image."[24] Writing begins, at least, to cure the cancer.

Another malignancy that Shange battles is her conflict as a Black woman writer with oppressive white male literary models. A longtime admirer of Bertolt Brecht's politically radical theater, yet angry at mainstream critics' narrow definition of *classic*, Shange decided to adapt Brecht's *Mother Courage* to a new setting, the post–Civil War American West. Why should a Black woman waste time performing or adapting the works of white men, she frequently asked herself during this process — yet she was obsessed with exploring the role of European drama in the lives of Third World people. "Involved in fruitless combat with myself about the works of dead white men," Shange chose a radical re-visionist strategy: she would "toy with one of Europe's precious sons."[25]

Her adaptation turned out to be "extraordinarily non-Brechtian," Shange explains, yet it gave her new power. Her particular focus was the intersection of racial and economic exploitation: "in our hemisphere race & class are im-

placably engaged and it is a duel to the death."[26] Shange's key character is
as ruled by greed and expediency as Brecht's Mother Courage was, but the
context in which she operates reflects the limited options made available to
enterprising Black women by the white patriarchy. One of the play's most
controversial elements is Shange's treatment of reconstruction Blacks' complicity in Native American genocide: troops of ex-slaves known as Buffalo Soldiers were recruited as mercenaries by whites in the Southwest Territories of
1866–67. For Shange, this contextual and thematic choice required a personal
facing of painful truths. "If i must come to terms with being a descendant
of imperialist assimilationists who were willing if not eager to murder & destroy other people of color, in the name of a flag that represents only white
folks, then let me use a vehicle conceived in the heartland of one of history's
most cruel ideologies, Nazism."[27] North Americans must acknowledge that
too often the oppressed become oppressors, Shange suggests; we must all accept responsibility for the machinations of an imperialist government. Shange's
Mother Courage examines the high costs individuals pay when co-opted by the
forces that undergird systemic violence. Yet, ironically, writing the play was
for her a violent act, a prolonged creative and cultural battle, as her language
in assessing the impact of the process reveals. "Now I have colored wagon
trains & towns, black conquistadores & hoodlums, wenches & ladies of refine-
ment embedded in the soils & myths I waz raised on, but excluded from. . . .
the battle is over. . . . the enemy has been banished from my horizons." In
rewriting *Mother Courage,* the playwright reached "relative aesthetic peace."[28]

As Shange realizes, not all the contemporary writer's battles are with others; she must also fight with herself to be a responsible, maternal artist. "I
hit my head against the wall because I don't want to know all the terrible
things that I know about . . . but if I don't get rid of them, I'm not ever
going to feel anything else."[29] Especially important to her is mothering young
girls through her writing, breaking silence about the truths of adult women's
lives, "feeding [children] poems on rye bread."[30] "It's the silence of mothers
that is so shattering," she explains. "The mothers know that it's a dreadful
proposition to give up one's life for one's family and one's mate, and, therefore, lose oneself in the process of caring and tending for others. To send one's
daughter off to that kind of self-sacrifice in silence with no preparation is a
mortal sin to me. . . . To break this silence is my responsibility, and I'm absolutely committed to it."[31] *For colored girls* ends, therefore, with the powerful
scene of young women comforting the bereaved Crystal, now childless but
also selfless, "missin' somethin'." Mothered first by a tree who took her up
in her branches and comforted her in the dawn light, the speaker is further

warmed by the nurturant sun, who "wrapped me up swingin rose lights everywhere." Most significantly, she learns through the "layin on of hands" ritual to mother herself: "i found god in myself / & i loved her, i loved her fiercely" (pp. 66–67).

This often quoted line takes on new meaning, I believe, when we reconsider the word "fiercely" in a warrior context. We must mother as rigorously as we fight, Shange implies; in fact, the fierceness of the woman warrior is matched by that of mother-love in its broadest guises as self-worth, daughter-devotion, and global sister-lust. Thus her collection of anti-imperialistic, revolutionary essays, *See No Evil,* begins with a personal admission of the difficulties of caring for her own daughter, Savannah, her sister in struggle as well as her child. "Worlds like words for a woman who is a poet and a mother are confusing / overlapping contradictory fatiguing and exciting," she asserts; she goes on to say that it is nonetheless her gravest responsibility to write as a mother and to mother through her embattled words. "i see no evil. i am / fighting demons in the dark and the energies of a free spirit / who must know / this world will do its best to take from her all she is unless she is / willing to struggle as she struggles with me for *the right to see.*"[32]

What she wills her daughter to see is the woman warrior's fiercely biophilic vision of global interconnectedness. *See No Evil* is dedicated not only to Savannah but to a host of female figures who can help her child strangle evil and therefore live afresh. These spirited foremothers include the goddesses Isis, Ishtar, Ochun, Yemaya, Diana, and Demeter, among others — Eastern, African, and Greek deities commingling now as sisters. "We need a god who bleeds," Shange asserts at the end of *Bocas: A Daughter's Geography,* who "spreads her lunar vulva and showers us in shades of scarlet / thick and warm like the breath of her" (p. 51). But matriarchal spirituality alone is not enough to enable her daughter, the poet implies, so she further dedicates *See No Evil* to "the 30 million african women / in the NEW WORLD OF WHOM I AM A PROUD SURVIVOR and the 500,000 murdered witches who were the first feminists" — women who fell victim to or resisted cultural aggression and in whose names we stake our own territorial claims. Finally, Shange's dedication reveals her willingness to embrace militant struggle if the situation demands it, for she is not a pacifist by any means. "I'm not saying that we don't have to struggle in physical ways but, of course, that should be a last resort."[33] Last-resort strategies are now underway in many countries, the poet recognizes; thus her dedication includes "the armed women in Nicaragua Guatamala el salvador mozambique angola namibia and South Africa" — women Audre Lorde has called "sisters in pain."[34]

To fight necrophilia and embrace biophilia, Adrienne Rich has claimed, requires of women that we "cast [our] lot with those / who age after age, perversely / with no extraordinary power, / reconstitute the world."[35] Similarly, Mary Daly concludes her *Wickedary* by urging us to join hands with "Other Archaic Adventurers / ventures of Weird women who cast our lot with the Fates, the Spinners of Stamina, the Forces who can save the world" (p. 284). This imperative to save the world lies at the heart of Ntozake Shange's choreopoems, essays, and feminist philosophy; and finally, I believe, she offers us a vision of angry optimism. "Acceptance of my combat breath hasn't closed the possibilities of hope to me / the soothing actualities of music n sorcery."[36] Creative combatants, biophilic sorcerers, must continue to do battle and thus protect ourselves and our children from the forces of necrophilia and oppression. "The planet is heaving mourning our ignorance," she cries at the end of *Bocas: A Daughter's Geography;* certainly the dangers confronting us could easily overwhelm. But the woman warrior recognizes that her blood-letting can also be a source of her power: "i am / not wounded i am bleeding to life."

NOTES

I would like to thank Sallie Bingham and the Kentucky Foundation for Women for grant support while I was writing this article.

1. Mary Daly, with Jane Caputi, *Webster's First New Intergalactic Wickedary of the English Language* (Boston: Beacon Press, 1987). *Necrophilia* is defined on 83–84; *biophilia* and *boundary* on 67; *crones* and *crone-ology* on 114–16. *Androcratic Assumers* and the like are discussed throughout Word Web Three as "inhabitants of the foreground," 183–235; see especially *wasters,* 234.

2. Gloria Anzaldúa, *Borderlands/La Frontera: The New Mestiza* (San Francisco: Spinsters/aunt lute, 1987), preface.

3. Daly discusses Amazons as warrior women in the *Wickedary,* 103–5, but the word *warrior* does not appear as an entry.

4. William Broyles, Jr., "Why Men Love War," *Esquire,* December 1984, 61–62. For a response to Broyles and a cogent analysis of women as warriors for peace, see Catherine Keller, "Women, Warriors and the Nuclear Complex," forthcoming in *Postmodern Visions,* vol. 2, ed. David Griffin (New York: State University of New York Press, 1988). For a thorough overview of war's "sedimented lore" in literature and social history, see Jean Bethke Elshtain, *Women and War* (New York: Basic Books, 1987).

5. J. Glenn Gray, quoted in Broyles, 61.

6. Mary Daly, *Gyn/ecology: The Metaethics of Radical Feminism* (Boston: Beacon Press, 1978), 370–71.

7. Judith Beckett, "Searching for Amazons," *woman of power* 3 (Winter/Spring 1986), 5. This "Woman as Warrior" issue offers an excellent variety of essays, interviews, poems, and artwork on this theme.

8. Cheris Kramarae and Paula A. Treichler, eds., *A Feminist Dictionary* (London: Routledge and Kegan Paul, 1985), 478.

9. The Combahee River Collective, "A Black Feminist Statement," in *This Bridge Called My Back: Writings by Radical Women of Color*, ed. Cherrié Moraga and Gloria Anzaldúa (Watertown, Mass.: Persephone Press, 1981), 210.

10. Barbara Smith, *Home Girls: A Black Feminist Anthology* (New York: Kitchen Table Women of Color Press, 1983), xxxii.

11. Maxine Hong Kingston, *The Woman Warrior: Memoirs of a Girlhood Among Ghosts* (New York: Random House, 1976), 24; Alice Walker, in Mary Helen Washington, "Her Mother's Gifts," *Ms.*, June 1982, 28; Toni Cade Bambara, foreword to *This Bridge Called My Back*, xvii; Cherrié Moraga, "It's the Poverty," cited in Gloria Anzaldúa, "Speaking in Tongues: A Letter to Third World Women Writers," in *This Bridge Called My Back*, 166; Audre Lorde, interview with Claudia Tate, *Black Women Writers at Work* (New York: Continuum, 1983), 102; Audre Lorde, "125th Street and Abomey," in *The Black Unicorn: Poems* (New York: Norton, 1978), 12–13; Adrienne Rich, "Sources XXII," in *Your Native Land, Your Life: Poems* (New York: Norton, 1986), 25; and Marjorie Agosin, "Needle and Thread Warriors: Women of Chile," *woman of power* 3, 35.

12. Audre Lorde, "The Women of Dan Dance with Swords in Their Hands to Mark the Time When They Were Warriors," in *The Black Unicorn*, 14–15. Other poems cited are "Harriet," "Chorus," "125th Street and Abomey," and "For Assata," in *The Black Unicorn*, 12–13, 21, 28, 44; "Dear Toni Instead of a Letter," in *Chosen Poems–Old and New* (New York: Norton, 1982), 58.

13. Audre Lorde, "Grenada Revisited: An Interim Report," in *Sister Outsider: Essays and Speeches* (Trumansburg, N.Y.: The Crossing Press, 1984), 189.

14. Audre Lorde, "Learning from the 60s," in *Sister Outsider*, 140.

15. Audre Lorde, "The Master's Tools Will Never Dismantle the Master's House," in *Sister Outsider*, 112.

16. The opening quote by Shange is taken from an interview with Stella Dong in *Publisher's Weekly*, May 3, 1985, 74–75. Shange plays cited are *for colored girls who have considered suicide/when the rainbow is enuf* (New York: Bantam Books, 1977); *Spell #7*, in *Three Pieces* (New York: Penguin Books, 1982); and *Bocas: A Daughter's Geography*, in *A Daughter's Geography* (New York: St. Martin's Press, 1983). Quotations from these works will be cited by page number in the text.

17. Foreword to *Three Pieces*, xiii.

18. Margaret B. Wilkerson, introduction, *Nine Plays by Black Women* (New York: New American Library, 1986), xxiii.

19. Interview in *Publisher's Weekly*, 75.

20. Ibid., 74.

21. Interview with Claudia Tate, *Black Women Writers at Work*, 157.

22. Adrienne Rich, "Power and Danger: Works of a Common Woman," in *On Lies, Secrets, and Silence: Selected Prose, 1966–78* (New York: Norton, 1979), 247.

23. Foreword to *Three Pieces*, xii.

24. Ibid.

25. "How I Moved Anna Fierling to the Southwest Territories," in *See No Evil: Prefaces, Essays and Accounts, 1976–83* (San Francisco: Momo's Press, 1984), 36.

26. Ibid., 35.

27. Ibid., 37.

28. Ibid., 38.

29. Interview with Claudia Tate, 160.

30. Eli says this in *Spell #7, Three Pieces,* 25.

31. Interview with Claudia Tate, 161–62.

32. Prologue, *See No Evil.*

33. Interview with Claudia Tate, 153.

34. Audre Lorde, "Meet," in *The Black Unicorn,* 33–34.

35. Adrienne Rich, "Natural Resources," in *The Dream of a Common Language: Poems, 1974–77* (New York: Norton, 1978), 67.

36. Shange, Preface to *Three Pieces,* xiv.

PART 2

Reformulating the Question

SUSAN CARLSON

Revisionary Endings: Pam Gems's *Aunt Mary* and *Camille*

When considering other writers, Pam Gems admires new forms: "I have such reverence for writers who are true explorers, who break form and content, who have that generosity which breeds vitality" (1983, 150). When evaluating her own writing, she voices the same commitment to structural experiment: "Form is a complicated game. I don't always write in the same genre, which baffles people. They tend to want tram-lines and to know where they are with a writer but I'm not interested in writing like that" (Gardner 1985, 12–13). And not surprisingly, her dramatic work is a collection of composite genres and novel structures in which, as she puts it, she breaks new ground (Betsko and Koenig 1987, 202). Joining Caryl Churchill, Michelene Wandor, Timberlake Wertenbaker, Sarah Daniels, Deborah Levy, and other British playwrights who are discarding conventional dramatic forms, Gems protests theatrical, social, and sexual conventions. Most insistently with her endings, Gems reinterprets theatre structures so that the disproportionate power of conclusions works for, not against, women and others on the margin of society.

While Gems's awareness of the possibilities for a spectrum of dramatic forms is reflected in the entire body of her work, I would like to study the structure of just two radically different plays. The one, *Aunt Mary*, was a comic, male-centered, off-beat stage failure while the other, *Camille*, written immediately after *Aunt Mary*, was a tragic, woman-inspired, ostensibly traditional stage success. While neither *Aunt Mary* nor *Camille* is obviously political,[1] both lobby for social and sexual changes through transformed structures and through endings not only revised but revisionary. In both, Gems demonstrates her belief in the transformative power of socially aware theatre: "of course words change everything" (Gems 1986a).

When *Aunt Mary* was first produced at the Warehouse theatre (London) in June of 1982, it baffled its audience. In his review, Charles Spencer complained of it as "an infuriating piece of whimsy," and bemoaned a "vestigial plot" that was "remorselessly comic" without a "single decent joke." Follow-up critical attention has been scant. Even a sympathetic reader like Michelene Wandor, although attracted to the play's anarchy, finds little to discuss once she has praised its campy style (Wandor 1986, 166). Gems herself seems to have been influenced by such critical doubts; she is surprised to hear the play praised (Gems 1986a), and is on the defensive in her afterword to the printed text, allowing her explanation of where and why the production went wrong to overpower her commitment to the play's anomalous theatre. In spite of the unenthusiastic, tentative response the play has generated, *Aunt Mary* retains a still unappreciated power that springs from its novel arrangements of relationship and its unconventional comic ending. The play brings to life Gems's belief that we need "new ways of living" to guide us through the relational upheavals of the late twentieth century (Gems 1986a).

The primary relationship in the play is that between two men, Mary, a transvestite bisexual, and Cyst, a transvestite gay. Desires, loves, insecurities, and sexual definitions are sorted out between the two of them during a series of conversations and celebrations at their "provincial" retreat outside Birmingham. Our attitude to them is conditioned by the other characters who cluster around them at their combination theatre–petrol station. Jack, a third middle-aged character, has joined Mary and Cyst for his convalescence after a recent sex-change operation, and Muriel, an elderly woman whose joy lies in hairdressing and weddings, completes the community. Martin and Alison, heterosexual and younger, appear as outsiders. Martin has retreated here to relax into his poetry writing, and his lover, Alison, has joined him, trailing the tawdry glory of her BBC television career. The play's direction and energy derive not from love intrigue or from any familiar linear narrative, but from the laughs and dilemmas caused by the clashing personalities and frequently incompatible sexualities of these six characters. The loose collection of interactions does, however, bend toward community and reconciliation, toward what is unambiguously offered as a happy ending: the three-way marriage of Mary, Cyst, and Muriel.

I need to preface my study of the play's ending with a review of the sexualities and relations that create the climate for a three-way marriage. From its opening moments, *Aunt Mary* (*AM*) refuses to allow familiar definitions of gender or sexuality. Mary's "sensational elegance" (*AM*, 15) in chic women's clothes and Cyst's "pale wig and sweet pea tulle dress" (*AM*, 15) immediately put us on notice that biological sex and sex-specific dress are unreliable guides to gender or character. And the tension also immediately apparent between Cyst and Mary results, in large part, from the open-ended options for relationship that these two characters lead the others in facing. Indeed, an exploration of sex and sexuality obsesses this whole community in the posing, proselytizing, and questioning of act 1. Mary oscillates between desires for men and for women, as evidenced in his connection to Cyst and his lusting after Alison. For Alison, the desire for options is feminist: she offers a woman's view of shifting sexual mores when telling the men that a young woman's sexual journey is motivated by the desire "to avoid buffoons and hooligans without ending up in a nunnery" (*AM*, 19). Again and again, a pattern of discussing or responding to various sexual urges swings the play from one relationship to another: Mary and Cyst contemplate sex when they hear Martin and Alison's "giggles and groans" (*AM*, 22); Cyst defends the "gay brotherhood" (*AM*, 23) as Mary denies he is gay; Alison and Martin struggle through the financial side of their heterosexual liaison (*AM, 25*); and Jack shares with Martin apprehensions about his sex-change (*AM*, 28–29). The viability of and necessity for these various relationships is reinforced by both the characters' attention to fashion and their passion for theatre. For Gems, both preoccupations are rich with subversive potential: "Fashion comes from the new, is the new. Like drama, it tends to be subversive. . . . Conformity . . . submission through fear . . . can never bring about the just society. The day our clothes submit, we submit" (*AM*, afterword, 48). The self-consciousness of roles necessary for the characters' dazzling cross-dressing and for their preoccupation with theatrical production (Mary and Cyst claim to work so that they can subsidize their tiny theatre) aids Gems in convincingly developing a world where roles—whether tailored, theatrical, sexual, or social—are accepted as necessarily changing, shifting commodities.

Thus, when, at the end of act 1, Martin offers his heterosexuality as a sign of superiority, his pleas to Alison—"Don't turn me down—I'm heterosexual" (*AM*, 30)—sound not only insensitive, but also dangerously misguided. The milieu of *Aunt Mary* discourages such smug self-aggrandizement and its narrow vision of gauging personal worth. Gems's reliance on comedy in creating her multi-optioned world helps explain why Martin sticks out—not because of his heterosexuality, but because of his exclusiveness. A comic structure, through its customary inversions, allows for the development of modes and moods not sanctioned in the ordinary course of events. Comedy is a "welcoming," inclusive structure and one which can, according to Catherine Belsey, "disrupt sexual difference" (1985, 167) through its diversity. Belsey finds such abandonment of conventional definitions of male and female sexuality in studying Shakespearean comedy. But while she meticulously sets her argument in the context of early seventeenth-century shifts in the definitions of family and sexuality, her findings transfer to a late twentieth century also in the midst of redefining its basic sexual and familial units. What happens in Gems's play is what happens in *As You Like It* or *Twelfth Night*—polar definitions of sexuality and gender give way, in the play's altered mode, to multiple options for assessing any individual's sexuality. Couplings exist that are not even conceivable in a world where male and female are fixed entities. As meanings in the existing system of sexual difference are unfixed in comedy, Belsey summarizes that "in the gap thus produced we are able to glimpse a possible meaning, an image of a mode of being, which is not a-sexual, nor bi-sexual, but which disrupts the system of differences on which sexual stereotyping depends" (1985, 190).

In Gems's play, a fluid first act in which the accepted system of sexual difference is discarded is followed by a second act in which Gems must propose connections and endings for her world of infinite possibilities. Although it has profited from the expansiveness of the comic genre, her play cannot share in a conventional reliance on heterosexual marriage as a certification of happiness. And so even in the first act, Gems begins to make us conscious of the particular effects of her plural world on such accepted social conventions as marriage. As he discusses book endings with Jack, Cyst isolates the idea of the expected happy ending—"They have to be married, it's that sort of book" (*AM*, 19)—and explains the predictability of such a conclusion by adding, "look . . . society is a structure" (*AM*, 19). These characters, however, perhaps because of their difference, know that such conventional endings do not operate as efficiently as they are imagined to, in any world. Nagging doubts about such structures and their power are voiced by various characters. Alison, for example, grumbles about the devastating effects of marriage on many women: "The patter of little feet . . . all mod-cons, three meals a day . . . 'hush kiddies, Daddy's writing.' Till my ass dropped . . . No thanks" (*AM*, 29). And more significantly, Gems ends the first act with a parody of conventional expectations that this play's social outcasts must be unassimilable. While there is full-blown melodrama with Cyst first chasing Alison with a knife and then attempting suicide, the expectations of diaster come to nothing, as neither Alison nor Cyst is hurt. And in act 2, the characters' first-act consciousness of social conventions and appropriate endings is transformed into their active pursuit of happy endings that will fit their lives.

The centerpiece of Gems's reconstitution of happiness is the marriage of Mary, Cyst, and Muriel, a *sui generis* mixture of the conventional and the experimental. In act 2, Mary's explorations of a formal union for him and Cyst culminate in a recognizably traditional marriage proposal. Kneeling at the side of Cyst's white-and-gold hip bath Mary queries, "Cyst, will you do me the honour of marrying me?" (*AM*, 38). As soon as Cyst accepts, the union is plotted on a conventional course; Mary immediately refers to Cyst as his bride and offers him an engagement ring (*AM*, 39). And the wedding itself includes the wedding march, the bride's entry, a wedding gown, a bridesmaid, and familiar words: "Dearly beloved . . . we are gathered here, in sight of God, to join together this man, and this man, in holy matrimony" (*AM*, 40–41). *Mostly* familiar words, that is. For of course, this is anything but a traditional marriage, since it features two men pledging their lives to one another. The subversive possibilities in a same-sex bride and groom are multiplied in the further alteration of the marriage, midceremony. When Cyst and Mary respond to Muriel's jealousy of their wedding by inviting her to join them in their vows, as a second bride, all three participants ignore the assumption that happiness comes only to twosomes. In a world where sexuality and the commitments it inspires have been established as various and mutating, marriage can be separated from its conventional "connotations" of heterosexuality and the nuclear family. Gems reserves for her use, however, marriage's connotations of happiness, union, sharing, and community; and she adds to marriage the possibilities of homosexuality, transvestism, and odd numbers. Gems does not dismantle marriage, but suggests that its more important values of love and commitment can and should be available to those the institution has excluded. Gems has reclaimed comedy's happy ending of marriage on the unusual terms of this play.

Behind the joy of Gems's reconstituted marriage in *Aunt Mary* lies her personal crusade for a restructuring of intimate relationship. While her models for what she considers a necessary commitment "to something and someone outside" ourselves (Colvin 1982, 9) include traditional notions of marriage and family, Gems has repeatedly proposed workable alternatives to the heterosexual nuclear family. Having found "great joy" in historical precedents for alternative families (Betsko and Koenig 1987, 209), she advocates an active search for new ways to live out our long lives: "we are living twice as long so we get restless and try to find other ways to" live with one another (Gems 1986a). And she offers as solutions communities of women and the same-sex marriage she brings to life in *Aunt Mary*—"Men should be able to marry men and women marry women if they want to" (Colvin 1982, 9).

One caution, however, is in order. Gems champions fresh relational possibilities in *Aunt Mary*, but at the same time, through an addendum to her happy ending, she registers her impatience with our slow progress toward such change. For while act 2, scene 4 ends with the emotional peak of the wedding vows and the visual excitement of cascading flowers, the play continues for one more scene. On the "day after," as we return to a stream of relational encounters, we must acknowledge that this new marriage is still an experimental union, not a relational panacea. Cyst and Mary's bickering is back, and Muriel's scattered behavior continues. Relational redefinition is possible, but never easy.

Through her formal experimentations in *Aunt Mary* Gems has exposed limitations to standard expectations of comic happiness while she has also satisfied our need for joy and community. She has used comedy without allowing it to determine her characters. And in her bending of the genre she has made theatre an avenue to social change.

Gems began writing *Camille* just after *Aunt Mary's* ill-starred production and consequent "terrible notices," and she explains *Camille's* aura of death and despair as part of her personal tendency to swing from a light-hearted play to a "heavy" one (Gems 1986a). With this darker play, Gems attempts to restructure not only genres, roles, and relationships, but also literary and historical precedent. She partakes in the "retelling" or "relighting" of the past that she sees as a primary task of the woman dramatist (Betsko and Koenig 1987, 204). The story of *Camille* comes from Alexandre Dumas fils's 1848 novel *Camille,* in which he tells the story of a Parisian courtesan, Marguerite Gautier (Camille), who has transformed herself from a peasant girl to a woman of dazzling beauty and stature, and who has earned the privilege of selling herself only to the wealthiest. For Dumas fils, her tragedy springs not from the personal compromises she has had to make, but from the tuberculosis that eventually kills her, and from her fervid, ill-fated love affair with Armand Duval. Dumas fils's story, which was based on his real-life love affair with Alphonsine Duplessis (and which has been reinterpreted in Verdi's opera *La Traviata* and George Cukor's 1936 film *Camille),* has given us our stereotype of the prostitute with a heart of gold who must pay, through death, for her flaunting of social protocol. In her play, Gems works to reclaim this character lost, for over 100 years, inside the series of ornate literary, musical, and filmic frames her various male admirers have erected. In this play as in *Aunt Mary,* Gems's revisionary focus is on roles and relationships, and on endings—those we may anticipate and those we may remake.

The complications in "retelling" Marguerite's story are reflected in the widely conflicting interpretations reviewers attached to their praise of Gems's play, first produced by the Royal Shakespeare Company in Stratford-upon-Avon in April, 1984. For some, Gems's *Camille* was successful because it made accessible to a modern audience Dumas fils's nineteenth-century stereotype.

Richard Edmonds applauded the absence of "contemporary nonsense" that would only "mar a classic theme"; and his sentiments are echoed by John Barber, who was delighted by the escape to "a world of corrupt sensual delight." For others, acclaim was grounded in Gems's "reclaiming" (Wardle 1984) of a woman through feminist and class-conscious angles of vision. These reviewers praised her "redistribution of emphasis" (Hoyle 1984), her "reappraisal of romantic love" (de Jongh 1984), and her efforts to "update and radicalize the myth" (Kelley 1984). That such opposite responses were generated by the same play suggests the entrenchment of the nineteenth-century Camille in our cultural attitudes.

Gems herself had been sensitized, from the beginning, to the power still so potent in Dumas fils's version of the story. Like Dumas fils, she admits to finding the real-life story of Alphonsine Duplessis hypnotic; and in her notes for the London playbill reports on the eerie way the historical facts made a place for themselves in her version.[2] For example, before she knew Duplessis had had a son, Gems had given her Marguerite one. But it was the story's prescribed ending that Gems had most to wrestle with. She realized that the melodramatic way in which Dumas fils's Marguerite dies makes pity the primary audience response and makes nearly impossible any response to Marguerite's difficulties as a woman and as a working-class wage earner: "It was a real problem that [the power of the death ending], you know. The first thing that hit me was the bloody TB because it is not a metaphor that will work nowadays, because TB is not a killer any more. And I was stuck with her death. It was a real problem because it is not dynamic . . . it's the woman as victim" (Gems 1986a). To short-circuit the pathos and victimization of the Camille she inherits, Gems revises the story and its format so that when she creates a death scene even Dumas fils would recognize, our impulse to pity must contend with our recognition of the social and sexual pressures that conditioned Marguerite's life.

The first way Gems asserts her reading of Marguerite's life is by multiplying the original story's limited notions of human relationship. As in *Aunt Mary,* male-female relationships are not assumed to be the sole possibility for togetherness. Before the impassioned love between Marguerite and Armand becomes central, *Camille's* (*C*) early scenes have offered same-sex friendships as the most satisfying and reliable bonds. Marguerite's friendship with Sophie—girlish, loving, supportive, and sexual all at once—has lasted through separation and pain; Marguerite's tie to Prudence has allowed for affection to accompany business transactions; and Armand's friendship with Bela, although easily unfixed by Bela's jealousy and Armand's inattentiveness, is the closest attachment either man knows. The sexual nature of two of these connections is explicit in Gems's calling for kisses "full on the lips" for both Sophie and Marguerite (*C*, 89) and Bela and Armand (*C*, 120). To stress the centrality of these unconventional connections Gems frequently uses impressionistic dance sequences to punctuate her dialogue. For example, at the end of act I, scene 4, in a "languid" (*C*, 103) late night mood, words give way to an opium-influenced swirling of partners; we see Armand dancing with Sophie, Bela with Clemence, Armand with Bela, Marguerite alone, and Armand with Marguerite (*C*, 103). Admittedly the sexual and relational freedom of such moments threatens to collapse into mere decadence, but more often there radiates an openness in which the stereotypes of male and female behavior in Dumas fils are transcended. Dumas fils sees all of his women competing with one another for men or money, and brings men together only to build defenses against the unpredictable passions of women. Dumas fils's Armand and Marguerite cling to each other against this bleak background. But when Gems directs our attention to Marguerite and Armand at the end of her act I, we can see their union as a matter of choice, not desperation or destiny.

By creating multidimensional women and a female context, Gems interrupts the original story's death-determined conclusion in a second way. Although Dumas fils chose to overlook the fact of Alphonsine Duplessis's child in creating a childless Marguerite, Gems not only makes her courtesan a mother, but also shows us both the boy and Marguerite's love and concern for him. In fact, it is her love for little Jean-Paul that must come before her love for Armand, when Armand's father forces Marguerite to choose between the two males in her life. Gems's Marguerite is further defined apart from her passions for Armand in her strong connections to her female friends. Throughout the play, the women who have survived and succeeded by trading on their bodies—Marguerite, Prudence, Sophie, and Clemence—depend on one another for support, love, and advice. Although they make room for men in their lives, their relations with men rarely compete with their womanly ties. Even when Marguerite is blissfully happy off in a country hideaway with Armand, she will confide to Sophie the doubts ("I am, almost persuaded. Some of the time," [*C*, 218]) she dare not share with Armand. That a collection of women is consistently the most prominent constellation of actors on stage is underscored by the appearance of these women around Marguerite's deathbed. She must die apart from Armand, but not apart from her female friends. The importance of Gems's female context in redirecting thinking about Marguerite's story is clear when the play is compared to its contemporary, a 1984 version aired in this country on commercial television. In this media updating, an exclusive focus on Armand and Marguerite and a traditional assortment of male-female relationships isolated the heroine and made unavoidable a Dumas-like vision of unredeemable female passion.

While both the female context and the expanded possibilities for relationship begin to diffuse the power of Dumas fils's melodramatic ending, in Gems's frame for her play is the clearest guidance for our reinterpretation of Marguerite Gautier. The frame consists of three scenes: the play's opening scene, in which Armand is befriended by Gaston de Maurieux when the two men meet at the auction of the deceased Marguerite's belongings; the first scene of act 2, during which Armand and Gaston witness the exhuming of Marguerite's body; and the play's final scene in which Gaston and Armand have a chance meeting with Marguerite's circle. Gems has borrowed the idea for the frame from Dumas fils's novel in which the story of Marguerite is framed once by the first-person testimony of the narrator (who is not directly involved with Marguerite), and again by the first-person narrative of Armand, embedded in the first narrator's revelations. The main effect of Dumas fils's double frame is to distance Marguerite, to reduce her to an object. Characteristically, the narrator, who certifies his tale as "truth" (1955, 3), equates the loss of Marguerite with the loss of a precious thing: "I regretted her death as one might regret the destruction of a beautiful work of art" (1955, 11). And the objectifying attitude persists in Armand's words, where Marguerite exists as a capricious but idealized figure he can only love or hate. In writing of Cukor's 1936 film, E. Ann Kaplan notes that the effect of certain filmic techniques is to prevent Marguerite from being perceived as a subject (1983, 40), and similarly, in Dumas fils's novel, the frame represents male control of Marguerite and her story. Yet Gems, who recognizes the "great strain" of an "inherited structure" (Gems 1986b) and who could have drawn on the frameless structure of Dumas fils's play version of *Camille* (1852), has chosen to build her version on the novel's framework. She retains its male voice and control, its early revelation of Marguerite's death, and at least some of its distancing of Marguerite. But it is by using Dumas fils's structure that Gems forces us to question not only its "truth" but also its limited vision of Marguerite.

For unlike Dumas fils, Gems has provided a point of view to challenge the male point of view in the frame. In the play's final scene (the last segment of the frame), we are tempted to believe that the time Armand and Gaston have so intensively shared has been devoted to Armand's story of Marguerite. Gaston graciously comforts Armand, "if it has been of the least assistance for you to tell me your story I am more delighted to have missed a few nights' sleep" (*C*, 151). We could infer from this that the story we have just witnessed is Armand's version of Marguerite. For Dumas fils, Armand's version *is,* indeed, the only one. But while in the novel the narrator can maintain his control of interpretation, on stage, Marguerite gains her own voice. And Gems has engineered her tale so that there is a clear distinction to be made between Armand's vision and other visions, including Marguerite's. Most importantly, the multiple perspectives in Gems's play qualify the traditional view of love and relationship omnipresent in Dumas fils's novel. Armand's view of love, which is valorized in the frame scenes where no one can contradict it, is also laid before us in his often agonizing interactions with Marguerite. For him, love is transcendent and can offer satisfactions that outweigh economic, class, or familial considerations: he tells Marguerite, "Why not? why not, if we choose. It's simple. We choose to live. . . . You are here, and I am here, and it is decided between us" (*C,* 125). While Marguerite is every bit as much in love as is Armand, she carries with her to this love realizations that his aristocratic standing can allow him to disregard. Relationships have economic and class dimensions, she repeatedly tells Armand, and for women such dimensions can be particularly brutal. A woman like herself, Marguerite tells him, must preserve her power by keeping her friends (*C,* 111) and by maintaining her economic independence: "it's in your interest, as it's in mine to guard my freedom. God knows it's cost me enough" (*C,* 112). Predictably, Marguerite's caution proves a more realistic interpretation of the play's central relationship than Armand's heedless passion will allow. And while Marguerite teeters on a complete embracing of Armand's all-for-love philosophy, she cannot shake off her knowledge that survival always requires compromise and that money does matter. By offering these conflicting visions of love between sexes and between classes, Gems does not desire to suggest that romance or love are outmoded or dangerous; she sees the play, in fact, as about "the paramount necessity for love" (Gems 1986a). But her two visions are meant to remind us of the filters through which we often choose to see love, filters that too often deflect considerations of money, class, or power. Gems has retained Dumas fils's frame to alert us to the powerful male version of Marguerite society has accepted for years and to counterpoint it with the female anarchy this frame has so carefully concealed.

Gems's critique of the patriarchal *Camille* is fragile, however. Helene Keyssar has noted that women's plays are often more subversive than the productions in which they are rendered (1985, 148). And *Camille*'s transfer from the Stratford-upon-Avon studio space of The Other Place to the proscenium-framed expanse of London's Comedy Theatre frighteningly demonstrated how Gems's counterpointed frame has a relative, variable power.[3] On the smaller stage, both the lack of definition in sexual roles and the feminist rhetoric of the female culture were fortified by the fluid and intimate production. In the London production, however, it was the vision of the narrative frame that was strengthened. The proscenium arch, by creating a distance between audience and actors, rendered Marguerite often no more than the object of Dumas fils's vision. Both literally and metaphorically, she was framed, and her radical rhetoric more easily contained and dismissed. The effect of the two different stage spaces on the play can be gauged more specifically in the subtle transformations of costuming. In The Other Place performance, the magnificent dress of Armand and Marguerite in early scenes was contrasted to their nakedness in the love scenes late in act 1. During their orgasmic encounter in scene 5, the lovers' physical exposure underscored the vulnerability they expose themselves to in their love. And as, in scene 6, the two slowly, humbly, and sadly accumulated their customary layers of clothing in preparation for again facing the world, an audience could visualize the disparity between the social facade that would part them and the emotion and desire that could bind them, so simply, together. "The nude scene," reported Francis Barber, the actor playing Marguerite, "was integral to the play" (Edmonds 1984). While the London production also depended on the characters' nudity, the decision to have Marguerite reclothe herself somewhat clandestinely, behind screens, detracted from her openness and emphasized, instead, coy motions. Such actions cast a pornographic light on the act 1 love scenes. And physically distanced from the action by the proscenium arch, the audience became voyeurs interpreting, and perhaps condemning, Marguerite's actions as shameful. Gems herself had predicted that the play would not "transpose." It succeeded in The Other Place, she noted, "because that's where the production was created. . . . If we had designed it from the beginning for the proscenium arch it would have been done differently . . . much more hierarchically" (Gems 1986a). So while Gems's framing of Marguerite's story allows her to critique its traditional world of romance, her formal reclamation of Marguerite remains dependent on careful production.

Nevertheless, Gems's addition of expanded attitudes to sexuality and her revision of Dumas fils's frame do aid her in reclaiming this story's ending. In both Gems's and Dumas fils's *Camille* we are told, from the opening moments, that Marguerite has died young. This foreshadowing of death delivered a clear message for Dumas fils, one that overpowered Marguerite's charm and eloquence: a freely sexual woman like Marguerite, no matter how beautiful or good-hearted, must die to pay the price for flaunting social protocol. In Dumas fils, we can temporarily accept, study, and admire Marguerite because both social and generic conventions assure us of her tragic end. Gems, however, was unwilling to accept this ending and its message. In her original script, she refused the death-ending and its relegation of one woman to her place. Finding the death scene neither "interesting" nor "useful," she concluded the play with "a prolonged scene which is a kind of mirror of their [Marguerite and Armand's] prolonged scene in the first half. . . . He seems hateful and has energy and she doesn't. And then she and her energy flare up and he becomes morose and in the end there is a kind of stand-off between them. And that was how I ended it. Problematically" (Gems 1986a). Such openness, reminiscent of *Aunt Mary*, did not satisfy Gems's director, Ron Daniels, however, who was "adamant that there should be a death scene" (Gems 1986a). While Gems delivered to Daniels the death scene he wanted (she justifies her concession by noting that the play had always been a "hybrid" done "on a whim" [Gems 1986a]), she struggled to curtail its effect. The play qualities I have discussed above—the broad definitions of sexuality and relation, the multidimensional female context, and the counterpointed frame—have all been designed as antidotes to the powerful death ending. Although we *do* see Marguerite die in Gems's play, we have been offered a socially and politically conscious framework in which to interpret the moment. Thus, in the play's final scene, which immediately follows Marguerite's death, Gems can ask us to consider the woman from a thinking distance. The "problematic" ending Gems originally conceived takes form in the final exchange of Prudence and Armand:

> *Prudence.* Ah, my friend, no more rapture? No more grand passion? Well, can it last? At least you lived it. For a while. At least now you understand. That it's all we have. Even I know that. Armand, don't betray what you had by destroying yourself. Do you know what she would have done if you had died? She would have gone away for a season—wasted a year of her looks. And then she would have remade her life. From necessity.
> *Armand.* I have no life.
> *Prudence.* Poor Armand. You thought to rescue Marguerite Gautier and you lost her. (*He does not reply.*)
> Perhaps, after all, she preferred her freedom. (*He looks up.*)
> Has it never occurred to you that some of us might prefer the life— given the alternatives?
> *Armand.* No. No. (*He rises.*) You killed her.

Were we so threatening? One man? One woman? It was the wrong
transaction.
There was a chance. A chance for something real. Something mutual.
There for the taking like an apple on a tree. Something ordinary.
Unnoticeable.
Prudence. A dream.
Armand. There was respect. Honour. Possibility. But you don't want
that. What do you want?
(*C,* 152–53)

Their debate is inconclusive, throwing up before us the various visions of love
Gems has counterpointed throughout the play. However, their disagreement does
transfer our attention from the issue of Marguerite's intrinsic worth to our interpretation of the social, economic, and sexual pressures that limited her options.

Structurally, Gems offers one further reassessment of Marguerite's death in
her ending to act 1. There the tour de force collection of exchanges, in bed, between the lovers Marguerite and Armand, encourages opinions and emotions dis-
allowed in the play's grander locales. And as Marguerite recounts the horrors of
her early life—poverty, sexual molestation, incest, and powerlessness—she can,
in this space, explain her feminist response to the world. Her idea of love, for example, has been materially conditioned: "Seven pregnancies in nine years? Arms
swollen with soda from washing stains from other people's linen? Ask my
mother. No. No love" (*C,* 108). And even Armand can offer, together with his
insistent passion, a growing acceptance of Marguerite's independence and self.
He's "at home with" her freedom (*C,* 110). We come away from act 1 with
doubts about the chances for this relationship's survival, but with no questions about the love itself. For something new is being tested here. In the
space of act 1, scenes 5 and 6, Gems links the ambience of Marguerite's bed to
enlightened attitudes about men and women's social and sexual connections.
In her bed, Marguerite is a powerful, eloquent, convincing feminist who earns
stature because of, not in spite of, her sexuality. Thus when Marguerite dies
in this bed at the conclusion of act 2 (it is symbolically if not literally the
same bed) we can read the loss not as necessary (as Dumas fils would have
it) but as regrettable. The memory of the earlier act 1 scenes cannot prevent the
death, but can empower us to view it other than tradition insists. We can
mourn the loss of the honesty, power, and control this woman eked out for
herself, and can cancel Dumas fils's lingering sense that Marguerite had to die.

Irving Wardle attempts to diminish the play's power by concluding that

"the piece remains the tubercular romance it always was rather than a tragedy." The crucial concern, however, is not whether Gems's play is a tragedy,
but how her Marguerite comments on *Camille* as tragedy. Susan Bassnett-
McGuire (1984) argues that a play like Gems's *Queen Christina* (or, by extension, *Camille*) will be irrevocably patriarchal, with its focus on a single heroine. I would counterargue, however, that Gems's *Camille* presents the single
figure of Marguerite Gautier just to reveal the patriarchal nature of Dumas
fils's tale. Discussing *Queen Christina* back in 1977, Gems noted, "what worries
me is that the woman's point of view . . . is not put" (Isaacs 1977). While
in *Camille* Gems keeps a male framework to remind us where point of view
did and still does lie, she spotlights efforts to subvert that control by building
for the story a woman's point of view. The tragedy in Gems's play is not just
Marguerite's death, but the way her story has been conscripted and her self,
strength, and power devalued. Gems herself still has doubts about giving way
to the death ending. Even as she was revising the play for its New York pre-
miere in December of 1986, she admitted: "it might really have been better
to bust the story out completely and not have her die" (Gems 1986a). And
so she leaves us with a play in which male power is acknowledged and subverted though not dismantled. The play is a sobering admission that changes
in social and sexual relationships are possible though slow in coming.

It is not as clear in *Camille* as it is in *Aunt Mary* that Gems is collapsing
her agenda for generic change with her drive for social reform. But to their
different degrees, both plays are predicated on Gems's concerns about our
world. "I think there have to be quite radical changes," she asserted in 1977
(Isaacs 1977); and in 1985 her specific goal was to favor "political plays" and
plays on "feminism today" (Gardner 1985, 13). Feminist drama, says Keyssar,
"aims to empower both the theatre and women" (1985, 184). In *Aunt Mary*
and *Camille,* as in most of her other plays, Gems is leading a struggle for a
feminist drama by pressuring old forms and proposing new ones.

NOTES
  1. Gems feels that "Politics, direct statements, belong on the platform not the
stage," but finds that most theatre is, by nature, political (Betsko and Koenig 1987,
208–9).
  2. The real-life story of Alphonsine Duplessis is not, however, to be equated with
the version of her life Dumas fils delivered. He neglected facts and events that did
not suit his purpose and invented others that did. Gems did the same. The two authors revised for different reasons, however.
  3. Gems originally wrote the play for a large proscenium theatre, and when the
Royal Shakespeare Company put the play on at its small studio space at The Other
Place, Gems played a large role in manicuring the script for that space.

REFERENCES

Barber, John. 1984. "Sybaritic Wallow." *Daily Telegraph,* April 13.

Bassnett-McGuire, Susan. 1984. "Towards a Theory of Women's Theatre." In *Semiotics of Drama and Theatre: New Perspectives in the Theory of Drama and Theatre,* ed. Herta Schmid and Aloysius Van Kesteren, 445–66. Amsterdam: John Benjamin.

Belsey, Catherine. 1985. "Disrupting Sexual Difference: Meaning and Gender in the Comedies." In *Alternative Shakespeares,* ed. John Drakakis, 166–90. London: Methuen.

Betsko, Kathleen, and Rachel Koenig. 1987. *Interviews with Contemporary Women Playwrights.* New York: Beech Tree Books.

Colvin, Clare. 1982. "Earth Mother from Christchurch." *Plays and Players,* August, 9–10.

de Jongh, Nicholas. 1984. Review of *Camille. Guardian,* April 13.

Dumas fils, Alexandre. *Camille.* Trans. Edmund Gosse, 1955. New York: Heritage Press.

Edmonds, Richard. 1984. Review of *Camille. Birmingham Post,* April 12.

Gardner, Lyn. 1985. "Precious Gems." *Plays and Players,* April, 12–13.

Gems, Pam. 1983. "Imagination and Gender." In *On Gender and Writing,* ed. Michelene Wandor, 148–51. London: Pandora Press.

———. 1984a. *Aunt Mary.* In *Plays by Women.* Vol. 3. Ed. Michelene Wandor, 13–49. London: Methuen.

———. 1984b. *Camille.* Notes for the 1984 Stratford production in Royal Shakespeare Company promptbook, Stratford-upon-Avon.

———. 1985a. *Camille.* In *Three Plays: Piaf/Camille/Loving Women.* Harmondsworth, Middlesex: Penguin. 73–153.

———. 1985b. *Camille.* Playbill to London transfer, Comedy Theatre, October.

———. 1986a. Interview with Susan Carlson, April 22, London.

———. 1986b. "The Stage Chronicle and the Play." From the program for *The Danton Affair,* Royal Shakespeare Company, Barbican Theatre, London, July.

Hoyle, Martin. 1984. Review of *Camille. Financial Times,* April 13.

Isaacs, David. 1977. "The Calm Gentle Woman Pressing for Change." *Coventry Evening Telegraph,* September 9.

Kaplan, E. Ann. 1983. *Women and Film: Both Sides of the Camera.* New York: Methuen.

Kelley, David. 1984. "Kinds of Surrender." *Times Literary Supplement,* May 4, 496.

Keyssar, Helene. 1985. *Feminist Theatre.* New York: Grove Press.

Spencer, Charles. 1982. Review of *Aunt Mary. Plays and Players,* August, 35–36.

Wandor, Michelene. 1986. *Carry On, Understudies: Theatre and Sexual Politics.* London: Routledge and Kegan Paul.

Wardle, Irving. 1984. "Agony and Ecstasy." Review of *Camille.* London *Times,* April 12.

JONNIE GUERRA

Beth Henley: Female Quest and the Family-Play Tradition

Commentators on dramatist Beth Henley almost uniformly have foregrounded the "southernness" of her plays—their colorful vernacular; their eccentric populations; the resemblance they bear to works by other southern authors, notably Tennessee Williams and Flannery O'Connor. If the southern bias in her reception initially obscured Henley's concern with women's themes, the recent surge of interest in female playwrights—created in part when, in the early 1980s, first she and then Marsha Norman won the Pulitzer Prize for Drama—has refocused the critical lens on Henley's representation of women and prompted feminist consideration of her theatrical achievement. This is not to suggest, however, that feminist critics observing the Henley landscape are equally impressed with its terrain.

Although Helene Keyssar finds in *Crimes of the Heart* "many of the . . . [themes] of a strong feminist drama" (1985, 157), she sharply attacks the play on aesthetic and political grounds. Keyssar specifically quarrels with the Broadway production in which the performance style of the actresses "yielded to caricatures" (1985, 159) and with Henley's lack of an ideological agenda.[1] On the other hand, Karen Laughlin blames productions of *Crimes* that "stress comical elements to the point of farce, thereby discouraging serious reflection on the play's potentially threatening revelations" (1986, 47) on the politics of a male-dominated theatre. And, in contrast to Keyssar, Laughlin contends that "Henley's script quickly transcends these limitations" (1986, 47) to deliver a powerful challenge to "an entire patriarchal vision of reality" (1986, 49).[2] Yet an examination of Henley's portrayal of women's lives, from a broader perspective than a single play can provide, points to serious shortcomings in her representation of women that Laughlin's argument disregards. Not only do Henley's subsequent plays, *The Miss Firecracker Contest* and *The Wake of Jamey Foster,* reiterate rather than expand the images of women she develops in *Crimes,* but also the patterns that recur have disturbing negative implications. At the core of Henley's failure to advance positive images of women lies her consistent and unimaginative dependence on the forms and modes of the dominant male tradition of American drama.

Like many plays inscribed into the canon of "good American drama," *Crimes, Miss Firecracker,* and *The Wake* all revolve around a family crisis and homecoming. In *Crimes,* the MaGrath sisters are reunited in the home of their dying grandfather after Babe shoots her husband; in *Miss Firecracker,* Carnelle Scott's effort to win the local beauty pageant coincides with the return to Brookhaven of the cousins with whom she was raised as a sibling — Elain Rutledge, who is running away from her wealthy husband and stifling domestic life, and Delmount Williams, just released from a mental institution; and, finally, in *The Wake,* the family and friends of the deceased Jamey Foster join his widow Marshael for a long, tension-filled "watch" over the corpse the day and night before the funeral. In her portrayal of women and the family, however, Henley departs from the mainstream American family-play tradition, which Carol Billman shows has privileged male characters and their familial and societal responsibilities and banished female characters to live in the shadow of their fathers, husbands, and sons (1980, 35–40). Henley turns a spotlight into the shadow and gives central importance to the dilemmas of women, to their conflicts and suffering within the family, and to their questions about personal identity and the meaning of life. Not only does she focus on seldom-dramatized dimensions of family relations such as the bonds between mother and daughter and between sisters, but also she recharts from a woman's vantage point such well-explored dramatic territory as marriage. Most significant is Henley's attempt to adapt the family play to portray the female quest for autonomy.

In *Diving Deep and Surfacing,* Carol Christ has analyzed the form and content of female quest in fiction and poetry by women writers, and her paradigm (1980, 1–26) is useful for evaluating Henley's plays. According to Christ, women progress through experiences of nothingness, awakening, insight, and new naming — each with a gender-specific meaning — on their journeys to selfhood. Because patriarchal society teaches women to question their own worth, she argues, women's experiences of nothingness are inescapable. If they embrace the models of female behavior prescribed for them, they learn self-negation and feel intense powerlessness. On the other hand, women whose lives do not conform to the conventional patterns suffer from both exclusion and self-doubt because they are perceived by society, and see themselves, as failures. Christ's term "awakening" designates the change in consciousness precipitated when women "come face to face with the nothingness they know as lack of self, lack of power, and lack of value for women in a male-centered world" (1980, 18). Since they understand the patriarchal image of woman to be a construct whose influence over their lives is within their own power to control, awakened women present a challenge to male definitions of reality. The insight on which awakening depends Christ explains as an experience of "seeing within" during which women recognize the split between the strong "real" self inside and the passive "other" self they are forced to enact within the repressive patriarchal structures of family and society. The final dimension of female quest—what Christ calls "new naming"—refers to the radical act of self-affirmation women engage in when they record their experiences through language. By putting into words the truth about their lives and refuting male versions of human reality that exclude or misrepresent their experiences, women validate their personal worth and that of other women. Moreover, concludes Christ, "as women begin to name the world for themselves, not only will they create new life possibilities for women, they will also upset the world order that has been taken for granted for centuries" (1980, 24).

The quests of Henley's female characters resemble the model Christ proposes. In the course of her plays, the heroines face their meaningless existences and struggle both to overcome oppressive definitions of themselves, in many cases stemming from their family relationships, and to become free persons.[3] Henley herself has underscored the importance of the quest motif in her work, describing her plays as being "about overcoming ghosts of the past and letting go of what other people have said you are, what they have told you to be" (Betsko and Koenig 1987, 218). Although all the experiences associated with female quest can be identified in her plays, Henley's decisions about form and dramaturgy undermine to some degree her thematic intention. In the first place, the conventions of the family-play genre perpetuate expectations about women's representation on stage that are inherently restrictive. And Henley does not re-vision the form in order to free herself to advance the kind of images of women as autonomous individuals that a female audience would like to identify with, to celebrate, or to become. That she accepts rather than reinvents the family-play structure predetermines her work to take as its central focus the nothingness women experience in their everyday lives. A corollary problem is Henley's adherence to a definition of realism so limiting that it compromises her ability to portray the multiple dimensions of women's awakening.

When Henley turns the spotlight into the shadow, her project, as Milly Barranger describes it, is to create on stage "presence" for women (1987, 9). But the images of women the audience confronts in Henley's plays are predominantly negative ones of suffering, self-destructive females whose lives and identities have been shaped by male family members and the sexist values of the small southern towns in which they reside. Indeed Henley makes fully visible women's experiences of nothingness.[4] In her world, there exists no marital happiness, nor is there intimacy or mutual understanding in the marriage bond. Rather, married females—Babe Botrelle, Elain Rutledge, Marshael and Katty Foster—openly acknowledge their discontentment and total emotional isolation from their mates. Henley's women characters also reveal their sense of personal meaninglessness through such stereotypically female behavioral patterns as self-sacrifice, submissiveness, and silence as well as through their negative self-images. Almost all exhibit obsessive insecurity with their bodies and physical appearance. Lenny MaGrath and Katty Foster, for example, feel inhabited by nothingness because they are unable to bear children. Meg MaGrath, Carnelle Scott, and Collard Darnell portray their nagging self-doubts through their reputations for promiscuity. On the topic of sexuality, the plays all support a society whose double standard punishes women who are sexually active, but averts its eyes from male misconduct. Whereas the local gossips censure Meg and Carnelle with the derogatory labels "cheap Christmas trash" (*Crimes*, 6) and "Miss Hot Tamale" (*Miss Firecracker*, 22), they criticize Marshael when Jamey starts an affair with a younger woman and deserts his family.

Henley's plays also portray women in confining roles outside the home: the jobs assigned to female characters sound dull and monotonous and reflect a low expectation of their capabilities. In *Crimes*, for example, Lenny "works out at a brick yard" (34) and Meg, after she fails to establish a singing career, pays "cold storage bills for a dog-food company" (23). Carnelle, in *Miss Firecracker*, is unprestigiously employed as a clerk in a jewelry shop; Popeye, as a seamstress. In *The Wake*, Marshael makes marching outfits for the "Prancing Ponies" and sells home improvement ornaments like "salt and pepper shakers shaped like crocodiles" (21). Her sister Collard works as a photographer, yet no creativity is expected in her job taking children's school portraits. In contrast, Henley's male characters often have important, professional careers as lawyers, state senators, and bankers. And men who have not succeeded at least have possessed grand ambitions: Jamey Foster to be a world-renowned historian; Doc Porter, in *Crimes*, to be a physician. Likewise, at the end of *Miss Firecracker*, Delmount announces his plan to "learn to be a philosopher . . . to let everyone know why . . . [they're] living" (102).

It is discomfiting that Henley traces the female characters' experiences of nothingness back to their mothers. The mothers all are dead and, therefore,

literally absent from the action on stage, yet through the stories of other characters, usually their daughters, they become a strong presence in the plays.
Since the daughters dwell primarily on very negative memories of their mothers, the images of these women that emerge from the shadow are consistently
atrocious. It is their mothers, reveal the daughters, who have instilled in them
destructive values and expectations and deprived them of the nurture, validation, and example with which to move beyond the limited possibilities for
women's lives sanctioned by the patriarchy. In *Miss Firecracker,* for instance,
both Carnelle and Elain have internalized the lesson of female inferiority
taught by their aunt and mother, Ronelle Williams—that a woman's only
sources of self-esteem are beauty and a rich husband. And, there is no doubt
that Ronelle's instruction has perniciously influenced each of their lives, contributing both to Carnelle's poor self-image and to Elain's narcissism. In *Crimes,*
the MaGrath sisters are haunted by their mother's emotional abandonment
and suicide; if she "felt something for anyone" (31), they recall, it was not
for her daughters, but for the family's old yellow cat. Their mother's rejection
has had a particularly devastating effect on Lenny and Meg, both of whom
continue to be afraid to risk feeling love for anyone else.[5] Finally, Marshael
in *The Wake* associates her mother's life with all the humiliating aspects of
female existence that she herself is determined to avoid.

In addition to these negative mother images, there is present in Henley's
work a recurrent pattern of women characters who perceive, much to their
horror, that their personal histories are repeating the stories of their mothers.
Marshael, for example, feels inexplicably cursed when, in spite of her resolution to the contrary, the details of her life with Jamey replicate her mother's
story: both had three children, two girls and a boy; both of their marriages
deteriorated into "yelling and crying in the night" (*The Wake,* 44); both Marshael's father and Jamey became alcoholics. Similarly, the MaGrath sisters recognize in themselves the same self-destructive emotional traits that caused
their mother's isolation and suicide. Although all three struggle to survive
the "real bad days" (*Crimes,* 120) they identify as their mother's legacy, Babe's
miserable marriage and suicide attempts most exactly recapitulate Mama Ma-
Grath's life. Because Elain has shaped her life to win her mother's approval,
her behavior exhibits the same self-division that characterized Ronelle's. Shack-
led by her mother's restrictive expectations of women's destiny, Elain becomes,
just as Ronelle had before her, "a saint or an angel" (*Miss Firecracker,* 11) in
society's eyes, but a monster in her most intimate human relationships. Unable to imagine a way out of her own spiritually dead existence, Elain also

fails to provide the nurture Carnelle needs during the younger woman's struggle to overcome the past.

In these portrayals of the mother-daughter relationship, Henley insists that inadequate mothers contribute to the continuation of incapacitating psychological traits and oppressive life patterns in the generation of their daughters. At the same time, she stops short of doing a feminist portrayal of these mother characters. It may be Henley's intention for the audience to interpret the repetition from female generation to female generation as proof of the patriarchy's power to prolong women's experiences of nothingness, but her scripts never clearly articulate a critique of the forces constraining the mothers' lives. Henley's daughters do not discern that their mothers, too, are victims, nor usually do they show sympathy with the older women's dilemmas. Instead the daughters express resentment of their mothers by developing "matrophobia," what Adrienne Rich describes as "a womanly splitting of the self, in the desire to become purged once and for all of our mothers' bondage, to become individuated and free" (1986, 236). As Henley envisions female quest, her women characters can progress, only if they reject their mothers' example.[6]

To fulfill their needs for nurture and guidance, for the positive mothering they have been deprived of, Henley's female characters turn to each other. Indeed some of the most powerful scenes in Henley's plays underline the integral relation in women's lives between breaking silence and survival. Central to Henley's vision of quest are female characters engaged in storytelling—sharing their lives through stories and discovering strength in the bond that their sharing creates.[7] A strong statement of this theme is spoken by Meg MaGrath to convince Babe to tell the truth about why she shot Zachary: ". . . it's a human need. To talk about our lives. It's an important human need" (*Crimes,* 46). Perhaps because her own experience in Hollywood has sensitized Meg to the stories that lie behind women's silence, she does not believe Babe's initial account of the shooting and determinedly breaks down her sister's resistance to naming herself an abused wife, the real motivation for the crime. In the same way, Meg also elicits Lenny's confession that she lied about the reason her affair with Charlie Hill ended. As listener and counselor to both her sisters, Meg displays extraordinary skill throughout *Crimes* in "hearing her sisters into speech."[8]

A similar portrayal of female community occurs in act 2 of *The Wake,* when all the women characters gather in Marshael's bedroom to console Katty, who has locked herself in the bathroom, in outraged response to catching her husband, Willy Wayne, embracing Collard. The women begin a ritual of storytelling: each relates a humiliating experience to prove to Katty that they have shared and, therefore, empathize with her feelings of worthlessness. And even after Marshael's story of how Jamey "fiercely hurt" (*The Wake,* 53) her pride in front of his twenty-two-year-old mistress finally brings Katty out of the bathroom to reassure Marshael: ". . . you are a woman. A beautiful woman. Don't let anyone tell you different from that" (*The Wake,* 53), the women persist in their self and communal examination. As they confide the worst deeds they have ever committed against another person and share their private feelings about having children, Henley captures how the story of one woman frees the next to "name" as her own experiences that she always before has kept secret. The female characters listen with attention and acceptance to each other's stories; from the validation of their individual experiences, each gains a new sense of self-worth.

Yet Henley's scenes of female interaction are not all celebratory or positive treatments. Until the end of *Crimes,* nearly all of the MaGrath sisters' conversations, especially between Meg and Lenny, erupt into arguments, the dialogue becoming a pattern of accusation and then retaliation against the other's attack. Moreover, a current of hatred runs through every scene in which their cousin Chick appears. A bastion of patriarchal values, Chick bullies, judges, and disparages the sisters until a rebellious Lenny battles Chick with a broom and literally sweeps her off the stage. In *Miss Firecracker,* Henley never presents a satisfying portrayal of female interaction. In fact, the play's focus on a beauty pageant emphasizes the destructive effect of the politics of appearance on women's relationships: that the looking glass sets women against each other, makes them enemies and rivals. The first scene of act 2 presents a case in point when Tessy Mahoney, the pageant coordinator, degrades each of the other finalists to Carnelle. Tessy's criticism of her own sister Missy is the worst of all: "She's not at all attractive. I'm amazed she ever got in the contest. . . . she looks like a tank in her swimsuit . . . she's hump-shouldered from practicing . . . [the] piano all day long" (*Miss Firecracker,* 59). Another sustained scene of female interaction (act 1, scene 2) brings together Carnelle, who thinks she has not been selected as a Miss Firecracker finalist; Popeye, who despairs that Delmount will never love her; and Elain, who exaggerates in self-pity her fears of a future alone. However, the crying jag the women share approaches farce and seems more mutually indulgent than supportive. Finally, although the security of the female bond during the women's collective "dark night of the soul" in *The Wake* permits Katty's revelation: "I hate the me I have to be with . . . [Willy Wayne]" (57), in the morning she forgets the self-affirmation she learned through sisterhood and becomes again the cloying wife who subordinates her own needs and desires to fulfill her husband's.

Henley's plays also are disappointing in their exploration of what happens when women get a clear vision of the nothingness of their lives. Too frequently the plays emphasize that women channel their anger and frustration toward themselves and become self-destructive. For example, in *Crimes,* Meg reports that during the Christmas holidays her silenced emotions "exploded": she went mad and ended up in the psychiatric ward of Los Angeles County Hospital. Both her melodramatic "awakening," Babe's suicide attempts, and Lenny's vomiting suggest the risk to women of facing up to their empty lives. Likewise, in *The Wake,* Marshael's internalized anger and anxiety are manifested in self-punishing physical effects: her painful canker sores, loss of appetite, and insomnia. This is not to say that Henley never subjects the outside forces restraining her female characters to attack. With her portrayal of the MaGrath sisters' victimization by Old Granddaddy's misguided plans for their lives as well as her consistent dramatization of the emotional confinement women characters endure in their marriages, Henley implies the destructive power of a male-dominated society. And, throughout her plays, oppressive men *do* receive their "just deserts": get shot in the stomach, go into comas, get kicked in the head by cows.[9] Yet under the guise of Henley's southern Gothic humor, such wish-fulfilling treatment becomes less recognizable as an attack on the patriarchal order.

Another weakness in Henley's portrayal of female quest is suggested by her habit of interrupting its presentation on stage: some heroines reach a crucial point in their development by going offstage and then coming back to announce the change that has occurred. Meg spends the night with Doc Porter and rediscovers the value of the heart's affections; Carnelle disappears on a solitary walk by the railroad tracks to come to terms with her last-place finish in the contest; and after her confrontation with Jamey's corpse, Marshael leaves the stage to seek under "the purple, purple trees" (*The Wake,* 62) something to restore meaning to her life. Henley's dilemma, of course, is to represent on stage situations of self-contemplation and insight, events that happen in mental space. However, her usual adherence to the unities of time and place and commitment to a view of character premised on logic and coherence make it difficult for Henley to dramatize the multiple dimensions of female quest. Since she chooses not to experiment with theatrical techniques that would take her outside the boundaries of realism, Henley must rely on expository dialogue and symbolism in details of character, stage business, setting, and language to communicate the new understanding of self her female quest-ers attain. These methods do help to define what takes place during a character's absence, but telling does not substitute for showing. One challenge that faces Henley as a playwright is to become innovative enough in her dramaturgy to render convincing portrayals of women characters as they awaken to the power within the self.

Perhaps the most damning criticism of Henley's treatment of the quest is that she never completes the "re-visioning" of her women characters' lives; indeed their surface realities alter little from the beginning to the end of her plays. Some, like Elain Rutledge and Katty Foster, actually forsake their quests. Although life on her own would give Elain an opportunity "to find out just why . . . [she's] alive" (*The Wake*, 92), she is overwhelmed by the terror, loneliness, and material loss that choice would entail. She resolves to return to her husband, even though she acknowledges that will be tantamount to "drop[ping] dead off this planet" (*The Wake*, 101). Similarly, Katty reconciles with Willy Wayne because she feels powerless to do otherwise. She rationalizes her decision to Marshael thus: "I don't have children or a career like you do. Anyway I don't like changes. My hair's still the same as I wore it in college" (*The Wake*, 58). To the audience such an outcome for female quest conveys a deeply troubling message: it affirms not only the limits imposed on women's lives, but also their helplessness to imagine positive alternatives for the future.

The other Henley heroines arrive only at the threshold of transformation: because they have recognized their self-worth, Henley suggests, they may in the future—but *after* the play's conclusion—take steps to restructure the exteriors of their lives. This strategy for ending her plays no more convincingly advocates character change than does her aborted quest motif. The conclusions are problematic, moreover, because they depend on symbolic scenes that permit contradictory interpretations. Henley ends *Crimes*, for example, with a scene of female community: Lenny's day-late birthday party. The play's conclusion also forecasts new life possibilities for the MaGrath sisters—non-oppressive relationships with men for Lenny and Babe, a new maturity for Babe signaled by her name change to Becky, the restoration of Meg's singing voice. On a symbolic level the birthday motif, too, seems to celebrate each sister's rebirth as an individual and their collective rejuvenation as a family. Lenny's description of her "vision" and Henley's concluding vision of the three sisters "in a magical, golden, sparkling glimmer" (*Crimes*, 125) would present powerful images of female bonding if Lenny's insistence that "it wasn't for every minute. Just this one moment and we were all laughing" (*Crimes*, 124) did not remind the audience of the uncertain fates of these women and raise doubts that either their new closeness or their new selves can be sustained.

In *Miss Firecracker,* Henley depicts Carnelle's "awakening" with a symbolic scene in the pageant dressing room. Alone, Carnelle gazes at her reflection in the mirror, imagines away her garish dyed-red hair, and finally articulates an acceptance of herself "as is": "It used to be brown. I had brown hair. Brown" (*Miss Firecracker,* 110). Unlike Elain, who accedes to spiritual death in order to repossess her clocks, Carnelle recognizes the presence within herself of "Eternal Grace" (*Miss Firecracker,* 110) and rejoices in her feeling of empowerment. Yet in Henley's script and the production of the play that I have attended, this scene loses force because it is juxtaposed on stage with a comical conversation between Delmount and Popeye about the temperature of the heavens. If the Fourth of July fireworks display of the play's final moments also seems to function symbolically to assert Carnelle's independence from other people's labels, it still remains difficult for the audience even to speculate what steps Carnelle will take in the future to complete the process of transformation.

On the one hand, the final scene of *The Wake* contains signs both of Marshael's greater security with herself and of her liberation from the expectations of others. That she firmly refuses to attend the funeral seems to suggest her decision to detach her life from Jamey's and from the forces which ravaged their marriage.[10] Marshael also sheds her martyr image; she stops behaving as if she has to "carry . . . the world on . . . [her] lonely shoulders" (*The Wake,* 45) and enlists help with her maternal responsibilities from Collard and Brocker Slade, her new romantic interest. At the same time, in typical Henley fashion, the play ends inconclusively as Marshael settles down to sleep while Brocker sings to her. Although Nancy Hargrove interprets Marshael's state of sleep as a promise of her awakening, and the play's time, the spring—specifically at Easter—as a prophecy of her rejuvenation (1984, 68–69), what is literally seen on stage—Marshael's exhaustion—would seem to leave a more lasting impression on the spectator than do the subtle implications of Henley's symbolism.

Beth Henley's family plays present important explorations of the lives of women, of the expectations that threaten them, and of their struggles to determine their own identities and destinies. In *Crimes,* Henley accomplishes much the same effect as Susan Glaspell does in *Trifles,* a play that creates audience sympathy for a female criminal who similarly has been driven to commit murder by an abusive husband and that also affirms the value of female community in women's lives. Although Henley has denied that her purpose in *Miss Firecracker* was "to judge the contest," the play nevertheless has been cited for its criticism of beauty contests and the warped societal values that promote

such female exploitation (Betsko and Koenig 1987, 220). And in *The Wake*
Henley provides a thought-provoking dramatization from a woman character's perspective of the emotional consequences of infidelity and marital failure. Despite the significant women's themes with which her work is concerned, however, there remain serious obstacles to Henley's quest to create
positive images of women in full control of their lives.

In her defense of *Crimes* as an important feminist play, Laughlin draws
on Elaine Showalter's explication of women's writing "as a double-voiced
discourse, containing a 'dominant' and a 'muted' story" (Showalter 1985, 266)
to support her judgment. Clearly, Henley's plays do fit into the tradition of
women's literature that makes use of symbolism to encode a message about
the relationship between women's experiences and the values and expectations
of a male-dominated family structure and society. But I take issue with Laughlin's conclusion that works that perpetuate restrictions on women's voices
truly can call into question "an entire patriarchal vision of reality" (1986, 49).
Such covert strategies as Henley employs throughout her plays affirm rather
than strike out against women's confinement.

Just as important, the quests for autonomy of Henley's heroines also are
crippled in their realizations by the formal limitations imposed by her dramaturgical decisions. Within the American family-play genre, as it has been
formulated by our premier male dramatists—O'Neill, Miller, and Williams—
the emphasis has been on stasis and repetition in the family-play structure,
and, conventionally, these plays have reached resolution in the literal death
or figurative "entombment" of a central character. Although Henley succeeds
in adapting the form to focus attention on women's dilemmas within the family, the family play ultimately provides an inhospitable context for her portrayals of women's journeys to autonomy. Indeed, within its framework, there
exists no potential for a constructive mother-daughter relationship, and women
characters' experiences of nothingness are privileged over the other more positive dimensions of their quests. Both the interiority and futuristic orientation
of female quest likewise resist representation in a dramatic form defined by
an adherence to the unities and a coherent view of character. When Henley
has the option of moving beyond images of women's thwarted lives and outside realism, of experimenting in her plays with other dramatic styles and techniques such as transformation, it is difficult to defend her choice of a vehicle
that embraces stereotyped habits of thinking about women, truncates the process of the quest, and only hints at rather than advocates metamorphosis of
character. If at Henley's best, her plays portray women who finally "just take
some sort of chance" (*Crimes,* 103) in the hope of changing their lives and

whose self-understanding deepens as a result, what she has yet to achieve is drama of the kind Keyssar has envisioned: one that not only "inspires and asserts the possibility for change . . . [but also insists] that we are what we do and what we become, and no one, neither woman nor man, is restricted from becoming other" (1985, xiv).

NOTES

1. Keyssar classifies *Crimes* as a "comedy of manners," for it reveals "the surfaces of sexual identity and sexism" without challenging "the deeper social structures that allow those manners to endure" (1985, 150). The interview with Henley included in Betsko and Koenig's collection seems to confirm Keyssar's assessment. Although Henley describes herself as a feminist, she does not comment on what that label means to her or how a feminist vision is manifested in her work (1987, 218). She also explicitly asserts that her plays are *not* political. "I don't really feel like changing the world," she explains, "I want to look at the world" (1987, 221).

2. For an extended discussion of *Crimes* as a challenge to patriarchal culture, see Laughlin (1986, 38–49).

3. Other critics who have identified the quest motif in Henley's plays overestimate, in my opinion, the success of Henley's heroines in achieving autonomy. See, for example, Barranger (1987, 9) and McDonnell (1987, 95).

4. In addition, Henley's plays support Christ's point that "women's intense perception of their own nothingness sometimes gives them acute perceptions of the larger forces of nothingness, domination, death, and destruction that operate in men's world" (1988, 17). For an informative analysis of the patterns of death and destruction that oppress Henley's female characters, see Hargrove (1984, 58–64).

5. For a discussion of the MaGrath sisters' relationship with their mother that focuses on their emotional detachment from her, see Harbin (1987, 84–85).

6. Henley's description of her plays as "emotionally autobiographical" (Solway 1987, 15) suggests a link between the recurrence of matrophobia among her female characters and Henley's acknowledged efforts to avoid reliving her own mother's story. She explains, ". . . I know I have a fear of being tied down. My mother was. I know my fear is based on her being trapped in with all that talent she had, by kids and husband and the world. I purposely . . . refused to do things that would make me into something I didn't want to be" (Betsko and Koenig 1987, 220).

7. McDonnell also discusses Henley's plot device of storytelling. Although she perceives the importance of the story to "an individual's quest for self-determination" (1987, 100), she fails both to see storytelling as an antidote for silence and to recognize the communal function it serves for Henley's women characters. For a brief consideration of the thematic similarity between Henley's treatment of female community and that of nineteenth-century women writers, see Laughlin (1986, 48–49).

8. This phrase is my variation on Nelle Morton's statement that women "hear each other into speech," from her unpublished sermon, "Hearing to Speech," delivered at Claremont School of Theology, Claremont, California, April 27, 1977, p. 1. (Quoted in Christ 1988, 7.) For a similar view of Meg's nurturing role in *Crimes*, see Harbin (1987, 87–88).

9. Babe's affair with Willy Jay, distinguished by his age, race, economic status, and gentle personality from her powerful husband, also poses a strong challenge to the patriarchal structure of which Zachary is representative.

10. The climactic scene of *The Wake,* when Marshael confronts Jamey in his coffin, however, is ambiguous. Although the experience may indicate that Marshael is now free to see her life in a new way, when she flees to the purple trees under which Jamey first declared his love for her, her self seems still invested in him and the past.

REFERENCES

Barranger, Milly S., ed. 1987. *Southern Women Playwrights.* Special issue of *Southern Quarterly* 25, no. 3: 1–117.

Betsko, Kathleen, and Rachel Koenig, eds. 1987. "Beth Henley." In *Interviews with Contemporary Women Playwrights,* 211–22. New York: William Morrow.

Billman, Carol. 1980. "Women and the Family in American Drama." *Arizona Quarterly* 36: 35–48.

Christ, Carol P. 1980. *Diving Deep and Surfacing: Women Writers on Spiritual Quest.* Boston: Beacon.

Glaspell, Susan. 1985. *Trifles.* Included in *The Norton Anthology of Literature by Women: The Tradition in English,* ed. Sandra M. Gilbert and Susan Gubar, 1389–99. New York: Norton.

Harbin, Billy J. 1987. "Familial Bonds in the Plays of Beth Henley." *Southern Women Playwrights.* Special issue of *Southern Quarterly* 25, no. 3: 81–94.

Hargrove, Nancy D. 1984. "The Tragicomic Vision of Beth Henley's Drama." *Southern Quarterly* 22, no. 4: 54–70.

Henley, Beth. 1982. *Crimes of the Heart.* New York: Viking.

———. 1983. *The Wake of Jamey Foster.* New York: Dramatists Play Service.

———. 1985. *The Miss Firecracker Contest.* Garden City: Doubleday.

Keyssar, Helene. 1985. *Feminist Theatre: An Introduction to Plays of Contemporary British and American Women.* New York: Grove.

Laughlin, Karen L. 1986. "Criminality, Desire, and Community: A Feminist Approach to Beth Henley's *Crimes of the Heart.*" *Women and Performance* 3, no. 1: 35–51.

McDonnell, Lisa J. 1987. "Diverse Similitude: Beth Henley and Marsha Norman." *Southern Women Playwrights.* Special issue of *Southern Quarterly* 25, no. 3: 95–104.

Miss Firecracker Contest, The. 1986. By Beth Henley. Directed by James D. Waring. Olney Theatre, Olney, Maryland. August 7.

Rich, Adrienne. 1986. *Of Woman Born: Motherhood as Experience and Institution.* 10th anniversary ed. New York: Norton.

Showalter, Elaine. 1985. "Feminist Criticism in the Wilderness." *Critical Inquiry* 8 (1981). Reprinted in *The New Feminist Criticism: Essays on Women, Literature, and Theory,* ed. Elaine Showalter, 243–70. New York: Pantheon.

Solway, Diane. 1987. "Creative Couples: Is Love Blind?" *New York Times,* July 19, sec. 2: 1, 14–15.

Lynda Hart

"They Don't Even Look Like Maids Anymore": Wendy Kesselman's *My Sister in This House*

Christine and Lea Papin's story is recounted in *Infamous Murders*. The sisters gaze at us from the pages of this collection of the world's most malignant and enigmatic killers. They are prim and immaculate in their white-collared, starched maids' uniforms. One is arrested by their gently contoured twinlike faces, their simplicity, their innocent ordinariness. "The Maids of Horror" leads us in:

> Everything appeared to be cut and dried. The brutally slaughtered bodies had been found, along with the murder weapons, and the two killers had immediately confessed to the crime. Yet something, surely, was wrong. These were not hardened criminals; they were not even psychopaths. They were ordinary housemaids. What had driven them to hack their employers to death?[1]

The demure women in the photograph are shockingly contrasted in a post-crime picture a few pages later where they are disheveled, chaotic, the neat outlines of their faces and hair replaced by unruly, indeterminate margins. There is something in the latter photograph—the maids become murderers—that suggests release: certainly in this photograph, "they don't even look like maids anymore" (54).

The "murderers of Le Mans," as they would come to be called, captured the imagination of journalists, psychologists, and novelists. They committed their crime in the small provincial town of Le Mans in 1933, the year that Hitler became absolute dictator of Germany and Freud wrote "Femininity." Christine and Lea were quietly performing their domestic duties, interrupted one otherwise unremarkable afternoon in February by an outburst of violence unparalleled in the annals of French history. Their story turned out to be eminently stageable, first by Jean Genet in the modern drama classic, *The Maids,* recently by Wendy Kesselman in *My Sister in This House.* Kesselman's fierce determination to restage the maids' story overrode her trepidation at reconsidering Genet's "masterpiece." She removed Madame Lancelin's husband from history and Genet's fictionalized male lover from literature because she "felt so strongly that it was to be a play about these four women, the interweaving lives of these four women."[2] From this history Kesselman creates a play that Helene Keyssar asserts "addresses almost every issue of consequence to feminist drama."[3]

The historical material that Kesselman reshapes scarcely lends itself to programmatic feminist articulation. Unlike the more didactic and highly controversial film *A Question of Silence,* in which three women brutally and ritualistically kill a man whom they do not know, *My Sister in This House* is about two women who kill their female employers, a mother and daughter. And unlike some critics of Gorris's film, it cannot be argued that the murder in *My Sister in This House* is symbolic or metaphorical and hence an "unrealistic" portrayal of women's responses to their oppression.[4] On the contrary, Kesselman's play is predicated precisely on a well-known and spectacular crime and her depiction of the incident restores much of the literal material as she found it in newspapers, court testimony, and personal interviews. It seems safe to assert that Kesselman's fascination with the sisters' story depends to a large extent on its having actually occurred.

In Keyssar's reading of the play, the sisters' crime becomes the "only appropriate response" when "the torture of constant condescension is taken into account." The fact that the Papin sisters murdered women supports Keyssar who finds the play demonstrating that "domination and abuse of power corrupt, no matter what the biological sex of the player," dramatically representing a world in which "class and gender oppression are inseparable."[5] For the contemporary French leftist newspaper, *L'Humanitie,* the sisters' gender was not particularly significant. They championed the maids' revolutionary revolt against the oppressive bourgeoisie: "This trial should not have been only that of the sisters, but also that of the sacrosanct bourgeois family in whose heart developed a baseness and wickedness, and a scorn for those who earn their living by serving them." *L'Humanitie*'s journalists looked no further than the "1001 vexations, the belittlements that the maids had endured at the hands of their employers, the life of slavery that lasted for seven years," to provide adequate motive for the sisters' explosive rage.[6] The American journalist in Paris, Janet Flanner, concurred: "When in February of this year [1933], the Papin sisters, cook and housemaid, killed Mme. and Mlle. Lancelin in the respectable provincial town of Le Mans, . . . it was not a murder but a revolution. It was only a minor revolution — minor enough to be fought in a front hall by four females, two on a side. The rebels won with a horrible handiness."[7]

Although Keyssar acknowledges that the sisters' crime was motivated by "a love that [could] no longer bear to see the other demeaned or in pain,"[8] she equalizes the significance of class and gender while Flanner's and *L'Humanitie*'s readings foreground class oppression. In the historical record, however, it was the sisters' sexuality that was painstakingly scrutinized. And in Kesselman's play, the question of the sisters' sexual relationship with each other and the complex subplot of all four female characters' sexual desire consumes the narrative. In the historical media coverage and in the trial record, the question of the sisters' motive was explored in direct relation to their sexuality. The jury apparently "missed [the famous Parisian Professor] Logre's illuminating and delicate allusion to the girls as a psychological couple, though they had understood the insane-asylum chief's broader reference to Sappho."[9]

The sisters' purported lesbian relationship was based on slender evidence, but much was made of the following "facts": Christine and Lea spent most of their time alone in their room; a trunk full of lingerie, presumably made by Christine for Lea, was found in their room; they had had their photograph taken together; following the crime they were found huddled together in the same bed (in some reports they were said to be naked, in others they wore identical blue kimonos — in any case they had washed themselves clean of the blood); during their incarceration Christine had screamed for Lea and when a sympathetic guard brought Lea in to calm her hysterical sister, Christine cried, "say yes, say yes, to me," and in one report she was said to have pulled up her skirt and exposed her thighs to her sister; Christine suffered from hallucinations while in prison and made the statement that she believed she was her sister's husband in a former life. When Christine was asked on the witness stand if there was "anything sexual in your relationship?" she answered that "they had merely been sisters."[10]

The issue of the sisters' guilt was resolved by their mutual confession. But the apparent absence of a motive (they had said that the murder was prompted by Madame's unexpected return and reprimand for blowing the fuse) led to extensive exploration of the sisters' sanity, which in turn depended on affirmation of their sexual "normality." In the provincial town of Le Mans, there were powerful incentives for proving the maids insane. Virtually every family employed domestic servants. The right-wing newspapers were full of warnings about the "Red Terror." It was two years before the formation of the Leftist Popular Party. Anarchists baptized the Papin sisters as "angels of the revolution." The courts were eager to suppress any analysis of the Papin murders as a class insurrection. If the "pearls of Le Mans," as Christine and Lea were called, could revolt, then all the bourgeois employers were in grave danger.

As the trial proceeded the lurid details of the murder were released and they offered material for speculation that the sisters had been motivated by more than class oppression. Monsieur Lancelin had come home to find the house in darkness and the door bolted. He summoned the police who found Mme. and Mlle. Lancelin's bodies

> lying stretched out onto the floor . . . frightfully mutilated. Mademoiselle Lancelin's corpse was lying face downward, head bare, coat pulled up and with her underpants down, revealing deep wounds in the buttocks and multiple wounds in the calves. Madame Lancelin's body was lying on its back. The eyes had disappeared, she seemed no longer to have a mouth, and all the teeth had been knocked out. The walls and door were covered with splashes of blood to a height of more than seven feet. On the floor were found fragments of bone and teeth, one eye, hairpins, a handbag, a key ring, an untied parcel, and a coat button.[11]

The instruments used to perform the murder were a pewter pitcher, a knife, and a hammer, ordinary household utensils transformed into deadly weapons. The sisters testified to cutting little marks in the women's thighs like the ones French bakers make in their loaves, a detail that suggests the maids' desire to manipulate their mistresses' bodies as objects, common objects that the women contacted daily. Christine and Lea ironically reversed the authoritative gaze of the Lancelins who viewed the maids as ordinary household objects. The maids as objects became subjects/seers in this reversal. As an end to the tyranny of their subjection to this gaze, they used their bare hands to gouge out their mistresses' eyes.

The condition of the murdered women's bodies certainly indicated that they were not killed in a sudden flash of passion/fury. Christine and Lea had evidently labored over the corpses for some time after the Lancelins' death. Professor Logre had colossal doubts about the sisters' sanity, but his testimony was dismissed when the prosecutor revealed that he had never interviewed the women in person. The local experts found the women to be of "unstained heredity," i.e., sane. They were "normal girls who murdered without a reason"; murdering without a reason was apparently proof of normality in Le Mans, as Flanner points out.[12]

The fact that the maids had partially removed the women's clothing and that menstrual blood was found on the women's bodies sparked debate about a sexual motivation for the crime that led nowhere in the historical trial record but was continued after the sisters were sentenced. The Papin sisters' crime occurred just a decade after the psychoanalytic shift to an obsession with female sexuality — the "great debate."[13] In the 1930s, the nature of female sexuality was at the center of heated controversy in intellectual circles. Six months after the trial in which Christine was sentenced to death (later commuted to life imprisonment) and Lea to ten years of hard labor, Jacques Lacan diagnosed the Papin sisters as suffering from *délires à deux,* a paranoid disorder that "is among the most ancient recognized types of psychosis."[14] In some cases, Lacan explained, the "insanity for two" depends on a stronger, actively insane subject acting upon a weaker, passive subject. Hence Christine's influence as the older sister accounts for Lea's passive obedience in the murder and her lighter sentence. Lacan's theory also accounts for the simultaneity of the sisters' assault and the exact duplication of the means and manner of the murders. The *délires à deux* theory thus accounts for the method, but not the motive, for the crime. For the motive Lacan seeks an answer in the women's sexuality.

Paranoid personalities sometimes exhibit aggressive, violent behavior. However, Lacan argues, the "urge toward violence or murder . . . would actually be only an abstraction if it were not controlled by a series of correlative abnormalities in socialized instincts." In the case of the Papin sisters, Lacan found correlative abnormalities in homosexuality and sado-masochistic perversions. The treatment of the victims amply demonstrated the sisters' sadism; Lacan does not further discuss their masochism. But he doubted "the reality of the sexual relations of the two sisters" because when "psychoanalysts derive paranoia from homosexuality they do so with the qualification that it is unconscious or latent homosexuality. This homosexual tendency is only expressed in a passionate negation of the self which gives rise to the conviction that one is persecuted and which finds the loved one in the persecutor." Lacan builds on Freud's basic assumptions about infantile sexuality, the repression of primitive hostility between brothers, and the abnormal inversion of this hostility into desire, producing a "special type" of homosexuality that dominates one's social instincts and activities. This affective fixation is often narcissistic and "must be overcome in order to achieve a socially workable morality."[15]

Genet's play is clearly informed by this psychoanalytic perspective. His maids, Solange and Claire, are a narcissistic pair who exchange roles and identities with stunning facility. They are "selves defined by another," as they alternately play Madame and servant. These sisters are locked in a pattern of self-loathing, unable to "escape the servitude save in self-laceration, and their revolt is only a criminal's folly which inevitably rebounds back on itself."[16] Genet sought to subvert conventional assumptions about gender and sexuality by insisting that the maids be played by male actors in order to radically "de-realize" the concept of the feminine. Sartre states in the introduction to *The Maids* that "Genet wished this feminine stuff itself to become an appearance." A male actor in the role of the maid would "make the defeminized and spir-itualized female appear as an invention of man, as a pale and wasting shadow which cannot sustain itself unaided . . . as the impossible dream of man in a world without women."[17]

Kate Millett identified Genet as a "rare male voice that seeks identifica-tion with the feminine," and Genet's "feminine conquest [as] a matter of over-coming rank with the miracle of spirit."[18] *The Maids* goes beyond drawing a strong parallel between sex and class oppression to posit an absolute equation between gender roles, regardless of the biological sex, and class rank. Millett recognizes Genet's attack on the source of homophobia—"the fact that sex role *is* sex rank."[19] The maids' insurrection in Genet's play is futile. They do not kill Madame, rather they project their hatred for her onto each other and move gradually, each time they instigate the game of killing Madame, toward self-destruction. Their self-hatred deepens and their loathing becomes increas-ingly internalized until it is released through the murder/suicide of Claire. *The Maids* ends with Solange describing Madame's discovery of her own body while the maids "rise up free, from Madame's icy form," or rather all that remains of them, "the delicate perfume of the holy maidens which they were in secret."[20]

Kesselman is also concerned with what the Papin sisters were in secret. *My Sister in This House* takes us inside the lives of Christine and Lea Papin to show us their world, and ours, from a point of view that no other represen-tation, historical or fictive, portrays. Her sisters commit two major, and I think related, taboos. First, true to the historical record, Christine and Lea violently kill Madame and Mademoiselle Danzard (Kesselman's fictive name for the Lancelins). Kesselman does not attempt to mitigate the atrocity of their act; in a voice-over the judge recounts a detailed description of the vic-tims' bodies in the final scene. The patriarchal prescription for women as non-violent is challenged by their act in much the same way that the women's crime in *A Question of Silence* disrupts the category of the feminine. The fact of their gender is of paramount importance here; women do not kill, by patri-archal definition. As Jeffner Allen points out, this definition is essential to the maintenance of heterosexual ideology.

The ideology of heterosexual virtue forms the cornerstone of the designation of women as nonviolent. The ideology of heterosexual virtue charges women to be 'moral,' virtuously nonviolent in the face of the 'political,' the violent male-defined world. The ideology of heterosexual virtue entitles men to terrorize—possess, humiliate, violate, objectify—women and forecloses the possibility of women's active response to men's sexual terrorization. Women, constrained to nonviolence, are precluded from claiming and creating a self, a world. The moral imperative established by heterosexual virtue, that women are to be nonviolent, establishes a male-defined good that is beneficial to men, and harmful to women.[21]

The male-defined monolithic category *Woman* is exclusive of violence—to be a woman means to be a person incapable of violence. Allen is, of course, not advocating that women adopt the patriarchy's violence. But what is interesting for the purpose of this discussion is the link between the definition of woman in patriarchal ideology as nonviolent, and *heterosexual* virtue, for it is precisely the break with heterosexuality that constitutes the second taboo with which Christine and Lea Papin were historically charged, and which Kesselman renders as not a supposition, nor a psychological latency, but an actuality in *My Sister in This House*. Whereas in Genet's play the maids' repression of their desire leads to self-destructiveness and hence locates them still as recognizable objects of heterosexual virtue "which binds women to male-defined nonviolence . . . leading to the sole form of action permitted to women: martyrdom and suicide,"[22] Kesselman's sisters direct their violence outward, onto their oppressors, and their action is constructed as a direct response to the immediate threat imposed by Madame Danzard's homophobia and threatened entry into the private world they construct in their room, where they are free to realize their fantasies of self and sexuality. Kesselman's maids do not see in each other the reflection of their own submissiveness and servitude. Instead, they risk that fearful confrontation, "that encounter, as in a mirror, with the reality of one's own true self."[23] In *My Sister in This House,* the maids' violence and their lesbianism are inextricably bound up with each other.

Sexual tension between the sisters is subtly rendered throughout the play, but it is in scene 14 that we see them making love. Madame Danzard and her daughter Isabelle are shocked when Christine and Lea come running into the house breathless with excitement. It is at this moment that Madame realizes that "they don't even look like maids anymore."[24] Their sexual freedom is read by Madame as an escape from their domestic servitude. Lea and Christine seek the privacy of their room where they laugh and whirl each other around, helping each other take off their gloves and hats. While their employers downstairs criticize the maids' appearance and housekeeping skills, Lea seduces Christine, slowly unbraiding her hair, unbuttoning her coat, pulling it open and revealing the delicate chemise that her sister has sewn for her. Christine watches as Lea moves provocatively around the room, then she pulls Lea down to her as the lights dim.

The seduction scene is the fruition of the sisters' developing sense of themselves as subjects that is depicted throughout the play. Christine and Lea begin to wear fine clothes, spend afternoons in the park together, dream of the day when they can buy a farm and be self-sufficient; they even dare to have their photograph taken together. They have quietly transformed the spare and shabby space that they are forced to inhabit into a home with personal possessions — a handmade white quilt on the bed, a braided rug on the floor. Madame interprets these signs of autonomy as evidence of abnormality, a transgression of their class, and then finally as signs of a sexual union between the sisters.

The fact that she and her daughter share similar comforts without any intimation of incest between them cannot be explained away by the legitimacy of their biological mother/daughter tie, for Christine and Lea are sisters and so must logically be granted the same immunity from the charge of lesbianism. Clearly, for Madame Danzard and her daughter, it is initially the sisters' transgression of their class that is troublesome. But madame's homophobic reaction to the maids does not come as a surprise in the last scene. Madame and Isabelle's repressed sexual desires are manifested in a number of scenes that come before. In scene 5, for example, Madame Danzard is alone in her sitting room, listening to the overture of Offenbach's "La Vie Parisienne." She smiles to herself and hums along, then sighs as she looks through old photographs in an album and begins dancing to the music. Isabelle intrudes on her solitude and startles her mother, who quickly changes to a station playing a Bach organ prelude. Aware that she has caught her mother in an erotic moment and thus in a violation, Isabelle takes a liberty herself — by eating a chocolate which she defiantly pops into her mouth as her mother glares. Since heterosexual virtue does not allow for the overt expression of sexual rivalry between mother and daughter, although it is set up by the patriarchy, Madame Danzard cannot retaliate against Isabelle, so she transfers her hostility to the maids, puts on the white gloves, and summons Lea to clean a speck of dirt she finds on the staircase. This transference of hostility to a member of the slave class is, of course, not just approved but prescribed by the patriarchy. As Christine passes her sister on the staircase, their hands touch for an instant, comforting and connecting each other in this moment of heightened oppression. Thus the maids' burgeoning desire and its incipient realization is strongly contrasted with the repressed desire of their employers and the hostility they feel in immediate reaction to the absence of love in their own relationship.

In Kesselman's play, Madame Danzard and Isabelle are destroyed by "heterosexual virtue," because they can never question its basic assumptions that control and suppress their lives, whereas the maids are temporarily liberated from it by constructing a counter-reality. Through the use of simultaneous staging, Kesselman dramatizes the two couples' lives, mother and daughter Danzard and the sisters Papin, as parallel and in many ways alike but finally as antithetical, incapable of coexistence. Christine and Madame Danzard share an appreciation of the sensual in material possessions—good food, fine clothing. They are both meticulous, precise in everything and judgmental of those who are not so controlled. They both enjoy power and tend to dominate those over whom they have some influence. They are serious women, pragmatic and somewhat cynical. The younger women, by contrast, are vulnerable, emotional, clumsy, disorderly, and inexperienced. Kesselman's play highlights the comparison and contrast between Madame and Christine and Isabelle and Lea. In scene 4, for example, the Danzards are eating in the dining room while the maids are working in the kitchen. Madame praises the maids for not prying, for being "discreet"; Christine praises Madame for not interfering in the kitchen: "Madame knows her place." The juxtaposition of the dialogue foregrounds the women's psychological similarities:

> *Madame Danzard.* They're extraordinarily clean.
> *Christine.* Madame is so precise, so careful.
> *Madame Danzard.* . . . it's the older one who fascinates me. I've never had anyone like her.
> *Christine.* I've never had anyone like Madame before.
> (Pp. 13–14)

The younger women are compared in their actions: Isabelle toys with her food and makes a mess of her plate; her mother chastises her. Lea is upbraided for her slowness and clumsiness by Christine. Lea spills the green beans she is preparing; Isabelle spills the seed pearls she is sewing onto a handbag. All four women are restrained by unlivable demands imposed upon them by the

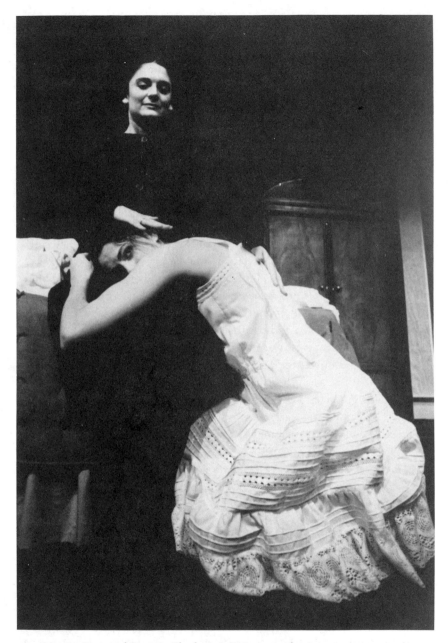

Cristine Rose and Patricia Charbonneau appear in the Actors
Theatre of Louisville's production of *My Sister in This House* by
Wendy Kesselman. (Photo by David S. Talbott.)

patriarchal category of *feminine*. But their class difference prevents them from sharing their oppression. As Rosemary Curb points out, "the four women are bound in a web of ambivalent narcissism as well as sado-masochism."[25]

The deterioration of Christine's excellence as a domestic servant signals her break with patriarchal order and duty; it also serves as a disruption that the holders of heterosexual virtue, the Danzards, will be unable to tolerate. In scene 15, immediately following the seduction scene, Christine departs from her consistent meticulousness by breaking a wine glass and leaving the broken pieces in the sink. Lea panics when she burns Madame's silk blouse that she is ironing when the fuse blows. Her sister's fear of their employers' reprimand prompts Christine to leave her domestic duties and comfort her sister in their room. Unexpectedly, Madame and Isabelle return to a darkened house with no maids to greet them at the door. Isabelle warns her mother not to go up to the maids' room, aware that the place is private and forbidden. But Madame asserts her property rights: "This is my house. Of course I'm going upstairs. Right now" (60). Kesselman's dialogue reflects the Lancelins' ownership of the maids. The sisters were supposed to be invisible unless commanded to appear. And at all times, they were expected to be silent. During the trial, Christine stated that the Lancelins had not spoken to the sisters at all in seven years. As Lacan points out, this was not an empty silence.[26]

In this next to the final scene, the silence is finally broken and Kesselman shows us what had filled it. Madame tells Christine, who will not allow her access to her room or her sister, that she will never find employ, "not after what I've seen tonight," and she calls the maids "dirt, and scum sisters." When Christine says that Madame has "seen nothing," Madame's rapacious homophobia is unleashed: "That face, that hair. You smell of it, my dear. Going to church every Sunday. Thinking you were a child of God. (*Raging, crossing herself.*) Forgive me God, for what I have harbored here." Lea strikes the first blow with the pewter pitcher as Christine leaps violently toward Madame Danzard's face, crying out repeatedly, "Not my sister, not my sister, not my sister" (62–63).

Catherine Clément calls the Papin murders "a single massacre, definitive, a feast day without an anniversary," as opposed to the repetitive structure of hysteria. Like Genet, Clément identifies the sisters as a "mirroring couple," but she also recognizes the presence of the other couple, the Lancelins, whom the sisters can no longer tolerate. Their crime then becomes "an exceptional act against the masters, a bloody saturnalia. But it is an attack that empties all possibilities of transference at once because it attacks the body of the other." According to Clément, the assault by the sisters in reality was an indication that transference had been broken: "two who were alike were bad enough already!"[27] In Genet's play there is only Madame; she does not have a daughter to make up the other half of the couple. Hence his maids each sees herself individually in the image of the other and Solange's attack is aimed at Claire and Claire's at Solange. It is only a matter of time, whose turn it is to play at being Madame, that selects Claire as the victim rather than Solange.

What happens in Kesselman's play is quite different. Her insistence that this play was to be about "the interweaving lives of these four women" is particularly significant when we look at the choices she makes with the historical material. Keyssar points out, as does Ann Kilkelly, that Kesselman eliminates the historical Monsieur Lancelin and Madame's lover in Genet's play. Her reasons for doing so, though, are more complex than simply writing an all-woman play. Kilkelly recognizes that it is the maids' "movement toward selfhood that the house cannot contain." But she goes on to argue that the women in the play, "bound by bourgeois social conventions and equally rigid religious conventions," are contained within a patriarchal structure in which "no movement outside of the system is possible."[28] I would qualify Kilkelly's reading by pointing out that Christine and Lea's sexual relationship *is* a movement outside of the system and that it is not only the "repressed passions" within the house that cannot be contained, but the *expressed* passions. Kilkelly assumes that the sisters were found, in history, "lying side by side in what was later discovered to be their incestuous bed."[29] And Keyssar asserts that Kesselman's dramatization "alters none of the original events."[30] But, in fact, Kesselman does make a very crucial choice that the historical record could not sustain — that the sisters were practicing lesbians. When Kesselman was asked if the sisters were lovers, she answered that she didn't know, though she did everything she could to find out.[31] Hence Kesselman's two artistic choices that deviated most radically from the "facts" as she found them were the elimination of the men and the creation of the sisters' sexual relationship. The sisters' lesbianism, then, historically and fictively, is culturally constructed.

Madame Danzard's husband seems to be dead, or perhaps never to have existed. There is talk in the play of an approaching marriage for Isabelle, but no suitor is mentioned by name and even the photographer who takes Christine and Lea's photograph seems to be skeptical about the impending marriage. In history Isabelle did have a fiancé. Thus in *My Sister in This House* Kesselman carefully makes the mother/daughter bond the primary and the single source of affection, or lack of it, between the mistresses. She also carefully constructs Christine and Lea's relationship so that it is more like a mother/

daughter than a sisters' relationship. Christine, the elder, nurtures "little Lea" and resents the letters that Lea receives from their mother. Christine, in fact, hates her mother whom she felt used her to make money and offered her no affection. In scene 4, Christine roughly braids Lea's hair, pulling and twisting it, hurting her sister just as her mother, in a letter, had warned Lea that Christine might. Then she is horrified by her behavior and says, "I'm a monster, aren't I? Just like she says" (21). Christine's hatred for her mother is complicated by her fear of becoming what her mother perceives her to be. And her mother's perception of Christine is very much like Christine's image of her mother. Each sees the other as cruel, abusive. Christine's relationship with her mother is "matrophobic," "a womanly splitting of the self, in the desire to become purged once and for all of our mother's bondage, to become individual and free. The mother stands for the victim in ourselves, the unfree woman, the martyr."[32] Christine vacillates between sheltering Lea from the harsh realities of a maid's life and resenting the additional burden of her own work due to Lea's clumsiness. In several scenes, she reprimands Lea like a naughty child, then comforts her and calls her a baby. In scene 6, the sisters return from a visit with their mother and argue briefly about why their mother ordered them out of her house, or if she meant Christine only. Lea says that it doesn't really matter since neither of them will ever go back to visit their mother. Then she takes the blanket that her mother had made for her when she was four years old and that she has carried ever since, and begins to unravel the strands and pull it apart. She offers a corner of the blanket to Christine, who hesitates at first, then enters into the game with her sister. They become frenzied as they run around the room, winding the wool around the sparse furniture, becoming entangled in the ropes until they fall down together on the bed. Both of them are laughing breathlessly on the bed when Lea uses what is left of the blanket to wrap her body close to her sister's. Christine calls an immediate halt to the game, stands up trembling, and answers a defiant no to Lea's "don't you want to play anymore?" (26).

The blanket pulling scene is clearly a ritual rejection of the mother, and with it comes Christine's awakening of sexual desire for her sister. It is also the moment when Christine moves fully into the mother's role. The incest between the sisters is thus primary; it is a return to, and an awakening of, the first primary love bond—between mother and daughter. The small room that Christine and Lea inhabit becomes their whole world: they dare to ask for heat to warm it, and they make it cozy with handmade rugs and blankets. They place the photograph of themselves on the nightstand. The servants' garrett is transformed into a womblike space, an image of "that earliest en-wrapment of one female body with another."[33] In this space Christine sings lullabies to Lea.

So we have in *My Sister in This House* the creation of two mother/daughter couples. The heterosexual Danzards have no male love objects but compete with one another's fantasies. Even the simple card game between Madame Danzard and Isabelle becomes a battle. Mlle. and Mme. Danzard's quarrel with each other is presented as a product of their social isolation based on the stultifying demands of patriarchal virtue. Christine and Lea, the "psycho-logical couple," dare to violate the fundamental taboo of patriarchy. The rela-tion between women's sexuality and evil has a long tradition in the Christian view that woman brought death into the world and sex perpetuated it. Les-bianism compounds the already dangerous carnality of women; in a phallocen-tric culture, they are women indifferent to the phallus.

Christine and Lea violate not only the patriarchal class hierarchy, but also, and more profoundly, they refuse the patriarchal psychological impera-tive by choosing to recreate the primary love bond between mother and daugh-ter rather than completing the patriarchal imperative that demands a woman's transference of affection from the first object, her mother, to a man. From a heterosexual, patriarchal perspective, Christine and Lea were "abnormal" long before they murdered, when they failed (refused) to give their primary and psychic energies to a man. Madame Danzard and Isabelle, on the other hand, are dutiful daughters. They seemingly accept the male-defined text for their lives, but their "virtue" victimizes them. They know that their maids have somehow transcended the limitations of heterosexual virtue, and they are envious and hostile.

In Ann Jones's essential study, *Women Who Kill,* she investigates the lives of women in American history, the infamous and the forgotten, who were murderers. Like Susan Glaspell in *Trifles,* Jones takes us behind the scenes to look at the lives of women who, in one way or another, failed to adjust to a life of oppression; failed to accept privilege as a substitute for rights; and, in a moment of fury or over years of quiet calculation, destroyed the image of their obstacle to freedom—usually a husband or a lover. Jones argues persua-sively that the "same social and legal deprivations that compel some women to feminism push others to homicide." The feminist and the murderer, each in her own way, "tests society's established boundaries."[34]

Like the psychiatrist in *A Question of Silence* who painstakingly examines the three women killers and reaches the conclusion that she shares directly with the eye of the camera—"I don't think those women are insane"—Wendy

Kesselman looks at Christine and Lea Papin and finds in their lives sisters to all of us who would dare to claim them. *My Sister in This House* asks us to reclaim the Papin sisters from the annals of French history where they reside as horrifying perversions of woman, and from the fictive representations that portray them as monstrous psychological aberrations. If we find "the rage of all women condensed to the point of explosion,"[35] horrifyingly unleashed in their actions, we also find the terror of their existence deeply woven into the fabric of a culture that denies them defense of the very boundaries of their bodies and minds.

NOTES

1. "The Maids of Le Mans," in *Infamous Murders* (London: Verdict Press, 1975), 112.

2. Lynda Hart, unpublished interview with Wendy Kesselman, June 1986, Cincinnati, Ohio.

3. Helene Keyssar, *Feminist Theatre* (New York: Grove Press, 1985), 181.

4. Jeannette Murphy, "A Question of Silence," in *Films for Women*, ed. Charlotte Brunsdon (London: British Film Institute, 1986). Murphy decides that the murder "cannot be discussed as metaphoric, or symbolic, or as a device (as I was initially tempted to do), as the director did in the press conference after its first screening, and as various feminist reviewers have done subsequently," 105.

5. Keyssar, 181.

6. *L'Humanitie,* "Le double crime du Mans devant les assises de la Sarthe," September 29, 1933, 3, trans. Kathleen Gallagher (unpublished).

7. Janet Flanner, *Paris Was Yesterday* (New York: Penguin Books, 1972), 98.

8. Keyssar, 182.

9. Flanner, 101.

10. *Infamous Murders*, 114.

11. *Infamous Murders*, 112. This information was verified in Kesselman's research in the town of Le Mans where she gained access to court testimony, personal interviews, and media coverage.

12. Flanner, 100.

13. See Juliet Mitchell's introduction to *Feminine Sexuality and the École Freudienne* (New York: W. W. Norton, 1982) for a discussion of the midtwenties shift in focus in the Freudian school. "In the midtwenties the focus shifted and a new epoch began. The crisis of the concept of the castration complex may well have contributed to a change of emphasis away from itself and towards the preoccupation with female sexuality," 20.

14. Jacques Lacan, "Motifs du Crime Paranoïaque: Le Crime Des Soeurs Papin," in *Minotaure: Revue Artistique Et Litteraire*, 15 February 1933, no. 3–4, 27, trans. Kathleen Gallagher. This disorder is listed on page 197 of the *Diagnostic and Statistical Manual of Mental Disorders*, 3rd ed. (Washington, D.C.: American Psychiatric Association, 1980) as a "Shared Paranoid Disorder: essential feature is a persecutory delusional system that develops as a result of a close relationship with another person who al-

ready has a disorder with persecutory delusions." It was noted in the court testimony that some months before the murders, Lea and Christine had been to the courthouse to request that Lea be removed from her mother's legal guardianship. A court official testified that the women seemed anxious and fearful and suggested that they were feeling persecuted. Nowhere in the local coverage, except for *L'Humanitie*'s report, was the point made that the maids were indeed multiply persecuted.

15. Lacan, 27–28.

16. Kate Millet, *Sexual Politics* (New York: Ballantine Books, 1969), 491.

17. Jean-Paul Sartre, introduction to *The Maids and Deathwatch* by Jean Genet (New York: Grove Press, 1954), 9.

18. Millet, 482.

19. Millett, 480.

20. Jean Genet, *The Maids,* trans. Bernard Frechtman (New York: Grove Press, 1954), 100.

21. Jeffner Allen, *Lesbian Philosophy: Explorations* (Palo Alto, Calif.: Institute of Lesbian Studies, 1986), 35.

22. Allen, 37.

23. Radicalesbians, "The Woman-Identified Woman," in *Radical Feminism,* ed. Anne Koedt, Ellen Levine and Anita Rapone (New York: New York Times Book Co., 1973).

24. Wendy Kesselman, *My Sister in This House* (New York: Nelson Doubleday, Inc., 1982), 54. Additional references in the text.

25. Rosemary Curb, "Re/cognition, Re/presentation, Re/creation in Women-Conscious Drama: The Seer, The Seen, The Obscene," *Theatre Journal* 37, no. 3 (October 1985): 317–28.

26. Lacan, 25. "Ce silence pourtant ne pouvait être vide, même s'il était obscur aux yeux des acteurs."

27. Catherine Clément and Hélène Cixous, *The Newly Born Woman,* trans. Betsy Wing, *Theory and History of Literature,* vol. 24 (Minneapolis: University of Minnesota Press, 1986), 18–19.

28. Ann Kilkelly, "Who's in the House?" *Women and Performance* 3, no. 1 (1986): 31.

29. Ibid., 29.

30. Keyssar, 180.

31. Hart, interview with Kesselman.

32. Adrienne Rich, *Of Woman Born: Motherhood as Experience and Institution* (New York: Bantam Books, 1977), 238.

33. Ibid., 218.

34. Ann Jones, *Women Who Kill* (New York: Fawcett Columbine, 1980), 12.

35. Radicalesbians, 244.

Jenny S. Spencer

Marsha Norman's *She-tragedies*

In the prologue to the *The Fair Penitent* (1703), Nicholas Rowe promises "A melancholy tale of private woes: / No Princes here lost Royalty Bemoan, But you shall meet with sorrows like your own" (I.156). The play is the first of Rowe's *she-tragedies,* a term that has come to be associated not only with Rowe's work, but with any eighteenth-century tragedy in which women are the protagonists or prominent in the pathetic situations depicted.[1] As the prologue suggests, Rowe's use of domestic themes, familiar settings, and more natural diction encouraged closer audience identification with the characters. His plots were constructed to emphasize the irony of the protagonist's fate; contrived situations and improbable actions were disguised by effective appeals to the emotions, especially pity. Despite Rowe's immense popularity in the eighteenth century,[2] a note of critical disapprobation is apparent in most twentieth-century criticism: in the standard edition of his plays, J. R. Sutherland writes that "the whole tone is shriller and more feminine. The blustering hero is replaced by the weeping heroine; the bold, challenging incident gives place to the sentimental situation."[3] Such a comment indicates a problem in shifting the focus of tragedy to the "weaker" sex, especially given the passive nature of conventional definitions of feminine virtue: maidenly purity, wifely obedience, saintly endurance, unobtrusive presence, and so on. Viewed as the "resting place" for family honor and morality, a women's scope of action was sorely circumscribed. Whether led astray by her own passions, beguiled by a seducer, or forcibly ravished by a villain, the female protagonist's most significant "action" was to suffer the consequences of her sexual activity. Because the heroine's power of attraction was also the source of her misfortune, her sufferings appear the inevitable burden of her sex. Rarely is a situation depicted that is in her power to change; the tragic heroine patiently suffers, waits to be saved (forgiven), and/or nobly commits suicide. While the focus on women changed tragic structure, tempo, and dramatic effect, the term coined to identify those differences also suggests the form's diminished critical reputation. Placing *she-tragedy* within a broader sentimental tradition, Arthur Sherbo defines it in opposition to "great " or "true" tragedy:

> The protagonists of these tragedies accept death and defeat in a spirit of acquiescent submission that is foreign to great tragedy. And the note of final triumph is conspicuously absent. . . . The protagonists of sentimental or pathetic tragedy are kept from achieving greatness by their recognizably exaggerated humanity, and nowhere is this brought home to us more clearly than in those scenes where far too much is made of emotions with which we ourselves are familiar from personal experience.[4]

To resurrect the term *she-tragedy* for Marsha Norman's women-centered plays is potentially misleading and perhaps unfair. Primarily written by male playwrights, eighteenth-century she-tragedies share dramatic and linguistic conventions that are alien to the modern stage: Banks, Southern, Otway, and Rowe have more in common with each other than with any contemporary playwright. And yet, as feminist historiographers have shown us time and again, cultural assumptions on which attitudes toward women rest prove far more resistant to change than the literary forms in which they appear.[5] Without belaboring the comparison, I would like to suggest that *she-tragedy* is an appropriate term for Norman's three most successful plays to date: *Getting Out* (1978), *Third and Oak: The Laundromat* (1980) and *'night, Mother* (1983).[6] These plays focus on female characters, address a female audience, and foreground issues of female identity. All three consider the problem of surviving in a patriarchal society, find limited hope in the connections between women, and chart the devastating emotional consequences of "self-realization" in a society that still defines and determines the feminine subject position negatively. As in earlier she-tragedies, far more time is spent elaborating upon the character's potentially pathetic situation than in advancing the action; so characters are revealed rather than developed. Thus the relation of women to "action" is still a problem. In a very real sense, nothing happens in these plays: the brief encounter between two women in *The Laundromat* provides a fleeting contact that changes neither woman's life; in *Getting Out,* the postprison experiences of Arlene prove the impossibility of the title's hopeful declaration; and even Jessie's suicide in *'night, Mother* is but the symbolic articulation of that character's perception of her living state. In all three, significant action happens elsewhere—offstage, in the past, or outside the enclosures framed by the play. Despite the gestures of self-affirmation that women come to make in each play, I would argue that in Sherbo's terms, "the note of final triumph is conspicuously absent."[7]

Such description is not intended as a criticism of Norman's work. The power of all three plays rests on the emotional dynamics that Norman explores and exploits for dramatic purpose, dynamics all too familiar to her female audience but rarely represented so effectively on stage. These plays are *about* female subjectivity, and since the conditions under which women assume and maintain their sexual identity in our society are often painfully contradictory, they are also she-tragedies. Clearly my use of the term would extend the meaning from its historical model to include modern plays that not only focus on women, but whose apparent or subtextual message also relates specifically to problems of being female, problems that can be interpreted as irresolvable because of their connection to a condition over which the characters have little control. If Norman's work is to escape the automatic assignment to minor status that she-tragedy has historically connoted, however, then attention must be paid to the ways in which her development of the form may affect our response to the plays.

Norman's naturalistic focus on women results in some remarkable similarities in structure, rhythm, theme, and emotional impact across three very different plays. First of all, all three plays consist primarily of women talking, usually to each other. The language is ordinary, the subjects familiar, and the emotional subtext very near the surface. This is not to imply that the characters speak alike. Norman's dialogue not only reveals social class, education, and personality, but emotional coping patterns as well. In *The Laundromat* (L), Deedee is a nervous and compulsive talker, "jittery when someone else is talking" (*L*, 13). While her unthinking chatter provides much of the play's humor, it also indicates the depth of her unhappiness and her inability to face it. Alberta, a former teacher, speaks precisely but reluctantly; and her conversational style quickly discloses the pattern of avoidance by which she suppresses her own emotional vulnerability.

In *Getting Out* (GO), Arlie and Arlene are distinguished most profoundly through their speech patterns. From the opening monologue, "Arlie girl" is established as an active, interesting, animated character in direct contrast to her meek, subdued, and tentative counterpart. The power of Arlie's speech lies in its apparent spontaneity, and in its contagious, adolescent, colloquial humor. However "perverse" her point of view, Arlie's anger and imagination is perceived by the audience as a strength; by dramatizing its verbal expression in prison rather than its physical expression in the acts of violence that brought her there, Norman permits her audience a point of identification that might otherwise be difficult to obtain. Indeed, it is by comparison to her garrulous, storytelling former self that the toll of Arlene's "rehabilitation" is most forcefully perceived. One can hardly imagine Arlie responding to Ruby's friendly chatter with "You think up all these things you say?" (GO, 49). Arlene not only seems a different person, but less of a person. The Arlie who begins a monologue with "No, I don't have to shut up, neither" (GO, 42) has been silenced, and we feel the same regret that Arlie voices about her released prisoner friend Frankie Hill: "They done somethin to her. Took out her nerves or somethin" (GO, 52).

In *'night, Mother* (NM), Norman's brief opening characterizations include revealing comments on verbal behavior: Thelma "speaks quickly and enjoys talking," is "chatty" and "believes things are what she says they are"; Jessie "generally doesn't like to talk" (NM, 2). Indeed, Mama believes that if she says the right words, Jessie will change her mind, and if that doesn't work, she can "get you someone to talk to" (NM, 17). Jessie's response ("I'm through talking, Mama. You're it. No more. . . . ") indicates both the strength of her resolve and the finality of the decision itself, the end of talk alluding to the end of life as well. On this particular night, talking will serve different functions for the two characters. Jessie wants, for once in her life, to speak and hear only truth, to establish with certainty the meaning and consequences of her act (a desire in many ways impossible). On the other hand, Mama recognizes that "Things don't have to be true to talk about them" (NM, 41). For Mama, as for Arlie and Deedee before her, conversation is social interaction and as natural as breathing. Talk prevents loneliness, satisfies emotional needs, and fills the time. When Mama *does* speak the truth, she expresses resentment at having her conversation ignored: "Agnes gets more talk out of her birds than I got from the two of you. . . . [the night he died] He didn't have ANYTHING to say to me. That's why I left. He didn't say a thing. It was his last chance not to talk to me and he took full advantage of it" (NM, 52–53). The cruelty of that moment is forcefully repeated at the end of the play when in order to commit suicide, Jessie must literally "stop talking" to her mother.[8]

Conversation is not simply the medium through which information about character and situation is relayed; in these plays, conversation IS the action. The dialogue between Alberta and Deedee, Jessie and Mama, Arlene and Ruby, constructs and mutually reconfirms reality for both the characters and the audience. While the gradual articulation of that reality is held out as positive, as turning points in the narrative, and as emotionally cathartic for the characters, the change of consciousness produced by "recognition" does nothing to alter their unhappy situations. Deedee's husband is still unfaithful, Arlene's life still a prison, and Mama still unable to keep her daughter alive; in each case, the characters' illusory hopes of somehow "getting out" of a bad situation turn more realistically to problems of "getting on," to surviving the personal losses and reduced expectations with which they are left by the end of the play.

In a woman's world, talk connotes collaboration, communication, social connection, and most importantly, survival. But talk can also be entertaining, can pass the time. Arlie misses Frankie Hill because as Bernie notes, she "ain't got nobody to bullshit with" (*GO*, 52), and it is far more true that talking and telling stories fills otherwise unendurable days than Bernie's ironic suggestion that "conversation is rehabilitatin" (*GO*, 51). Despite the apparent progress that Arlene's release from prison involves, we find that life "outside" is comprised of the same daily rituals as life inside: Arlene moves into a cell-like apartment,[9] cleans up a mess she didn't make, eats food she doesn't want, fends off undesired sexual advances, and awakes to the noise of a loud siren. The day that we watch onstage is a taste of her future, and the prospects are as depressing as the droning tones of the play's opening broadcast: "Kitchen workers. All kitchen workers report immediately to the kitchen. Kitchen workers to the kitchen. . . ." (*GO*, 7). Arlie is not the only female character "doing time," however. In both *The Laundromat* and *'night, Mother*, Norman makes her audience conscious of time passing by the presence of an onstage clock marking the real passage of the plays' uninterrupted action; but within this linear time frame, the action is marked by the rhythm and tempo of domestic work. Thus conversations are motivated, maintained and framed by repetitive, unrewarding, interminable routines that in these plays constitute the sphere of female activity. Alberta and Deedee, for example, meet each other in one of the few places outside the home women might be found alone in the middle of the night. Alberta has had trouble doing the last load of laundry for her recently deceased husband; Deedee is trying to fill the time she suffers waiting for her unfaithful husband. They talk, get to know each other, tell stories, offer advice. The play's ending is as definite, as emotionally satisfying, as finishing a load of clothes. Alberta leaves with one shirt still to wash; Deedee continues to wait for her wash and her unfaithful husband. Nothing has changed, but Alberta finds her lonely task more pleasant and Deedee finds she can survive the waiting. As Mama says of laundry in *'night, Mother*: "Whatever else you find to do, you're still mainly waiting. The waiting's the worst part of it. The waiting's what you pay somebody else to do, if you can" (*NM*, 22).

For most of the female characters, time goes on, unmarked by significant action, filled up with meaningless activity. Only Jessie is "clearly aware of the time passing moment by moment" (*NM*, 2), a sense of time that results from her active purpose, from having a definite end in view, from taking control. But Jessie's decision is intended to stop time, not redeem it. Early in the play, she explains that her decision is like stopping a bus ride headed nowhere:

> . . . if I ride fifty more years and get off then, it's the same place when I step down to it. . . . And I can't do anything either, about my life, to change it, make it better, make me feel better about it. Like it better, make it work. But I can stop it. Shut it down, turn it off like the radio when there's nothing on I want to listen to. (*NM*, 33, 36)

The charged time of *'night, Mother* simply reinforces the emptied time that Jessie and Mama have passed until this evening, time marked by the repetitive rhythms of housekeeping and holidays. The insistent patter of all three plays reinforces this notion of emptied time; as it is ordinarily used, female conversation diverts the character's attention from what the audience cannot help but see.[10] The psychological problems of the characters are thus positioned within, and in part attributable to, time itself — here represented by Norman as static and unchanging, without historical significance, unnatural, oppressive, man-made.

Already, then, we can assume some difference between the audience's perception of the character's plight and that of the characters themselves, between the individual pathetic situations depicted and the tragic elements that link them all. At least one of the characters in each play suffers from an identifiable psychological problem made naturalistically plausible by more than ample exposition. In *The Laundromat,* the play closest of the three to comedy, Alberta is depressed over the death of her husband, but hasn't cried for forty years, while Deedee is angry over her husband's infidelity, but unable to deal with it directly. In *'night, Mother,* we find that Jessie's suicidal depression follows a series of losses, from her dog King to her husband, with congenital epilepsy thrown in for good measure. Arlie's "case" is the most clinically complicated, involving sadistic crimes, attempted suicide, and a schizophrenic "recovery" from aggressive to withdrawn behavior; but she is also the classic juvenile delinquent, a victim of child abuse in the form of paternal rape and maternal neglect. As experienced emotional "survivors," Alberta, Mama, and Ruby offer varying degrees of comfort, help and advice to their younger counterparts. And interestingly, the lesson from each seems modeled on the insights of "reality therapy."[11] When Arlene breaks down at the realization that life outside is as intolerable as life in prison, Ruby, an ex-con herself, can only agree: "[You thought] it was gonna be different. Well, it ain't. And the sooner you believe it, the better off you'll be" (*GO*, 60). To Deedee's more reasonable desire to have her husband come home, Alberta notes: "People just can't always be where we want them to be, when we want them to be there. . . . You don't have to like it. You just have to know it" (*L*, 16). Mama's desperate appeals to her daughter are similarly tempered by demands to "shape up" and "face reality." "Whoever promised you a good time? Do you think I've had a good time? . . . you're miserable and it's your own sweet fault" (*NM*, 33). The irony of Jessie's response ("And it's time I did something about it," *NM*, 33) is that her action reconfirms her mother's point of view: life is tough and little can be done to change it.[12] As in *Getting Out* and *The Laundromat*, the dialogue moves toward the point at which the main characters take responsibility for their own lives without consideration of who is "responsible" for the situation they face. In other words, despite the emphasis on exposition, the question each character faces is not really "why am I unhappy?" but "what should I do?" And with this question, we return again to the problem of women and action found in the earliest she-tragedy.

While the dialogue reveals the various causes that have led to the characters' problems, and it is in apparent grappling with them that the action of the plays consists, the conversation itself is offered to the audience as a discourse ripe for deeper analysis. Through it, we find that the problem of women and action is inseparable from the problem of female autonomy, the contradictory nature of feminine subjectivity itself influencing Norman's dramatic structure and linking the characters of the play and the women in the audience to powerful effect. Let us look, for example, at *Getting Out* where the issue is foregrounded by Arlene's literal identity crisis, visually represented on a split stage that alternates between past and present versions of the same person, played by two different women.[13] In the opening stage directions, Norman notes that "Arlie moves through the apartment quite freely, but no one there will acknowledge her presence" (*GO*, 6). As the phrasing suggests, Arlie is real, but not seen — there, but deliberately unrecognized until the end of the play. In other words, Arlie's onstage presence is not merely an expressionistic device with which to explore Arlene's memory and present mental state; rather Arlie and the incidents she plays out are concretizations of Arlene's past, and their meaning depends on the reality we grant them. More importantly, the self is split almost entirely along lines associated with gender differentiation: the tomboyishly "masculine" (aggressive, angry, violent, willful, and "bad") Arlie is juxtaposed to the "feminine" (meek, quiet, withdrawn, indecisive, and "good") Arlene. Only Arlie has the power to "act" in the sense we usually attribute to "causing things to happen." Since Arlene's "proper" position in society is a passive one, getting out involves a giving up of the very strength she would seem to need outside.[14] While reviewers complained that Arlie's "conversion" is schematically represented, it is the moment's metaphorical referents that are important here. Against the persistent sexual abuse that Arlie endures, the attention of the male chaplain is temporarily empowering; but he recognizes a self Arlie doesn't know (Arlene), a self she must become to gain his approval and ultimately her "freedom." Like Jessie's suicide in *'night, Mother,* the very act that establishes Arlene's identity is also a self-destructive one. Nearly dying from self-inflicted stab wounds, Arlene's dramatic "recovery" involves learning to knit and being praised as the best housekeeper in the dorm (*GO,* 61–62), her "rehabilitation" thus represented by Norman as a kind of self-destructive feminization.

The manner in which Norman frames the action of *Getting Out* not only undermines our sense of Arlene's personal accomplishment, but further problematizes the issue of female identity and its relation to patriarchal authority. The play opens with two offstage voices in succession. The first, a woman's, occurs before the act 1 curtain and thus outside the proper action of the play. With its droning tones, its repetitive and simplistic directives, its unexplained restrictions, its reading error (significantly, a misreading of names), and its focus on the unglamorous details of day-to-day prison life, the announcement not only strikes a curiously comic note, but also characterizes the limited sphere of approved female activity both inside the prison and out.[15] The male voice that follows, however, not only initiates the play's actions, but also identifies the "subject" (Arlene Holsclaw) and establishes the standards by which she is judged. The warden's announcement of Arlene's release sounds suspiciously like a prison sentence: "Subject will remain under supervision of Kentucky parole officers for a period of five years. Prospects for successful reintegration into community rated good" (*GO,* 9). Indeed, if Arlene "succeeds," it is only to take up the role and place assigned to her from the opening moments of the play.[16]

Moreover, Arlene is shown to be no more personally "responsible" for her criminal self than she is for her rehabilitated one. Raped by her father, exploited by her boyfriend, sexually harassed by the prison guards, and emotionally manipulated by the chaplain, Arlene's female identity is shaped, damaged, conditioned and reconstructed *by* and *for* the representatives of patriarchal authority. In other words, no separation is made (or possible) between self and sexual identity: Arlie's sex determines the particular forms of abuse she suffers, just as Arlene's rehabilitation depends on the management of her sexual behavior and the appearance of a presentably feminine demeanor. In this respect, one moment of the play is particularly telling. Arlene awakes to her first full day of freedom by the sound of a loud siren, "bolts out of bed, then turns back to it quickly, making it up in a frenzied, ritual manner." The Pavlovian response is followed by recognition of "the habit she has just played out" and another sequence of gestures:

> The sound of a jackhammer gets louder. Arlene walks to the window, and looks out. There is a wolf-whistle from a worker below. She shuts the window in a fury, then grabs the bars. She starts to shake them, but then her hand goes limp. She looks around the room as if trying to remember what she is doing there. . . . (GO, 44)

One one level, the actions naturalistically connect the two figures in the play, Arlene reacting as Arlie would in her half-awakened state. But the furious bar-shaking that follows a wolf-whistle not only reinforces the association between prison life and life "outside," but connects Arlene's feeling of anger and powerlessness specifically to her sexual objectification by an anonymous male "look." The sequence is significantly preceded by Bernie's offer of chewing gum (the single gesture of kindness shown Arlene in prison), the subtext of which is indicated by Guard Evans's unanswered question: "You screwin' that wildcat?" (GO, 44).

In this play, the gaze of men is the gaze of institutional power, a gaze that *subjects* Arlene, for better or worse, to a sexual identity against which personal rebellion is futile. Even Norman's stage set emphasizes the psycho-sexual dynamics of Arlene's identity crisis. Using catwalks manned by prison guards, the entire play is put under the gaze of men, and their objectifying look provides a disturbing frame for Arlene's private struggles. This subjection to the male look, this sense of always being watched but never being recognized (i.e., acknowledged, accepted, understood, or even seen) is central to the emotional dynamics of all three plays. Here it is doubly reinforced: under the chaplain's influence, Arlene cannot "see" the former Arlie; and the figures from Arlene's past have trouble remembering her new name or accepting the change it indicates. Again, that change is charted in primarily sexual terms. Bernie misunderstands Arlene's acceptance of help as an invitation to move in ("You don't want me to go. You're jus beginning to git interested . . ." GO, 38), Arlene's mother reads Bernie's hat as proof of sexual misconduct ("You ain't changed a bit . . . same hateful brat." GO, 30), and Carl assumes not only that Arlene has gotten out of prison by sexual favors, but will resume work for him. The list of examples could go on, but the point is clear:

Getting Out is not about the contradictions of the humanist self, but a specifically female one. Arlene may get out of prison, but her tragic plight involves a socially constructed identity that assigns her permanently to a powerless, passive position, to a female "self" she hardly recognizes. The end of the play suggests that Arlene, at best, will survive the damage done to her. In Ruby's words, "Arlene's had about all the help she can stand" (*GO*, 63). But the physical, emotional, and economic cost involved in Arlene's "socialization" makes us question the very standards by which her acceptability is finally judged. Represented here in extreme and inescapable form, the issues of sexual identity directly address the female audience member and make the experience of the play for her a thoroughly depressing one.[17]

The problems of feminine identity and female autonomy are perhaps more disturbingly represented in Norman's two naturalistic plays *The Laundromat* and *'night, Mother.* Here the social worlds narrow to the interactions of a mother-daughter pair[18] who talk about themselves, their family, their relationships, their domestic life, and their past; and who reveal through their conversation the unworked-through grief and anger that the talking itself is intended to alleviate. However, the promised emotional catharsis is undermined by endings that stop the conversation without solving the problems, a structure that reinforces the very irresolvability of the problems *as* they are posed in Norman's plays.[19] As duologues, *The Laundromat* and *'night, Mother* appear to focus on women unmediated by the gaze of men, but a closer look reveals the action to be crucially determined by absent male characters. Alberta and Deedee find themselves doing laundry *because* their husbands are not around. As Deedee so eloquently puts it, "if they were both home where they should be, we wouldn't have to be here in this crappy laundromat washin' fuckin' shirts in the middle of the night!" (*L*, 16). Jessie's suicide is committed with her father's gun (although Cecil's would have done), loaded with ammunition that Dawson unwittingly provided. Both literally and metaphorically, men have encouraged and enabled Jessie's act. Jessie describes her death wish in reference to her father, "I want to hang a big sign around my neck, like Daddy's on the barn — GONE FISHING" (*NM*, 27) while Dawson makes her "feel stupid for not doing it ten years sooner" (*NM*, 17). Although no single male character is to blame, the hopelessness of Jessie's state and the inevitability of her suicide is defined primarily in terms of the absent men to which most of the dialogue refers. From Mama's point of view, Jessie's deliberate exclusion of male witnesses is itself an exclusion of hope, Mama's inability to prevent her daughter's suicide sadly counterpointed by her persistent belief that Dawson, Cecil, Ricky or even the ambulance driver could have. Because

Susan Kingsley and Lynn Cohen in a production of Marsha
Norman's *Getting Out* by the Actors Theatre of Louisville. (Photo
by David S. Talbott.)

the sphere of significant "male" action (of self-assertion in the most positive sense) lies elsewhere, for Norman's women to "act" they must physically leave the set. Significantly, such action is undermined by the fact that in each case, the character's movement is simply to an invisible extension of the same set: Arlene will go upstairs, Deedee will go next door, Alberta goes home, and Jessie locks the bedroom door behind her. Despite the closure each ending provides, the final tableau presents an isolated woman mindlessly clutching a "prop" (Arlene's grocery item, Deedee's Dr. Pepper, Mama's hot chocolate pot) in the face of irreparable loss.[20]

Because the apparent cause of the characters' unhappiness lies outside the plays, dramatic conflict in the traditional sense is replaced by differences of opinion and personality, with the misunderstandings and illuminations that arise from *within* the powerless position women share. Indeed, the female bonding that occurs in each play results from the often humorous acknowledgment that in relation to men, they all share similar experiences. To Arlene's complaint that Carl doesn't listen, Ruby responds, "Funny, ain't it, the number a' men come without ears" (*GO*, 59), and their friendship is cemented with the "Queen Victoria's hat" story about being "taken" by a man and sent to county jail for it. From priest to prison guards, the men in *Getting Out* reduce Arlene to a sexual identity that corresponds to their own desires, a situation that seriously confuses Arlene's sense of self and with it, her ability to act in her own interest. Ruby survives analogous experiences with men by learning to mistrust everyone. In *'night, Mother,* Jessie indicates a similar unwillingness to accept the passive, feminine position to which she has been assigned; self-negating as it may be, her suicide is an attempt to establish an identity, over and against the power of Dawson that Mama so mindlessly accepts.[21] In fact, we share Jessie's action in part as a joke at Dawson's expense, Dawson who thinks all women share his wife's foot size, and who "just calls me Jess like he knows who he's talking to" (*NM*, 23). Jessie wants to do something that her brother isn't privy to, won't understand, and whose fatal consequences are a direct result of his ignorant self-absorption: "He took it as a compliment. He thought I might be taking an interest in things. He got through telling me all about the bullets and then he said we ought to talk like this more often" (*NM*, 15). Jessie and Mama not only share private knowledge of this evening, but share the conditions that have led to it. Thus Mama's humorous description of never being the woman her husband wanted to see (*NM*, 46) is mirrored in Jessie's admission that leaving Cecil was a relief: "I was never what he wanted to see, so it was better when he wasn't looking all the time" (*NM*, 62). In *The Laundromat,* Alberta reveals a similar uneasiness with her story of sending Herb to the store every Thanksgiving to avoid having him watch her work. Whereas women constantly acknowledge and validate male authority, male attention, however well-intended, has the opposite effect on these characters. According to Deedee, Joe finds her mere presence "there watchin'" at the drag races a "real big help" (*L*, 13), an experience Alberta clearly recognizes: "I never understood that, men wanting you to watch them do whatever it is. . . ." (*L*, 13). In the forms it is experienced, male attention is so rarely empowering that each woman will at some point in the plays express a preference for solitude. As Alberta puts it, "Your own face in the mirror is better company than a man who would eat a whole fried egg in one bite" (*L*, 25).

As the women relate their experiences across three plays, a pattern of male behavior emerges that is far more damaging than any sexual infidelity. Whether father, husband, son, brother, friend, or lover, the recurrent theme is misunderstanding, misreading, or misrecognition of women. Since women's perception of themselves, and with it their ability to act, depends on male recognition, patriarchal power is shown to be based on a kind of deliberate blindness—on men's inability to properly "see" women, coupled with their need to see them in a particular way. Although the seriousness of the complaint varies, from the sleeping male attendant in *The Laundromat* to the sexual exploitation of *Getting Out,* every male character provides a case in point. While Norman's plays turn on the issue of emotional self-awareness, what the characters recognize and what the audience does is not necessarily the same. The issues Norman raises go beyond the wish that men were different so that Harlequin romance endings (invisible women finally recognized and valued by the men they love) could come true. Rather, we are asked to consider the ways in which male misrecognition itself shapes and determines female subjectivity, to see how women are betrayed by their own socially constructed sexual identity.

Whereas the expressionistic techniques of *Getting Out* help foreground these issues, the comedy of *The Laundromat* provides the audience with the distance necessary for a similar feminist perspective. As in Norman's other plays, the stage set is not merely a backdrop for the action, but in some sense defines, contains, and determines it, reminding us of the very limitations imposed on the characters. Here the "standard dreary laundromat" with its "dirty ashtrays" and "ugly chairs littered with magazines" presents in hyperrealistic tones the bleak reality of those women whose dreams are formed by *Better Homes and Gardens.* While the actions and dialogue between Alberta and Deedee are "natural" and familiar, the opening theme song "Stand By

Your Man" underscores the pathetic and potentially absurd nature of the loyalty their behavior eventually illustrates. As the coincidental sharing of names (their husbands') indicates, their only real connection to each other is *as* women, a condition that in this play cuts across differences in age, social class, and education. The play opens with another absent male voice, but this time addressing the women in the play (and audience) in a personal, even intimate tone:

> This is your Number-One-Night Owl saying it's 3 o'clock, all right, and time to rock your daddy to dreams of delight. And Mama, I'm comin' home. And the rest of you night owls gonna have to make it through the rest of this night by *yourself,* or with the help of *your* friends, if you know what I mean. And you know what I mean. (*L, 5*)

The patter simultaneously lures the listener with its promise of sexual satisfaction and prepares the audience for the theme of solitude that the lack of such fulfillment here entails. As in the opening song lyrics, the "real" women of the D.J.'s address will be rewarded for waiting. Deedee later denies that these women exist; she, Deedee, is the waiting woman, and it is to her desire that the D.J. speaks. The moment reminds us of Rosalind Coward's analysis of popular radio: "Nowhere is sexual desire more obviously scripted and stage-managed than in the mishmash of music and chat directed at women . . . on popular radio. Sexual desire, attraction and love dominate not just as themes in the music but also make up a large part of the D.J.'s chatter."[22] And indeed, it is as "generic" woman, addressed and positioned by the media institution, that the two characters in the play, otherwise so different, connect. Deedee shares Alberta's problem of not feeling "quite herself" without her husband, of having trouble "being" on her own; their loneliness and isolation is not an existential metaphor, but the direct result of emotional dependence on "absent" men. Thus while both women reveal a need to talk about themselves, to establish the sense of independent identity that their "getting out" so late at night suggests, they do so primarily by talking about their husbands.

Focused on her relationship with Joe, Deedee's free-associative chatter is unwittingly humorous, emotionally self-revealing and easily interpreted by Alberta (and the audience). The self-deprecating humor reveals her insecurity just as her response-demanding conversational style indicates loneliness. Like both Jessie and Arlene, Deedee's barely repressed hostility is inseparable from the feelings of impotence associated with low self-esteem; and as in *Getting*

Out, Norman highlights this female identity problem with the use and misuse of characters' names. Deedee recalls:

> The guys in high school always kidded me about my name. (*Affecting a boy's voice*) Hey, Deedee, is Deedee your name or your bra size? . . . That ain't the worst of it. . . . David's locker was right next to mine and Ricky's say, "Hey, did you have a good time last night?" And David would say, "Yes, In Deedee." Then they'd slap each other and laugh like idiots. (*L,* 11)

But equally telling is Deedee's admission that she wouldn't change lockers because the basketball players passed it on their way to practice. Deedee's identity, her sense of herself *as* a woman, depends on male recognition, but the look that positions her is hardly validating. When Deedee gave her husband a doll imprinted with an image of her own face, Joe "laughed so hard he fell over backward out of the chair and cracked his head open on the radiator" (*L,* 15), then gave the doll away. A modern Nora, Deedee must lie about her part-time job and fully recognizes that Alberta's suggestion to "tell him how you feel" (*L,* 21) will exacerbate rather than cure her marital problems. Norman's deliberate allusions to *A Doll's House* take the audience back again to the relationship between action and female identity: Deedee's emotional and economic dependence on her husband is represented as the cause of her sentimental and childlike behavior, just as Alberta's responsible advice arises from the undesirable necessity of surviving on her own. What emerges from this play, however, is not simply an image of "needy" women, but of women whose needs are represented as incapable of satisfaction: of women betrayed by the very desires that arise from occupying the female subject position in our society.

The self-defeating nature of female desire itself provides the tragic dimension to Norman's plays. In all three plays, the male gaze that defines female identity, validates female behavior, and empowers women to act is represented as both necessary (desirable) and unattainable (absent). In other words, what women want (a strong sense of self) and what women need to have it (male recognition) is contradictory. From a male point of view, women provide the castrated "other" against which phallic authority and male sexual identity are defined. From the female perspective provided in these plays, however, such authority is imprisoning, blind, or indifferent. As a result, the women in the plays turn to each other for self-validation. But if male misrecognition shapes and informs female (self) consciousness, then such connections can provide no solution. As we have seen, despite their apparent differences, the women in these plays share the same problems and position in relation to men, and the mother-daughter dynamics that inform their interactions make the female identity issue even more problematic. All the protagonists suffer from feelings of inadequacy, impotence, repressed anger, and low self-esteem. But if the very sense of self that makes action possible is in danger, it is not the mother's mirroring image that can provide the source of originating identity and power. And yet for Arlene, Deedee, and Jessie, this is precisely the role that the mothering figure is asked to play. Moreover, the emotional dynamics that result from foregrounding issues related to gender identity may understandably have a different impact on men and women.[23] While men cannot directly identify with any of the plays' female characters, the female audience can identify with them all; and when the struggle is as sharply contested and as undecidable as it is in 'night, Mother, the experience of the play can be painful indeed.

Are Norman's plays feminist? The question itself falsely assumes that a play's social and political meaning is inherent, detachable from the social moment of its production and reception. As Colin McCabe argued about film over a decade ago, a work's theoretical and political interest cannot be decided by internal factors alone. Norman's plays are woven from conventional material, using traditional forms, and embedded in cultural assumptions that both the form and content carry with them. Moreover, their emotional effect depends on an immediate recognition of reality on the part of audience members, and Norman goes out of her way to maintain that illusion with onstage clocks keeping real time, familiar sets and dialogue, and the tempo of domestic routine. As she notes in the stage directions to 'night, Mother, *Under no circumstances should the set and its dressing make a judgement about the intelligence or taste of Jessie and Mama* (NM, 3). Even the potentially distancing devices of *Getting Out* are used to bring us closer to understanding and identifying with what otherwise might appear as an interesting and unusual "case." And yet, like "lived experience" itself, these plays offer us the raw material for alternative and "critical" readings of the reality so powerfully depicted on the stage. Whether deliberate or unwitting, the problem of "misreading" women that is reiterated in each play is an issue that necessarily involves audience response. Because the focus on female characters and gender-specific identity issues may result in very different effects upon male and female audience members, we need be especially wary of the ways in which the plays are interpreted and judged. (That each of these plays lends itself to both conventional and alternative readings may in fact account for their success.) But if Norman's work can make us aware of the extent to which our own subjectivity—our pleasures, desires, needs, and anxieties—are laden with unexamined assumptions about women and sexual identity, then the re-evaluation of she-tragedy as a significant literary form has already begun.

NOTES

1. See, for example, Arthur Sherbo, *English Sentimental Drama* (East Lansing, Mich.: Michigan State University Press, 1957), 139. The term *she-tragedie* is coined in the epilogue to Rowe's *The Tragedy of Jane Shore* (1714), which begins "Ye modest matrons all, ye virtuous wives, / Who lead with horrid husbands decent lives; . . . What can we say your pardon to obtain?" The word appears in the following context:

> There are more ways of wickedness than
> one. If the reforming stage should fall to shaming
> Ill-nature, pride, hypocrisy, and gaming;
> The poets frequently might move compassion,
> And with she-tragedies o'errun the nation.

2. In the revised edition of the *Biographia Dramatica, Vol. II* (London: T. Walker, 1782), David Baker notes that "this play is so well known, and is so frequently performed, and always with the greatest applause, that little need be said of it" (113).

3. Quoted in Sherbo, 139.

4. Sherbo, 139–40.

5. See, for example, Sandra M. Gilbert and Susan Gubar, *The Madwoman in the Attic* (New Haven: Yale University Press, 1979).

6. Marsha Norman, *Getting Out* (New York: Dramatists Play Service, 1978); *Third and Oak: The Laundromat* (New York: Dramatists Play Service, 1980); *'night, Mother* (New York: Hill and Wang, 1983). References to these plays hereafter cited parenthetically within the text.

7. Sherbo, 140.

8. When the moment comes, Jessie says, "Let go of me, Mama. I've said everything I had to say" (*NM*, 87).

9. Norman makes a special note that "The apartment must seem imprisoned" (*NM*, 5). Not only is Arlene appalled to find burglar bars on the window, but the catwalks that frame the stage set, as well as Arlie's ability to move through the space of the entire set, make Arlene's apartment room appear even smaller than it otherwise might.

10. Only men have the power to "make time," a notion brought home with particular poignancy in Norman's *Traveller in the Dark*. Here the main character, a famous male surgeon, appears guilty of not "making time" for his head nurse and most loyal friend, Mavis. But in Sam's version of the situation, Mavis caused her own death by not attending to her own symptoms "in time" for Sam to be able to save her. In

this play, the audience witnesses Sam work through his own confused feelings of anger, guilt, and grief while his wife knowingly "waits" for the storm to pass.

11. See William Glassner, *Reality Therapy* (New York: Harper and Row, 1965). This popular, atheoretical, behavioral approach to clinical psychiatry has been the model for many drug and criminal rehabilitation programs in the last two decades. The reality therapist denies the existence of the unconscious mind and has little use for the patient's own account of his/her past history or present emotional state; the patient is offered love and emotional involvement in exchange for accepting the therapist's version of realistic and appropriate behavior. Reality therapy's embrace of the status quo and use of emotional blackmail to produce "responsible" behavior make it, in the opinion of this writer, a potentially dangerous form of therapy, especially for women. Although Glassner's psychology pervades the dialogue and consciousness of Norman's characters, I would suggest that the plays themselves offer a critique of this overtly pragmatic approach to women's problems.

12. One of Mama's cruelest statements comes near the end of the play when she realizes there is nothing she can do to change Jessie's mind. Here she tries to make Jessie face the fact that even her suicide will change nothing, that Jessie's attempt to accept responsibility for her own life simply reconfirms a pattern of emotional manipulation and physical dependence that is "just like you" and will surprise no one (*NM,* 79). The audience recognizes the truth of Mama's depiction of reality. Because by the end of the play Jessie's action seems both inevitable and somehow justified, we will, as Mama says, pity her rather than Jessie.

13. See also Madonne Miner, "'What's These Bars Doin' Here?'—The Impossibility of Getting Out," *Theatre Annual* 40 (1985): 115–37, for further examples of the way in which Norman foregrounds the identity theme. Miner suggests that the desire to identify with Arlene at the end of the play is related to our desire for integrated selfhood, a desire embedded in patriarchal and capitalistic ideology that Norman's play undermines. While Norman's play can be persuasively read as a critique of the humanist self, I would suggest that such a postmodern stance does not necessarily make it "radically feminist." For a view that uses both Freud and Foucault to consider the libidinal dynamics of audience reception and focus more theoretically on the postmodern identity theme, see Timothy Murray, "Patriarchal Panopticism, or The Seduction of a Bad Joke: *Getting Out* in Theory," *Theatre Journal* 35 (October 1983): 376–88.

14. Arlene is left virtually defenseless, for example, against Bernie's attempted rape. Saved by Bernie's own guilty conscience, the first act closes with Arlene's quiet and painfully spoken words: "Arlie coulda killed you." The use of the word "coulda" for the more expected "woulda" underscores the feeling of loss and powerlessness that accompanies Arlene's changed personality.

15. The repetition of the loudspeaker announcements at the beginning of act 2 also underscores the cyclical time pattern associated with women and their activities in this play. See above discussion of Norman's handling of time and its relation to women.

16. As Timothy Murray (1983) puts it, the real subject of this play is "less the Arlene who has righted her wrongs by doing institutional time than 'subject Holsclaw'—who is subject to the judgement of the Alabama State Parole Board, the supervision of Kentucky parole officers, the evaluation of an institutional shrink, and the

unknown contents of her textual self, Appendix C. . . . the freedom of her mind and body is relational to social structures and institutions which continue to master them . . . a figure of the judgement of an absent voice of institutional power" (378–79).

17. While it is reasonable to assume that men may also find the experience of the play a depressing one, I would suggest that it is for different reasons. Generalizing in a different metaphorical direction, one can see the play as an individual against society struggle, for example. On the other hand, without questioning the institutional values depicted in the play, the audience might see Arlene's struggle precisely as the Board of Parole does—as a bad woman who is now good and whose prospects for "reintegration" are promising. Only by such acceptance can I understand critical comments that assume we "root" for Arlene or find any comfort in the notion of her "making it." (See not only reviews of the play's first production but also the two articles cited above that critique initial responses from a different angle.)

18. Alberta and Deedee are not biologically related, but they have the same last name, and enact patterns so typical of mother-daugher interaction that Deedee twice makes the telling comparison: "I wish Mom were more like you" (*L,* 20) and later, "You're worse than Mom" (*L,* 22).

19. As we shall see, since female subjectivity is itself the problem, ambivalence and irresolvability are central to the plays' emotional dynamics.

20. In each case, that loss is inseparable from the self-recognition that accompanies it. In *The Laundromat,* Deedee is left with Alberta's refusal to give her phone number (and therefore establish any lasting relationship) and the realization of what she must do (leave Joe). While Alberta gives her some courage to face this decision, Alberta's departure leaves Deedee (and the audience) conscious of the overwhelming odds against such self-initiated change. In *'night, Mother,* Mama is left with the realization that not only she has failed to save Jessie, but also that Jessie is right—that they share the very condition that has led to Jessie's action. Arlene's final moments are perhaps the most positive since the two sides of her personality communicate for the first time in the play, the laughter suggesting a "female bonding" process in which both mother and daughter, past and present selves, may merge in the interest of mere survival.

21. For a further discussion of the psychological underpinnings of Jessie's suicide, see my article, "Norman's *'night, Mother:* Psycho-drama of Female Identity," *Modern Drama* 30, no. 3 (September 1987): 364–75.

22. Rosalind Coward, *Female Desire: Woman's Sexuality Today* (London: Granada, 1984), 145ff.

23. While both men and women share the problem of detaching themselves from the mother in order to assume a separate identity, only the female must both *reject* her mother (as original love object) and *become* her mother (take her place) in order to assume a "normal" sexual identity. If the authority of the Father is both necessary and unattainable for women, the authority of the Mother is both necessary and insufficient.

PART 3

Alternatives to (His)tory

JAN BRESLAUER AND
HELENE KEYSSAR

Making Magic Public: Megan Terry's Traveling Family Circus

When Megan Terry moved to the Omaha Magic Theater in 1974, she began a new phase of the feminist discourse she had begun to shape in the experimental theatre of the 1960s. The energy that she had directed for more than a decade toward collaborative production endeavors, primarily in New York City with the Open Theater, now became more precisely focused on joint endeavors with her colleague, Jo Ann Schmidman, and on efforts to engage and address the local community in Omaha. While Terry was one of the few feminist playwrights to have had her work from the sixties and early seventies published, after 1974 fewer of her texts were commercially printed, even though she and the Omaha Magic Theater made serious efforts to arrange for low-cost script publication and willingly made copies of new scripts available to anyone who asked. Awareness of Terry's work since 1974 has also been limited because, although the Omaha Magic Theater has toured extensively in the Midwest and occasionally on the East and West Coasts, it has remained remote from the mainstream Boston–New Haven–New York–Washington, D.C. theatre circuit.

It is not, therefore, surprising, that when, in the 1980s, the press discovered the "new women playwrights," Megan Terry was ignored or overlooked. At the same time, there is good reason to claim, as one of us did in *Feminist Theatre*,[1] that Terry is the "mother of American feminist theatre." Evidence for this claim abounds in Terry's more than fifty plays. As a body of work, these dramas have explored a wide range of feminist issues: production and reproduction, the language of patriarchy, gender roles inside and outside the family, the victimization and heroism of women, and the pain and power of women in a repressive society are all essential elements of Terry's dramatic discourse. Her plays persistently criticize and subvert specific institutions and events in American society—from the war in Vietnam to the hypocritical behavior of parents toward adolescents—but these critiques are not merely casual gestures at topical issues or facile assaults on patriarchy and sexism. Rather, they are specifications of a vision that emphasizes a transformation of morality as the basis of social and political change.

Although critical of the particular instances of violence and oppression against women, Terry's plays have never insisted, as has the work of some feminists working in other media, that revolution is necessary in order to improve the stature of women in society. Her objections to inequality are not usually couched in terms of an economic system that creates such situations, but rather emerge as protests against individual circumstances, institutional corruption, or verbal and conceptual distortions, notably common in occurrence as these may be. Even, for example, in a play like *Babes in the Bighouse* (1979), which harshly condemns both the treatment of women prisoners and, metaphorically, the pervasive imprisonment of women in the codes and practices of modern society, the challenge is to the audience's sense of responsibility and dignity, not to the economic and political systems that support such prisons. Terry's outlook in this regard has been archetypally American and may be a strategic choice given that her audience, too, is, for the most part, assertively American. Enacting her own feminist version of American romanticism, Terry has chosen in most of her plays to highlight the positive, though incremental, change that is available: women, in her dramas, are "alive and well" and on the way to doing even better.

This belief that things can be better took form in Terry's work as magic even before she joined forces with the theater of that name. *Calm Down Mother* (1965), one of Terry's first plays to be explicitly concerned with women as women, depicts the tensions as well as the attachments between mothers and daughters, but ends with a ritual-like chant that invokes woman's reproductive capabilities as a source of difference and almost mystical strength. *Viet Rock* (1966) concluded in "deathly silence," but the intense ambiance of community in the acting ensemble deliberately encouraged spectators to believe that they—we—could overcome the various oppressions represented and enacted in that war. The most memorable moment in *Approaching Simone* (1970) occurs when each member of the acting company takes on a piece of Simone's clothing, symbolically taking on her pain and her struggle for women's freedom. Simone Weil, like theater itself in Terry's hands, is a model, but, as dramatized, her heroism can join her to others rather than separate her from them.

It is possible, then, to comprehend Terry's move to Omaha, Nebraska, as a geographical expression of her conviction that possibilities exist outside the norm. It is also important to note that this move came at the beginning of a decade that was to see both the rise and the retrenchment of feminism, including, in the eighties, a new generation of women content to identify themselves as "post-feminists." From the retrospective view of 1988, however, those changes are dated, and even for some who embraced "post-feminism," that label is showing itself not only as inaccurate but invidious.

As if sensing such a trend in the offing, Terry's 1983 collaboration with JoAnne Metcalf, *Mollie Bailey's Traveling Family Circus: Featuring Scenes from the Life of Mother Jones,* represented a new and increasingly politicized direction for her drama. Retaining the basic optimism of her previous work, while venturing into one of the most contested arenas of contemporary American society, Terry dares in *Mollie Bailey's Traveling Circus* to show the possibility of authentic communication and mutual support between two types of successful women who, in today's world, would appear to be unyielding foes. The central figures and the orchestrators of events in this drama are Mollie Bailey and Mother Jones, both born in the nineteenth century, the former out of Terry's imagination, the latter out of history. In Terry's staged world, Mother Jones, a political activist, socialist, and organizer for the rights of women and children, is not the evil enemy but the star performer and ally of Mollie Bailey, a woman who is a traditional housewife and, ironically, the ringmistress of a traveling "family" circus.

In this world, dramaturgically and politically, transformation and possibility are key motifs, as they have been throughout Terry's work,[2] but their explicit presence has been augmented by an increased attention to the social-political cosmos. The onstage transformations that were oppositional conventions in Terry's dramas of the sixties (and that became accepted theatrical practice in American experimental theatre before vanishing, in the seventies, from the work of most male playwrights) are revitalized in *Mollie Bailey's Traveling Circus* as circus feats. More eloquently than in Terry's previous work, these transformations are also now the feats of American women recovering and reconstructing their history. Even the production history of this drama diverged from the pattern Terry had established in the previous decade: first produced in the Plays in Process series of the Mark Taper Forum in Los Angeles, *Mollie Bailey's Traveling Family Circus* was then produced at California Institute of the Arts and in Santa Barbara, California, before appearing onstage "at home" at the Omaha Magic Theater.

The prologue to *Mollie Bailey's Traveling Circus* signals the ironic tone and mythic frame for this play. Suspended on a wide trapeze or platform held aloft by "invisible" stagehands, two Celtic queens, who are, simultaneously, Mollie Bailey and Mother Jones, are crossing the Irish Sea on a raft in the midst of a fierce storm. Lashed to their raft are other, unconscious members of their tribe. Mother Jones's opening line—"Did you lash down the males?"—instantly establishes the inversion of conventional power relations between men and women; the men are not only physically subjugated to the women but are treated as sexual types, as "males." (A few lines later, Mother Jones confirms this conception when she reassures Mollie that they will reach land with at least one male "in good condition.") The prologue also establishes a mother-daughter relationship between Mother Jones and Mollie Bailey: literally fulfilling the role suggested by her ironic, historical name, "Mother" Jones commands, instructs and nurtures Mollie, who, in turn, proclaims her love for "Mother" and her confidence that she will be empowered by her mother's attachment and support:

> *Mollie.* Mother, I love you so. Let me stand against the storm and spell you. If you hold my hand I'll be able to feel the way to steer. (P. 2)

Theatrically and culturally, this prologue is at once familiar and disconcerting. The sea-storm setting and the playful echo of "Take in the topsail" in "lash down the males" blatantly recall Shakespeare's *The Tempest,* which, like Terry's play, is situated in both the historical context of the discovery of the new world and the mythical context of a separate space of spectacle where time and place are magically construed. The raft of the two Celtic queens is a far cry, however, from the sailing ship of *The Tempest,* and the two women steering the raft's course would have had no place, even as passengers, on Shakespeare's all-male ship. Perhaps even more unsettling, where Gonzalo ended the prologue of *The Tempest* longing for any piece of dry land, Mother Jones bypasses an island, seeking greener fields. Contrary to gender stereotypes, the men of *The Tempest* quickly lose patience, blame others, and surrender to fear and chaos, whereas Mother Jones concludes the prologue of the contemporary drama warmly reassuring Mollie that "If we're not in trouble, we're not going in the right direction."

The right direction in *Mollie Bailey's Traveling Family Circus* is rarely straight forward, or straight backward. In keeping with many contemporary feminist plays, this prologue and the two acts that follow exploit theater's liberty with time and place to conjoin previously disconnected elements of culture and history. Such temporal and spatial reconfigurations orient the spectator toward alternative ways of viewing the present and the past. Terry has subverted conventional representations of chronology and history repeatedly in her work, beginning with *Calm Down Mother,* but the particular juxtaposition in *Mollie Bailey's Traveling Family Circus* of a historical figure with a fictional character has even more striking affinities with several of Caryl Churchill's dramas than with Terry's own previous work.

Churchill's *Top Girls,* like Terry's *Mollie Bailey's Traveling Circus,* begins with an imagined ritual of passage that requires a new understanding of gender roles. The similar emphases in Terry's and Churchill's dramaturgies on unprecedented historical representations and on explicit intertextual gestures suggest that the most potent emergent element of feminist theater may not be the recovery of women's history but what Mother Jones calls "getting into trouble," and what I have elsewhere described as doing dangerous history.[3] Where many feminist endeavors, in the theater and in other media, have aimed to recuperate women's history as an inspirational resource for women and men, dangerous historical explorations seek not only to recover the forgotten achievements of women but also to examine the conditions under which gender conflicts have repeatedly arisen and repeatedly been resolved such that women have remained subordinate to men. Dangerous historians, and dramatists doing dangerous history, confront the illusions of the past, including those that conceal women's complicity in the recurrent subjugation of women to men. Dangerous history also refuses to ignore women's violence at key moments in that history. The processes and effects of doing dangerous history in drama are increasingly evident not only in plays by Churchill and Terry, but in other feminist dramas such as Wendy Kesselman's *My Sister in This House* (1982), Louise Page's *Salonika* (1982), Ntozake Shange's *Three Pieces* (1981) and Sharon Pollock's *Blood Relations* (1981).

If, then, Terry's prologue to *Mollie Bailey's Traveling Circus* is a warning that we are about to enter the realm of dangerous history, it is therefore appropriate that the setting into which Mother Jones and Mollie Bailey are lowered for acts 1 and 2 is a circus, a place whose attraction is inseparable from its embrace of danger. That Terry sets this play in a circus is at once a logical extension of her long-term association of magic, theater, and spectacle and an assertion that what has once been implicit in her own dramaturgy and in American culture will now become explicit, theatrically and substantively. At least in modern societies, the circus is the ultimate world of possibilities, paradoxes, and perversions; it is a reminder of the lost world of carnival, a world that Soviet cultural critic M. M. Bakhtin has recalled to our attention as the locus of folk humor and unofficial culture in Western societies from the Greeks through the Renaissance.[4] Because the circus separates the audience from the performer/participants, it is not a true carnival, but in its irreverent conjoining of laughter and fear, its deployment of popular imagery, its love of exaggeration, its pleasure in the grotesque, and the promiscuity of its attachments, the circus, like the Rabelaisian novels that attracted Bakhtin's attention, signifies a symbolic opposition to the dominant values and practices of patriarchal societies.

Mollie Bailey's circus partakes of these essential attributes, but it also evokes a uniquely American understanding of circus: an exotic incarnation of the American rags to riches dream in which anyone can be anything and all is attainable. The American circus is the archetypical carnival that we run away to join, hoping to belong to a world in which our fantasies become real and we're freed from normative constraints. So Terry, in *Mollie Bailey's Traveling Family Circus,* dreams for us, envisioning a society with new rules that embrace diversity. Once we enter this world, it will metamorphosize us in such a way that we neither want nor are able to return to our previous lives.

Traditionally, and in Terry's play, the circus is the realm of a liberated Saturnalia in which identity is redefined. As in most forms of carnival, the masters may become servants and vice versa, but there are possibilities even beyond this. Anyone can become anyone, then, in turn, become someone else. Identity is no longer fixed, especially when performers adopt new personages for their various "acts" or roles within the performance as a whole. Combining a familiar circus routine and a transformation technique often used in the sixties and seventies by improvisational theatre companies like the San Francisco Mime Troupe and Paul Sills's Story Theater, Terry is able to stress this fluidity of identity in *Mollie Bailey's Traveling Family Circus* with far less stylistic self-consciousness than in her previous works: within the circus setting, one man can stand on another's shoulders to play the Father; the Mother can be similarly performed; the actress and the actor playing Mollie and her husband, Gus, can grow older and younger within a minute's time; other actors in the company can transform from trapeze artists to canaries. The circus setting naturalizes these transformations because within the bounds of circus the notion of who one is within the group is in Heraclitian flux: age, gender, and authority are constantly redefined.

The circus not only has performers who transcend the circumscription of labels, it also has clowns, indefatigable warriors who conquer the impossible, recovering from falls that in everyday life would bring men and women down. Mollie Bailey herself displays some of the attributes of the clown in the first scenes of act 1, when, as she introduces her children, "endless streams of people seem to keep coming out from under her skirt." And, although the circus life is controlled by metaphors of the family, often with the ringmaster as patriarch, in this play, Mollie Bailey is ringmistress and a matriarch who is able to share her power without diminishing it.

Mollie's ability to share her power is explicitly attributed in the play to her gender identity, but the drama suggests that, even for a woman as strong as Mollie, this might not be possible in the ordinary world. The circus, however, is, also, importantly, a cooperative, a collective in which interdependence is all, and, frequently, a matter of life and death.[5] The benefits of cooperative effort are announced in the prologue of *Mollie Bailey's Traveling Family Circus,* but it is in the arena of the circus itself that the particular possibilities and originality of the cooperation between Mollie Bailey and Mother Jones are revealed.

Following two scenes that introduce the audience for the circus (and the drama) to Mollie Bailey's personal history of escape from an authoritarian father to love, marriage, and centerstage in "Women's Eternal Circus," Mollie, as ringmistress, introduces "for the first time anywhere" an act that "has never been staged in America or on the continent." The "act" is a scene from nineteenth-century American history, starring Mother Jones, and, as Terry blatantly reminds us, this is not a scene commonly played on the stages of American history or theater. In stark contrast to the frivolity and resurrection symbology of the initial circus scenes, Mother Jones first appears as a herald of death, carting the dead bodies of four children on top of coffins in a procession of carts drawn by old women. The image recalls the travels of other famous and weary souls, particularly the journeys of Brecht's Mother Courage with her wagons and children who die in the face of overwhelming adversities. In a speech to the audience, Mother Jones narrates the story, which is, indeed, a true story, of the epidemic that took the lives of her husband and four children. She tells of her grief, then sings to us of her determination to "find a way to fight for the living." As Mollie made a new life for herself with Gus and the circus after leaving her parents, Mother Jones reincarnates life from death. What Mollie does for a nuclear family, Mother Jones creates for the communal family of the poor and oppressed.

By embracing theater's ability to realize the impossible, to blur borders between the "real" and the imagined, Terry creates a dream juxtaposition of the lives of two outstanding women from history "who didn't know each other, [but who allow us to] know more about ourselves by knowing them."[6] This juxtaposition sharpens the sad irony of Mother Jones's name: it was not until after she had lost her four children and husband to a yellow fever epidemic and had become an extraordinarily successful labor organizer that Mary

Harris Jones became known as "Mother" Jones. The lives and works of Mother Jones and Mollie Bailey are thus inverses each of the other, but are also analogues; both demonstrate the force of nurturing activities and the empowerment possible through what anthropologist Nancy Chodorow has called "the reproduction of mothering." (I am thinking here of mothering, not as the institution that presently determines women's experience, but as it might be imagined in a non-gender-biased society.)

By showcasing Mother Jones, Mollie Bailey reveals her to be an object of her admiration, though there is never any suggestion that Mollie is dissatisfied with her own life. Notably absent is any indication of competition between the two women. Instead, mutual respect and collaboration between Mother Jones and Mollie Bailey implies a personalized version of the triumph of a feminism based on responsibility and attachment to others over a patriarchical social system grounded in ideas of rights and competition. This is not a feminism that excludes men, that requires an alternative lifestyle or is biologically constrained. The dialogue between Mollie and her husband, Gus, emphasizes that the pleasure they take in the life and family they have created for themselves is informed rather than threatened by Gus's recognition of Mollie's strength. And Mollie can be strong and still value "clean family fun" and a "down-home good time show."

Equally important, Mollie Bailey can be strong in her ways while fully acknowledging the different strengths of Mother Jones, whom we see in the first act as an "agitator, aggravator, hellraiser," crusading against starvation wages for child and women laborers. Mollie attempts to delight little children and provide them with the gift of laughter and life while Mother Jones struggles for downtrodden children and fights the police. But while Mollie's voice is sweet and often expressed in song and Mother Jones's voice is harsh and inclined to cursing, each woman is able to hear the other, and neither sees herself or the other as victim.

The episodic, non-narrative structure of the play supports the audience's understanding of the differences as well as the interdependencies between Mollie Bailey and Mother Jones. After Mollie's initial introduction in act 1 of the "Mother Jones act," scenes from the life of Mother Jones are intercut with scenes from Mollie's life. The connections between these scenes are often not explicitly articulated by an on-stage character, but are implicit in the similarities or contrasts between the events in Mother Jones's life and those in Mollie Bailey's. Two scenes in act 1, for example, juxtapose Mother Jones's instruction of a young soldier with Mollie's instruction of her daughter. Functioning much like an Eisensteinian montage in film, the audience learns from the collision between the two scenes more than from the separate content of either situation.

On a larger scale, act 1 and act 2 of *Mollie Bailey's Traveling Family Circus* have only a minimal narrative relation to each other but interanimate each other by contrasts and continuities of roles and themes. Where Mollie was the initiating voice of act 1, it is Mother Jones who begins act 2, and, notably, it is now Mother Jones who uses song to present her message. Her song repeats a refrain: "I was born in Revolution . . . " that reminds us of the changes in her life and in the historical context of her life, but that also reassures us of some continuity: " . . . And I'll never leave you. . . . Til we've seen these troubles through." Like Brecht's women, when she is not changing herself, Mother Jones is the emissary of change; and like Brecht's Widow Begbick (*Man Is Man*) and Jenny (*Threepenny Opera*), as well as Mother Courage, Mother Jones's survival and success are predicated on her adaptability. Unlike Brecht's women characters, however, Terry's bringers of change are not only changed themselves by circumstances but are also able to transform themselves.

This openness to change is as true of Mollie as it is of Mother Jones. Mollie transforms herself most obviously by leaving home and then creating her circus/family. The actress's onstage transformations from middle-aged woman to young girl and then again to older woman heighten and defamiliarize these commonplace changes, giving them dramatic equivalence with the radical alterations of Mother Jones's life. This is not to say that Terry conflates the tragedies of Mother Jones's life with the traumas of growing up and separation from parents, but that the models of change we are offered range, importantly, from the heroic to the ordinary. Mollie's attitude toward change, rather than her circumstances, provide a way to understand our own capacity to transform ourselves. She has a propensity for change, she tells us: "I was born when I was already ten thousand years old."

Mollie also celebrates complexity and eventually dismisses the archetypal purity ascribed to women; by so doing, she suggests we do the same. When her son, Eugene, presents his intended bride for her consideration, Mollie destroys his expectations of what is to be thought valuable:

> *Eugene.* She'll expand me! She has a beautiful soul, so clean, so pure, so white.
> *Mollie.* (*To audience and all*) Right away I'm alarmed!
> *Eugene.* But those are all perfect qualities. . . . She has a clean soul.
> *Mollie.* Then don't marry her.
> *Eugene.* I don't understand you.

Mollie. You can marry her if her soul is as patched as our tent.
(P. 31)

Mollie again invokes the circus as a source of imagery and meaning when she
goes on to explain to Eugene her position on freedom from the tyranny of
perfection:

> You think to sell us your bride by showing only her pure points. That's
> not what circus is all about. Where are the falls? Falling and almost fall-
> ing and recovering from falling. That's our job. (Pp. 32–33)

From a lifetime of "acts" inside the bigtop of Mollie Bailey–Mother
Jones's Family of Women's Eternal Circus, Mollie has learned the lesson with
which she concludes her sermon to her son: "If the soul is a soul that is
whole, it must be made up of all aspects, dark and light, of the human/animal
possibilities." Stage directions indicate that Eugene is frightened by his mother's exhortation. No wonder, since what Mollie proposes is no less than a
dismantling of the secure matrix of role-playing on which society has come
to depend. Perhaps most threatening, Mollie's admonitions are pointedly addressed to her son at the moment he wishes to marry, and they are called
forth, specifically, by Eugene's unquestioning assumption of the value of a
pure soul.

Eugene's vision of a perfect marriage modifies the patriarchal stereotype
by insisting on his own purity as well as that of his bride-to-be, but Mollie's
revisionist gender values call not only for equality but for transformations of
values for both men and women. Authentic transformations necessarily bring
a genuinely brave new world. Eugene senses the terror of the unknown in
this projected cultural revolution, and his explosion: "Mother. . . . You ask
for everything!" is not unlike the shriek of the isolated daughter in Caryl
Churchill's *Top Girls,* whose final cry is "afraid."

Mollie's only fear, the fear that grounds her advice to her son, is of a
life lived without risk. As she explains in her final "introduction" of Mother
Jones, Mollie admires and wants her audience to "experience" Mother Jones
because, "Mother Mary Harris Jones is one first-class risk-taker. . . ." She and
Mother Jones each have "a different way of living in this world" and "a different philosophy of life," Mollie continues, but with or without the labels and
diverse "philosophies" of capitalism and socialism, of homemaker and agitator, as mothers, they share an understanding that "sometimes to minimize
the danger, you have to take risks" (42).

Mollie Bailey and Mother Jones each acknowledge for themselves and for the audience that "history" as we know it is as much a human creation as any other enterprise. The task, therefore, is to rewrite a history that will enable rather than circumscribe those that come to be influenced by it. In the past, men have written the histories, but in the world of Terry's play, Mollie is the author of herself and of her story, a story that is unlike that of many authors because it is not, finally, a monologue but a dialogue. Aware that others will be suspicious of this mode of telling, and will demean her and her story as "woman's work," when you come to watch her circus, you will hear her say:

> Some people have put forward the notion that women don't know how to organize, don't know how to make decisions, don't understand logic, nor can they even tell a story with a beginning and a middle and an end. I confess, to the last accusation, because the way I see it the story has no beginning and it not only hasn't ended for me, it's always starting all over again. (P. 41)

Speaking here for the first time in the play "for women," Mollie's "confession" affirms the episodic, circular structure of her circus and of the play itself, while simultaneously reclaiming Terry's basic belief in the regenerative powers of women and the epiphanic stories they tell. Life does go on in Mollie's stories: in the final scene of the play, Mollie's husband, Gus, dies in the arms of the couple's very pregnant daughter, Minnie. Terry then deploys the most theatricalized transformation of the drama to play this motif out fully: all of the actors drape garments on Mollie that before our eyes, change her into a seventy-five-year-old woman. The individual women, Mollie Bailey and Mother Jones, are as vulnerable to time's tolls as we are, but in parting from the audience, speaking in one voice for the first time, they encourage us: "Go on—go on and open / Open that door you've never opened before!"

Mollie Bailey's Traveling Family Circus: Featuring Scenes from the Life of Mother Jones ends on this chord, but the legacies of Mollie and Mother Jones do not. They are part of a re-engendered society and of a new history in which lives and acts transform rather than simply end. In this play, as in her previous work, Terry pushes boundaries, but here she not only imagines anew a universe in which people may effect their own transfigurations, she also takes the risk of reconfiguring the terrain of women's relations to each other. The ordinary moments of our contemporary lives are made extraordinary both by replacing women in history and by imagining difference among women as well as between men and women as a source of strength rather than weakness. In Terry's hands, familiar dramatic tools and cultural practices are made strange and magical by combining signs and conventions from differing forms of discourse and diverse value systems. The songs, transformational acting techniques, dialogic discourse, and wondrous feats of *Mollie Bailey's Traveling Family Circus* together make everyday existence alien, but rather than making us remote from our own society, they urge us to reenter our own worlds through new doors.

Like a magician who is freed to show the audience how she pulls the rabbit out of the hat, Terry, like Mollie Bailey and Mother Jones, shows women and men *how* to work to make a difference. Mother Jones and Mollie Bailey will, indeed, "be back again," to haunt us and inspire us, as will all the previously hidden struggles, defeats, and triumphs of women when today's women own their pasts as their inheritance, an inheritance that is rightfully ours but for which we also must accept the dangers of responsibility.

NOTES

1. Helene Keyssar, *Feminist Theatre* (London: Macmillan, 1984, 1986), 53–76.

2. For a different introduction to the idea of transformation in Terry's dramas, see June Schlueter, "Keep Tightly Closed in a Cool Dry Place: Megan Terry's Transformational Drama and the Possibilities of Self," in *Studies in American Drama: 1945–Present,* vol. 2, 59–69.

3. Helene Keyssar, "Hauntings: Gender and Drama in Contemporary English Theatre," *Amerikanische Studien,* December 3–4, 1986, 461–68.

4. Mikhail Bakhtin, *Rabelais and His World* (Bloomington, Ind.: Indiana University Press, 1984), especially 432–74.

5. Op cit. 153, 255–56. Bakhtin comments frequently on what he calls the "wholeness" or collectivity of carnival. For example, "The individual feels that he is an indissoluble part of the collectivity, a member of the people's mass body. In this whole, the individual body ceases to a certain extent to be itself; it is possible, so to say, to exchange bodies, to be renewed (through change of costume and mask)" (255). We might note that this description of the spirit of carnival is similar to Nietzsche's notion of the Dionysian in *The Birth of Tragedy.*

6. Megan Terry, author's note to script of *Mollie Bailey's Traveling Circus: Featuring Scenes from the Life of Mother Jones* (New York: Broadway Play Publishing, 1983).

STEPHANIE ARNOLD

Dissolving the Half Shadows: Japanese American Women Playwrights

The musical play, *Pacific Overtures,* which explores the forced opening of Japan to the West, is probably the most prominent, recent (1976), American theatre piece about Asians. Written by Stephen Sondheim and John Weidman and produced by Harold Prince, *Pacific Overtures* is remarkable as a majority-culture-produced theatre work that gave minority culture members such as Mako and Soon-Teck Oh the opportunity to take major roles in the commercial theatre that were not blatantly stereotypical. However, although women characters are part of the plot, no real women appear on stage until the last scene. All of the women's parts, scheming mothers, noble daughters, prostitutes, are played by men. The appearance of women on stage is created by a male-invented and -executed code of behavior. Actual women are completely absent. One can argue that the concept is based on Japanese tradition, but this is the very tradition and attitude that has denied women a public voice in the East and the West. The tradition of the Japanese male actor creating a persona to represent the Japanese female has been recreated in a dehumanizing way in majority American film and stage images of Asian and Asian American women. The roles may be played by women, but they are merely inhabiting personas created by men to reinforce exploitative stereotypes of submissive and/or erotic women defined only by their relationsips to men. All women share this condition of absence in the traditional theatre. For women of color, the stereotyping has been narrower and more cruel.

The Asian American woman has just begun to speak on stage in her own voice, to act in her own person. Asian American women have been writing plays for a little more than ten years, encouraged by the development of the Asian American theatre movement. The first plays are largely autobiographical, an attempt to document the experiences of the playwrights and the experiences of their mothers. Wakako Yamauchi says, "My mother died and I felt I had to put something down for my daughter to remember me because mothers don't tell their kids everything; but at least if she read my stories, my plays, she'd know what kind of person I am . . . or was.[1]

In Los Angeles in 1965, East West Players, the first Asian American theatre company, was founded by a small group of Japanese, Chinese and Korean American actresses and actors discouraged by the limited and degrading opportunities for them in theatre and film. They began by performing adaptations of Asian stories and traditional Western plays until new plays could be written by developing Asian American playwrights. Mako, the prominent stage and film actor, who played the lead in the Broadway production of *Pacific Overtures,* has been the artistic director of East West Players since its founding.

In 1973, under the auspices of the American Conservatory Theatre in San Francisco, Frank Chin, a Chinese American playwright, started the Asian American Theatre Company and two years later Northwest Asian American Theatre grew out of an umbrella organization called Asian Multi-Media in Seattle. The only other permanent Asian American theatre is Pan Asia Theatre in New York. Frank Chin was the first artistic director of the Asian American Theatre Company in San Francisco and later was replaced by an artistic committee which has been chaired for substantial periods of time by Judy Nihei and then Emilya Cachapero. For much of its existence Asian American Theatre Company (AATC) has been run as a collective in which women have played a major role. AATC has recently reorganized and returned to a single artistic director, at this writing, Lane Nishikawa. Bea Kiyohara has been director of Northwest Asian American Theatre since 1978. All three theatres produce full seasons of five plays or more each year with various community outreach activities.

The first production of a play written by an Asian American woman was *When We Were Young* by Momoko Iko in 1974 at East West Players, supported by a Rockefeller Foundation Playwright-in-Residence grant administered by East West Players. Although relations between the administrative staff at East West Players and women playwrights have been strained at times, a significant number of playwriting grants at East West Players have gone to women playwrights including Momoko Iko, Wakako Yamauchi, and Karen Yamashita.

Although Asian American women have been writing plays for only thirteen years and East West Players has been in existence for a little more than twenty years, the Asian American theatres are part of a history of theatre in the West representing the diverse populations of this area for over a century and much more if one includes Native American rituals. Traditional theatre histories usually consider the origins of theatre in the West as the coming of Eastern players to tour the gold rush camps and any significant, subsequent developments as tours or transplants of an English–New York model. Professional Mexican theatres that were led by women were touring the Southwest in the mid–nineteenth century and later Italian and Chinese theatres were founded in California.[2] Now, the Asian American theatres are part of a vibrant diversity of theatre throughout the West that includes chicano theatre, black theatre, and feminist theatre as well as what could be termed traditional anglo theatre.

While the participation of women from a broad range of Asian Pacific backgrounds continues to grow in the Asian American theatre, Japanese American women have made the primary contribution as playwrights thus far. Playwrights Wakako Yamauchi, Momoko Iko, and Velina Houston write about the experience of two waves of immigrants, the Issei women (first generation): those who came before World War II and were incarcerated, and those who came after the war as war brides. In the Issei plays the writers document their mothers' histories, dramatizing modes of survival. The playwrights also write about their own experiences as Nisei, second generation, in plays that focus on the psychological ramifications of youth terminated by the camp/war experience. In the Issei plays, Wakako Yamauchi and Velina Houston write about isolated women whose strength comes from the mother/child relationship. In the Nisei plays of Yamauchi and Momoko Iko, the playwrights examine the uneasy relationships between women and men whose reliance on traditional roles has been shattered by the war.

Wakako Yamauchi grew up as a farm child in California's Imperial Valley in the 1930s and was interned at Poston, Arizona, with her family during World War II. She has written eight plays in addition to her highly regarded short stories. *And the Soul Shall Dance, 12-1-A, The Music Lessons,* and *The Memento* have had productions at East West Players, Asian American Theatre Company (San Francisco), Northwest Asian American Theatre and Pan Asia Theatre in New York. *The Music Lessons* has had a reading at the Public Theatre in New York and *The Memento* a production at the Yale Repertory Theatre. *And the Soul Shall Dance* was selected as one of the ten best regional plays of 1976–77 and was produced on PBS in 1978. Yamauchi has had several major playwriting stipends granted through East West Players and the Mark Taper Forum and for 1988, a Brody Arts Award.

Momoko Iko was born into a farm family in the Yakima Valley in Washington. After internment her family moved to Chicago as did many other internees including Wakako Yamauchi. The Japanese were forced to relocate to

the Midwest and East upon leaving the camps because people were allowed
to leave the camps before the war's end only if they had work and the Japanese were restricted from returning to the West Coast during the War. Momoko Iko did not return to the West Coast until the early 1980s.

Velina Houston is the daughter of a black American soldier and a Japanese war bride. Houston, who was born in Japan, grew up in Kansas, where
the American government sent many of the men in the military who had married Japanese women after World War II. She has written a trilogy based on
her parents' lives, *Asa Ga Kimashita* (*Morning Has Broken*), *American Dreams,*
and *Tea* and, more recently, *Thirst,* which examines the relationship between
three Japanese American sisters after their mother dies. Houston's plays have
also had productions at the Asian American Theatres. In 1987 *Tea* was produced at Stage II of the Manhattan Theatre Club and is scheduled for a 1988
production at the Cassius Carter Theatre at the Old Globe in San Diego.
American Dreams has been produced at the Negro Ensemble Company in New
York.

While Yamauchi and Iko write from within the Japanese American community, Houston writes of Japanese women in an integrated segment of society. Together the plays chronicle the struggle of Japanese and Japanese American women for a self-determined identity in the face of shifting cultural values,
racism, economic oppression, and patriarchal family structures.

Japanese women immigrating to the United States were met by a blatant
racism fueled by Japan's defeat of Russia in 1905 and exploding with Japan's
bombing of Pearl Harbor. Economic exploitation of Asian immigrants was
conveniently supported by racist attitudes as were denials of the rights to citizenship and the purchase of property. The immigrant Japanese women were
caught between conflicting cultures and hostile governments. They came
from a tradition-bound society that had locked the doors against emigration
for centuries. The Japanese were as critical of those who left as the Americans
were unwelcoming. In *Shirley Temple, Hotcha-cha* by Wakako Yamauchi, Japanese Americans (Nisei) visiting Japan before World War II are stoned and in-
sulted.[3] In *Tea* Velina Houston writes of the bitterness of both Japan and the
United States toward the Japanese women who married American soldiers.

> We are a casualty the Japanese do not care to count.
> Excess baggage Amerika does not want to carry.
> And so the country watches as thousands of us leave Japan behind.
> And it aches.
> And it cries.
> And it hopes we will not be lucky.

Or brave.
Or accepted.
Or rich.
But in between the hate they have for us.
The disdain.
The contempt.[4]

In the plays of Yamauchi and Houston, there is a sense that the women who came were independent, adventurous, or were strong enough to have committed some transgression that made their families eager for them to emigrate. Of the last group, even though their arrival in the United States was forced upon them, it was their rebelliousness that prompted the family action. These are women who set themselves apart. The women in these plays are often alone or are presented as they struggle to define themselves rather than fit a pattern of their husbands' or the larger society's creation.

In *And the Soul Shall Dance,* about Issei farmers in California's Imperial Valley in the 1930s, Emiko is regarded as an aberration. She observes none of the traditional formalities or courtesies such as serving visitors tea or making polite conversation. More significantly she will not provide companionship to her husband or his daughter (her niece) by a previous marriage and makes clear that she participates in sexual relations reluctantly. She is sullen and withdrawn. Her husband beats her and she makes no effort to hide the bruises. Sometimes they drink together, an illegal liquor that they brew, and then drunkenly fight each other.

Emiko hangs on to an inner ideal of love and beauty which allows her to resist the severe circumstances and abuse. If she gave in in any way to her husband or tried to make the best of immigrant farm life, it would mean compromising her sense of herself which she must keep intact to survive. She refuses to accept her parents' and her husband's view of her as property. Because she was a beautiful young woman, Emiko was groomed by her parents for marriage to a rich man, thus there were lessons in music and dance. But she fell in love with someone her husband suspects was Korean or *etta*[5] and by physically consummating the relationship she became worthless, damaged goods. She was therefore sent to California to marry her dead sister's husband.

Oka, the husband, has also been badly damaged by the economic and social structures of Japan and then the United States. As an impoverished young man, he was apprenticed to Emiko's and her sister's family where the harsh labor was accompanied by constant degradation from the sisters' father. Oka chooses emigration as an escape from humiliation. He is scarred by the economic exploitation of Japan and the racism of the United States. But although both Emiko and Oka suffer from inequitable economic and social structures in Japan and the United States, Oka is still in a position to regard Emiko as his possession. When she claims some control over her body, "just because I let you . . .", Oka scoffs, "Let me (*obscene gesture*) you? I can do what I want with you. Your father palmed you off on me—like a dog or cat—an animal. . . ."[6] He takes the money Emiko has saved to return to Japan and buys American-style clothes, a permanent wave, and movie magazines for his newly arrived daughter who has been raised by the grandparents in Japan.

The final image of *And the Soul Shall Dance* is of Emiko dancing alone in the desert watched at a distance by the girl, Masako. Dressed in a kimono and carrying a branch of sage she sings

> Akai kuchibiru
> Kappu ni yosete
> Aoi sake nomya
> Kokoro ga odoru
> Kurai yoru no yume
> Setsunasa yo
> Aoi sake nomya
> Yume mo odoru
>
> The soul shall dance
> Red lips against a glass
> Drink the green wine
>
> In the dark night
> Dreams are unbearable
> Drink the green wine
> And the dreams will dance[7]

Emiko remains focused on her inner vision, a fantasy she has created to sustain herself.

And the Soul Shall Dance was written in 1976, *Tea* by Velina Houston, in 1983. They are set twenty years apart, *Soul* in the 1930s and *Tea* in the 1950s. In *Tea*, Houston creates another woman whose behavior is in sharp contrast to the "nice, Japaneezy"[8] women around her who "never say something is bad, never express anger towards someone, hold it inside, keep smiling and nodding and bowing."[9] Himiko smokes cigars, drinks, wears a blonde wig, and uses obscene language. She went to work in a dance hall in Japan after the war and then found herself rejected because she worked in a less than respectable occupation. Like Emiko she was controlled by her father.

Himiko. Here, father. Here's all the money I made at the cabaret this week. No, I swear I didn't keep any of it for me. All for you. . . . Father, may I come home next weekend? No, of course. People would talk. They all know I've been working at the cabaret. I'd miss work too. I know you need the money.[10]

Because she cannot go home, Himiko marries the Puerto Rican American soldier by whom she becomes pregnant. Her husband proves to be racist and abusive. When they move to the United States he tries to keep her from maintaining Japanese traditions and from leaving the house. She is to be his spiritual and physical prisoner. He frankly claims he married her to have a "good maid."[11] In *And the Soul Shall Dance* Emiko expresses her anger by withdrawing. In *Tea* Himiko verbalizes her anger.

I wasted my life in this stupid Kansas hick town. Not Kansas City, but Kansas. The state of mind. Do you know where Kansas is? In the crotch of the United States. Somebody should have warned us. Junction City, Kansas, where the Kansas River meets the Smoky Hill River and where the Japanese meet hell.[12]

Emiko dances in the desert by herself. Himiko kills her husband.

Emiko and Himiko are both Issei who carry a struggle against externally imposed role from Japan to the United States. Each has stepped far outside the prescribed role and away from the community to preserve a sense of autonomy. The limitations presented by the new circumstances serve to intensify the terms of the fight.

A third overtly rebellious character emerges in Momoko Iko's postwar play, *Flowers and Household Gods,* set in the early 1970s, about the lingering effect of the camp experience on the Nisei. Three adult children of Issei parents gather for the funeral of their mother. Mazie, the younger sister of Mas, now in his fifties, and Junko, in her early forties, rejects what she sees as her brother's and sister's reverence for misunderstood Japanese values.

Mazie. You want to make mama a saint and put her into a museum . . . the noble self-sacrificing, uncomplaining, gentle Japanese woman. . . . She never chose to live in the half-shadows of American life.[13]

She also rejects the reconstruction of family hierarchy based on a social order that ended in the camps. She claims the camps "froze Japanese American val-

ues to 1941 adolescence" and accuses her brother of spending his energy asserting himself as the "captain of a non-existent ship."[14]

Mazie has removed herself from the accepted behavior of the Japanese
American community and physically distances herself from her family. She has
not married, has no children, and will not accept the code of "obligation"
to family members that the other characters claim guides their actions. She
denounces the concept of *gaman* (endurance) and *giri* (indebtedness) as barren.
She has spent time in Mexico in a community of artists in San Miguel Allende
not only searching for a means of articulating her alienation but also trying
to break the hold of the past. Mazie lacks the decisiveness of Himiko or
Emiko, perhaps because her situation is less hostile than theirs. But clearly
the camp experience has added a layer of confusion to the difficult question
of identity already facing members of a minority, immigrant group. Mazie
is at the beginning of a process of taking selectively from her Japanese past
in order to construct a new reality.

The playwrights present a number of different situations in which the
intersection of Japanese and American cultures produce conditions that isolate
the women characters. We have many impressions of what it meant to be in
an internment camp for a Japanese American during World War II: loss of
freedom; loss of any sense of equal protection before the laws; loss of life's
work, savings, property, business; humiliation. In Wakako Yamauchi's play
about the camp experience entitled *12-1-A* (a barrack number), Mrs. Tanaka,
a widow with two children says, "This is the first time I don't worry about
shoes, clothes. . . ."[15] Mrs. Tanaka is not a shallow woman. She understands
the implications and consequences of Japanese American imprisonment. Ultimately her son refuses to enlist in the American armed forces and she chooses
to be transferred to Tule Lake with him for possible deportation to Japan. But
her life in the United States has been spent "alone, going to work in restaurant every night, every night come home, soak feet, count tip money"[16]
in order to support her family.

Mrs. Tanaka's widowhood may reflect the unbalanced immigration of
Japanese to the United States, before exclusion ended all immigration from
1925–52, an imbalance that resulted in a generation of marriages in which
husbands were considerably older than their wives.[17] But there is a recurrent
pattern in Yamauchi's and Houston's plays of men escaping harsh circumstances through alcohol and death. In the barrack next door to the Tanakas',
Mrs. Ichioka's husband is dying of an unidentified illness, but which the
other characters recognize as a broken heart.

> *Mitch.* You say it's the water that makes him sick. His heart's breaking, man, don't you know?[18]

Wakako Yamauchi's father died at the camp in Poston, Arizona, after the news came that the Japanese Americans would be released. She says it is her father dying in Mrs. Ichioka's room. "He just couldn't start again."[19]

These were men who may have struggled as impoverished farmers or apprentices in Japan before they went first to Hawaii as laborers and then on to California to work for subsistence wages, where they were unable to buy their own land and were aliens ineligible for citizenship. The loss of what they had built up and the defeat of Japan proves to be overwhelming for Yamauchi's Issei men. The Japanese male conditioning is too rigid for the change in circumstances. Whatever the combination of age, racism, economic disappointment, and loss of pride that defeats the male characters, the women assume the responsibility for their families' survival while the men abandon the struggle.

In *The Music Lessons,* set in 1935, Yamauchi further explores the life of a widowed Issei, Chizuko, who now wearing her dead husband's work clothes, does all the farm work while she raises her three children. The husband, an alcoholic, fell or jumped into the canal and drowned.

> *Chizuko.* He never paid attention to them — to any of us. Well, I guess this work wasn't suited for him. . . . When I left Japan I never knew it would be like this. The babies came so fast . . . and me, by myself, no mother, no sister — no one — to help . . . Never thought my life would be so hard. I don't know what it is to be a woman anymore . . . to laugh . . . to be soft . . . to talk nice.[20]

In the first play of Velina Houston's triology, *Asa Ga Kimashita (Morning Has Broken),* which takes place in Japan after the war, Fusae, wife and mother (modelled on Houston's grandmother), runs the family hotel and related business while her husband, Kiheida, retreats to his *sake.*

> *Fusae.* You will take care of this? Since the war has been over, you haven't taken care of anything.[21]

With the marriage of their daughter, Setsuko, to a black American soldier, Kiheida commits suicide. Setsuko, whose life is traced through Houston's trilogy, is affected by a similar pattern. She becomes an immigrant widow raising her two daughters alone in Kansas. In *Tea* Setsuko's daughter says, "The war destroyed our fathers."[22] As an enlisted black man, Velina Houston's father was sent immediately to the front in World War II where he was acutely aware of his position as a man of color killing people of color. Attempting to numb the self-loathing that followed, he became an alcoholic who subsequently became mentally absent from his family even before his premature death.[23] And finally in Momoko Iko's *Flowers and Household Gods,* Mazie mourns the death of her mother who sustained her "cause Papa was too hurt and angry to do anything but drink."[24]

In *12-1-A,* Wamauchi's play about internment, a fundamental part of the texture of the play is the wind. At the beginning of the play the characters are physically thrown together by a dust storm that blots out the light and makes movement outside impossible. Throughout the play the wind howls and the dust swirls. Here, as in *And the Soul Shall Dance,* there is a sense of great distances. The camp is set in a physical and emotional void, cut off from contact with the outside world. In *And the Soul Shall Dance* and *The Music Lessons,* both set in the Imperial Valley, the characters' houses are remote. Each home is a world unto itself. The vast space reinforces the emotional isolation the characters feel. If warmth and support do not come from within the household, they do not exist. These are not plays in which women characters are sustained by women friends. The conditions of the land and the endless work required to eke out a marginal existence combined with the characters' inclinations to turn inward to family rather than outward to neighbors creates an intense loneliness.

The isolation that Yamauchi symbolizes spatially is cultural as well as emotional and physical. The characters are cut off from Japan as they are cut off from each other. The racial resentment that culminates in the camps separates the Japanese from the rest of America. As the prewar immigrants are segregated in the camps, the postwar immigrants are segregated in isolated military posts like Fort Riley, Kansas. Emiko in *And the Soul Shall Dance* is cut off from the world of *natori,* ceremony and tradition. Himiko in *Tea* is stopped from buying tea and rice. In *American Dreams* Setsuko is locked in a dark room to prevent her contaminating the family; in *Tea* Himiko is locked in the house in her husband's effort to enslave her.

The isolation of the war brides (*Tea*) is particularly acute because not only are they cut off from Japan and America, but many have been rejected by their own families and their husbands' families. They also do not have the opportunity to join the Japanese American community. Each feels the need to create an entirely new and insulated world which includes their non-Japanese husbands and Amerasian children.

> We survive
> Not as Amerikans
> Or as Japanese Amerikans
> But as new Japanese in Amerika
> In our own new world we built.[25]

The characters speak of living in shells, in silent gardens. The women acknowledge that only sorrow brings them together. "Whenever anything bad has happened to a Japanese 'war bride' we have tea and realize how little we know about each other." Setsuko regrets her inability to comfort Himiko. "She was Japanese. One of us. I like her very much. I wish I could have told her, just once."[26]

The position of the Nisei women after World War II is deceptive. They have lived through the obvious shocks of immigration, the economic deprivation of their childhoods, the imprisonment during their adolescence. But instead of being less isolated, the plays suggest that their separation is more profound. They are not only caught between cultures, but suspended between generations, slipping into a kind of invisibility of frozen smiles and town-and-country clothes. The camps have inspired a self-doubt requiring endless proof of satisfactory Americanization. Relationships with husbands hollow into formalities with little understanding or common purpose. Relationships with children become vague and unsatisfying.

In *Flowers and Household Gods,* Fred, an upwardly mobile Nisei real estate salesman in all-white Albuquerque, New Mexico, describes his wife as "the perfect Japanese-American mother [who] got our kids everything from Playskool educational toys to Adidas to Head skis, . . . and the future . . . BMW dreams and Nikon zoom lenses and mother-coddled arrogance."[27] The Nisei women miss the earthiness and fun of their own childhoods but can't create a feeling of connection in their magazine-picture-perfect kitchens. They see themselves as part of their husbands' acquisitions, subservient to men who are re-establishing their self-esteem by becoming economically successful in a white world "so they can act like cocks of the walk, one of a kind, special, while girls get traded in for new models."[28] Yamauchi has written a play about the long term effects of camp on the Nisei generation entitled, *Not a Through Street,* in which paralyzed characters live on a dead-end street.

What tempers the isolation of the Issei women is the relationship between mothers and children and particularly mothers and daughters. The Issei women have a fierce obligation to family which allows them to cope with extraordinary conditions in order to provide for their families: Mrs. Tanaka who sees camp as a vacation after the exhausting struggle to make ends meet; Himiko who in spite of a lifetime of accumulated suffering commits suicide only after her daughter's death. More than obligation is the mutual love that sustains children and mothers alike. In *The Music Lessons* Chizuko is left with the burden of having alienated the daughter she dearly loves through the effort to make a life for her.

And the Soul Shall Dance offers contrasting views of the destructive relationship of Emiko and Oka and the warmth in the Murata family. The Murata parents and their daughter Masako weather the disappointments and deprivation of immigrant farm life through the comfort of each other's company. Hana finds deep satisfaction in the closeness of daily interaction with her daughter. In a few carefully selected, understated details, Hana demonstrates the pride and regard she has for her daughter. "Your hair is so black and straight . . . nice."[29]

Masako, supported by her mother's love, is at the same time drawn by the intensity of Emiko's feelings which suggest a poetic sense of life beyond the drudgery of desert existence. Emiko, erratic and rebellious; Hana, practical, consistent, present; Masako will grow up to recreate both women's experiences, to find the survival instincts of both inspiring. For the Nisei, like Masako the child and Mazie the adult, it is their own resources, their own determination to pursue a new sense of self beyond their Japanese past and American present that allows them to transcend the loss of any certainty brought on by the camps.

A clearly articulated social critique emerges from the plays as a group. The family is seen as the only significant social unit. National systems (i.e., Japanese traditions, American institutional racism: ineligibility for citizenship, ineligibility to buy property, forced incarceration, forced relocation) influence what becomes of the families, but the families are not examined as part of a larger community because of their physical and cultural isolation. Even the community that might have been formed in the camps is sharply divided by the issue of conscription into the American military. Each individual within the family must chart her own territory, make her own way.

The plays present a clear indictment of patriarchal attitudes which regard women as property and military victory as necessary to the successful male self-image. While the plays as a group place the struggles of the women characters in the foreground, the destructive effect of militarism, racism, and economic exploitation on both the male and female characters is continuously apparent. The characters are seen against the coordinates of two clashing patriarchal societies. However, the social critique forms the context rather than the focus of most of the work. The plays serve as documentation of individual histories, in part representative of Issei and Nisei experience in America, but only beginning to eliminate the obscurity of a people and time that have gone largely unrecorded.

NOTES

The material for this paper was collected over a period of years including attendance at performances at East West Players, Los Angeles; Asian American Theatre Company, San Francisco; and Northwest Asian American Theatre, Seattle, and interviews with playwrights, producers and performers from all three theatres. Since only two plays by Asian American women have been published to date, *And the Soul Shall Dance* by Wakako Yamauchi in *West Coast Plays 11/12* (California Theatre Council) and Act I of *The Gold Watch* by Momoko Iko in *Aiiieeeee!* edited by Frank Chin, my research has been greatly enhanced by the generosity of the playwrights in providing me with copies of their scripts. I regret not including a lengthier discussion of the work of Momoko Iko, but only limited access to her work was available.

1. Author's interview with Wakako Yamauchi, April 27, 1985.

2. See *Ethnic Theatre in the United States,* ed. Maxine Seller (Westport, Conn.: Greenwood Press, 1983), for discussions of the Mexican and Italian theatres.

3. Wakako Yamauchi, *Shirley Temple, Hotcha-cha,* manuscript, 10.

4. Velina Houston, *Tea,* manuscript, 22.

5. In the Tonzai *Times* 1, no. 8 (May 1985): 7, J. K. Yamamoto explains that prejudice against those whose "jobs involved contact with death, disease or animal by-products" began during the Edo or Tokugawa period (1600–1868) and developed into the segregation of a class of people called *eta* or, more recently, *burakumin,* "regarded as being lowly, dirty and inferior to other Japanese."

6. Wakako Yamauchi, *And the Soul Shall Dance,* in *West Coast Plays 11/12,* California Theatre Council, 138.

7. *And the Soul Shall Dance,* 163.

8. *Tea,* 6.

9. *Tea,* 32.

10. *Tea,* 42–43.

11. *Tea,* 5.

12. *Tea,* 6.

13. Momoko Iko, *Flowers and Household Gods,* manuscript, 53.

14. *Flowers and Household Gods,* 73.

15. Wakako Yamauchi, *12-1-A,* manuscript, 19.

16. *12-1-A,* 19.

17. In the *Politics of Prejudice* (Berkeley: University of California Press, 1977), Roger Daniels reports "statistical [support] can be found in the data compiled when the West Coast Japanese were incarcerated during the Second World War. At that time most of the Issei males were between fifty and sixty-four years of age, and most of the Issei females were between forty and fifty-four. The major group of the Nisei

were between twenty and twenty-four years of age. When these and other data are plotted on a chart, it becomes apparent that there was a 'missing' generation of Japanese, i.e., the generation which, under conditions of a normal population–sex ratio, would have been born in the years 1905–15" (14).

18. *12-1-A*, 78.

19. Author's interviews with Wakako Yamauchi, April 1982 and August 1985.

20. Wakako Yamauchi, *The Music Lessons*, 38.

21. Velina Houston, *Asa Ga Kimashita*, 5.

22. *Tea*, 48.

23. Author's interviews with Velina Houston, October 1985 and January 1988.

24. *Flowers and Household Gods*, 64.

25. *Tea*, 55–56.

26. *Tea*, 62.

27. *Flowers and Household Gods*, 90.

28. *Flowers and Household Gods*, 88.

29. *And the Soul Shall Dance*, 162.

ANITA PLATH HELLE

Re-Presenting Women Writers Onstage: A Retrospective to the Present

> It would be ambitious beyond my daring, I thought, looking about the shelves for books that were not there, to suggest to the students of those famous colleges that they should rewrite history, though I own that it often seems a little queer as it is, lop-sided; but why should they add a supplement to history? calling it, of course, by some inconspicuous name so that women might figure there without impropriety? For one often catches a glimpse of them in the lives of the great, whisking away into the background, concealing, I sometimes think, a wink, a laugh, perhaps a tear.
>
> —Virginia Woolf, *A Room of One's Own*

Considering the complexity of the woman writer's relationship to language and literary history, Virginia Woolf speculated that nothing less than an alternative form of history would be required to catch a glimpse of her.[1] I argue here that the creation of a new literary history remains at issue in a number of biographical dramas about women writers. The current popularity of the biographical genre alone might make it appear that women's role in cultural production is at least being recognized, for we now have biographical dramas about women writers from Emily Dickinson to Gertrude Stein and Sylvia Plath. But do women become subjects of their own discourse when they are re-presented on stage? Exactly what is being commemorated? And for whom?

The territory is vexed with difficulty, for the hierarchical opposition of man to woman in language and culture has most often precluded the possibility of alternative female self-representations. In short, the stage has belonged to him. For this reason, I find the most satisfying examples of historical revisionism to be those in which women onstage actively question and resist the context of assumptions by which authority and authorship are gendered and maintained. But this does not mean that all authors, subjects, and identities are being swept away with a deconstructive turn. Biographical dramas about women writers are particularly illuminating for they recognize the possibility of the female subject as a fact of experience: women *have* written and continue to write poems, novels, plays, even when it has been difficult. For the same reason—in order to guarantee the possibility of a female writer-subject—it would appear that feminist theatre must suppose a relation of identity between the women on stage and a recognizable historical personage. If biographical drama is to effect change, it would seem for the time being that the identity of actor and proper name—"Gertrude Stein," for example—must be supposed. In the manner and effect of the plays, spectators are prompted to move from the assumption of an identity in language to reexamine and re-imagine the meanings *she* creates onstage.

Dramatic treatment of the theme of female authorship is a twentieth-century phenomenon, emerging alongside the modernist challenge to canons and periodicities, but reaching well beyond modernisms's apocalyptic claims. Nineteenth-century history looms large in two important precedents, Susan Glaspell's *Alison's House* (1930) and Gertrude Stein's *The Mother of Us All* (1947), minefields of misogynistic myths about "anomalous" women writers and the naturalized role of women in culture.[2] Many more recent plays appear to spring directly from the politics and culture of the current women's movement, reflecting the increasingly broad influence of feminist criticism and theory in popularizing lives and work of women writers, as well as calling attention to the commonalities women share whether they consider themselves geniuses or not. I've also read and seen performed a number of innovative and experimental scripts fashioned by actresses or other creative women new to the playwriting business;[3] these give added emphasis to the notion that theory may be playing an advance role, helping women break into theatre and creating audiences more receptive and informed about alternative, imaginary, utopian visions.

Biographical dramas create opportunities for challenging the context of assumptions that constitute the fiction of male authorship, for reasons having uniquely to do with the difference between the construction of the subject in the text and on stage. In semiotic terms, authorship in both cases might be described as a symbolic production of subjectivity, articulated in relation to points of reference, terms, and analogies that come to be taken for granted as defining woman.[4] But as feminist literary criticism has helped us understand, the constituting analogy for textual representation is a masculine term that predetermines just which sex an author should be. If the dominant paradigm for textuality is the masculine subject as father-author-god, his feminine counterpart by default must conform to the blank space of the page—a space in which woman is written but cannot write herself.[5] Furthermore, since difference is one of the ways we constitute meaning, the hierarchy of male presence and female absence is problematically kept in play through the processes of reading and identification.

The materiality of the stage offers unique opportunities for breaking out of the textual construct and context of masculine authority in two ways. First, women's voices and bodies may be part of what Teresa de Lauretis, by analogy to the semiotics of film, has described as a "cultural set-up." This is to say, women's voices and bodies occupy gendered discursive roles in relation to points of articulation and terms of reference which regulate the degree of freedom and the kinds of meanings that may be ascribed to their acts. But women's voices and bodies are not necessarily fixed in this set-up. What women say and do onstage may also contradict, exceed, or otherwise mark off a space of difference between the static symbolic construct, "women," and "women" as historical subjects.[6] Second, theatre sets up conditions for identification between actor and spectator that are different from those that obtain in the relation of texts to other texts that confer authority and meaning upon them. The identity of female spectators as actual historical beings, as de Lauretis has proposed, is certain in the sense that what we see and hear allows us to be caught up and moved along as "subjects-in-process"[7] through a series of spatial and temporal positions. All the more intriguing, then, is what happens or fails to happen when a woman appears in the place of the writer on stage and offers her own version of history.

In many of the plays under consideration here, something *has* already happened—a woman stands as a "figure for" a recognizably famous author. But it does not automatically follow that the woman writer becomes the subject of her own discourse by being thematized into the central character role. This becomes especially clear when historically specific discourses are scrutinized as part of the play. For example, in William Luce's popular monodrama, *The Belle of Amherst* (1976)[8] the point of view is set up through domestic space and assignments given to women within it. The play appeals by offering an intimate view of the writer at home, celebrating the artistic sensibility behind the hermetic mask of seclusion. But when Julie Harris places a morsel of her homemade cake on the end of a fork and tilts it toward the audience while reciting her recipe, we are being dished up a very traditional formula for feminine success. The trouble is not so much that Dickinson can cook as that the representation never exceeds the domestic frame. What might at least have been, in Dickinsonian irony, "The Soul selects her own Society— /

Then—shuts the Door"[9] becomes a cheery parting salvo, "And when next
we meet—I'll give you my recipe for gingerbread!"[10] In an even more blatant
way, narrative omniscience aborts possibility in *Stevie; a play* (1977) by Hugh
Whitemore. An anonymous male figure narrates the action from one side of
the stage, and at other times plays the role of Stevie's friend. As we watch
with and through him, Stevie appears most "lovable" when she is fluttering
about stage helplessly and childishly dependent, a sad-eyed, rumpled "elderly
Shirley Temple":[11] but what else could we expect from the perfect gothic
set-up, a narrative that superimposes masculine control over a hapless female?

Just how difficult it may be to challenge the semiotics of authorship
within the canons of historical realism is apparent in Susan Glaspell's *Alison's
House*.[12] The sexual and political content is very much on the surface here,
for the audience, through the characters, must decide whether Dickinson's
"quarrel with the world" should be decided according to the nineteenth-
century standards of bourgeois morality or the more permissive values (presumably) of the 1920s. Dickinson never appears on stage, a move that may
have been dictated in part by circumstance. Arthur Waterman claims that
Glaspell created the play after reading Genevieve Taggard's *The Life and Mind
of Emily Dickinson,* one of the first biographies of the poet that attempted a
sympathetic presentation of Dickinson as a passionate woman. The Dickinson
estate refused permission to quote directly from Dickinson's poems or to use
her name.[13] Consequently, Dickinson is Alison Stanhope and the Amherst
setting is transposed into a variation on the Glaspell homestead in Davenport,
Iowa. To an extent, Glaspell makes the conditions work for her, using the
play to create a context that demands a new kind of social awareness of wom-
en's needs, even where clear solutions don't emerge. But there can be no more
obvious indication that Emily's "world" of authority is a gender-divided one
than the silence and invisibility of the woman writer whose destiny is to be
decided in the course of the play.

When the play opens, Emily/Alison has been dead eighteen years, but
the household is still organized spatially according to the grammar of nineteenth-
century family life. In his first act Father Stanhope, the male head of the
household, decrees that his daughter's room is off-limits to change: everything
must remain as it is, in spite of the fact that the family is moving. As the
characters pack their belongings, considering what they must hold on to or
give up, we also perceive a shift in the sexual ideologies that have kept women
in their place. The female characters divide into two groups: good women,
like Alison/Emily and a favorite daughter-in-law, who have presumably sac-
rificed sexual expression to retain moral superiority; and the "new women"

of the 1920s, notably Alison's niece, Elsa Stanhope, a restless spirit for whom the free exercise of sexual will is identified with the new ethic of personal autonomy. Each family member is in his or her own way haunted by the notion that Alison/Emily's "house" contains a hidden manuscript, buried evidence of a past affair with a married man. Uncontained fires burning mysteriously offstage in Alison's bedroom hint at the chaos that such knowledge might unleash. The Stanhope patriarch jealously guards Emily's virginal memory, while the new women in the play urge that the manuscript be brought into the open, arguing that Alison's creative gifts belong to the world because they speak for women.

Glaspell's clear grasp of the anomaly of nineteenth-century female authorship, the undergirding sexual double-standard, and the controversial status of the "new woman," caught in the cultural crossfire — all these lead us to expect a more challenging ending. Glaspell's careful adherence to the classic dramaturgical model returns us twenty-four hours later to Alison's room, where Elsa and her father are reconciled. Here, questions of female identity, authorship, and difference are finally reduced to the same old difference, the opposition man/woman on masculine terms. The manuscript containing the damaging evidence is eventually found and entrusted to Elsa, but only after she makes peace with the family. The quiet fires burning in Alison's bedroom are meant to impart a domestic warmth and ease which has eluded the family so far, but the message is clear: it's up to women to provide the moral glue of human relationships. A study in sexually compromised and compromising positions, *Alison's House* restates the divisions of experience with which it began: Alison/Emily could never have "dwelled in possibility" within this rigidly prescribed role.

The Mother of Us All (MUA)[14] is one of Gertrude Stein's serious comedies, an opera portraying all she most deeply loved and bitterly resented about her native land and culture: its noise, vastness, ambition, and the troublesome fathers she wished would let her speak her mind. For Stein, theater was an expository mode, an opportunity to consider history, language, gender as ideas that could be questioned through the immediacy of performance. Of course, Susan B. Anthony is primarily known as a suffrage leader, not a writer. But the play is important to this discussion because Anthony's reputation as a speechmaker on behalf of constitutional representation for women is just the sort of semantic pun Stein could use to exploit the possibilities of rebellious play on self-representation. Stein's serious subject, then, is the politics of self-representation, for she had often seen herself as a missing person in the defining structures of literary history: "I always wanted to be historical, from almost a baby on, I felt that way about it."[15] As if to underscore the link between the biography of Susan B. Anthony and the autobiography of Gertrude Stein, Stein includes a cameo self-portrait, a bit part for the young "G.S.," who comments on the difficulty of fathers.

Stein's analysis of dominance in representational structures, social and linguistic, is presented through a cubistic composition of gendered speaking places, public for men and private for women. These spaces have implications for who can speak to whom, and for what purposes. Fathers and authors of the constitution such as John Quincy Adams and Daniel Webster can speak on any occasion for everyone. On numerous occasions it is also clear they are speaking self-interestedly, as they lecture on the pursuit of life, liberty, and happiness, while women are denied votes. Female speakers transgress a boundary when they appear in public spaces to speak on behalf of themselves, for they are in a contradictory position as nonsubjects in a man-made space. This contradiction is most apparent when Susan B. mounts a public platform and attempts to speak on behalf of women. Dispiritedly, she realizes she is addressing "those who are not there who are not there who are not there" (*MUA*, 182). Among themselves, women in the play constitute a discourse community muted within the dominant culture. Susan B. and her companion Anne (an obvious allusion to Alice Toklas) can address each other only when they are alone, and during interludes of the play. Thus the play works its way back to a deadlock.

Stein's "revenge" against history[16] is finally to use language paradoxically against itself. She does this first of all by carnivalizing male speech, undermining lofty messages in comic verbal compositions, parodies, and burlesques. A particularly hilarious chorus of "The Three V.I.P.s" (Andrew G., Thaddeus Stevens, and Daniel Webster) boasts:

> We you see we V.I.P. very important to any one who can hear or you can see, just we three, of course lots of others but just we three just we three we are the chorus of V.I.P. Very important persons to anyone who can hear or see. (*MUA*, 178)

Finally, Stein also mocks those who make up the community of memory, for in giving too much power to the past, she fears female biography will be reappropriated. In the end, the various characters clump together around a statue commemorating suffrage effort. We are now in the present, and Susan B. is dead; but time is always slipping away and Stein wants her language to be able to outstrip history. Susan B.'s voice has the last word, seven times speak-

A scene from Salli Lovelarkin's *Maud Gonne: A Terrible Beauty Is Born*. (Photo by Jay Bachemin.)

ing and lapsing into silence: "My long life, my long life" (*MUA,* 202). The tone is akin to a dirge; but the final speech is also a song which celebrates and justifies Stein's choice of expatriation, the only position from which she could imagine having her say.

In a number of contemporary plays, we can be more hopeful that women are constructing their own stages for semiotic production. This seems most likely to happen when: (1) the stage becomes a meditative, reflective, intersubjective space where difference can be broken down, analyzed, and reinterpreted; and (2) texts themselves are broken into or given subversive readings in performance. In these plays, it is not the author who disappears with the deconstruction; rather, it is the political context that shapes our perception of authority and textuality that is exposed. Salli Lovelarkin's Cincinnati production of *Maud Gonne: A Terrible Beauty Is Born* (1987) is in some ways typical of an attempt to combine deconstructive technique with reconstructive purposes. The script is only one ingredient in a multimedia mix that helps us disentangle our memory of Maud Gonne from the image of her as demonic muse in W. B. Yeats's celebrated poems. Maud and Yeats occupy separate spaces: as Yeats reads, Maud Gonne recites her own mystical meditations on the Celtic past from another platform, apart and above. History goes on around them, and what is more important, it keeps on moving, through a series of spatially and temporally dislocated frames. Gonne's identity is never fixed within a single frame, but appears thematically and structurally interwoven. We see her struggles repeated as those of Ireland's women, dishonored figures from Celtic folklore as well as ordinary women, ragpickers and political prisoners.

In Rose Leiman Goldemberg's *Letters Home* (*LH,* 1979)[17] the stage is already an intersubjective and intertextual space. According to Goldemberg, performance takes place "in the mind of Aurelia Plath . . . and in the audience, as Aurelia, in telling and remembering her story, struggles for and achieves understanding," (*LH,* n.p.). The script is ingeniously fashioned from two disparate but related texts: Sylvia Plath's letters to her mother and Aurelia Plath's introduction to the posthumously collected *Letters Home,* intended to set the record straight after more than a decade of Plath criticism dominated by an interest in the daddy-complex. In fact, neither the mother's or the daughter's version turns out to tell all. Rather, the transformation of a naive reading of the texts into a complex performance opens up vantage points from which we can analyze the political content and contexts of their relationship. Goldemberg's drama persuasively demonstrates the truth of Nancy Chodorow's thesis in *The Reproduction of Mothering:* the preoedipal bond of mother and daughter is one of such profound kinship that it survives into adulthood as a source of power and ambivalence. Furthermore, paternal authority in family structure drives a wedge in each woman's attitude toward her mother, and herself by impairing the capacity of women to think of themselves as cultural actors.[18] In the play, mother and daughter speak from different sides of a stripped-down stage: there are letters, desks, bookshelves, little else. Both women appear caged and restless, looking to each other for help when there is no other source. Their speeches are often simultaneous, as one breaks in upon the other, speaking *for* her in a dialogic interplay—they may as well be putting words into each other's mouths. And this mother and daughter love words: part of the pathos is that writing is so evidently bond and bondage.

The political content emerges when the same definitions and terms of reference are evoked from different points of view. To a large extent, mother and daughter share a lexicon: terms such as *home, family, error, disappointment* are uncannily repeated. We hear Aurelia recalling the pains she takes to cater to her husband Otto Plath's demands, and a few moments later Sylvia picks up the definition, this time reflecting upon the "pains" (*LH*, 8) she is taking to achieve a standard of beauty. By comparing contexts of use with points of articulation, we come to a critical awareness of the cultural pressure on both women to "measure up." One of the earliest and most telling indications of destructive symbiosis is established on romantic terms. Aurelia is rereading one of her daughter's glowing reports of a college dance; as she recalls her daughter's words, Aurelia Plath sweeps up her skirts, and swirls around the stage in trancelike imitation of the language of the letter: "so all I could see was a great cartwheel of colored lights . . . What a divine way to die!" (*LH*, 13). The scene is one of the most unnerving in the play for more than one reason. If we are familiar with Plath's self-destructive bent, we watch the mother's delusion uneasily, for it all too readily equates the fantasy of love and death with having a good time. But a social taboo is also being violated here: Aurelia looks slightly ridiculous because aging mothers *don't* dance. The miming of identity exposes the perilousness of both women's positions when they are caught up in romantic postures.

More hopefully, *Letters Home* finally reveals that when women speak for and through each other their pains of *enunciation* may also be *annunciations*—growing pains and signs of new life. Eventually, both characters recognize the need for greater separateness. Simultaneity diminishes as psychic distance grows. What we learn by watching the mother separate from the daughter and the daughter from the mother is a need for resistance to patriarchal definitions from both sides. The drama does not externalize its solutions, but it does celebrate the dignity of taking responsibility for oneself, surviving the struggle, and re-examining the contexts in which femininity is reproduced. Furthermore, the effects of re-presenting the mother as a woman who writes cannot be underestimated. Considering that mothers have more often been the "others" of masculine representation, this aspect of the drama also has revisionary power.

In striking contrast, *Virginia; a play* (*V*, 1981) by Edna O'Brien comes close to privileging the subversive potential of "feminine writing."[19] The drama is particularly worth considering as an adaptation of an avant-garde theory of textuality. Spatially and temporally, "Virginia" is often a liminal presence onstage. Directions specify that *"when she is talking her writing is in another vein altogether—reflective, rapturous, dreamlike"* (*V*, n.p.). Such a writing-effect operates through gesture and articulation, as well as numerous asides to the audience. What counts is the capacity of the body to rearticulate and reorient a history of representation by writing itself.

The play is particularly concerned with differentiating the effects proper to a woman of Virginia Woolf's class and upbringing from those that pre-occupied her as an artist, and in her relationships to other women. In one sense, this is accomplished by making us take a second look at the canon of Woolf's writing as well as at the body of the writer, but the two are connected, as I will explain in a moment. Stripping large chunks of the dialogue from Woolf's autobiographical writing as well as her fiction, O'Brien gives a more personal, intimate view of the texts and contexts that inspired Woolf's distinctive literary style. For instance, Virginia's first speech breaks directly into the schizophrenic ramblings of the shell-shocked and hysterical Septimus Warren Smith in *Mrs. Dalloway:*

> I dreamt that I leant over the edge of the boat and fell down. I went under the sea, I have been dead and yet am now alive again—it was awful, and as before, waking the voices of the birds and the sound of wheels chime and chatter in queer harmony, growing louder and louder, and the sleeper feels himself drawing toward the shores of life, the sun growing hotter, cries sounding louder, something tremendous about to happen. (*V,* 9)

Even if we recognize this passage from the novel, the terms of reference have shifted. In the context of the play this passage functions as a screen memory, reverberating with overtones traceable to the unconscious maternal signifier. It soon becomes clear that Woolf is not thinking about Septimus Warren Smith but meditating on the meanings of her mother, Julia Stephen, another woman described as "there" and "not there" in "Virginia's" memory:

> My mother, his wife, not at all the same thing . . . sitting there writing a letter at the table, and the silver candlesticks and the high carved chair and the three-cornered brass inkpot and then not there. (*V,* 10)

In this altered context, Woolf's elliptical manner reveals a woman almost beside herself with desire to recapture this ghostly, elusive, maternal femininity, a signifier hidden but never emptied of content, continually reactivated through Virginia's own fluid manner of self-definition. Like the child who so mourns the loss of undifferentiated, preoedipal union that s/he continually rolls a spool out of sight and delights upon reeling it back,[20] Virginia treats language itself as the primary vehicle for transforming a relation of otherness into a relationship of closeness, identity, and presence.

While *Virginia; a play* takes quite literally Woolf's speculation that a women who writes thinks back through her mothers,[21] we are also made to see that the struggle for self-representation takes place within historical circumstances common to women as political subjects. We witness this first of all in a scientific discourse that treats female acting out and acting up as a medical problem. While Leonard Woolf marks a daily chart of Virginia's fluctuating moods and regulates her social activities accordingly, what worries him is precisely her ecstatic unreasonableness: as he puts it, when Virginia is ill, she "leaves the ground, she follows her voices, she stumbles after them . . . she goes beyond reach" (V, 44). The man of reason soon becomes suspect, however, for what is most apparent about Virginia is her open sensuality, the availability of her body to continued redefinition, the undercurrent of excitement behind her "trembling." Resisting the rest-cures, she "walk-talks" excitedly across the stage, embellishing words and phrases with rapidly shifting inflections of voice that seem to take in a multiplicity of voices. Her wandering, trancelike states of supposed madness also resist linguistic and gender determinations. The counterinsurgent role of female desire is particularly apparent when Virginia the "hysteric" makes a "scene of herself" by flirting with Vita Sackville-West. Flirting with a woman onstage may constitute par excellence an example of what Luce Irigaray has described as a "mimicry of male discourse."[22] It becomes impossible within this context to "pin down" Woolf's sexuality in gender-polarized terms, as biographers have often done. Onstage together Virginia and Vita play at romance, sometimes using "acting" voices. Each alternately masquerades as courtier and object of desire, jokingly picking up and putting down gendered participles: *whoring, cutting up, throwing oneself overboard*. At the same time, Virginia makes most sense of her "madness" when she mocks Harold Nicholson's letters, reading them aloud for Vita: "I am glad that Vita has come under an influence so stimulating and so sane (*She lets out a hoot of laughter*)" (V, 45). Reversing the terms of a discourse in which male reason is set up to oppose female madness, the play makes fun of those who are unaware of the secrets women share. When Virginia drops to one knee and appears to be composing *Orlando* aloud and in Vita's presence, an alternative literary tradition begins.

Gertrude Stein's quarrel with history has inspired several new plays, all of which celebrate Stein's love of performance and her fascination with the performative aspects of language. Marty Martin's monoplay, *Gertrude Stein Gertrude Stein Gertrude Stein,*[23] aptly illustrates how much is to be gained from a script that itself borrows heavily from Stein's experimental writing. In Martin's play, Stein's poetics of "insistence" relies primarily on sound, rhythm, repetition. Our attention is pulled away from and against expectations of conventional literary experience. When the voice does the acting, we are prompted to reflect on the differential effects created within language, effects capable of being used subversively. As "Gertrude" explains in this play (and in her words), the habit of constantly repeating herself becomes its own ritual: "a *no* can become a *yes* if it is done right." Of the new Stein plays, only Pat Bond's *Gertie Gertie Gertie Is Back Back Back*[24] works against both textual *and* gender determinations at the same time. Bond's Stein is a clownish time-traveller who crosses boundaries between gay and straight worlds. In a recent interview, Bond told me she had been driven to create the play out of anger and frustration: after years of researching critical opinions on Stein, and even writing the draft of a book about her, Bond was possessed by the feeling that Stein's texts were "all locked up." Bond explained, "[Finally] I put the type-writer in the background and began to fill in with my own ideas of what Stein might say, especially to women, if she were alive today." Hundreds of performances later—most of them at colleges, universities, and alternative community theater settings—the play still derives its effects from laughter and a degree of improvisation. Mimesis is the brunt of Bond's jokes. The play opens with a montage of many wise and absurd things said about Gertrude Stein by her contemporaries, along with blown-up photos. "Stein" steps out against a famous photographic profile when she makes her entrance, mocking the representation: "Tell me, do I really look like Julius Caesar?" Above all, Bond delights in creating saturnalian shock effects. She particularly enjoys the sequence—an invented one—in which "Gertrude" tells us that Mary Pickford once leaned over and asked to have a picture taken with Gertrude Stein—"America's sweetheart and Gertrude Stein, together at last!" There's no point in wondering whether Stein is a mannish woman or a womanish man. She's both and neither at the same time. The overall effect is a fusion of Bond's personalities and Stein's in look-alike bodies, confronting the audience with a dialogue about our own gender-determined expectations.

Biographical dramas such as Goldemberg's, O'Brien's and Bond's perform a cultural intervention by refusing to memorialize the terms and conditions of authorship set up around sexual oppositions. We cannot think such plays important merely for presenting "images" of women writers onstage, but for documenting and examining the ways in which the anomalous woman writer is created and maintained. All of this is so crucial, of course, because feminist theory has often sought to understand the relationship of power to knowledge by asking what it might mean that women have written and continue to write within historical definitions of authorship that are masculine-centered. In theatre, as I have shown, we must finally go beyond the question, "who is the author?" in order to see that authorship, history, and difference are socially constructed. Furthermore, it is necessary to do so while continuing to acknowledge the empowering potential of identity in language. There appears to be no consensus about whether an alternative form of female authority is being produced, or whether women may indeed be writing beyond authority, whatever that might mean. What does appear certain is that the terms and conditions of the presentation are shifting.

NOTES

1. Virginia Woolf, *A Room of One's Own* (New York: Harcourt Brace, 1929), 47.

2. See Joanna Russ, *How to Suppress Women's Writing* (Austin: University of Texas Press, 1983), especially 76–86 for a description of "anomalousness" and its effects.

3. For example, see the discussion later in this essay of Salli Lovelarkin's unpublished script, *Maud Gonne: A Terrible Beauty Is Born,* performed in Cincinnati, Ohio, Xavier University, March 27, 1987. I am indebted to actress/director Merril Lynn Taylor, Portland, Oregon, for suggesting a number of other recent scripts.

4. Teresa de Lauretis establishes the relevance of these semiotic terms for feminist theory in general and cinema in particular in *Alice Doesn't: Feminism, Semiotics, Cinema* (Bloomington: University of Indiana Press, 1984), 16–17 and 31–35. Like cinema, theater can be said to have a metonymic relation to language, and voices and bodies can be said to be the aural and visual components of its meaning making. De Lauretis's semiotic approach is useful in getting at what happens when a woman becomes a figure for the author and is at the same time caught up in signifying practices and codes over which she may not have control. And, theater, like cinema, can be said to perform a kind of "writing" of material reality.

5. Sandra M. Gilbert and Susan Gubar, *The Madwoman in the Attic: The Woman Writer and the Nineteenth-Century Literary Imagination* (New Haven: Yale University Press, 1979), especially 17.

6. These are de Lauretis's terms, equally applicable to theater, 5–6.

7. I am speaking here of voices and bodies on stage as "already significant images" in that they are constituted by discursive practices, de Lauretis, 31, 145.

8. *The Belle of Amherst: A Play Based on the Life of Emily Dickinson* (Los Angeles: Creative Image Company, 1976).

9. Emily Dickinson, poem 288, in *The Norton Anthology of Literature by Women,* ed. Sandra M. Gilbert and Susan Gubar (New York: Norton, 1985), 846.

10. Luce, 78.

11. *Stevie; a play* (London: Samuel French, 1977), 38.

12. Susan Glaspell, *Alison's House* (London: Samuel French, 1930). Eve LaGalliene directed and played Elsa Stanhope.

13. Arthur E. Waterman, *Susan Glaspell* (New Haven: Twayne, 1966), 86–87.

14. Gertrude Stein, *The Mother of Us All,* in *Selected Operas and Plays of Gertrude Stein,* ed. John Malcolm Brinnin, 159–202 (Pittsburgh: University of Pittsburgh Press, 1970). I discuss only discourse patterns in Stein's libretto; Virgil Thompson's piano-vocal score was composed after her death. For a general analysis of Stein's use of theatre as an expository mode, see Betsy Alayn Ryan's excellent study, *Gertrude*

Stein's Theater of the Absolute (Ann Arbor, Mich.: UMI Research Press, 1984), especially 33–66.

15. Stein, "A Message from Gertrude Stein," in *Selected Writings of Gertrude Stein,* ed. Carl Van Vechten (New York: Random, 1946), vii.

16. Neil Schmitz discusses the theme of revenge in Stein's work, though not with reference to the plays, in "Portrait, Patriarchy, Mythos: The Revenge of Gertrude Stein," *Salmagundi* 40 (1978): 69–91.

17. Rose Leiman Goldemberg, *Letters Home* (Hollywood: Samuel French, 1976). Subsequent citations to this work will appear in the text.

18. Nancy Chodorow, *The Reproduction of Mothering: Psychoanalysis and the Sociology of Gender* (Berkeley: University of California Press, 1978).

19. Edna O'Brien, *Virginia; a play* (London: Hogarth Press, 1981). Subsequent citations appear in the text. On the concept of a "feminine writing," see *Hélène Cixous: Writing the Feminine,* by Verena Andermatt Conley (Lincoln: University of Nebraska Press, 1984), especially 129–61.

20. I allude to the subject's determination through displacement, as observed by Freud and theorized into language by Jacques Lacan, *Ecrits: A Selection,* trans. Alan Sheridan (New York: Norton, 1977), 30.

21. *A Room of One's Own,* 79.

22. For a summary of Irigaray's position, see Toril Moi, *Sexual/Textual Politics* (New York: Methuen, 1985), especially 139–43.

23. Marty Martin, *Gertrude Stein Gertrude Stein Gertrude Stein: A One-Character Play* (New York: Vintage, 1979), 41.

24. Bond's script is unpublished. All subsequent quotations are from an interview with Pat Bond, San Raphael, California, October, 1987.

Yolanda Broyles González

Toward a Re-Vision of Chicano Theatre History: The Women of El Teatro Campesino

The numerous social and political struggles of the 1960s and 1970s—such as the civil rights movement, the United Farm Workers' movement, the antiwar movement, or the women's liberation movement—were the source of inspiration to a multifaceted cultural renaissance. Perhaps the single most inspirational struggle for Chicanos was the David and Goliath standoff between the emergent United Farm Workers' Union and the agribusiness giants in California and other states. The 1965 grape strike which highlighted the determination and moral strength of the nation's poorest segment of the population inspired and directly influenced all sectors of Chicano political activism. One manifestation of that spirit of activism was the Chicano theater movement which spread across the Southwest (and parts of the Midwest) in the 1960s and the 1970s. In virtually all centers of Chicano population as well as on the campuses everywhere emerged theatre groups dedicated to portraying the life, heritage, and problems of Chicanos in this country. Under the wing of the United Farm Workers' organization based in Delano, California, emerged El Teatro Campesino (The Farm Workers' Theater) in 1965, conceived as an organizing and fundraising tool of the union. In its beginnings El Teatro Campesino performed numerous highly improvisational skits (called *actos*) which gave humorous expression to the labor problems of farmworkers in bold words and actions. In addition to regular performance before farmworkers—often on the back of flatbed trucks—the group also played college campuses and toured Europe repeatedly. The group's satirical presentation of the conflicts between farm bosses and farmworkers was highly entertaining and also pragmatic: they invariably ended with a pitch for unionism. A selection of these early works entitled *Actos* was published in 1971, the only Teatro Campesino publication to date.

In the course of the 1970s the composition of El Teatro Campesino changed from a farmworkers group to a predominantly student group. As the group's thematics broadened to include a variety of Chicano issues — educational, cultural, spiritual — Teatro Campesino plays became longer and more intricate. Yet the basic vivacious performance style established in the early years remained a constant throughout its development. It was a form of performance deeply rooted in the centuries-old tradition of Mexican popular theater, particularly the *carpa* (itinerant tent show) tradition which was popular both in urban centers and farm labor camps until the late 1950s and early 1960s. *Carpa* elements evident in El Teatro Campesino from its beginnings in 1965 to its dissolution around 1980 are the use of political satire, of comic sketches, stock characters, music, binguality, double entendres and other verbal play, as well as bawdy humor, exaggerated gestures, voice quality, and body movement. Intense audience participation is also a hallmark of that tradition. Above all, El Teatro Campesino shared with the *carpa* the collective creation process characteristic of the Mexican oral performance tradition. Unlike the phenomenon of individual authorship within print culture, the oral performance tradition generates performance material through group improvisation and reliance on memory. Various elements from the oral performance tradition form the core of other forms of theatrical expression cultivated by El Teatro Campesino even after its disassociation from union involvement in 1967. The inordinate strength of El Teatro Campesino was not as much a function of innovation as of its reliance on tradition. The revalorization of the popular working-class performance aesthetic by El Teatro Campesino constitutes one of the most striking acts of cultural reaffirmation by Chicano intellectuals threatened with cultural extinction.

Among the popular traditional genres adopted by El Teatro Campesino were the seasonal sacred pageants performed in Chicano/Mexican communities for hundreds of years. Most notable among these are the *Pastorela* (Shepherds' Play) and *Las cuatro apariciones de Nuestra Señora del Tepeyac* which re-enacts the story of Mexico's most revered deity, the Indian goddess Guadalupe-Tonantzin. Other traditional forms cultivated by El Teatro Campesino after the early *actos* were the *corrido* (traditional narrative ballad) form and *mito* (myth) form. Plays using combinations of these forms were also performed. The staged *corrido* — popular in turn-of-the-century Mexico — features a narrational play that unfolds through the singing and brisk-paced dramatization of a *corrido*. The most successfully staged Teatro Campesino play in *corrido* form was *La gran carpa de los Rasquachis* which went through five rewritings between 1973 and 1978. El Teatro Campesino toured Europe and the United States with two of those versions. Integrated into the final versions of that epic story of a Mexican immigrant family were elements of the so-called *mito* (myth) form which sought to foreground the fundamental correspondences between the particulars of everyday human existence and the larger cosmic forces. In its final years, the Teatro Campesino collective continued to experiment with the *mito* and *corrido* forms in *Fin del mundo,* for example, which was performed in numerous different versions between the years 1974 and 1980. The dramatic portrayal of linkages between the historical, socio-political, and the spiritual domains is among the most striking achievements of El Teatro Campesino. During its years of intense theatrical activity the ensemble remained a spiritual, cultural, and ideological standard bearer of the Chicano movement.

Chicanas in Theatre: A Lost Legacy

In the summer of 1980 I witnessed a performance of El Teatro Campesino's *Fin del mundo* in Europe. That production marked the end of the ensemble known as El Teatro Campesino, a name that had stood as a trademark representing a way of performing and a way of living, both intimately linked. The spirit of group commitment was still alive in that production, and that energy obviously contributed to the rare power of that performance—a power that was visibly transmitted to German and French audiences in spite of language or other cultural barriers. My own dissatisfaction with the piece sprang from the portrayal of Chicanas. The women characters in the show felt like an eerie rerun of earlier Teatro plays: the saintlike wilting wife, the sleazy whore, and the grandmother figure. Compared with the male characters, the females seemed one-dimensional and relatively insignificant. Among the male characters, the most notable in terms of expressivity was the Pachuco youth nicknamed *Huesos* (Bones). It was Huesos who most controlled the audiences and the motion on stage. I was astonished backstage after the performance when I discovered that the extraordinary Huesos was played by a woman: Socorro Valdez. Her performance was unforgettable. And yet her presence in the Teatro had never been described by scholars or historians of Chicano drama. Why?

The history of women's participation in the long tradition of Mexican theatre in the Southwest constitutes a neglected cultural legacy whose contours have yet to be mapped. Virtually nothing is known concerning the participation of Chicana women in the two-hundred-year history of Mexican theatre in what is today the southwestern United States. Secular and of course ritual performance forms have existed for the past two centuries and much longer, but the role of women has become a lost legacy. As is well known, numerous realms of women's historical experience have been lost due to the (male) gender-specific interpretation of past reality. Women have—through omission—been erased as agents in history. The erasure born of gender discrimination is exacerbated in the case of Chicanas; race and class discrimination have made their performance history appear triply insignificant to mainstream keepers of the historical record, in this case theatre historians. The contributions and struggles of the women in El Teatro Campesino are a part of that rich legacy that, once exposed, will alter the established version of Chicano theatre history.

History—and that includes theatre history—has frequently been reduced to a chronology of the doings of "great men." Similarly, the history of El Teatro Campesino has been canonized as the history of the "life and times" of Luis Valdez. The tendency to place individuals—usually male individuals—and not groups at the center of history constitutes a radical simplification by which the dynamics of a life *process* are filtered out, leaving behind names, dates, and places. Beyond the more obvious distortions attendant to creating monuments to individuals, that conceptual framework serves to eclipse the memory of group achievement. As individuals reading history, we are more likely to feel dwarfed by all the "great men" instead of learning of the strength we have through community and collaboration.

The reality of collective creation of plays within El Teatro Campesino has been noted by some researchers; but that has not altered their overriding historical framework, based on the great-man concept, similar to the hierarchical division of labor with a supposedly omnipotent boss at the top. It is a way of looking at the world. It is a way of writing history. In the voluminous literature that exists on El Teatro Campesino, that collaborative activity is often overlooked entirely or considered of secondary importance; references to "Luis Valdez's Actos" or to "Valdez's characters" or to "his teatro"[1] are descriptive inaccuracies reflecting the age-old method of conveniently subsuming the work of a group of people under the name of one man. One noted critic frequently mentions the "collective process" or "collectivity," yet the reality of collective authorship is consistently subsumed under the individual rubric of Luis Valdez and reduced merely to something that happens under the aegis of a genius:

> Perhaps the success of this creative genius' collaborations with his ever-evolving troupe is due to the fact that Valdez is a poet, playwright, actor and director who can see all of the elements necessary for effective theater and who can transpose those visions to the stage.[2]

It appears the anonymous "ever-evolving troupe" possessed no genius or vision.
Theater historians' fixation upon a great man has snowballed into an ac-

count distortive of the simplest facts. Anthologies of Chicano theater, for example, usually name only Luis Valdez as the author of works that were in fact collectively authored.[3] The most widely anthologized *acto, Soldado razo* (Buck Private), for example, runs without exception under the name of Luis Valdez, and not of El Teatro Campesino. Yet Olivia Chumacero recalls how this *acto* was written by various members of the ensemble:

> Once we were working on *Soldado razo,* working on the idea. In fact I remember we were going to do this *acto* specifically for the Moratorium against the war in Vietnam. . . . *Entonces* [well] there was a girl in the Teatro who told us what had happened in her family. . . . And so the *acto* is based on a real story. Well, Luis introduced the *calavera* [skeleton] character into one of the improvisations; and Phil [Esparza] did the *calavera* in the improvisations. He started doing various numbers. And we immediately thought that this is a great tool to use in this *acto.* And it worked. I remember that was when Luis actually wrote the dialogue that the mother and the son have in the letter . . . for the rest of the *acto* we were working off improvisations that we were doing. Luis was teaching at the University and he didn't have as much time to help put it together. So I remember that he wrote that part. But all the other parts were done collectively. Everybody's ideas, everybody's input, the improvisations. Luis functioned as sifter. . . . Things came out from *you,* from what *you* thought, from what *you* had experienced in life. . . . It was your life.[4]

The vital facets of history that become blurred or erased by the great-man perspective are the very forces that shape the "great individuals" and sustain them in a position of prominence.

I would like to put aside the heroic and monolithic vision of El Teatro Campesino and momentarily destabilize that image by describing facets of a struggle that has been carried on by some of the women in the group—with varying degrees of success. By presenting those conflicts and contradictions and their resolutions in all their human breadth, I hope to rectify the history of El Teatro Campesino so that *process*—the full range of human action, including women's contributions—becomes visible.

In the years since the European tour of *Fin del mundo* I have explored the dynamics of Teatro Campesino and of other *teatros,* and I have developed a closer understanding of those dynamics, based not so much on what I have read as on what I saw then and have observed since then. My understanding is also based on long conversations and interviews and on day-to-day living experiences with the women and men of El Teatro Campesino in California.

During my two years of research residence in San Juan Bautista, I was able to observe and to develop an understanding of the realities behind the appearances. Day-by-day behind the scenes inquiry has opened my eyes to the creative process that predated production of *Fin del mundo*—and the roles of women in that process. It is the roles of these *women* and their significance within the history of El Teatro Campesino and—by extension—within the history of Chicano theater that I address here. In reconstructing that history I rely principally on those *teatristas* (theater workers) who have never been viewed as prominent. I have chosen to focus on the oral testimony of various Teatro women, particularly Socorro Valdez, as well as on my own observations. The present essay represents a preliminary version of a much more extensive essay. The full version includes the testimony of several more Teatro Campesino women and focuses on various other questions concerning the work of women in *teatro*. In its final form, the essay will constitute one chapter in a book on various dimensions of El Teatro Campesino. The composite story of the roles of women in the Teatro Campesino is only one of the unwritten chapters of its history.

Women's Roles in El Teatro Campesino

It cannot have escaped the attention of those who followed the development of El Teatro Campesino through the years that the female roles have remained fairly constant. In the course of the evolutionary process from *actos* to *mitos* to *corridos* to combinations thereof, from the days of the *actos* performed by farmworkers for farmworkers atop flatbed trucks to the days of *Zoot Suit* in Hollywood and on Broadway, the female characters have consisted of variations of the same three or four types. Women are first of all defined in a familial category: mother, grandmother, sister, or wife/girlfriend. All women are also divided into one of two sexual categories: whores or virgins. Depending on the circumstances of any given play—all of which have male protagonists—the handful of female traits are mixed or matched to create the desired effect. The spectrum of female characteristics is narrow; female roles are one-dimensional stereotypes. Most common are the prostitutes and the virginal wife or mother, but there can also be prostitute mothers, for example. For the sake of brevity I dispense with a discussion of examples of this form of female characterization in the Teatro Campesino repertoire.[5] Suffice it to say that female characters typically engage in activities that are accessory to those of males. Women's roles do not enjoy the dramatic space necessary for the unfolding of a character. Never is the world seen through the eyes of women, the other half of humanity.

In my interviews with Teatro women I explored the genesis of these roles and the women's views of them. In elaborating on their views of these roles, the women—without exception—placed these roles within the context of their own personal development. There is agreement among them that the stereotyped roles found in the work of El Teatro Campesino are in many ways related to the stereotyped views of Chicanas found within society at large. The women who joined the company in the 1970s basically inherited stereotypical female roles as givens. The roles had been largely preestablished and were neither submitted to scrutiny nor questioned, owing to two major factors. On the one hand, most women entered the Teatro in their teens. Therefore, their consciousness of themselves as women and of their theatrical roles as women were not highly developed. In the words of Teatro member Diane Rodríguez:

> At the beginning we were playing various types, like the "supportive wife," you know, or the "virginal" type, like an icon, literally, she was just a statue—and that was a character; that was one of the main roles. *We* were playing these roles, *we* let that happen. And we had some input. But where were we, as women, at that point? Somehow at that point we didn't have the consciousness and we played these cardboard roles. Or maybe we did have some consciousness but we didn't know how to get it on the stage. There was *something* that was not as strong as it is now, of course. There is more of a consciousness of women—in oneself— that there wasn't then.[6]

Socorro Valdez, who performed her first Teatro Campesino role at fifteen, also feels that age prevented her from questioning female roles with which the men in the company apparently felt comfortable:

> I was growing up, you know. So for me to confront Luis at that time and say: Look, your writing about women is no good . . . well, that is not where I was coming from; he was much older than me and had more life experience. But he didn't have *female* experience.[7]

A historical factor also made the roles of women appear a secondary consideration. During the 1960s the efforts to address *raza* (Chicano people) and the reality of *raza* as a *whole* somehow precluded a special consideration of women's roles or problems. In the words of Diane Rodríguez:

> It seems that because we have always worked for a certain goal, we have overlooked some things. I admit that. I admit that very much . . . we perform his [Luis Valdez's] view of women, basically. Now there is some input. But in order that the show go on . . . well, we have said: OK we'll go with this and we have performed these roles. . . . We have talked about this and I think all of us are very conscious. But I don't think that we have found the answer yet either.[8]

Putting women's issues second, or discounting them altogether, was common among leftist groups of the 1960s in the United States and around the world. The liberation of people "in general" was considered the chief priority. Ironically, those engaged in struggles for human equality were slow to recognize that class struggles and ethnic struggles would not necessarily better the lot of women. *Movimiento* (Chicano Movement) women who raised women's issues—which are, dialectically speaking, men's issues as well—were accused of being divisive.

With the passing of time and the development of consciousness as women, the sense of working within confining roles became increasingly apparent and increasingly frustrating. Socorro, the youngest of the group, described it in this manner:

> It was like walking the same path over and over. There was the mother, the sister, or the grandmother or the girlfriend. Only four. You were either the *novia* [bride], *la mamá* [mother], *la abuela* [grandmother], *o la hermana* [sister]. And most of the time these characters were passive. The way those females are laid out are for the most part very passive and laid back, *y aguantaban todo* [and they put up with everything]. I think that is what really chewed me up at the time.[9]

The women's dissatisfaction with these roles led to one of the longest and deepest struggles in the development of the Teatro Campesino. I would even venture to say that the question of women's roles became the most enduring contradiction within the company, a contradiction paralleled in various ways within the Chicano movement. It was a contradiction between what was, on the one hand, a constant process of renewal in the form of new genres and new techniques, new visions and experimentation, and what was, on the other hand, a static clinging to well-worn stereotypes of gender roles. The Teatro Campesino repertoire, with its strong progressive strides in the treatment of labor issues, of Chicano culture, of historical issues, consistently demonstrated stagnation in its treatment of women.

Resistance to change was in some ways anchored in the makeup of the company, which had been predominantly male since its founding. Socorro Valdez describes how the women struggled to be viewed and treated as equals:

> At one time there were only three women in the whole darn thing: Olivia Chumacero, myself, and a third I don't remember. That was a real interesting time. We were either going to remain members of the company, or just be "the women of the company." That made a real difference, you know, because I hated to be put into a mold like "These are the ladies of the Teatro." Aw, shut up! Don't gimme *that*! They would separate you without needing to. And so Olivia fought for her own, as I did. You know we were both very young. We both ended up in the role of *fighters* because that's what was needed to get the men's heads to a place where they would be able to discuss something with you. We would have open meetings where the shit would fly across the room. . . . But I know how important those three women were at that period, because there was no other female voice in the company.[10]

Administrative decision-making power was, to a large extent, in the hands of the men. In time women learned to question the division of labor along gender lines:

> We even got down to questioning who was going to be telling who what to do; because I personally got very tired of being under the thumb of a man. We had a male touring manager. We had a male booking agent. We had a male director. We had a male stage manager. We had a male everything. And there are women there that are just as strong . . . I could pick up a house if I had to, you know. . . . But they just never thought I could. And it was up to me to show them that I could. There was no fault to bear; just responsibility.[11]

The aspect of male dominance in administrative matters was reinforced by the patriarchal organization of El Teatro Campesino. Luis Valdez typically worked with persons much younger than himself. And the relationship between the members of the ensemble, a group that *worked and lived* together, was defined as a familial one. The group was officially defined as a *familia*;

Luis Valdez was the symbolic father or person in charge. The process of changing the portrayal of women, of developing fuller roles and images of women, was perceived by the women as a challenge both in theatrical terms and in terms of human dignity. Yet the men did not share that sense of urgency in the women's challenge. Perhaps it was alarming to the patriarchal structure of El Teatro Campesino. Socorro Valdez describes the challenge created by women:

> Luis has seen a lot of stuff through the work that the women have done in this group. They've always given him a little more . . . to *challenge* him. And there were times in the group that the women were just outraged. We'd say "What are you doing? I'm sick of playing mothers! I'm sick of playing sisters!"[12]

The question of redefining female roles, however, met with passive resistance. For one thing, it never really found acceptance as a problem. Far from being taken up as a challenge, it was treated as an unnecessary provocation. Women's efforts to dramatize a new vision of women were frequently countered by the suggestion that they write their own plays, a subtle form of ostracism. Clearly, the collective spirit suffered a collapse when gender roles were questioned. Suddenly an individual solution was suggested for what was a collective problem. That response was indicative of the lack of ensemble commitment to the creation of adequate roles for women. Women of the Teatro view that resistance — on one level — as a function of the men not having "female experience." But a more complex dimension of that resistance is also articulated: the narrowness in the perception of women by males is linked to the narrowness in the men's self-perception: "He [Luis] can't experience women any other way except as a man. And no one else can do that either, unless they are willing to *stretch their own image of themselves.*"[13]

Male resistance to female self-determination, however, should not be personalized or considered the special problem of this or that man or group. In truth, it is not unique to El Teatro Campesino. Male supremacist ideology and practice, in all sectors of society, have been the focus of extensive discussion and investigation within the women's movement. A prime manifestation of that ideology is the inability to accept women beyond their biological roles: wife/mother/lover; it is a form of blindness that prevents many from perceiving the vast spectrum of experiences that in reality comprises womanhood. The virgin/whore dichotomization of women is the distorted projection of male supremacist ideology. Maintenance of male power *needs* a fragmented (i.e., nonthreatening) image of women. Although various women in the Teatro Campesino ensemble were a living antithesis to the male stereotypes of women, there is virtually no evidence of a new understanding or "stretch." The women's self-image remained at odds with the images of those unable to see women in their wholeness: the issue of women's roles was consistently deflected.

The growing desire of some Teatro Campesino women to create and try out roles with greater depth to some extent coincided with Luis Valdez's gradual striving to assume greater power within the organization. That striving was not without implications for the women engaged in redefining the roles of women. Casting decisions became the exclusive right of Luis Valdez. And casting decisions became a conscious and/or unconscious tool in the perpetuation of the classic stereotypes of women. In the last Teatro Campesino ensemble production (*Fin del mundo,* 1980) the female lead character of Vera—companion to the drug addict Reymundo Mata—was played in the highly incongruous but characteristic ingenue style. This was the result of a casting decision: a novice actress was chosen over the more experienced Teatro women. As in so many productions, a role that promised a great deal delivered very little:

> The one role that all of us women tried out for was the role of Vera, the pregnant wife-girlfriend. Unfortunately that role was handled by a very weak actress. . . . She was *physically* maybe suited for the role: a pretty face. But in terms of the *guts* I think that Olivia or Diane were much better suited. . . . It was a real hurt for us, because we would try to coach her: "Don't act like such a clinging vine!! Leave us a little bit of pride!!" It had the makings of a wonderful role, but it didn't get developed. Luis cast her in that role.[14]

The same practice of casting weak actresses in pivotal roles was repeated in subsequent productions, to the detriment of the plays as a whole. The production of *Rose of the Rancho,* which inaugurated the Teatro Campesino Playhouse (1981), featured a wilting Juanita character in the play's center. That role was a result of a casting decision and of playwriting. A powerful and expressive actress in the role of Rose might well have created a character highly incompatible with the general thrust of this lightweight melodramatic comedy. The drama seeks to entertain and to attract a broad audience by offending no one. As such, it follows a stereotyped entertainment formula: the weak Mexican Juanita character and her "rancho" are saved by an Anglo whom she then marries. All live happily ever after.

The same novice who played the Rose character then played the principal female role in Luis Valdez's *Bandido!* (1981), a play about the 1860s California Chicano heroic outlaw Tiburcio Vásquez—with predictable results. The historic figure's legendary quest for social justice becomes insignificant as Valdez highlights Vásquez's quest for women. All three women in the play are Vásquez's satellites and are defined solely in terms of men: the highbrowed Rosario is wife to Leiva and lover to Tiburcio Vásquez; California Kate is a whore madam; Rita Madrid is a "feisty camp follower" (*Bandido!* script) in competition with Rosario for the love of Vásquez. Much of her dialogue centers around winning him.

The reality of physical and spiritual stereotyping of women within El Teatro Campesino extended to include factors such as skin color. This is even true of a play such as *La Virgen del Tepeyac,* which occupies a very special place in the history of El Teatro Campesino. Playing the revered Mexican deity Guadalupe-Tonantzin was regarded as much more than a "role" by the women of the company. It was an honor and a deeply spiritual undertaking. It is not the Roman Catholic institutionalized version of Guadalupe that gives the pageant its power, but rather the adoration of Guadalupe-Tonanztin as the Native American deity that she is: the symbol of a cosmic force. The role of Guadalupe is perhaps the one female role that was loved by all the women of the company. Unlike other roles, it represented a tribute to female potentiality. Yet the role also fell prey to stereotyping. An unspoken casting taboo altered the appearance of the Indian goddess. Yolanda Parra tells of the alteration:

> In the *Virgin del Tepeyac* they should have a real Indian-looking woman because that's the *whole point.* She appears to Juan Diego in the image of an *india,* and I mean hardcore stone-ground Mexican Indian. . . . But the women they pick for the role look like little Spanish madonnas. I've always thought Olivia Chumacero would make a great Virgen del Tepeyac; because there is a certain amount of ovaries that go into that part. You're talking the guts of the Universe there. You're talking somebody who can really feel the power.[15]

Control over casting decisions provided a kind of insurance policy for the director. It assured that the roles would be played in accordance with *his* view of women. Within the three or four role types available to women, only

certain predetermined women could play certain predetermined roles. Just as
female roles in plays had become cemented, women also became stereotyped
along rigid lines *offstage*. A vicious circle of typecasting was created. In the
words of Socorro Valdez:

> As it were, the actresses that were "soft" offstage and just *muy buenas,*
> *muy muy buenas* [tame; real, real tame] got the "soft" roles. And the ladies
> that were *medias cabronas* [the ones who wouldn't take shit from anyone]
> and had a beer and a cigarette hanging out of their mouth, well you
> know what role they got. . . . I always ended up with that other stuff.[16]

Women were divided basically into "soft" types and "hard" types—into good
and bad. Yet this division did not go unquestioned. What is more, it deep-
ened the women's understanding of themselves and of their roles. In the words
of Socorro Valdez:

> Now I know these choices. And I know there were moments in the
> group when there was to be a "girlfriend." Well, can Socorro be the
> girlfriend? No, Socorro can't be the girlfriend. Socorro is either the old
> lady or she's the jokester. But I was never seen in this company as a
> "soft" woman, because they confuse softness and hardness and they at-
> tach those two things to strength or weakness. But there is no such thing
> in *my* mind. . . . You can't put those two things together like that. They
> fluctuate.[17]

El Teatro Campesino continued to re-enact all varieties of virgins, mothers, and sleazy whores throughout the decade of the 1970s. This is not to
imply that the women stayed in the company in the position of martyrs.
There were various other dimensions of activity that made the experience very
rewarding. Truly, the flowering of creative capacities afforded by the collective
process within the Teatro was seemingly limitless, as long as it did not pertain
to the expansion of women's roles. Even the eventual entry of women into
administrative positions did not trigger a modification of the portrayal of
women on the stage.

In discussing the nature of women's roles, it should not be overlooked
that the rigid views of gender roles both on and off the stage created a special
set of problems peculiar to women in theatre. These problems illustrate the
close relationship between the private and public spheres in theatrical life. One

obstacle the women had to overcome was the negative response of many to the very presence of women in *teatro*. The prejudice against women actors manifested itself even among some Teatro Campesino supporters:

> It got wild when people started saying: Those broads are nothing but a bunch of *tú sabes* . . . *que actrizes ni que actrizes* [you know what . . . actresses, my foot]. Only *guys* could be actors. For some reason we were still only women. . . . Somehow or other. Critics of the Teatro, people that were close to the company, people that were around: they wondered what kind of women we were. We were just cheap broads. *Now* the idea is different; but traditionally women in theater—even way back to the dark ages—were considered just whores.[18]

In many cases Chicanas also encountered parental resistance to their work in theater. Olivia Chumacero tells of this situation: "It's been eleven years since I left the house . . . but when my parents think of theatre they think of loose women. In Mexico if you are into the arts in this way *eres mujer de la calle* [you're a woman of the street]. . . . Women have it harder and they have to be strong."[19] In the course of time, motherhood also became an issue affecting the participation of women in El Teatro Campesino. Specifically, child bearing and child raising were considered incompatible with theatrical touring. Rather than accept elimination from the company, women struggled to demonstrate that touring with children was possible and necessary:

> We wanted to have more say in certain decisions. For instance: touring and babies. How about taking babies out on the road? So-and-so couldn't travel because she had a baby. Now that's ridiculous. Olivia was one of them . . . the forerunners of the mothers in the company. They had their babies . . . and they proved it, not only to themselves or to their in-laws or to their parents, but to Luis, that it could be done. They proved that women—even now—with all the pressures of motherhood could be seen performing on the stage and then breast-feeding their kid in the van the next hour. It was possible. It wasn't easy. . . . I use Olivia as an example because she just trudged right through it in the best way she knew how. And it wasn't always easy for her. . . . I don't have any children but I do know how *I* want to be now that I've *seen* how they could do it. They proved certain things for me. And that was during the *hard* times when we had to go cross-country to New York in one van, and the baby diapers and all that. . . . You know, that was a hell of a point that the

women made. It affected me a great deal to see that. The company had to' make it possible for children to go with us. That's what it had to do. Staying home had to be a matter of *choice* and not a matter of having children. That point was very important: the establishment of an acting mother.[20]

Although acting mothers became a common thing in El Teatro Campesino, a policy of equal sharing in child-care responsibilities was not established. Each couple with children had to work out its own strategy for dealing with the added responsibility of child care. Particularly in the case of infants, primary or sole responsibility usually rested with the mother. As such, acting mothers found themselves with a work-load disadvantage within the company. In the women's or men's testimony there is no mention of difficulties in the establishment of an acting father.

Breaking the Mold: Creating New Pathways

Having devoted a good deal of attention to the limitations imposed upon women and women characters on stage, I would now like to examine the other side of that long-smouldering contradiction. The efforts — of *some* women — to break through the confinement of stereotypic female roles had, to some extent, been thwarted. Yet their determination and consciousness remained unaltered and became a compelling force in other directions. New avenues had to be explored. From the backstage perspective of theatre history I witnessed dramatic breakthroughs. Some of them had immediate consequences for centerstage action. Others had their impact in areas of less media visibility.

Let us briefly follow the strivings of Socorro Valdez, whose breakthroughs have been dramatically inspirational. The first role that Socorro ever played in the company was the grandmother role. I offer her own recollection of that activity:

> I was fifteen years old — my first role in the company was that of an old lady about eighty years old. And I jumped on it real quick because it was character, it was character work. It was real big broad acting. That was my point of beginning. And so when I played my first character I immediately relied on my strength. And the old lady I played was by no means a whining old lady. She was a very powerful character . . . maybe the way I'm going to be when I'm eighty, because I don't see myself coming from a weak place.[21]

Although that performance is not noted by historians of Teatro, it is alive in the memory of all Teatristas. Olivia Chumacero recalls:

> Socorro, for example, created the mother and grandmother characters in the Teatro. She was sixteen years old and she used to do the most fantastatic old lady that you had ever seen. Incredible. Really incredible: *el movimiento, la forma, el estilo de hablar, las expresiones* [her movements, her form, her style of talking, her expressions] everything. It was wonderful.[22]

In spite of the vitality of the performance process, the female roles became stagnant after they began to repeat themselves in various guises for over a decade. Socorro Valdez describes one manner in which she resolved to break the mold:

> At the time there were no men in the group who could be made to play pachucos, or old men, etc. And it was important to play the men's roles well; because the truth is that Luis writes for men. He always has. His point of view is male and it will always be so. But it was kind of strange that he had no men to play the men. So I figured, "Hell, what's holding me back? Just let me put on a pair of pants and jump into it and see." And in fact I ended up playing men better than the men! . . . It wasn't that I was trying to get the role; I was trying to *establish* the role within the group. Those characters of men needed to be played. But unfortunately the men in the group at the time were not able or capable or free or whatever the problem was.[23]

Assuming a male role represented a major step in the exploration of new possibilities as a performer. And that step was an outgrowth of the living, creative impulse that had become frustrated within the narrow confines of stereotyped women's roles. The male roles enjoyed a major part of the lines. For Socorro, playing a male role provided a new adventure in role-playing: as a male she was now in an *active* position. In the Teatro Campesino repertoire, action was typically centered around male protagonists, with women characters generally functioning as auxiliary figures. The women figures were those *affected* by men; they were peripheral: the ones *to whom* things happened. Not that the reverse would be desirable. The overpowering centrality of one character (usually male) creates limitations of dialogue, space, and action in the development of other characters. In Teatro Campesino plays in which the main character (male) has been balanced by other characters, those other characters are invariably also male (such as in *Fin del mundo,* 1980; or *La Gran Carpa Cantinflesca*) or they are sexless characters like La Muerte (Death) or El Diablo (the Devil) (such as in *La Carpa de los Rasquachis*). Women characters fill the spaces in between.

Socorro Valdez's appropriation of male roles provided an opportunity for her to stretch her own self-image, to grow.

> [The female roles] are very limiting. There is the mother type, and then there is the "mutha": the whore type, sleazy, cheap. There is always the mother, the sister, the girlfriend, or the grandmother. That's very limiting. And that's one of the reasons I dove so deep into aborting the fact that I was female and only female. I need exploration in my work.[24]

The exploration and imagination involved in the creation of new characters was considerable. To play a role or character did not mean to follow the script or another person's directions. It meant literally to *create* a character, to bring it to life virtually from scratch. That included the creation of the dialogue and movement through the improvisational process. Playing each role entailed a degree of creative responsibility for performers very much unlike that of dramatic traditions whose fixation rests with written scripts. To perform a play was to *generate* a play. Even the classic *actos*—which have been adopted for performance by Chicano theatre groups throughout the United States and in Latin America—were never rehearsed by El Teatro Campesino using a script. Contrary to popular belief—and contrary to the spirit and practice of the oral performance tradition—the published collection of *actos* does not represent "definitive" texts. The concept of *definitive* is not applicable within the oral tradition, in which plays change markedly with every performance—based on the improvisational fancy of the performers and their relationship with that evening's audience. Olivia Chumacero describes the process:

> When the *actos* book was done, no scripts existed. Felix Álvarez went around with a tape recorder asking people what their lines were so that he could write it down and put the *acto* book together . . . even though those lines changed a lot as we went along, depending on who was doing the character and depending on the situation. The parts would change a lot.[25]

Clearly, Teatro Campesino plays were collaborative exercises that changed with each performance and with each rehearsal. Much of theatre criticism and theatre history divorces these pieces from the human beings who created them. Yet the texts uttered did not exist separate from those people. They did not exist as a fixed text in "dramatic literature" fashion. The text alone is not even half the story. For much of Chicano theatre it holds true that academic textual analysis cannot unfold or reveal the artistry involved. Socorro Valdez describes her view of bringing expression to a "crude image" (i.e., role):

> The roles are like an old rock, but crack that baby open and you have intricate, intricate layers of evolution. *That* is what has been my goal: it is to take these very crude images that were there, that have their own form of artistry, and break them open so that the inside is expressed. It makes me work harder, it makes me push more to get inside of a *cholo* [street dude] or to get inside of that *campesino* [farmworker] who seems so obvious.[26]

Similarly, the role of "director" of El Teatro Campesino had a function very much unlike that within print culture or mainstream theatre. The dynamics of collective authorship created a process in which the director was more often engaged in taking direction than in giving it. This relationship of reciprocity prompted Yolanda Parra to indicate that "Luis Valdez was created by El Teatro Campesino," when historians of theatre always put it the other way around. In her words:

> He [Luis] pulled a lot of stuff out of them and they *gave* him a lot of material, tons of material in the improvisations. And you see that material appear even in shows like *Zoot Suit*. He took characters that had been developed within the group in a collective situation. As director he might come out and say: "This is the situation." But then it was the *actors* that made it happen for him. . . . In a lot of ways Luis was created by El Teatro Campesino. The unquestionable loyalty of the members also created him.[27]

Given the extraordinary acting skill of Socorro Valdez, it would be no exaggeration to speak of her as a leading figure in the history of El Teatro Campesino. In the entire history of her work with the Teatro Campesino, however, Socorro Valdez has never played a lead female part, only numerous male leads. That is a startling fact considering not only Socorro's almost legendary talents as a performer but also her yearning to explore many roles. Yet the stereotyped casting within the company eliminated her, and other women who look like her, from various female lead roles. There is sadness in her voice when she indicates that she was never allowed to play Our Lady of Guadalupe in *La Virgen del Tepeyac:*

> I never even got close to it. They wouldn't let me. . . . I could never have the role . . . because Luis doesn't see me that way. They see the Virgen de Guadalupe as a soft, demure, peaceful, saintly, ingenue type. The really incredible part was when it turned out that I have too many teeth. I was told "You got too many teeth. The Virgen didn't have that many teeth." It appears the Virgen de Guadalupe had no teeth. I thought to myself: "That is the stupidest thing I ever heard of!" *¿Apoco estaba molacha la Virgen de Guadalupe?* ["Do you mean to tell me Our Lady of Guadalupe was toothless?!"][28]

The truth, however, was that Socorro did not meet the standards of beauty that had been set for the dark-skinned deity, La Virgen Morena: Socorro has strong *indígena* (Indian) features and dark brown skin. That also partially explains how she and other Teatro Campesino women ended up creating numerous roles that camouflaged their natural appearance. In addition to the male roles, they created numerous sexless characters. Socorro's portrayal of *La Muerte*—in *calavera* (skeleton) costume—became a classic. She comments herself: "In all these years I was always under heavy makeup or under heavy costume, you know. And one role that I pretty much made my handle was the *calavera* because it was sexless; it was of neither sex."[29] The sexless roles became numerous, and they were pursued as a creative outlet for women to escape the confinement of female roles. Olivia Chumacero created the *Diabla* during the *corridos* dramatizations of the seventies and also the Angel role in *La Pastorela*; Yolanda Parra's performance as St. Michael in *La Pastorela* (1981) is remembered by many as one of the finest renditions of that character. Several women also played male roles, but not as consistently as Socorro. In the course of seeking new channels for creativity, Olivia Chumacero and Socorro Valdez also began directing. Socorro directed many productions of *La Virgen del Tepeyac*.

Olivia Chumacero has also developed alternative pathways for applying her acting and directing expertise. She performed with the Teatro regularly until 1980, while also pioneering in theatre work with children of Chicano migrant workers. She continues to do that work today, while also conducting a program of drama workshops for women in battered women's centers and for youth in drug prevention centers. She has also taught dramatic techniques to future bilingual teachers at the University of California at Santa Cruz, while at the same time learning the technique of filmmaking. Olivia's work can serve as a model for the application of theatre skills in ways that directly benefit disenfranchised sectors of society. Her theatrical commitment is tailored to fit the needs of the community in which she lives. The paths taken by Socorro Valdez and Olivia Chumacero provide us with but two examples of the new roles that women have assumed and created, in an effort to break the mold of distorted and fragmented images of Chicanas. But at different times and in different ways virtually all the women have consciously engaged in the effort to create new spaces and models in which they and other women — and men — can move. Many have managed to transform old frustrations into new options. These are women who are keenly aware of the possibilities within themselves — as performers and as human beings. The history of El Teatro Campesino must include the history of its contradictions and of the emergence of women who have charted new territory for subsequent generations.

Chicanas Onstage into the 1980s

The long history of El Teatro Campesino's collective work had ceased entirely by 1980. When Luis Valdez went to Hollywood and then to Broadway, the members of the ensemble for the most part went their separate ways. Many of them continue to fuse performance and life, in classic Teatro Campesino fashion. Most of them apply their skills within the processes of everyday activities: be it in schools, with community groups, in workshops or in theatre productions around the San Francisco Bay area. Although El Teatro Campesino still exists on paper, the name no longer stands for an acting *ensemble* that is strongly committed to specific cultural and social ideals; Luis Valdez has long since left the arena of alternative theatre and is committed to mainstreaming — a process he sometimes likens to a narcotic injection: "I see it as mainlining into the veins of America."[30]

I would like to focus attention on Luis Valdez's major stage creation of the 1980s: a production entitled *Corridos*. The show has enjoyed considerable box office success both in San Juan Bautista (1982) and at the Marines' Memorial Theater of San Francisco (1983). It also traveled to the Old Globe Theatre in San Diego and the Variety Arts Theatre in Los Angeles. *Corridos* harvested the critical acclaim of the establishment press and received virtually all Bay area theater awards for the 1983 season. A brief examination of *Corridos* corresponds with the trajectory of the present inquiry: the stated goal of *Corridos* is "to explore the relationship between men and women."[31] Let us examine the results of this exploration, especially as they pertain to women.

The *corridos* (traditional ballads) chosen for performance are "*Rosita Alvirez*," "*Cornelio Vega*," "*Tierra sin Nombre*," "*Delgadina*," and a Luis Valdez weaving of "*La Rielera/La Valentina/La Adelita*" entitled "*Soldadera.*" What, then, is the nature of the relationship between men and women? One prominent feature common to these *corridos* is the murder of a woman. One exception is "*Cornelio Vega,*" where a man is murdered "*por amar a una mujer* [for loving a woman]." Valdez himself indicates in an interview: "*Hay un tema central que tiene que ver con la violencia en contra de las mujeres que desgraciadamente es real, hasta hoy en día. Es parte de nuestra historia como es parte de nuestro presente*" ("There is a central theme having to do with violence against women that unfortunately is real, to this very day. It is part of our history as it is part of our present").[32] The theme of violence against women, however, is in no way treated as an issue or a problem. To the contrary: it is used as a comic element or simply as a dramatic climax. And through the very choice of *corridos,* violence against women occupies a prominent and almost exclusive role in "the relationship between men and women." In fact, male/female relationships seem to exhaust themselves in violence. In the San Francisco production, the *corrido* of "*Doña Elena y El Francés*" was added; Doña Elena is of course shot by her husband. In an effort to establish a kind of equality between the sexes, a *corrido* in which a woman murders her husband was also added: "*El Corrido de Conchita la Viuda Alegre.*" The heavy focus on shooting and blood project the image of Mexicans as a bloodthirsty, vengeful crowd. In spite of the abundance of existing *corridos* in which no one is murdered, only *corridos* with violence between men and women are dramatized. The desire to exploit the dramatic tensions of violence takes precedence over the desire to provide a balanced portrayal of a people and of their ballad tradition.

The excessive violence in the vision of relationships between men and women is not startling, given Luis Valdez's mythical and violent vision of what he terms "basic human experience." Within that vision, historical process is put in terms of the sexual imagery of rape. And, by implication, sexual experience is likened to the historical process of raw conquest. In his own words:

We who are of the Third World and are victims of colonization have been subjected with the rest of the world to the phenomenon of Europe for the last five hundred years. These people left that section of the world and they went out and conquered other vast sections of the world. Now conquest and that warriorlike stance is not peculiar to this period of history, it has been all throughout the history of the human race and also in the Americas. Perhaps what is upsetting us is that we are still in this period, that we are still stuck. The modern Genghis Khan is still with

us and he came from Europe in all of his forms. He came in a particularly masculine form. In the case of the Spanish he came in iron armor.
The male erection made flesh, if you will, *"Chingate, Cabron!"* ["Fuck
you, you bastard."] If I may refer to basic mythical experience of the male
in the sex act—that is what it takes. In order to do your stuff as a man,
you have to have armor and a spear and you have to penetrate and the
more you penetrate the better it is. *Dime que no* [Tell me that's not true].
On the other hand, there is the other part which is just as natural which
is the female experience which is *"Vente, Cabron"* ["Fuck me, you bastard"]. Those two fit together. I am not trying to embarrass you. I am
talking basic human experience.[33]

Related to the presence of violence is the *Corridos* production narrator's
statement that the *corridos* portray types such as *la coqueta* (the coquette) or
el valiente (the brave-but-foolhardy). The type that emerges in the course of
staging a *corrido,* however, is very much a result of dramaturgic interpretation.
Attaching one label to a *corrido* figure involves a choice by which one characteristic, among many possible ones, is singled out. It is the essence of stereotyping. One example of this procedure can be seen in the decision to charac-
terize Rosita Alvirez as a coquette. Instead of focusing upon the *hija desobediente*
(i.e., the mother/daughter relationship), she emerges as a loose and reckless
woman. Highlighted action includes, for example, Rosita seductively lifting
her dress in front of a mirror and flashing her legs. At the dance, Rosita is
lewdly flirtatious and then seems to "get what she deserves." In other words,
her provocative behavior seemingly justifies Hippolito's violence against her.
However, Rosita could also have been typed as the *hija desobediente,* the diso-
bedient daughter, highlighting the mother/daughter relationship. Yet that relationship, and the traditional Mexican value of a mother's advice, are sabotaged
from the outset by the willful decision to portray the mother as a stumbling
drunkard.

The dramatization of *"Tierra sin nombre"* distorts the *corrido* text by pro-
jecting a male fantasy of female submissiveness. Its plot consists of a love tri-
angle; a woman loves two men and finally chooses one over the other. At
the wedding she is murdered by the man she did not choose. The dramatized
corrido distorts the text in various ways. For example, the successful suitor is
portrayed as a rich, "handsome" Spanish-type gentleman whereas the rejected
man is a barefooted *indio-campesino* (Indian-farmworker) type. Thus, through
a dramaturgic sleight of hand, the woman character is subtly maneuvered out

of legitimately choosing between two men based on emotional considerations. She bases her decision on money (class) and looks (race): she chooses the rich, tall, "handsome" man, who symbolically throws around a bag of coins. But is it really *her* decision? Cast in the ingenue mold, the female character cannot resist the advances of the good-looking rich man. He actively pursues her and she passively submits, her eyes lowered in shyness. We are left with the stereotype of the passive Mexican woman. None of that is in the original *corrido* text. As a comment on the nature of relationships between men and women, and as a comment about women, it projects a male fantasy of female submissiveness. Throughout the show the narrator emphasizes the point that "*corridos* are macho in viewpoint." Commentary such as that would appear to indicate that the images of men and women we see before us simply represent a retrograde Mexican tradition. That is also what the script indicates to us when we are told that "the *corridos* are reproduced with loyalty to the *corrido* tradition." Such statements seek to equate what *corridos* are with what is in reality one interpretation of them. A sharp distinction between the two must be drawn, however. Otherwise, not only a number of female and male *corrido* characters are stereotyped but also the entire *corrido* tradition. The images of women for sale, women as passive victims, women as drunkard mothers are not a creation of the *corrido* tradition but a projection of the *Corridos* production.

Valdez's emphasis on so-called machismo could easily have been balanced by the inclusion of other neglected non-*machista corridos* such as "*Juana Gallo*," "*Agripina*," "*El Corrido de las Comadres*," or "*Maria y Julian*," all of which provide multifaceted, narrative ballad portrayals of women. The *corrido* "*Juana Gallo*" describes the heroic actions of a young woman warrior in various battles of the Mexican Revolution. Agripina—after whom the *corrido* is named— also engages in battle.

One segment within the *Corridos* production is entitled "*Soldadera*," a *pastiche* of three famous *corridos* about women. It is of special interest because Luis Valdez conceived it as a corrective to his own interpretation of the *corrido* tradition as "macho":

> In search of some justice to the true role of women in Mexican history, we now go to the period most *aficionados* consider to be the high point . . . of the *corrido*: the Revolution of 1910. . . . And there we find three legendary songs about three legendary women—*La Adelita, La Valentina* and *La Rielera*. . . . These, together with a character inspired by

the dispatches of an American journalist riding with Pancho Villa back in 1914, a man by the name of John Reed, now combine to give us a portrait of Mexican woman at war.[34]

"*Soldadera*" is of further interest because Socorro Valdez plays a lead female role. For Socorro the piece marks another breakthrough in her career as a performer. After 1980 she went to Hollywood in search of other acting opportunities. Her return to San Juan Bautista was not unconditional. She demanded to play a role that she had long been denied. In her words:

> He [Luis Valdez] put the *corrido* together and he wanted me to play the role, because I had been after him for a length of time. You know, I wanted to play a young girl. And I didn't want makeup on my face. I didn't want lipstick. I didn't want false eyelashes or fake boobs or nothing. I just wanted to be myself up there, just wanted to be the Indian person that I am. . . . I came back to him [Luis], but I said: "That's it. No more masks, no more *calavera* [skeleton] face, no more *calavera* bones on my face. None of that shit. I'll go out there in a plain cotton dress and I'll have those people going."[35]

She did, in truth, have *Corridos* audiences going. Her stage presence and commitment to the work at hand were unique within the cast. Yet the strength of her performance was diminished by the script's vision of women. What is Valdez's vision of women of the Mexican Revolution? One of the striking features within "*Soldadera*" is that it is not female characters such as La Adelita, La Valentina, and La Rielera who address women's role in history. The production does not draw from even *one* female testimonial source concerning the Mexican Revolution of 1910. Nor were historians of women consulted. The result is a highly superficial and distorted portrayal of women's participation in the Revolution. The character of John Reed (*Insurgent Mexico*) does most of the talking in the piece entitled "*Soldadera*." John Reed, the only Anglo in the production, also functions as white savior: he is the only male in the production who does not engage in violence against women. He is a heroic man who speaks gently and protects Elizabeta (Socorro Valdez) from her surly Mexican companion.

Reed's manner stands in strong contrast to that of the three *soldaderas* and the Mexican men. The verbal exchanges between these men and women are almost exclusively aggressive and/or abusive. Men and women fall into the categories of conqueror or conquered. Some effort is made within "*Soldadera*" to demonstrate diversity in women—but that diversity is external: La Valentina is the hip-swaying, hard-nosed companion to the colonel. In the San

Juan Bautista production she also displays a strong inclination toward attire highly unsuited to the rigors of the Mexican Revolution: she wears spiked-heel boots and tight pants. La Adelita carries a rifle; La Rielera (Socorro Valdez) is a gentle-souled Indian woman who follows men. The semblance of diversity collapses entirely when the women engage in dialogue. Their contribution to the narrative line consists entirely of discussions concerning the finding and losing of men, about following men, about holding on to men. There is nothing in their dialogue or actions to reveal any depth in their character nor in understanding of the revolution around them. Mexican women are not shown in their true roles as thinking historical agents but only as helpmates to men.

John Reed, for all his talking, provides no insight into the social forces within the revolution. He has been edited in such a way that he portrays battles without causes. The Mexican Revolution, and history in general, is reduced to a backdrop, a foil for song numbers and centerstage chatter. La Rielera engages in two activities: sleeping with her man, Juan, and making tortillas. The Valdezian portrayal of *soldaderas* (the soldier women of the Mexican Revolution) constitutes a distorted simplification of the historic role of these women. For although some women did cook for men on the revolutionary campaigns, many women also fought in battle; and many joined the revolutionary forces on their own. It is fair to conclude that Luis Valdez's "search of some justice to the true role of women in Mexican history" was conducted less than halfheartedly, for it produced meager findings. The professed search amounted to little more than a rhetorical device aimed at paying lip service to women's presence in history. Notwithstanding the vast critical acclaim that greeted the piece, with it the stage portrayal of Mexican women has reached a new low.

The deplorable representation of Mexican/Chicana women is a chronic weakness and signature of Luis Valdez's mainstream productions such as *Zoot Suit, Corridos,* or the recent film *La Bamba* (1987). In *Zoot Suit,* which earned widespread recognition as a landmark play and movie (1980s), we again encounter the stereotypic dominant mother, the whorelike Bertha, the virginal Della, and a white savior, here Alice Bloomfield. Most lamentable, the true historical role of the Chicana Josefina Fierro in organizing the Sleepy Lagoon Defense Committee in 1942 on behalf of the zoot suiters was completely erased. Historian Bert N. Corona sharply criticizes Luis Valdez's distortion of the facts:

> In 1942, Josefina Fierro, as national secretary of the Congreso Nacional de los Pueblos de Habla Española, carried out two very significant actions. One was the formation of the Sleepy Lagoon Defense Committee (contrary to the distorted version in Luis Valdez's play *Zoot Suit*) which

conducted the public defense of the twenty-two Mexicans who were tried for the death of one. Josefina traveled all over the nation, assisted by Luisa Moreno, to develop the broad national campaign against the racist and divisive indictments and yellow journalistic press descriptions of the Hearst Press. . . . It is to be deplored that Luis Valdez could find insufficient drama in the true facts about the Defense of the Sleepy Lagoon and Zoot Suit victims, that he had to rely upon Hollywood gimmicks of a fictitious melodrama between two persons [Alice Bloomfield and Henry Reyna] that never took place in order to tell his story.[36]

Truth and substance have taken a back seat to melodrama in *Corridos* as well. In spite of the production's undeniable entertainment qualities — the visual effects, the dancing, musical performance, the fast pace — it is entertaining without being thought provoking. What is worse, *Corridos* affirms Hollywood images of men in sombreros and on horseback engaged, for the most part, in violence with colorful señoritas defined in terms of men. The tradition of such images and their marketability in the entertainment business was recently described by Luis Valdez:

> Now there was a time when this country reveled in Latino images — commercially — and that was in the 1940s of course, parallel with the Zoot Suit era. . . . The U.S. . . . turned its attention to Latin America and said, "How can we sell more movies in Latin America?" and obviously they said "Let's put more Latin images on films, but let's make them 'safe' images." So what we ended up with was Carmen Miranda. What we ended up with was the Latin Night Club and Rhumbaing down to Rio or what have you. . . . Desi Arnaz came out of that era, you know. But nothing came from the Mexican Revolution . . . at least not during World War II.[37]

With *Corridos,* the Mexican Revolution has now entered the ranks of safe (i.e., caricature) commercial "Latino" images such as those projected by Desi Arnaz, Carmen Miranda, and various others. The media may well revel in these well-worn images, now marketed as "New American Theatre." Some may thrill at the visibility the show provides for so-called Hispanics. Others may take pride in seeing Mexican-Americans perform in what is known as legitimate theatre in show business circles. But, El Teatro Campesino in the 1960s set the standard to demand more than that.

The highly visible professional Chicano productions of recent years offer little that is inspirational or alternative. With regard to the representation of Mexican/Chicana women, productions such as *Zoot Suit, Corridos,* or the film

La Bamba are nothing short of devastating. It would appear that the absence of a collective work context has left Luis Valdez wholly unrestrained in giving expression to his vision of women. The division of labor inherent to professional theatre and commercial film, with its hierarchy of personnel and constant turnover of hired actors, does not foster discussion nor the development of a critical consciousness, let alone disagreement or a challenge to established models. The production team recruits from a generation of entertainment actresses/actors for whom the portrayal of Mexicans on stage is not an issue. In my conversations with the cast members of *Corridos* it became apparent that the images of women (and men) they project are not a matter of particular concern. In the absence of a group of actresses who have learned to question and reject shallow roles, the emergence of a broader vision of women within the new Teatro Campesino production company seems unlikely. El Teatro Campesino is now the name of a small administrative apparatus that puts on an occasional play in which the spirit of group commitment and the performance energy characteristic of the Teatro Campesino ensemble is altogether missing. The tight-knit acting ensemble has been displaced by actors who do their jobs and then return to Los Angeles in search of the next gig. The model for the new organization comes from business administration. Theatrical production is streamlined: actors act, the director directs, administrators administrate. In the arena of glittering lights, the struggle to establish new women's roles has dissipated. Yet far from the limelight we can perceive the efforts of Chicanas who continue to explore and create dramatic alternatives for women. The dream to reflect the vast spectrum of Chicana womanhood on the stage will in time find creative expression. After the *Corridos* production, Socorro Valdez described her dream of reflecting the vast spectrum of Chicana womanhood on stage:

> I'll tell you what my dream is—one of my dreams. And I know I'll get to it because it's a driving thing in me. . . . My dream is to be able to do a theatre piece on the phases of womanhood. It's something that has not been done yet. All the times that I've seen women's programs or women in this or women in that, it somehow has never been quite satisfactory for me, you know. No one can take womanhood and put it into *one* thing. But that is precisely what I want to do. I want to put womanhood into every form that I can express: in singing, in crying, in laughing, everything. That role is not yet there. That role has not been written. Maybe it has been written in a Shakespearean way. But I don't relate to those European images of women. . . . Women are obviously in a

type of great void. They are balanced, but in terms of the way the world looks at us they've put us in this position where we've accepted the condition of doing one role instead of many. If there were some way of taking that and putting it into words that are theatrical, I would like to do that. I don't believe a man is going to write that. I don't believe that for one single minute. And I sure can't wait for Luis to write that role.[38]

The activities of several of the women from El Teatro Campesino—Olivia Chumacero, Socorro Valdez, Diane Rodríguez, Yolanda Parra—and the work of Silvia Wood in Tucson, Arizona; Nita Luna and El Teatro Aguacero in New Mexico; the women and men of El Teatro de la Esperanza; the now dormant Valentina Productions; Cara Hill-Castañon's one-woman shows; and the plays of Estela Portillo Trambley, Denise Chavez, and Cherríe Moraga all mark the entry into a new cycle of theatrical activity for Chicanas. We are not without inspirational models, nor without the example of women who question and who strive to reclaim a fully human female identity onstage. We do well to acknowledge that activity in the writing of theatre history.

NOTES

I use the term *Chicano* as it is commonly used: to refer to persons of Mexican ancestry in the United States, also known as Mexican-Americans. I deliberately avoid the use of the hegemonic term *Hispanic* because it obscures our Indian ancestry, also because it seeks to identify us with a colonial power of the sixteenth century, and because it is so general in its usage as to be meaningless.

The research for this and other portions of my study on El Teatro Campesino was conducted under a grant from the National Research Council/Ford Foundation. In its preliminary form, this essay was presented by invitation of the University of Arizona's Renato Rosaldo Lecture Series. I would like to thank the women of El Teatro Campesino for their encouragement and collaboration on this project.

This essay appeared in a different form in *Chicano Voices: Intersections of Class, Race, and Gender* (Austin, Texas: CMAS Publications, 1986).

1. These are recurrent phrases in writings on Teatro Campesino. I have used these for the sake of illustration. They are from Carlota Cárdenas de Dwyer, "The Development of Chicano Drama and Luis Valdez's Actos," in *Modern Chicano Writers,* ed. J. Somers and Tomás Ybarra-Frausto, 160–66 (Englewood Cliffs, N.J.: Prentice-Hall, 1979).

2. Jorge Huerta, *Chicano Theater: Themes and Forms* (Ypsilanti, Mich.: Bilingual Press, 1982), 17. Huerta has been the most prolific writer on El Teatro Campesino. In all of his writings the dynamics of the creative process are blurred by his linear vision of a great man directing the anonymous masses of actors. Teatro members who devoted ten or more years to the intense collective undertaking of El Teatro Campesino are never named, let alone quoted, in Huerta's history.

3. See, for example, Antonia Castañeda Shular, Tomás Ybarra-Frausto, Joseph Sommers, eds., *Literatura Chicana* (Englewood Cliffs, N. J.: Prentice-Hall, 1972); *Chicano Voices,* ed. C. Cárdenas de Dwyer (Boston: Houghton Mifflin, 1975); Dorothy Harth and

Lewis Baldwin, eds., *Voices of Aztlan, Chicano Literature of Today* (New York: Mentor, 1974).

4. Personal interview with Olivia Chumacero (TS), Core Group Member, El Teatro Campesino, San Juan Bautista, California, 19 January 1983, 11–12.

5. The characterization of women in the Teatro Campesino repertoire is discussed in the full version of this paper. Also, selected examples of writings on Teatro history are scrutinized.

6. Personal interview with Diane Rodríguez (TS), Core Group Member, El Teatro Campesino, Strasbourg, France, June 7, 1980, 5.

7. Personal interview with Socorro Valdez (TS), Core Group Member, El Teatro Campesino, San Juan Bautista, California, March 1, 1983, 6.

8. Ibid., 8.

9. Interview, 4.

10. Interview, 30.

11. Socorro Valdez Interview, 33.

12. Interview, 7.

13. Socorro Valdez Interview, 7.

14. Personal interview with Yolanda Parra of El Teatro Campesino, San Juan Bautista, California, December 31, 1982, 6–7.

15. Interview, 6–7.

16. Interview, 6.

17. Interview, 6.

18. Interview, 31.

19. Personal interview with Olivia Chumacero and Diane Rodríguez (TS), El Teatro Campesino, Strasbourg, France, June 7, 1980, 13.

20. Socorro Valdez interview, 32.

21. Ibid., 5.

22. Interview, 13.

23. Interview, 3.

24. Interview, 4.

25. Interview, 12.

26. Interview, 29.

27. Interview, 4.

28. Interview, 5.

29. Interview, 11.

30. Interview with Luis Valdez by María Emilia Martín for California Public Radio, May 5, 1983.

31. Luis Valdez's statement in the role of narrator during the San Juan Bautista workshop production run of *Corridos,* September 16, 1982, through October 31, 1982. The San Francisco production ran from April 20 to July 4, 1983.

32. Interview by María Emilia Martín, May 5, 1983.

33. *Final Report to the National Endowment for the Humanities* (TS), "Califas, Chicano Art and Culture in California," Oakes College, April 18, 1982, 43.

34. Luis Valdez, *Corridos: A New Music Play* (TS), Final Draft. Marines' Memorial Theater, San Francisco, April to July, 1983, 59.

35. Interview, 12.

36. Bert Corona, "Chicano Scholars and Public Issues in the United States in the Eighties," in *History, Culture and Society: Chicano Studies,* ed. Mario R. Garcia et. al., 16 (Ypsilanti, Mich.: Bilingual Press, 1983).

37. *Final Report to the National Endowment for the Humanities* (TS), "Califas, Chicano Art and Culture in California," Oakes College, April 18, 1982, 43.

38. Interview, 36.

REFERENCES

Chumacero, Olivia. 1983. Personal interview, January 19.

Chumacero, Olivia, and Diane Rodríguez. 1980. Personal interview, June 7.

Condon, Frank, director. 1981. *Rose of the Rancho.* By David Belasco. Adapted by Cesar Flores and Luis Valdez. El Teatro Campesino Playhouse, San Juan Bautista, California.

Final Report to the National Endowment for the Humanities. 1982. "Califas, Chicano Art and Culture in California." Oakes College, April 18.

Interview with Luis Valdez. 1983. María Emilia Martín. California Public Radio, May 5.

Parra, Yolanda. 1982. Personal interview, December 21.

Rodríguez, Diane. 1980. Personal interview, June 7.

El Teatro Campesino. 1971. *Actos.* San Juan Bautista, Calif.: Menyah Productions.

——. n.d. *La Carpa de los Rasquachis,* TS. El Teatro Campesino Incorporated. San Juan Bautista, California.

——. n.d. *La Gran Carpa Cantinflesca,* TS. El Teatro Campesino Incorporated. San Juan Bautista, California.

Valdez, Luis. n.d. *Bandido! The American Melodrama of Tiburcio Vásquez, Notorious California Bandit,* TS, second draft. El Teatro Campesino Incorporated. San Juan Bautista, California.

——. 1980. *Fin del mundo,* TS. El Teatro Campesino Incorporated. San Juan Bautista, California.

——. 1982. *Los Corridos.* TS. El Teatro Campesino Playhouse. San Juan Bautista, California. September 16 through October 31.

——. 1983. *Corridos: A New Music Play.* TS. Marines' Memorial Theater. San Francisco. April 20 through July 4.

Valdez, Socorro. 1983. Personal interview, March 1.

Yarbro-Bejarano, Yvonne. 1983. "Teatropoesía in the Bay Area: Tongues of Fire." *Revista Chicano-Riqueña* 11, no. 1 (Spring): 78–94.

JANELLE REINELT

Michelene Wandor:
Artist and Ideologue

Perhaps more than any other single woman, Michelene Wandor has made it possible to perceive and understand the relationship between the women's movement and theatre in Britain. She has accomplished this task through her multiple roles as critic, historian, playwright, and activist. While most of the other women included in this book are known primarily through their fictional writing for the stage, Wandor is better known for her historical and critical writing, and also as the editor of several anthologies of plays linked by the issue of sexual politics. She is, however, equally serious about her own writing for the stage and radio, and about her poetry. Recently, Wandor's five-hour play enjoyed a run on the Lyttleton stage at the National Theatre. Written in association with Mike Alfreds, *The Wandering Jew* is one of the first plays by a contemporary British woman opening on a main stage of the National Theatre.

Although possessing her own specific personal history, Wandor's experiences provide a prototype for the experiences of many women who began to work seriously in the British theatre and in politics during the ferment of the 1960s. She had been interested in theatre since childhood. In London during her adolescence, a dedicated English teacher took her to see the whole of Shakespeare at the Old Vic and her brother took her to see Joan Littlewood's productions at Stratford East.[1] She read English literature and acted extensively at Cambridge, but did not start writing until after she graduated and returned to London. Between 1968 and 1975, she began writing poetry, plays, and poetry and theatre criticism. In 1971 she became the Poetry Editor of *Time Out,* for which she also wrote theatre reviews. In 1974, she went back to school to do an M.A. at the University of Essex in the sociology of literature. Working part time to support herself and two small sons, she completed her degree in 1976.[2]

During the second half of the 1960s, Wandor experienced many of the passions and contradictions associated with that period. She was writing poetry, but was also in two Marxist study groups, one with women and one mixed. The New Left's commitment to direct political action created certain dilemmas for creative artists. Wandor recalls, "There was a kind of puritanical approach to art—it was OK if you did collective agit-prop work on housing estates, but poetry was kind of reactionary because it was all this interior, individualist bourgeois rubbish. And writing plays as individuals was also rubbish because we had to break down hierarchies and be very collective; companies had to control their own work."[3] New feminist critiques also stressed the importance of collective work and pointed out the link between patriarchy and hierarchy. Wandor experienced a contradiction between politics and her writing, but was also receiving vital stimulation and challenge from her political study/activity. She went back to graduate school to further investigate some of the social theories she was reading, and by the time she finished, the political climate had changed: the "puritan" position had been rethought; poetry and individual writing had a role in building the revolution.

In the late sixties when Wandor started to write, she found herself in the middle of a general burst of vitality and theatrical experimentation. As she has documented in *Look Back in Gender,* the end of censorship in 1968 was a major event that, linked with a favorable financial climate, spawned myriad projects and groups. The Living Theater and La Mama visited from New York, and the bed-sitter domestic drama was replaced with many different styles and forms of theatre, produced on tour in pubs, halls, or in the street. Politics and theatre were inevitably intertwined: "The general raising of the political temperature meant that all playwrights, even those who did not see themselves as 'political' or who tried to keep their distance from various political ideologies, were influenced by the public nature of the political debates and the visibility of political activism—socialist and feminist—at the end of the 1960s and the first part of the 1970s."[4] In her own case, Wandor describes the feeling of openness and possibility. She walked into *Time Out,* more or less "off the street," to approach them about writing and within a week found herself on the staff, where she remained as theatre critic and poetry editor until 1982. Malcolm Griffiths saw a pub production of *The Day After Yesterday* (1972), Wandor's play about the sexual/moral dilemmas of the Miss World contest, and asked her to write something for his company, the Portable Theatre. (The Portable Theatre became one of the most important political theatre groups of the period, where Howard Brenton, Snoo Wilson, and David Hare among others developed some of their early work.) She wrote *Spilt Milk* and *Mal de Mere* in a fluid, nonrealistic style suitable for the touring practices of the Portable. The year 1972 also saw the publication of the first anthology of British Women's Liberation writings, *The Body Politic;* Wandor was editor and contributor.

Writing/Making History

Michelene Wandor has documented the confluence of theatre and sexual politics during this period and through the seventies in *Understudies* (1981) and its revision, *Carry On, Understudies* (1986). These books provide a historical survey of the emergence of feminist and gay theatre and a catalogue of theatrical activity on sexual political issues. Because much of this work has taken place on the fringe, in touring situations, or in Theatre-in-Education, it is subject to exclusion or oversight in traditional theatre publication. Wandor's book results in legitimation of the existence and extent of activity in this arena, ensuring that the history is publicly acknowledged and recorded for the future.

The differences between the first monograph and the revised and expanded edition consist not only of scope but also of approach. The first book provides the political and social context for understanding the development of feminist and gay theatre in the 1970s. The revision develops Wandor's critical theory with respect to feminism and includes assessments and analysis of plays. She explains the differences in a typically historical fashion, pointing out that in the first book, she was in the position of justifying a new kind of theatrical expression that depended on positive audience reception for survival. "It meant that I soft-pedalled on some developing ideas about theory, and refrained (very generously, I think, in retrospect) from making value judgments."[5] The second version, published this year, appears when the feminist and gay movements have had fifteen years to consolidate their goals; their imprint on theatre is unmistakable, if always precarious. The historical situation having shifted, it becomes important to engage in serious critical analysis of established plays and writers. She has a strong counter to the notion that women should not criticize each other's work: ". . . if women do not activate, initiate and take as much control as possible of their own work, then they/we are simply reproducing the associations between the female-equalling-the-feminine-equalling-the-natural/instinctive-equalling-the-anti-intellectual. We may write more plays and creep up to being somewhere close to ten percent of the total of contemporary playwrights . . . but we are not contributing to the way those plays are discussed, perceived and understood."[6]

In both books, the goal is to provide "a critical history of the relationship between theatre, class and gender."[7] Wandor documents three phases of theatrical development (adding a fourth in *Carry On*), highlighting the most notable companies, playwrights, and plays to emerge in each period. The first phase, 1969–73, saw the mingling of theatre and politics as the Women's Street Theatre Group and the Gay Street Theatre Group demonstrated at the Miss World contest. The political point of the plays was the overriding concern of this early work. Groups often held discussions with the audience after performances, and style varied from naturalistic to exaggerated depending on the message conveyed.

During the second phase, 1973–77, some permanent companies formed that are still active a decade later. The Women's Theatre Group, Monstrous Regiment, and the Gay Sweatshop had their first productions. Several women gained access to the prestigious subsidized theatres during this period: playwrights Caryl Churchill and Pam Gems, and director Buzz Goodbody. In her discussion of the second and the third phase (from 1977), Wandor focuses on the three groups in order to describe the "different emphases on the political theatre axis, reflected in their audiences, their ways of working, the class content of their work, and the theatrical forms they took on and explored."[8]

The chapter on the third phase ends with a section entitled "Organization." The Feminist Theatre Study Group and a series of conferences under the title "Women in Entertainment" carried a set of issues into the sphere of public debate. These included sexual representation in West End shows, women and humor, women and creativity, and women in the profession — as writers, directors, and administrators. Wandor reports on the financial and professional status of women theatre workers, drawing on a 1983 survey commissioned by the Standing Conference of Women Theatre Directors and Administrators.

It should be clear from the preceding discussion of Wandor's historical method that she brings tools from her study of the sociology of literature to bear on the theatre. In recognizing and making explicit the relationship between audience, material, and financial support, Wandor constantly keeps an analysis of theatrical modes of production in the foreground of the discussion, although she never uses this term. In contrasting the grass-roots base of the Women's Theatre Group (WTG) to the relative professionalism of the Women's Group, she provides a context for understanding the WTG's commitment to the experience of working-class women. She contrasts the styles developed out of rough, agit-prop beginnings with the more polished work of those whose background was the professional theatre, not in order to make some ill-considered remarks about quality, but in order to illustrate the links between various theatrical styles and the economic and artistic conditions that produce them.

Wandor provides another tool for gender/class analysis in her account of three different types of feminism. This theory and its application first appeared in an essay for the magazine *Drama,* accompanying the results of the survey conducted by the Standing Conference of Women Theatre Directors and Administrators.[9] She expanded the discussion into a chapter for the *Understudies* revision, "Political Dynamics: the feminisms."

In characterizing tendencies within feminism as (1) radical feminism, (2) bourgeois feminism, and (3) socialist feminism, Wandor did not break new theoretical ground.[10] However, in popularizing these notions (especially in her journalism), she provides a wide audience with some critical tools for developing a feminist perspective on aesthetic experience. She recognizes the strengths of all three types of feminism insofar as they all challenge male dominance, promote self-determination for women, and seek social change.

As might be expected, Michelene Wandor is a socialist feminist and believes that it is the only kind of feminism that can offer the possibility of achieving revolutionary change because socialist feminism acknowledges that power relations are based on class as well as gender and that these interact in various, sometimes contradictory ways. Strategies for change have to take into account both the instances when women can achieve solidarity across class lines and also the instances when women must work with men to challenge political power based on class.

The three-part schema forms the basis for Wandor's analysis of contemporary plays by women. Caryl Churchill's *Vinegar Tom* is seen as possessing two dynamics: a socialist feminist one in the emphasis on class and gender oppression in the seventeenth-century narrative of women labeled as witches, and a radical feminist one in the contemporary songs which are intercut with the narrative. "The difficulty . . . is that the complexity of the narrative is undermined by the crudeness of the songs. The narrative indicates very clearly where men are responsible, but it does so in a context which makes class and gender sense. The songs simply imply that all men are to blame and the two messages actually contradict one another."[11] *Trafford Tanzi,* Claire Luckham's popular play about a lady wrestler who effectively overthrows the oppression of her family and her husband to make it to the top, is set in a working-class context, but has a bourgeois feminist dynamic, according to Wandor, since it celebrates women's equality with men, taking male values as the norm.[12] A play with a radical feminist dynamic like Nell Dunn's *Steaming*—portraying a community of women struggling against the male membership of the local council which wants to close the baths where the women meet — loses its feminist dynamic because of the terms of its representation. The cast of women who spend large amounts of stage time in the nude becomes vulnerable to voyeurism as the audience is positioned to become voyeur. Only a very careful and strong production could circumvent this pitfall, which the original production did not succeed in doing, in Wandor's judgment.

Michelene Wandor's most recent book, *Look Back in Gender,* is an extension of her analysis to some of the most prominent plays by both men and women of the postwar years. The book has two foci: to understand how a play's controlling gender shapes its meanings and to understand how historical changes affecting the society as a whole affect the portrayal of gender.

In her discussions of gender, Wandor is careful to distinguish her perspective from a schematic biologism which simply asserts that the writings of men and women are fundamentally different. She finds that they *are* different, but only in the sense that gender is "one of the fundamental imperatives in the imaginative creation of the world on stage." Playwrights write out of their own experience of the world as gendered, and the choices they make about the representations of gendered characters (which of course they all are) reflect ideological assumptions that may or may not be conscious.

Look Back in Gender divides postwar drama into two phases, separated by the abolition of censorship in 1968. The book itself is divided into two parts; the last chapter of Part 1 reprints Kenneth Tynan's classic essay, "The Royal Smut-Hound," which details and harangues the practice of censorship in Britain. Allowing her readers to see a before-and-after effect, Wandor makes visible the shifts that occur. While material dealing with sexuality is always present, the repression of it in the first phase (with censorship) resulted in more ambiguous and symbolic treatments of those themes. Obviously, freedom to use graphic language and bolder images is explored in the second phase (after censorship ended). Also, the family unit, which dominates most plays she studies from the earlier period, is absent in the latter, replaced by social, public spaces and relationships. While politics is treated more extensively in the second phase, it is often divorced from personal life.[13] In the plays Wandor studies, by both men and women, heterosexual relations are absent or not central. The single exception appears to be plays by men treating homosexuality, in which sexuality is itself political. Thus a pendulum swing seems to have resulted in which the new taboo is on family and emotion, creating the same old polarity between intellect/emotion, political/personal, men/women.

There are problems in accepting Wandor's conclusions because they are, of necessity, based on a selection of only some plays from the period, and not others. She offers the criteria of success, presence on exam syllabi, and wide production. But the temptation to find other plays of equal stature that do not fit the terms of her analysis is great. Churchill's *Cloud 9,* for example, seems to treat specifically issues of the family, the relationship of the personal to the political, and of course, sexuality.

The decision to discuss well over thirty plays is itself a liability in that the discussions must perforce be very short and often more summary than substance. *Look Back in Gender* is caught in a double bind, not including enough material to support its general conclusions about the period on one hand, and covering too much material, making substantive analysis impossible on the other. Wandor is planning to write a sequel or second part, which may alleviate one or both of these problems.

Wandor's particular readings of a variety of plays from the 1970s and 1980s are often open to question and argument, but that is in some ways the point: she has laid the groundwork for a serious and detailed discussion of the effect of sexual representation in performance, a ground that includes the current social codes operating in society, the makeup of the audience, and the content of the text itself. She invites a semiotic analysis of production meanings and engages in this lively debate.

Providing a socialist feminist framework for the perception of theatrical production is no small feat. In fact, it links Wandor's work as a journalist with her work as a critic/scholar and as an editor. Her reviews for *Time Out* during the seventies offered the audience a number of critical reference points. In a piece on *Anna Laub,* for example, she points out how the gender of the protagonist leads to a gender-bound message: "The play's general thesis is that people should be able to choose themselves whether to live or die—and Anna's fate is sealed accordingly. While the philosophical argument is intriguing, its concentration on Anna as the key symbol means that statements are also being made about women's role, as well as about life and thought; the conclusion therefore has the extra dimension of anti-feminist content."[14] This kind of analysis helps produce a theatre-going audience sensitized to the encoding of gender in the production of meaning. Commenting on the defeat of the social-ist option in *Dusa, Fish, Stas and Vi,* Wandor praised the production's "remark-able confidence and subtlety," but also criticized "a perilously under-thought-out approach: the play could too easily be used to prove that socialist feminism is a dead end, all the more so since Pam Gems writes so well about women's supportiveness."[15] The reviews of these two plays may illustrate Wandor's own description of her journalism in this period. In *Carry On, Understudies,* she writes about developing a strategy of couching critical comments within a positive overall assessment. However, perusal of Wandor's journalism does not support the self-judgment that she "soft-pedalled" her reviewing. If she found fault, she tended to spell it out—writing about the Sadista Sisters' 1976 show, "the new butch decadence does little more than show that some women can be as bad on stage as some men."[16]

Between 1982 and 1985, Michelene Wandor made a series of playscripts available to a wide public through her editions of *Plays by Women,* published by Methuen. Together with accounts in the two *Understudy* books of plays that have not been published (e.g., *Kiss and Kill,*' *Calamity Jane, Enslaved by Dreams*), these four volumes put feminism's contribution to theatre before an audience just beginning to be aware of changing sexual representation. She published the work of established playwrights like Caryl Churchill and Pam Gems, but also of relative newcomers like Debbie Horsfield and Claire Luckham. Wandor also edited a collection of group-devised scripts for Journeyman Press, *Strike While the Iron Is Hot* (1980), bringing to attention the work of the Gay Sweatshop, Red Ladder Theatre, and Women's Theatre Group. Always, in introductory essays in these volumes, Wandor sets a context for their reception that stresses the social and political conditions of their production. Addressing the leftist readership of *Strike* she writes, "The intellectual left has given far more attention to the mass distributed arts than it has to theatre; rightly in terms of analysing what is beamed out to large numbers of people by the dominant culture. But theatre must not be dismissed simply on statistical grounds. The fact that theatre is still a labour intensive medium, the fact that there is live contact between producers and consumers, the fact that political theatre can with great assurance seek out new audiences, and the fact that drama is being used more and more as an educational medium, makes it a vital area for cultural struggle."[17] Wandor combines the roles of advocate for the artistic work, theatre historian, and sensitive critic in all her journalistic and critical/scholarly writings. What remains is to consider her own creative writing for the stage.

Writing/Making Plays

Michelene Wandor has written over fifteen stage plays since 1970. They range from lunchtime theatre offerings to a five-hour extravaganza at the National. Stylistically, Wandor has experimented with melodrama (*The Wandering Jew*), domestic comedy (*Scissors* and *AID Thy Neighbor*), verse drama (*Aurora Leigh*) and occasional realism (*The Old Wives' Tale*.) She is not partial to realism, however, feeling that the challenges and satisfactions for the writer are not great. Helene Keyssar has characterized her as a realist writer,[18] but Wandor disagrees. Clarifying her position, she says that realism describes what people were writing in the seventies, but not her own commitment to it. She thinks this seventies trend is understandable and can be compared to the rise of the nineteenth-century novel when it seemed that "the most political way to write about the conditions of ordinary people was to record the details of it."[19] Sometimes the minutiae of domestic realism is employed in a symbolic way. Wandor experienced Marsha Norman's *'night, Mother* as a case in point. "She used the everyday experience of women's lives to go on about a very painful existential dilemma . . . so it was almost like the realism was a screen, although it was also the way in which they managed their lives together—so it became symbolic." She objects to, and is not interested in, material that confuses realistic detail with message, when something is "given to you for its own sake. I have no time for that writing."[20]

She does have time for a variety of styles and projects. Rather than trying to survey her work here, which would result in little more than cataloguing the plays, I will discuss three plays that represent different dimensions of her work.[21] *Whores D'Oeuvres, AID Thy Neighbor,* and *The Wandering Jew* represent various subject matter, staging experiments, and working conditions, and can serve as a useful introduction to Wandor's playwrighting.

Two whores on a makeshift raft sailing down the Thames after a hurricane: one of them wears a rented policewoman's suit, intended to lend respectability to a leafleting campaign in support of legalizing prostitution. On the way to do politics, they become stranded in the downpour. This situation is the premise of *Whores D'Oeuvres* (*WD*, 1978), Michelene Wandor's most surreal play. She wrote it for two of Malcolm Griffiths's Trent Polytechnic students, and he directed the first production. Like the other plays she wrote for him and/or which he directed (*Spilt Milk* and *Mal de Mere*, Portable Theatre 1972, and *To Die Among Friends,* Paradise Foundry, 1974), *Whores D'Oeuvres* entails stripped-down space-staging suitable to touring, which provides the appropriate scenic representation for a play that takes place on several symbolic and theatrical levels.

The narrative line of the play is simply the women's attempt to survive the storm and find help, although the urgency of being "stranded at sea" is not foregrounded. The play has seven scenes, alternating day and night; the night scenes are marked in the script as dream sequences. These segments work on three levels: as actual dreams or rather nightmares of women in this line of work (e.g., a simulated rape in scene 4), as repressed emotions and attitudes, normally kept at bay, and as the "dark" or hidden realities behind prostitution.

When Griffiths approached her to write something for his two students, Wandor was intrigued with the possibility of writing about prostitution: "the arguments [were] flying around about it at the time—'it's only a job'— and it seemed to me that sexuality is a lot more fraught and complicated than that, and you can't simply reduce it to an economic argument as an easy way for women to get money back from men as though it's not affecting them."[22] Scene 5 pits the two women in an argument about whether prostitution is just a job:

> *Pat.* My punters pay a fair price and they know how to treat a woman.
> *Tina.* We can't all do escort work.
> *Pat.* There you are—you've got no ambition. Anyone can get to the top now if they really want to. We've all got our preconditions now.
> *Tina.* Our what?
> *Pat.* Preconditions for prostitution with a smile. Home is the sailor, home from the sea, and the prostitute's on the pill. If more women took the pill they wouldn't be so bothered about rape.
> *Tina.* Helen got her face slashed last week. (*WD*, 83)[23]

This exchange provides characterization and criticism of bourgeois feminism. Pat is the upwardly mobile hooker who believes that anyone can get ahead; Tina is the street slag. The scene develops this class tension. Tina challenges Pat for her political action: since Pat doesn't work the street, she's not in danger of getting arrested. Pat says she organizes because she wants Tina to be able to pay her rent. She is acting from a bourgeois ideology that sees economic gain as the great equalizer. Tina names the cost of playing by the male-constructed rules of the "game," and not only pinpoints the hidden emotional and physical costs of this view, but also associates accommodation of the sexual status quo with acceptance of the status of hooker. Wandor reinforces these associations in the dream sequence that follows. First the two women play a wife and a prostitute receiving telephone calls from a man telling his wife he will be home late, and then soliciting the hooker. Then Pat and Tina play wife and hooker disparaging each other. Pat/hooker tells Tina/ wife that she is a scab, undercutting the rates. Tina charges that Pat is a thief. For Tina, Pat smells of hate while for Pat, Tina "stink[s] of cowardice and guilt" (*WD,* 87). The scene ends with the decoding of the policewoman's uniform:

Pat. You should have been a policewoman.
Tina. You've got one for your shadow. (*WD,* 87)

The costume of policewoman takes on an ironic meaning on Pat's body. By rationalizing the role of prostitute, legitimizing it, she acts as the watchdog for the status quo. She is literally engaged in legalizing prostitution, instantiating the male system in which women are objects of commerce. The dream sequence portrays class tension behind the two women's positions, making their ideological consequences visible. At the end of the play, the women are going to be rescued, but the differences between them are not resolved. Tina has decided to quit the game, even though she has a daughter to support and no skills. Pat, however, exits with the line, "I've always liked a nice uniform" (*WD,* 89).

AID Thy Neighbor (*ATN*) is totally different from *Whores D'Oeuvres* in tone and technique. The opening stage directions have the familiar ring of an Alan Ayckbourne comedy, which Wandor admits is deliberate: *"The set is two London living rooms, with the dividing wall, as it were, knocked down. It functions on demand as either the home of Sandy and Georgina or Mary and Joseph. At the back of the set are sections which represent separate kitchens of the two houses. At an upper level of the set are the two couples' bedrooms. Downstage there is a table set for a foursome dinner party."*[24] In place of Ayckbourne's slick comedies of class, Wandor has devised a comedy based on sexual preference and the desire to have babies. One straight couple and one gay couple are trying to get pregnant. The play features a series of comparisons: both couples have trouble becoming pregnant, both of the partners to the would-be mothers have ambivalent feelings about parenting, both mothers eventually have artificial insemination by donor (AID). The gay woman becomes pregnant; the straight woman feels resentment until she decides she doesn't really want to be a mother after all. Of course, her husband has meanwhile decided he does want children. In the end, they agree to knock down the wall dividing their flats and, together with a single mother and her school-aged daughter (perfect for babysitting), set up a group living situation. Along the way they foil a would-be investigative reporter who passes herself off as gay in order to do an expose of lesbian couples who try to have children by AID.

This scenario has much that might end up as melodrama, if Wandor did not treat it with such high humor. The first act features a send-up of conventional attitudes toward sexuality as the couples get to know each other. At a first dinner party, Sandy shows up in plastic motorbike trousers, a leather bomber jacket, helmet, and gloves. Playing on the "butch" image, Wandor makes fun of both the familiarity of the stereotype and the inevitable reactions. When Georgina and Mary first overtly discuss Georgina and Sandy's relationship, the dialogue comments on the typicality of the straight woman's response.

> *Georgina.* I'm sure it's not as though you disapprove.
> *Mary.* It isn't as though I disapprove.
> *Georgina.* It's more that you probably never knowingly had a lesbian in
>   the house, let alone entertained a couple round to dinner . . . let alone
>   consoled one after she's had a miscarriage.
> *Mary.* Yes, well, I think you've put that rather well. . . . (*ATN,* 130)

In the second act, after the audience has become familiar with the reality of the characters, the lesbian couple puts on an exaggerated act for the journalist impersonating a gay woman wanting information about AID. They insist on calling themselves and her by male nicknames. They preach slogans at her, "I love consciousness raising over supper" (*ATN,* 148). They get her thoroughly drunk and take compromising pictures of her. The scene is very funny, but what is most striking about it is the way in which it punctures stereotypes of lesbian behavior and celebrates them at the same time. Roles are being consciously assumed and enjoyed, but they are clearly roles. The similarities between Sandra and Joe (Joe wishes he had a motorbike like Sandy, and both whip out to the bar for a quick one when they have fights with their mates), combined with the send-ups of stereotyped behavior, provide a critique of gender construction and its nonintrinsic status.

Wandor has done a good deal of adaptation work over the last ten years. In addition to *The Wandering Jew,* she has adapted Elizabeth Barrett Browning's verse-novel *Aurora Leigh,* first for radio and then for the stage. Many of her adaptations have been radio plays including a three-part dramatization of Jane Austen's *Persuasion* and an eight-part serialization of Dostoyevsky's *The Brothers Karamazov.* When Mike Alfreds was invited to join the National with his own company, he asked Wandor to adapt Eugene Sue's lengthy and complex novel, *The Wandering Jew.* Although both Alfreds and Wandor are credited with the script, the procedure was one of joint consultation and planning followed by Wandor's actual writing (and later editing) of the text. Alfreds was primarily responsible for the production, including casting, staging, and cutting. They worked on it for almost a year, including rehearsals that began in April, 1987; it opened in August, 1987.

The original text was written for serial publication and needed particular work on dramatic shape. Alfreds and Wandor considered making the play into two evenings in the theatre, but it finally became a five-hour performance featuring fifty speaking characters. In the introduction to the published text, Wandor describes the challenge of the adaptation: The story "draws on the potent images and conventions of its time, combining the gothic novel, the adventure story, anguished, semi-pornographic sexuality, romance and innocent faith. At one level the sheer apparent impossibility of the project was what appealed to me most. The question boiled down to the simple one of how to find a theatrical form and a language that retained the heightened melodramatic spirit of the original, and yet would still appeal to a modern audience."[25] She evolved a simple narrative style designed to move the plot and provide description in an impersonal cool mode, intercutting it with alternately expansive and short scenes of stylized action—gothic, melodramatic, even cinematic. Sometimes scenes are played out entirely in visual terms while a scene with spoken dialogue happens simultaneously. The result is the true hybrid of styles and techniques that the novel demands.

The story pits a scattered family descended from seventeenth-century exiles against the powerful, greedy Jesuits. A huge fortune is to be returned to the remaining heirs only if they can assemble for the reading of the will 150 years later, in the narrative present of the play. These family members include two young, innocent sisters, a young, beautiful priest (named Gabriel), and an Indian prince, among others. Their chief adversary is the Jesuit Rodin, as melodramatic a villain as could be imagined.

The text of *The Wandering Jew* (*WJ*) captures the quality of old fairy tales and romantic novels in the diction of the characters and the composition of the scenes portrayed. The girls are fifteen-year-old twins. In the description provided, which Wander indicates may be spoken as narration or not, she invokes the old genres: "Rose's lips are like a carnation damp with dew. Blanche's eyes are as blue as forget-me-nots. Their hearts beat in unison" (*WJ*, 9).

The complex requirements of the play, which Alfreds conceives as "a tribute to plot," provide many challenges for a would-be adaptor. A panther kills a white horse within the first section of the play. In another scene, a theatre full of Parisians come to see the panther and his master in mortal combat. Clearly not possible as stage realism, Wandor describes the scene with cool restraint, leaving the production possibilities indeterminate. At the National, two actors in frock coats played the horse and panther, providing an elegant, nonrealistic representation of their struggle.

The Wandor-Alfreds collaboration became somewhat problematic. As rehearsals progressed, Wandor was disappointed to feel herself more and more excluded from the creative process. Her suggestions were not, from her point of view, taken very seriously or were swept aside. For Alfreds, accustomed to scripting his own work, the difficulty of working with a writer may have contributed to the problems. For Wandor, "the rehearsal process was very difficult and traumatic . . . the script was long at the beginning and needed cutting but it had a very strong sense of style. In the end, it came down to a territorial squabble."[26] Reviews were mixed, some critics like the *Guardian*'s Michael Billington finding the complexity of the novel too unwieldy for the stage: "For almost an hour I could barely work out what was going on. . . ."[27] Others, like Ruby Cohn who viewed the second night performance, were especially pleased with the adaptation: "I think Wandor and Alfreds were exceptionally clear in staging the intricate plot-strands. Not for a moment was I confused about them, and I have no recollection at all of the novel."[28] Perhaps it is inevitable that a project of this magnitude and complexity will engage a variety of responses from its audience.

The politics of the piece are similarly ambiguous. Cohn thought they were able "to put in a plug for workers, while poking sly fun at orthodoxies."[29] Wandor describes Sue's politics as "dodgy, reactionary." She tried to be attentive to the contradictions of bourgeois ideology in the dynamic of melodrama, playing down the "noble savage" stereotype in the characterization of the Prince and finally cutting a section of the book about a benevolent employer who "builds lovely dormitories for his workers who then work terribly hard six days a week and sit around by the fire in the evening singing hymns happily." Along with all the other challenges of adaptation, she enjoys struggling with the implicit politics: "You can take what seems to be a reactionary text and work with it in some ways that make it more interesting."[30]

These three plays indicate the range and scope of Wandor's writing for the theatre. In addition to her playwrighting and her critical journalism, she writes for radio and television and has also published extensive prose fiction and poetry. In an afterword to her poems in *Touchpapers,* she writes, "I know (roughly) who I am, and am certain of the fact that feminism, and my involvement with it, have been crucial to my sense of purpose and audience in my poetry."[31] True of all her work, from poetry to prose to plays, Wandor's work is unified however much the differences in her audience (popular, academic, theatre people) or her voice (journalistic, scholarly, creative) may suggest otherwise. Underlying all of it is a commitment to giving expression to the variety of crosscurrents developing in the artistic practices of feminist socialists and gays, to providing a socialist feminist critique of the existing state of these arts, and to actively involving herself in creating the new art.

NOTES

1. At age eleven she was living with her family in Israel for a period, and acted her first role in a community production of *The Man Who Came to Dinner.* Thoroughly caught up in the experience, she promptly decided to become an actress. Personal interview with Michelene Wandor, London, July 8, 1987.

2. Her thesis helped consolidate some tools for an analysis of the relationship between ideology and art: "Literary Theory and Literary Criticism in Britain in the 1930s: *Scrutiny* and *Left Review.*"

3. Interview, July 8, 1987.

4. Michelene Wandor, *Look Back in Gender* (London: Methuen, 1987), 90.

5. Michelene Wandor, "Culture, Politics and Values in Plays by Women in the 1980s," *Englisch Amerikanische Studien* 3–4 (1986): 441.

6. Ibid.

7. Michelene Wandor, *Carry On, Understudies,* (London: Routledge & Kegan Paul, 1986), xv. Cf. *Understudies: Theatre and Sexual Politics* (London: Methuen, 1981), 7.

8. *Carry On, Understudies,* 61.

9. Michelene Wandor, "The Fifth Column: Feminism and Theatre," *Drama* (Summer, 1984), 5–9.

10. See, for example, Alison M. Jaggar's full discussion of these categories in *Feminist Politics and Human Nature* (Totowa, N.J.: Rowman and Allanheld, 1983).

11. *Carry On, Understudies,* 170.

12. "The Fifth Column," 7.

13. This finding surprised Wandor who writes, "far from demonstrating the slogan that 'the personal is political', Phase Two has again and again demonstrated (in plays by men *and* women) that the personal is the opposite of political, must be separated from it, and cannot be explored in relation to it." Michelene Wandor, *Look Back in Gender: Sexuality and the Family in Post-War British Drama* (London: Methuen, 1987), 162.

14. Michelene Wandor, rev. of *Anna Laub,* by Jacov Lind, *Time Out,* November 22–28, 1974, 64.

15. Michelene Wandor, rev. of *Dusa, Fish, Stas and Vi,* by Pam Gems, *Time Out,* December 17–23, 1976, 25.

16. Michelene Wandor, review of Sadista Sisters, *Time Out,* December 3–9, 1976, 7.

17. Michelene Wandor, ed., Introduction to *Strike While the Iron Is Hot* (London: Journeyman Press, 1980), 14.

18. Helene Keyssar, *Feminist Theatre* (Hong Kong: Macmillan, 1984), 136ff.

19. Interview, July 8, 1987.

20. Ibid.

21. Helene Keyssar's book includes discussion of several of the other plays and Wandor talks about her own work in chapter 11 of *Carry On, Understudies.*

22. Interview, July 8, 1987.

23. Michelene Wandor, *Whores D'Oeuvres, Five Plays* (London: Journeyman Press, 1984).

24. Michelene Wandor, *AID Thy Neighbor, Five Plays,* 117.

25. Michelene Wandor and Mike Alfreds, *The Wandering Jew* (London: Methuen, 1987), introduction.

26. Interview, July 8, 1987.

27. Michael Billington, "Wandering through the Plot," *Guardian,* August 8, 1987.

28. Personal letter from Ruby Cohn, August 11, 1987.

29. Ibid.

30. Interview, July 8, 1987.

31. Judith Kazantzis, Michele Roberts, and Michelene Wandor, *Touchpapers* (London: Allison and Busby, 1982), 95.

WORKS BY MICHELENE WANDOR

Stage Plays

Sink Songs. Playbooks, 1975.
Care and Control. In *Strike While the Iron Is Hot.* London: Journeyman Press, 1980.
Mal de Mere and *Spilt Milk.* In *Plays Nine,* ed. Robin Rook. Edward Arnold, 1981.
Aurora Leigh. In *Plays by Women,* vol. 1. New York: Methuen, 1982.
Five Plays. (*To Die Among Friends, Whores D'Oeuvres, The Old Wives' Tales, Scissors, AID Thy Neighbor.*) London: Journeyman Press, 1984.
The Wandering Jew. With Mike Alfreds. New York: Methuen, 1987.

Edited Anthologies

Strike While the Iron Is Hot: Three Plays on Sexual Politics. (Red Ladder Theatre, *Strike While the Iron Is Hot;* Gay Sweatshop, *Care and Control;* Women's Theatre Group, *My Mother Says I Never Should.*) London: Journeyman Press, 1980.
Plays by Women. Vols. 1–4. New York: Methuen. Vol. 1. 1982. *Vinegar Tom* by Caryl Churchill, *Dusa, Fish, Stas, and Vi* by Pam Gems, *Tissue* by Louise Page, *Aurora Leigh* by Michelene Wandor after Elizabeth Barrett Browning. Vol. 2. 1983. *Rites* by Maureen Duffy, *Find Me* by Olwen Wymark, *Letters Home* by Rose Leiman Goldemberg, *Trafford Tanzi* by Claire Luckham. Vol. 3. 1984. *Red Devils* by Debbie Horsfield, *Aunt Mary* by Pam Gems, *Blood Relations* by Sharon Pollock, *Time Pieces* by the Women's Theatre Group and Lou Wakefield. Vol. 4. 1985. *Objections to Sex and Violence* by Caryl Churchill, *Rose's Story* by Grace Dayley, *Blood and Ice* by Liz Lochhead, *Pinball* by Alison Lyssa.

Criticism

The Body Politic. First anthology of British women's liberation writings. Editor and contributor. Stage One, 1972.

Dreams and Deconstructions. Edited by Sandy Craig. Essay on feminism and theatre. Amber Lane Press, 1980.

On Gender and Writing. Essays by twenty-one writers (male and female). Editor and contributor. Pandora Press, 1983.

"The Fifth Column: Feminism and Theatre." *Drama,* Summer, 1984, pp. 5–9.

Women's Writing; a Challenge to Theory. Edited by Moira Monteith. Essay on roots and language. Harvester Press, 1986.

Understudies: Theatre and Sexual Politics. New York: Methuen, 1981. Revised and expanded as *Carry On, Understudies.* London: Routledge and Kegan Paul, 1986.

"Culture, Politics and Values in Plays by Women in the *1980s.*" *English Amerikanische Studien* 3–4 (1986): 441–48.

Look Back in Gender: The Family and Sexuality in Post-War British Drama. New York: Methuen, 1987.

PART 4

Disruptions

ELIN DIAMOND

(In)Visible Bodies in Churchill's Theater

Writing is for you, you are for you; your body is yours, take it.
—Hélène Cixous, "The Laugh of the Medusa"

Alice. I hate my body.
—Caryl Churchill, *Vinegar Tom*

Hélène Cixous's "The Laugh of the Medusa," the controversial manifesto of *l'ecriture feminine,* opens forcefully: "I shall speak about women's writing: about *what it will do*" (1981, 245). Revolutionary myth as much as practice, "feminine writing" celebrates the libidinal multivalence of a woman's body and imagines a uniquely female writing that disrupts, mimics, exceeds, and dismantles what is known in feminist discourse as the patriarchal symbolic.[1] Since the 1975/1976 publications of "The Laugh of the Medusa," Cixous has been accused of ahistorical essentialism, of conceptualizing a female body-scene that keeps offstage political and material differences within and between genders.[2] For Caryl Churchill, who began writing professionally in the activist climate of the post-Brecht British fringe and the socialist debate in the women's movement, Cixous's scorn for empirical gender categories would probably be repugnant.[3] Churchill's own work of the mid-1970s (*Light Shining in Buckinghamshire, Vinegar Tom, Cloud 9*) places historical contradiction, class ideology, and sexual politics at the center of action and rhetoric. Alice of *Vinegar Tom* hates her body because in the play's fictional seventeenth-century village, where poverty and terror are displaced into misogynist scapegoating, her body is materially and sexually abused, her desire inexpressible.

Yet to think about theatre writing is to envision immediately a writing that "will *do,*" that empowers speakers with vital words, incites bodies to move in space. The "unheard songs" Cixous imagines in the female body have a place in Churchill's theatre writing, a curious place. From her early theatre texts, but especially in the recent *Fen* and *A Mouthful of Birds,* the body be-

comes a kind of limit-text of representational information, a special site of
inquiry and struggle. What I am isolating for discussion is a double strain
in Churchill's work: on the one hand, a commitment to the apparatus of representation (actor as sign of character; character as sign of a recognizable human
fiction) in order to say something *about* human oppression and pain—the capitalist greed that underwrites bourgeois feminism in *Top Girls,* for example,
or the cyclical exploitation of workers in *Fen;* on the other hand, a consistent
though less obvious attention to the powers of theatrical illusion, to modalities within representation that subvert the "aboutness" we normally call the
work's "content." I am referring to various representations of corporeal violence—Worsely's hacking, burning, poisoning, shooting his body, and constant reminders of stinking meat in *Owners;* the witch hunting in *Vinegar Tom*
that involves onstage pricking and hanging; Angela forcing Becky to drink
boiling water in *Fen,* among other examples. I am referring also to self-reflexive
play on illusionism, from card tricks to telepathic summonings and telekinesis,
and, after *Top Girls,* to a dialogue style of overlapping speeches that fractures
the language of the individual subject into near-cacophonic vocalizations. This
incomplete list of effects may not add up to a demonstration of Artaudian
cruelty, magic, or sonority, but it indicates a certain obsession with the signifying limits of the performing body.

  Mention of performance raises the question of the differences in contemporary theory between "performance" and "theatre," and the place of feminism in those debates. With the enormous influence of Brecht and Artaud on
western experimental theater since the late 1950s, with the revival of theater
semiotics and its poststructuralist modifications,[4] the body, common to both
performance and theater, marks a crucial point of division. Certain formulations are by now axiomatic. Theatre is governed by the logos of the playwright's text; actors re-present fictional entities of that text to produce a
unique temporal and spatial framework or dramatic "world." Theatre spectators are encouraged in pleasurable narrativity: prompted to identify with the
psychological conflicts of individual subjects, to respond to the lure of suspense, reversal, and deferral, to decode gestural and spectacular effects.[5] Performance, on the other hand, dismantles textual authority, illusionism, and
the canonical actor in favor of the "polymorphous thinking body" of the performer (Blau 1982, 30), a sexual, permeable, tactile body, a "semiotic bundle
of drives" (Féral 1982, 177) that scourges audience narrativity. In performance,
linear fictional time gives way to spatial intensities or projections of the performer's thought, gesture, movement, and voice. Theatre, the art of *representation,* transforms this polymorphous, drive-ridden, repressed, instinctual—can

we call it an "orificial?"—body into what Roland Barthes calls an "emphatic formal body, frozen by its function as an artificial object" (Barthes 1972, 27–28).

Simple binaries like "orificial-artificial" are of course dangerous; the performer's body in a performance piece is arguably no less artificial than an actor's body in a production of *The Wild Duck*. My interest here is not to uphold an opposition but to suggest that the distinction is useful for pointing out the *ideological* nature of representation. In theatre the sexual and historical specificity of the actor's body is absorbed into a representation of the body of a character, as defined and delimited by the author's text. This absorbtion, as Brecht pointed out repeatedly, is one of theatre's most destructive mystifications since it produces a seamless (i.e., ahistorical, apolitical) illusionism. Though an art constructed from (among other elements) human bodies, theatre demands a certain distance in order for the truth of its illusions to be believed.[6] At the most basic perceptual level, the body transforms into a sign of a character only when its bodily markers are erased, when facial lines, the veins in the hand, the wrinkled stocking, all the boundaries between body and adornment, body and history, are made invisible.

This seeing from a distance has profound implications for feminism. In drama studies, feminism has moved from an empirical concern with images of women in plays to a critique, fueled by deconstruction and psychoanalytic "French feminism," of the phallic economy that underlies representation. With its apparatus of curtains, limelights, perspectives, trapdoors, exits and entrances, theatre exists in a perpetual dialectic of appearance and disappearance; thus it tends to feed the structural demands of the castration complex.[7] Seeing is never a neutral act. In psychoanalytic theory, scopic desire is directed toward substitute objects and images that compensate for the (repressed) loss of the breast, the absence of the penis on the mother's body, and, more complicatedly at the oedipal moment, the feared or acknowledged absence of the penis on the child's own body.[8] Representation, the making visible (again) of what is lacking or what has disappeared, has been called "phallomorphic" (Irigaray 1977, 26) because it relieves, at the unconscious level, castration anxiety and, at the cultural level, reinscribes the authority of patriarchy. As Michel Benamou puts it, representation relies on "two vanishing points: God absent in the wings, the King present in his box" (1977, 6).[9]

Churchill's contribution to this discussion is the burden of this essay. What I would suggest at the outset is that her texts have become increasingly attentive to the ideological nature of the seeable. Specifically, the mystification of the body in representation has come to serve as a metaphor for the concealments of human, and especially female, experience under patriarchy and capitalism. In other words the lighted stage queries the world of *permissible* visibility, what can, and more importantly, what cannot be seen. Churchill does not sketch out performance scenarios; she works within egocentric logocentric representation, but she stretches and reconfigures its conventions. In what I consider to be Churchill's feminist project, there is no "writing the body," but rather a foregrounding of the apparatus that makes the writing impossible.

Before turning to *Fen* (1982) and *A Mouthful of Birds* (1986), I want to look briefly at Churchill's *Traps* (1976), *Vinegar Tom* (1976), *Light Shining in Buckinghamshire* (1976), *Cloud 9* (1978), and to consider theoretical discourses that have operated powerfully on the margins of her dramaturgy since the mid-1970s. Apart from her receptivity to socialist-feminist discourse, Churchill encountered Brechtian alienation and historicization techniques through working with two theatre collectives in 1976; in 1978 she adapted Michel Foucault's concept of disciplinary technology from *Discipline and Punish* for her play *Softcops*. It is not my intention to demonstrate direct influence, but I do suggest that Brecht and Foucault provided Churchill with ideas and tropes that have shaped her concern with the body-limits of representation.

In Churchill's *Owners* (O) (1972), the butcher Clegg's stinking meat is a metaphor for capitalism gone putrid; but the conversion of animals into commodities has wider analogies when Lisa gives away her newborn to the childless real estate developer Marion, and Lisa's husband Alec resumes his affair with her; in exchange, though this is not Lisa's wish, Marion allows Lisa and Alec to stay in their rented apartment. Attempts to "own" or exchange babies or husbands are shown to be as misplaced as property manipulations. At the close of act 1, Lisa lies on a bed with pregnancy contractions while her senile mother-in-law administers to an imaginary child. The scene alludes to birth and death but also implies the irrelevance and powerlessness of female nurturance in an exchange economy. At the end of the play, Alec, whose passivity suggests a version of Eastern mysticism as alternative to Judeo-Christian getting and spending, walks into their burning apartment building to save a neighbor's child. His demise is described by Worsely:

> At this point I thought myself of going back in. Fire has a terrible attraction. As it leaps and licks up, like a creature taking over, when really of course it was the house turning into fire because of the high temperature it was reaching, rather than a fire consuming the house. . . . It was very hot. I was just coming out when Alec came in through the door,

walking quite calmly considering the heat. "The other baby, you see" is what he said and set off—I would say up the stairs but I couldn't exactly see them in the flames. But he rose as if climbing the stairs. Turning into fire quite silently. We waited but of course he didn't come out and nor did the Arlingtons' baby. It was too hot. (*O,* 66)

Alec is apotheosized ("he rose . . .") for the play's one nurturing act. What interests me here is that Churchill attempts through the clearest realistic diction to make us believe in excruciating heat even as she gives the lines to the perverse Worsely, whose suicide attempts and Swiftian detachment have become a running gag through the play. When seconds later, Worsely fires into his brain with a pistol, then says "Missed" (*O,* 67), the point about the limits of seeing is subtly made. The phenomenal body has an equivocal function when it is called upon to represent pain or to stop "being there." The actor's body is a site of experience that cannot in fact *have* experience; physical death is always a matter of a toy gun while in language the body can be immolated and resurrected. Artaud reviled the theater of representation because it cannot "break through language in order to touch life" (1958, 13). But as Herbert Blau notes, language, not body, "has the amplitude we long for, and the indeterminacy in its precisions" (1982, 149). In this finely wrought, quick-paced farce, Churchill encodes a mistrust of the very illusionism that makes theatrical farce effective.

This mistrust is thematized in *Traps* (*T,* 1976), perhaps Churchill's least-admired play. In her introductory notes, she describes it as "an impossible object, like an Escher drawing, where things can exist on paper, but would be impossible in life. . . . In [*Traps*], the time, the place, the characters' motives and relationships cannot all be reconciled—they can happen on stage but there is no other reality for them" (*T,* 71). The play refers only to itself. This is of course true of any written text, but the relation to referentiality in *Traps* is unusual. Characters are completely recognizable; what they do is not surprising, narrativity seems absolutely appropriate, yet nothing coheres. The clock on the wall tells "real time"; time presses inexorably forward, but characters move backward and forward temporally with no transition or justification. At the beginning of act 2 Albert is discussed as dead but later enters to no remarks: like illusionism itself, impossible but true. The magic of the card trick fails, but not Jack's telepathic powers when he summons his sister and she arrives, like the actor summoned by the script, on cue. Lacking the moral resonance of absurdism and the serious playfulness of surrealism *Traps* is an exercise, a self-reflexive parable of theater logic.

However, in the closing image Churchill raises the stakes. She invokes the possibility of a "polymorphous thinking body" or at least a phenomenal "lived body" in Merleau-Ponty's sense, existentially present, orificial, and conscious. With perhaps a sly glance at another self-reflexive theater artist, Churchill revises the "real" pond where the child "dies" at the end of *Six Characters in Search of an Author (SC)* and calls for a tub of water to be placed onstage, its material reality asserted by the fact that naked actors climb into it, get wet, climb out, and dry themselves. The one-by-one bathing ritual injects, for the first time, an impression of temporality and focused space. Dialogue, until now unverifiable, takes on a kind of transparency as it relates to the bathing: "Come on, out you get." "No it's warm." "Hey it's cold, I want some more water" (*T,* 122). The final bather eats and smiles in what has been described as, and what we feel surely *is,* dirty warm water. At this point the spectator might also insist that the illusionistic surface has cracked; the orificial time-bound body of the actor, not merely the character, has become accessible, a marker for what Blau calls "the one inalienable and arcane truth of theater, that the living person performing there may die in front of your eyes and is in fact doing so" (1982, 105). Such "arcane truths" are intrinsic to performance art when serial repetitions, devoid of motive, produce a kind of spatial intensity whose only referent seems to be the death drive. In this sequence, Churchill choreographs a small performance using bodies who have "characters" only in a fragmentary sense. The smiling inertia of the final bather seems to gesture beyond the pleasure principle to the "absolute repose of the inorganic" (Laplanche and Pontalis 1973, 102). But of course this is just another sleight of hand. Our belief in an orificial nonillusionistic body is *produced* by a representational system. The "body" we see is perceivable not only because of its presence, but because the *water,* which "frames" the body, has taken on a character, a narrative, of its own.

Churchill's work after *Traps* contains versions of that play's obsessions but *Light Shining in Buckinghamshire* and *Vinegar Tom,* written the same year, mark a political and epistemological shift. Simply the actor's body became, for Churchill, a thinking, laboring, socio-political reality, and her own labor became implicated in dismantling hierarchies in the theatrical mode of production. She has frequently expressed gratitude for the working methods of Joint Stock (with whom she wrote *Light Shining in Buckinghamshire*) and Monstrous Regiment (*Vinegar Tom*). Both groups start with workshop cum study periods in which the company and writer discuss central themes, read historical material, travel, talk to experts, and explore character possibilities. This is followed by a solitary writing period, followed by rehearsal and text revisions, then touring, and finally a London production. While the solitary writing period and the author-position on the published text seem to suggest that key hierarchies have remained in place, Churchill's notes on the Joint Stock experience reveal a complicated authorial process for *Light Shining in Buckinghamshire* (*LSB*, 1985b):

> It is hard to explain exactly the relationship between the workshop and the text. The play is not improvised: it is a written text and the actors did not make up its lines. But many of the characters and scenes were based on ideas that came from improvisation at the workshop and during rehearsal. I could give endless examples of how something said or done by one of the actors is directly connected to something in the text. . . . (*LSB*, 184)

At a later interview she commented: "Though I still wanted to write alone sometimes, my attitude to myself, my work, and others had been basically and permanently changed." (*LSB*, 131)

Change is the key to Brechtian historicization and to the theme and construction of *Light Shining in Buckinghamshire.* Representing the conflicting forces in the British Civil War not as seamless narrative but as a colloquy of texts drawn from Winstanley's writings, the Putney debates, a Leveller newspaper, and the Bible, Churchill attends to the unique conditions that shaped the conflicts and discourses and, through textual fragmentation and subjective commentary, demonstrates the volatility of the period, its susceptibility to a genuinely revolutionary consciousness. Through now-familiar alienation techniques (actors serving as onstage audience; speaking as "actors," not characters; different actors playing the same role) spectators are prevented from identifying emotionally with any single action or character, but are encouraged to make connections between a previous historical moment and their own.[10]

The legacy of Brecht is not simply a series of provocative theatrical tricks but an insistence on the link between bourgeois ideology and conventional modes of theater representation. Drawing on this critique, Churchill has tried to foreground for discovery the gender ideology that governs sexual representation. The spectacular, theatrical elements of *Cloud Nine* (*CN*)—the time compression by which "historical time" leaps 100 years between acts 1 and 2, while the Victorian colonial family has aged only 25 years—demonstrates causality and change in sexual politics; cross-gender and cross-racial casting demonstrate that gender and servitude are culturally coded effects that effectively erase the body and its desires. As a male-centered, male-subservient angel in the house, Betty in Churchill's conception is literally man-made (played by a man). Serving the white colonial economy, Joshua in representation takes on the color of that economy (the African is played by a white). Important for this discussion is the way in which the theatre apparatus becomes a point of reference in these inversions. Each character's sexual and racial position is marked by appropriate dress and is introduced by doggerel verse, including the phrase, repeated by each character "as you can see" (*CN*, 251–52). What we *see* is what, given sexual and racial politics, cannot be seen.

The signature costumes of the trans-historical dinner party in *Top Girls* (*TG*) function similarly. The five "top girls," eating and drinking together in an expensive London restaurant have entered Western representation, but at a cost. Each points to the elaborate historical text that covers her body—Nijo in geisha silks, Joan in regal papal robes—but their fragmented speeches, the effect of the words of one being spoken through and over words of another, refer to need, violence, loss, and pain, to a body unable to signify within those texts. After much drink, Pope Joan delivers a long speech in Latin, a fragment from Book II of *De Rerum Natura* (*On the Nature of Things*) by Lucretius that begins by extolling detachment from human striving and the "tranquil sensation[s] of pleasure" only to plummet into speculation about the "horror of death." Joan forgets her text toward the end (*"Quod si ridicula*— something something on and on and on" [*TG*, 17]), and though the passage she quotes concludes that "terror and darkness of mind" are like children's nightmares and will be "scattered . . . by the outward display and unseen workings of Nature" (Lucretius 1950 trans., 45) Joan stumbles on the word "terrorem," then *"gets up and is sick in a corner"* (*TG*, 17). For the Epicurean Lucretius knowledge is based on sense perception; Pope Joan's vomiting (the representation of her vomiting) reminds us of the unseeable, unknowable female body wrapped in a male costume, a metonymy for cultural as well as theatrical invisibility.

How theatrical concealment or mystification relates to sexual oppression is suggested by a short scene in Churchill's play about poverty, religious superstition, and "witch"-hunting. In scene 13 of *Vinegar Tom* (*VT*), Alice avenges her sexual loneliness by constructing a mudman representation of a lover who has abandoned her, and as her friend Susan watches, Alice pricks between its legs "so he can't get on with his lady" (*VT*, 162). Then Jack, a married neighbor who has tried unsuccessfully to seduce Alice, arrives and accuses her of bewitching him, removing his penis. He chokes her until she *"puts her hand between his thighs."* Alice: "There. It's back." Jack: "It is back. Thank you, Alice. I wasn't sure you were a witch till then" (*VT*, 164). This Brechtian

A scene from *Top Girls* by Caryl Churchill. Cast members include Mary Dierson, Glynis Bell, Yolanda Lloyd, Amelia White, Elanie Hausman, Judy Yerby, Christina Moore. Production by the Cincinnati Playhouse in the Park. (Photo © Sandy Underwood.)

gest demonstrates the crude double-bind logic by which innocent women were condemned as witches. But it also reveals the male terror that fuels such logic. As mentioned earlier, the economy of sight (as of commodities) is a phallic economy based on castration fear or the disavowal of a feared absence. The female shores up that economy by functioning as a lack (absence) in relation to phallic presence; as the male's complement and opposite the female acts as guarantor against castration. Jack endows Alice with the power of the phallus in order to repossess his organ, but then, newly authorized and empowered, he must subdue her by "seeing" her as, labeling her, a witch. If Jack hardly seems in a phallic position of knowledge and authority, Susan as spectator believes that he is. He authorizes the truth that condemns Alice to demonic power and persecution. In this parable of female oppression, the lie is a truth if it is believed, which is another way of describing the theatre apparatus itself. The theatre wants us all to believe—or at least accept—its representations, and in doing so we ratify the power that authorizes them. In this case Jack stands in for Christian doctrine whose institutionalized misogyny, especially virulent in the *Malleus Malificarum* (on which Churchill drew for the Kramer-Sprenger duet), condemns not only women but difference itself:

> If you complain you're a witch
> Or you're lame you're a witch
> Any marks or deviations count for more.
> Got big tits you're a witch
> Fall to bits you're a witch
> He likes them young, concupiscent and poor. (*VT,* 170)

The referent for "he" is unnamed and, like the devil, invisible. But "he," the authorizer of all violent binaries, whether in gender, in politics, or in religion is shored up by every pricking and hanging. In scene 19, Alice's outspoken old mother and a woman healer are hanged on stage and Margery, Jack's wife, prays to "dear God" whose power is rearticulated precisely by this "destroying [of] the wicked" (*VT,* 174).

The power of unseen systems to control human thought and behavior, the use of ritual spectacles of punishment to regulate, govern, eliminate resistance, the conception of the body as a site of disciplinary control for a turbulent population—all this and more Churchill would have found in Michel Foucault's *Discipline and Punish,* on which she bases *Softcops* (1978). Foucault's concept of "docile bodies," those objects of "useful trainings" capable of being "manipulated by authority" (1979 trans., 155), produces a long series of chain reactions in her post-1978 work. The subject of Foucault's study is not simply the genealogy of the prison system, but of discipline as a type of power with a particular set of instruments, techniques, procedures, levels of application— a "technology" of the body, essential for the operations of modern society. Foucault begins in the preclassical era with the "spectacle of the scaffold": public torture, mutilation, and spectacular confessions that rearticulate the power of the sovereign. A period of reform follows when punishment becomes a matter of highly skilled "penalty-representations" (114), staged events using scenery, *trompe l'oeil* and other optical effects for the moral instruction of spectators. Finally, there is the decisive shift in discipline symbolized by Benthem's panopticon, a means of incarceration and confinement for mass control whereby one man centrally placed can observe many. For this latter account and throughout *Discipline and Punish* Foucault's tropes are theatrical.

In the panopticon, the cells are backlit like "so many small theaters, in which each actor is alone, perfectly individualized and constantly visible" (200). The panopticon becomes a polyvalent disciplinary tool applied "to reform prisoners, . . . to treat patients, to instruct schoolchildren, to confine the insane, to supervise workers" (205); the goal always is to turn human beings into "docile"—and productive—bodies. Though this is not a principal theme in Foucault's argument, disciplinary control, the making and manipulating of docile bodies, is inextricable from the rise of capitalism. The "massive projection of military methods into industrial organization" (221) *harnesses the worker's body,* "forces[s] it to carry out tasks, to perform ceremonies, to emit signs" (25).

Foucault has been taken to task for his account of power as a vast network to which the subject can never be exterior,[11] for this account eliminates dialectical and historical analysis, class struggle, and gender as explicit categories of power relations. Yet Foucaultian formulations on exclusion and sexual legitimation can be suggestive for feminist criticism[12] and I would guess *Discipline and Punish* "excited" Churchill because it gave her evocative ways of understanding gender oppression as the production of "docile bodies" in the family that, by extension, buttresses the schools, the military, and other branches of state power (Churchill 1985b, xii). *Softcops* is a reductive but respectful gloss of Foucault's study; but *Cloud Nine,* written the same year, explores more fully the disciplinary methods of gender as a multivalent form of body control. The male playing Betty and the female playing her son, Edward, foreground the ways in which culture, through its custodians in the family, discipline the body, force it to "emit signs" of clear masculinity and femininity. The notion of body discipline in the theatre has been part of our argument from the outset: the transformation of a sentient, thinking—what I have been calling an orificial—body into an artificial sign or representation of a fiction. The inability of the orificial body to *appear* in a representational space takes on specific political resonance in *Fen* and *A Mouthful of Birds;* indeed the link between the theatre of representation and processes of social discipline will be my concern for the remainder of this essay.

Fen

Named for the once-wild swamp land of England's East Anglia, *Fen* is divided into twenty-one brief scenes, each bearing the scars of social and familial discipline. The fen women's body-wracking labor (potato picking, onion grading), combined with their housekeeping, rearing, and feeding chores, create a closed system of repetition and self-defeat. The love affair between Val and

Frank bogs down in its own repetitions, Val attempting to leave her husband and daughters only to leave her lover because she can't live without her children; and in near-monosyllabic exchanges between the generations of women in Val's family, birth and blood create an ongoing cycle of denial, guilt, and rage. Churchill's interest in inertia, both political and emotional, goes back to *Objections to Sex and Violence, Owners, Traps,* and *Top Girls,* but early in the play *Fen* brings stasis and defeat to the very edge of representational truth. Frank, alone on stage, monologues an imagined conversation with the landowner Tewson, and as he works up to the fantasy of hitting him, he hits himself. This self-hitting, this self-discipline, marks a change in Churchill's writing. Now the body enters decisively, the body that can be hurt. I do not mean that the actor gives himself actual pain, rather that his body has become an explicit site of his character's struggle and suffering. The historical and political pain of life in the fens is concentrated into that slap, Frank punishing himself for even considering confronting the boss.

Fen (*F*) grows out of a particularly depressing moment in British politics. The Falklands war of 1982 brought unprecedented popularity to the Thatcher government, which in 1983 was returned to power with a landslide majority. In bitter homage to Thatcherite economic policies, *Fen* opened in January 1983 with a speech by a "Japanese businessman" who praises the "beautiful English countryside" and the "beautiful black earth" of the fens and all the multinationals (Esso, Equitable Life, Imperial Tobacco, etc.) that own a piece of them. With this unembarrassed reference to technocracy fresh in our minds, we meet the fen women "*working in a row, potato picking down a field*" (*F,* 5), an immemorial image of peasant labor. The ironic juxtaposition of businessman and laboring women, multinational financing and a cash crop of potatoes, becomes a social gest for the double alienation of the women. Tewson, on whom they rely for minimal day wages, is bought out by a multinational, and becomes a tenant himself.

Fen might best be compared to *Vinegar Tom.* Set in the 1970s and the 1640s respectively, each play investigates economic subjugation and female oppression; each shows the impossibility of heterosexual love (Alice-Man in *Vinegar Tom*; Val-Frank in *Fen*), each condemns religion as destructive ideology (Christian doctrine reinterpreted through Kramer and Sprenger in *Vinegar Tom*; the evangelical Mrs. Finch in *Fen*). However, while *Vinegar Tom* shows the possibility of growing consciousness and possible change (Alice: "I'm, not a witch. But I wish I was. . . . I should have learnt [from the cunning women]" [*F,* 175]), the *Fen* women are studies in abjection. Nell, the "witch" and "morphrodite," is utterly isolated in her objections to the exploitative conditions under which the women labor. At the play's midpoint, she narrates a long story about a runaway boy (her grandfather), a living corpse, and a vengeful farmer who skewers an adulterous couple with a pitchfork as they lie naked together in bed, then axes them to death. The story's gothic details—the boy's terror, the old man rising from a coffin, the gruesome central image (" . . . suddenly he raised the pitchfork and brung it down as hard as he could directly over their bare stomachs, so they were sort of stitched together" [*F,* 13])—strike Nell as "funny" and her listeners as evidence of Nell's eccentricity.

However, the narrative has an important correlative in the enacted play; the ax murder is carried out on Val, the adulteress, by her lover Frank, and her murder produces not just another good story but access to a new, if tenuous, representational space that alters our perspective on the play's "world." Frank places Val's "dead" body in a wardrobe and then suddenly, unexpectedly, she walks back onstage from the other side and begins talking. (Apparently on the opening night, her reappearance caused several spectators to scream.) In an episodic but coherent text concerned with mimetic accuracy in diction, gestures, referents, what is the purpose of raising the dead? The answer lies I think in the analogies set up between cyclical economic exploitation, the erasure of female desire, and the regime of permissible visibility in theatrical representation. Unable to "write" her body in the sense of representing its desires, Val literally writes on her body—marks her chest with a pen indicating where her lover should stab her. However, Churchill rejects a romanticized closure that would require the body to represent itself as dead. She also rejects the foregrounding of theatrical illusionism: Worsely's shooting himself with a prop gun in *Owners.* Rather she *extends* the boundaries of what can be seen and said as representation. Val re-emerges not as a prophetic ghost or a misty mystified body but as a consciousness that instantiates a new theater space ("There's so much happening. . . ."). She ventriloquizes the stories of other dead, but more importantly *by her bodily presence* makes a space for her fellow laborers to explore and change their suffering. Val summons Becky by speaking her nightmare—another episode of the stepmother's sadistic abuse—and when both appear, Churchill comments on two modalities of representation.

> *Angela:* Becky, do you feel it? I don't, not yet. There's a pain somewhere. I can see so far and nothing's coming. . . . Let me burn you. I have to hurt you worse. I think I can feel something. It's my own pain. I must be *here* if it hurts.

Becky: You can't, I won't, I'm not playing. You're not *here*.
(*Angela goes.*)
(*F,* 24, emphasis added)

Angela's "here" refers to self-awareness arrived at by inflicting pain while Becky's "here," in the heightened context of what I am calling Val's death-space, refers both to the dream fiction that they are both enacting and to the theatre whose illusionism has become an explicit datum of the play's epistemology.

Angela banished, *Nell crosses on stilts.* A visual echo of the seventeenth-century fen-dwellers who used stilts to cross the swampy earth. Nell converses with her own inveterate enemy.

Nell. I was walking out on the fen. The sun spoke to me. It said, "Turn back, turn back." I said, "I won't turn back for you or anyone." (*F,* 24)

The sun's earthly cycle figures a constant process of turning back, but human beings, as historical agents, can change their condition. Equally hopeful is the final sequence that begins Val's announcement, "My mother wanted to be a singer. That's why she'd never sing." Suddenly "May is there. She sings" (*F,* 24). Characters appear like the return of the repressed, and in these liminal moments a nightmare is redreamed, a life rerouted, an old woman's voice freed for expression. The death-space permits a representation of the unrepresentable, what Cixous has called the "unheard songs" of the libidinal (and revolutionary) female body. Yet there is no affective triumph in these songs, rather a grim awareness of the conditions that prevent their singing. Nell's political self-consciousness has no projection outside this death-space. Walking on stilts she merely echoes the fen-dweller's historical defiance of— and failure to halt—exploitation that goes back to Charles II's scheme to drain the fens for grazing land. If the spectator loses track of spatial-temporal markers, *Fen* is not a dream play—no Strindbergian chrysanthemum blooms; in fact Frank sits gloomily throughout these summonings and denies any transcendence to his actions:

Frank. I've killed the only person I love.
Val: It's what I wanted.
Frank: You should have wanted something else.
(*F,* 24)

The female bodies in Val's death-space reach across the play to a nameless female Ghost in scene 9, a witness to 150 years of working women's suffering who appears to reproach the landowner Tewson. As with the appearances in Val's death-space, this ancient ghostly voice does not rupture representation, but marks a signifying space, the marginality of which bears witness to the ideology of permissible visibility—and audibility. The capitalist has always refused to see this woman, to hear this voice. In scene 16, the actors gather to sing in unison an excerpt from Rilke's *Duino Elegies,* which provides a gloss on the unarticulated despair of the fen-dwellers and on the logic of Val's death-space. Less Brechtian intervention than communal dirge, Rilke's elegy is another "unheard song," a portion of which I cite below:

> Who, if I cried would hear me among the angelic orders? And even if one of them suddenly pressed me against his heart, I should fade in the strength of his stronger existence. . . . And so I repress myself, and swallow the call-note of depth-dark sobbing. Alas, who is there we can make use of? (*F,* 19)

If we judge this play for its ability to alienate and historicize the fen-women's material and political pain, *Fen* is a provisional success, not because a redemptive socialism is asserted, but because the representation apparatus has been suggestively implicated as a tool of social oppression *and* as a means of resistance. The partial visibility of the death-space in which women's bodies are reinvested with stories, secrets, and mythic powers alludes to—and attempts to correct—the violent repression in the visible world (in and out of the theatre) where their bodies and others like them are disciplined into silence.

A Mouthful of Birds

A Mouthful of Birds (MB) makes space for the body's "unheard songs" in a register of pain and suffering that Foucault might have seen as the revolution of the docile and Cixous as a rupture of patriarchal constraints. Seven characters, identified specifically by social and professional roles (a Switchboard Operator, a Mother, an Acupuncturist, a Vicar, a Businessman, an Unemployed man) over thirty-two short scenes find themselves overtaken by passion, obsession, habit, such that law, sovereign reason, strict regulation of gender roles—all the ballasts of patriarchy—are dislodged in a violent release of psychic and sexual energy. The pre-text for *A Mouthful of Birds* is Euripides' *The Bacchae,* which

Churchill and her collaborator David Lan allow to overtake their own text. Scenes marked "Possession" intercalated with the monologues and enactments of violent behavior give all actors double identities drawn from the Euripides text. Structurally *The Bacchae* becomes a source of momentum and expectation; when Derek is possessed by Pentheus and puts on women's clothes; when the women gradually become possessed by the Bacchae, we know that the violent dismembering of Pentheus is inevitable. *The Bacchae* also supplies a reference point for a kind of historicizing of the psyche: "We could have left the play as the seven stories without including anything from *The Bacchae* itself, but would have missed the presence of the horrific murder and possession, something not invented by us or by Euripides, so we kept it as something that bursts from the past into these people open to possession, first the voice of an unquiet spirit telling of a murder, finally the murder itself happening as the climax to all their stories" (*MB*, 5). This violent "burst from the past" suggests the libidinal and psychic turmoil within each docile social entity; more importantly Churchill inscribes this overtaking of the body through the nonrepresentational, nonlogocentric alterity of dance. Thus the common action of eating a piece of fruit produces a "Fruit ballet" whose movements invoke what will become the ecstasy and horror of Pentheus: "*sensuous pleasures of eating and the terrors of being torn up*" (*MB*, 28). At the end of act 2 the actors, "*as their main character,*" dance their "*memories of moments of extreme happiness*"; this dance develops into "*a moment of severe physical pleasure*" (*MB*, 49). The transformation of "characters" into "dancers" suggests an attempt to intrude the orificial into the artificial, to overthrow the repressiveness of a representational system (the characters lose themselves in the dance). To what extent these dances "read" to the audience is less important than the startling range of physical signification Churchill and Lan make visible. They also attempt what Freud (in *Civilization and Its Discontents*) says cannot be done; they give the body, and the spatiality it instantiates, the "past of the mind" (*MB*, 71). In the contemporary secretary lurks the memory of "severe physical pleasure" which connects her to the killing ecstasies of Dionysian maenads. The final lines of the excerpt from Rilke's *Duino Elegies* seem to offer appropriate metaphors for how Churchill and Lan have imagined these turbulent bodies: "Fling the emptiness out of your arms to broaden the spaces we breathe—maybe—the birds will feel the extended air in more fervent flight" (*F*, 19).

But even the "extended air" has a politics. No sooner imagined (or recovered) it will immediately reveal its own boundaries and rules. The beauty of the "characters," the fictional identities that actors represent, function within specific cultural and sexual constraints. Thus we understand why the moment of possession and ecstasy for the businessman Paul, who traffics in pork in international markets, will be the discovery that the commodity he fetishizes has a history and temperament of its own: a beautiful shape "cut in the air" (*MB,* 46). For the Trinidadian Marcia, possession means a fall from spiritual grace. A switchboard operator in a London office, she also operates a psychic switchboard as medium to her Trinidadian gods. But in a white sexist culture, her otherness lames her powers; a spirit in the shape of a white upperclass woman inhabits her, steals her West Indian accent and rejects her gods. Marcia's Baron Sunday has become barren; she can only writhe and scream at her loss.

At different moments in scene 15, the androgynous Dionysos appears to and dances to nameless men and women: "*This dance is precisely the dance that the woman in the chair longs for. Watching it she dies of pleasure*" (*MB,* 37). Simultaneously, two prison guards use a ludicrously inadequate institutional discourse to try to account for such a body that cannot be clearly gendered.

> *Male Prison Officer.* It was him when we admitted her. I can guarantee that.
> *Female Prison Officer.* Guarantee? (*MB,* 37)

These moments preface the play's central agon, when the intrusion of the orificial into the artificial becomes a pointed gender critique. Derek's social identity is "unemployed"; he rejects his father's own form of identification—"He thought he wasn't a man without a job"—but Derek's scene of possession is an ambitious and self-reflexive comment on the processes of representation. Having revealed a susceptibility to possession by Pentheus, Derek is then possessed by the language and desires of a nineteenth-century hermaphrodite, Herculine/Abel Barbin. In other words, his double identity is doubled and strikingly divisive: sexual confusion is precisely what Pentheus struggles to eradicate.[13] The orificial body, despite its gender discipline, retains the unconscious memory of and a yearning for the plenum of androgyny, what Lacan calls the "real lack" that occurs at the moment of sexual differentiation in the womb, when "the living being is subject to sex" (Silverman 1983, 152) and separated from originary, primordial wholeness. The Herculine Barbin passage, spoken by a woman dressed as a man, records the physical and emotional agony of separation from the plenum of androgyny: "Sara's body, my girl's body, all lost, couldn't you have stayed?" (*MB,* 52) as well as the social torture it has brought her/him: "Hermaphrodite, the doctors were fascinated how to define this body, does it fascinate you, it doesn't fascinate me, let it die" (*MB,* 51). We noted earlier that representation, in its function of bringing *back,* or compensating for the threat of disappearance, participates in a phallic economy, the economy of castration. It is also a form of ideological control. Indeed Pentheus in the Euripides text reviles the Dionysian Bacchantes until the disguised god offers him the chance to be a voyeur, that is to violate the women's ecstatic rites by transforming them into a spectacle for his pleasure. With the Pentheus/Derek/Herculine/Abel Barbin layering comes the implication that Pentheus's attack on the Bacchae signifies the repression of a lost female nature that he himself parodies by putting on a dress. For Pentheus the girlish god and the sexual confusion he represents will produce civil anarchy, but the contemporary play suggests that repression of ambivalence, self-division, and difference is also violent, and tragic. Civilization, Freud notes, requires that "there shall be a single kind of sexual life for everyone, disregards the dissimilarities, whether innate or acquired, in the sexual constitution of human beings; it cuts off a fair number of them from sexual enjoyment, and so becomes the source of serious injustice" (Freud 1961, 104). Abel the cursed male who lost his unsocializable, uncivilized "girl's body" dies inhaling gas; Pentheus, whose name (we are twice-told by Euripides) means "grief," is torn to pieces.

The scene between Derek and Herculine/Abel extends the body's representational limits more definitively than ever before in the Churchill canon. The fragmented history of Herculine's hermaphroditism is delivered by an actress dressed as a man. Considering Churchill's interest in the effects of cross-dressing, the choice is predictable. What is new is that the male actor playing Derek, while he takes the objects that signify Herculine's life, does not make the image symmetrical—does not dress himself as a female. Yet he repeats her monologue verbatim and upon reaching the rhetorical question that closes the speech—"Sara's body, my girl's body, all lost, couldn't you have stayed?" (*MB,* 52)—the actress playing Herculine turns back and, standing behind him, kisses him on the neck. The image (reproduced as a photograph in the text) startlingly resembles a two-headed hermaphroditic body, an "impossible object" like a Mobius strip, a Medusa's head, or an unheard song.[14]

In part 3 of *A Mouthful of Birds,* the characters speak from the moment of postpossession and mark what Freud refers to as their "expedient accommodation" (1961, 96) to the rigors of civilized representation. Lena, the Mother who has drowned her child, struggles with her remembered pleasure in killing as well as giving birth. Paul, having lost his beloved pig, becomes a destitute alcoholic: "Days are quite long when you sit in the street but it's important not to do anything. . . . I stay ready" (*MB*, 71). But Derek/Pentheus who has been torn apart, celebrates here his surgical tearing, his transsexual body: "My breasts aren't big but I like them. My waist isn't small but it makes me smile. My shoulders are still strong. . . . My skin used to wrap me up, now it lets the world in. . . . Every day I wake up, I'm comfortable" (*MB*, 71). This body ruins representation. It undermines a patriarchy that disciplines the body into gender opposition; it dismantles the phallomorphic economy that denies visibility to the female (except as opposite or complement to the male). The hermaphroditic body is excessive to itself—there is not "self" but selves, the other in the one—orificial, literally: "My skin used to wrap me up, now it lets the world in."

Derek's narcissism and his "comfort" must be seen as part of a dialectic; he does not have the last word. The character Doreen, a secretary, and also Agave (the mother of Pentheus who in frenzy tears off his head), closes the monologues and opens again the question of the untenable discipline, the ideological repression that is representation. We might look at a major trope common to the texts in our discussion. "Flying is woman's gesture," Cixous claims, pairing women with birds and robbers (*voler* in French means to fly and to steal):

> [Women] fly the coop, take pleasure in jumbling the order of space, in disorienting it, in changing around the furniture, dislocating things and values, breaking them all up, emptying structures, and turning propriety upside down." (1981, 258)

The bird/robber trope is central to Euripides' description of the Bacchae:

> Then like birds, skimming the ground as they ran, they scoured the plain which stretches by the river Asopus and produces a rich harvest for Thebes; and like an enemy army they bore down on the villages of Hysiae and Erythrae . . . and ransacked them. They snatched children out of the houses; all the plunder they laid on their shoulders. . . . (1967 ed., 204)

Doreen has been violent; she has summoned powers to make objects fly around the room (scene 23), but the flying/robbing have produced trauma and further repression:

I find no rest. My head is filled with horrible images. I can't say I actually see them, it's more that I feel them. It seems that my mouth is full of birds which I crunch between my teeth. Their feathers, their blood and broken bones are choking me. I carry on my work as a secretary. (*MB,* 71)

The woman's bird-body, freed into murderous choreography, now stands in repose and swallows itself, or tries to, in order to "carry on." When Doreen finishes her speech, Dionysos dances again, libidinally, ferally, but she, docile, productive, capitalized, does not. The cracks and fissures in the representational surface have been explored in *A Mouthful of Birds,* but the structure of disciplinary control remains. Ecstatic, dying, dancing, screaming, possessed bodies attempt to represent the release from representation, and in the futility of that endeavor a feminist politics is made visible.

NOTES

This essay originally appeared in *Theatre Journal,* May, 1988, 189–205.

1. In Jacques Lacan's formulation, the human child takes up a subject position in culture at the oedipal moment with the entry into language or the symbolic order. As the oedipal conflict is synonymous with the male child's acceptance of the father's law or prohibition, the symbolic order is inscribed with the Name-of-the-Father; hence the "patriarchal symbolic." See Jacques Lacan 1977, 67ff, 199ff. Cixous believes that the subversion of the law of meaning is possible only if woman "blazes *her* trail in the symbolic" by writing from her otherness, her body. For objections to Cixous's position, see n. 2.

2. The best rebuttal to *l' ecriture feminine* is still Monique Wittig's "One Is Not Born a Woman" (1981), a Marxist-feminist attack on the biologism that ultimately underpins the privileging of the body. "Our first task, it seems, is to always thoroughly dissociate 'women' (the class within which we fight) and 'woman,' the myth. For 'woman' does not exist for us; it is only an imaginary formation, while 'women' is the product of a social relationship," 50–51. For an excellent summary of these issues and an analysis of the ways in which *ecriture feminine* might still prove an enabling myth for feminism, see Ann Rosalind Jones, "Writing the Body: Toward an Understanding of *l' ecriture feminine*" in *Feminist Criticism and Social Change: Sex, Class and Race in Literature and Culture,* ed. J. Newton and D. Rosenfelt.

3. See Michelene Wandor, *The Body Politic: Writings from the Women's Liberation Movement in Britain 1969–1972* (1972), and for a more specific study of theatre and feminism with a section on Churchill, see Wandor's *Carry On, Understudies.*

4. See especially the work of Patrice Pavis in *Languages of the Stage,* which breaks away from both systematic communication models and exclusive focus on *mise en scène* to consider problems of ideology and desire in performance and reception.

5. In the antimimetic tradition of expressionism, surrealism, and absurdism, narrativity is challenged, spatial and temporal referents are confused but, with the pos-

sible exception of Brecht and Artaud, the dominance of the text as antecedent to performance is accepted. As in much modernist writing, the conventions and centrality of representation are reaffirmed by their seeming violation.

6. Brechtian theater also demands distance — he preferred conventional proscenium space — not for the sake of illusionism but to allow the audience sufficient freedom for reflection and analysis.

7. Michael Goldman broaches these same issues but draws different conclusions in *The Actor's Freedom* (1975), 35ff, 113ff.

8. I am not proposing symmetry in the male and female experience of the oedipus but since split subjectivity applies to both sexes so too does the longing for originary wholeness. The discussion of whether castration is one of many separations human beings undergo on the road to subjectivity or *the* complex which may refer back to other separations is beyond the scope of this essay. See Juliet Mitchell's discussion in *Feminine Sexuality: Jacques Lacan and the école freudienne,* trans. Jacqueline Rose, 13–16 (New York: Pantheon, 1982).

9. For a feminist view of nonphallomorphic representation see Jill Dolan, "The Dynamics of Desire."

10. Brecht discusses historicization throughout his theoretical writings. See especially "On the Use of Music in an Epic Theatre" (84–90); "Alienation Effects in Chinese Acting" (91–99); "A Short Organum for the Theatre, #33–40" (189–91), in *Brecht on Theatre.*

11. For Foucault's own synthesis of the power network see *The History of Sexuality,* 92–97.

12. See, for example, Mary Ann Doane's use of Foucault in *The Desire to Desire.*

13. Though the Methuen text of *A Mouthful of Birds* never mentions this source, Churchill and Lan probably made use of the memoirs and dossier on Herculine Barbin, first published in 1978 as *Herculine Barbin, dite Alexina B.* by Gallimard, then in 1980 as *Herculine Barbin: Being the Recently Discovered Memoirs of a Nineteenth-Century French Hermaphrodite,* introduced by Michel Foucault, translated by Richard McDougall, Pantheon Books, New York. For Foucault, the case of Herculine/Abel Barbin illustrates juridical attempts to regulate sexual identity in the 1860s and 1870s after centuries of relative tolerance for hermaphroditism. The nineteenth-century concept of a "true sex" buttresses a medical ethical discourse across diverse cultural practices, from biological science to religious confession to psychiatry; thus Herculine's doctors and judges force her to leave the "happy limbo of . . . non-identity" and become "himself" (Introduction, xiii). Churchill and Lan pare down Herculine's effusive prose to narrative fragments and unanswered questions, suggesting the unbridgeable gap between non-identity and a medically acceptable, legally "true" sex/self.

That such issues fascinate Churchill is evident from her radio play *Schreber's Nervous Illness* (first performed 1972), which deals with Freud's case history of Judge Schreber, whose physical sufferings stemmed from his belief that God planned to turn him into a woman and impregnate him in order to produce a new race of men.

14. The two-headed but divided figure has a parallel in the divisions of this co-authored text. Compare Churchill's introduction to Lan's on the fate of Agave. *A Mouthful of Birds,* 5–6.

REFERENCES

Artaud, Antonin. 1958. *The Theater and Its Double*. New York: Grove Press.

Barthes, Roland. 1972. "Baudelaire's Theater." In *Critical Essays*, trans. Richard Howard, 25–31. Evanston, Ill.: Northwestern University Press.

Benamou, Michel. 1977. "Presence in Play," in *Performance in Postmodern Culture*, ed. Michel Benamou and Charles Carmello. Madison, Wis.: Coda Press.

Blau, Herbert. 1982. *Blooded Thought: Occasions of Theatre*. New York: Performing Arts Journal Publications.

Brecht, Bertolt. 1964. *Brecht on Theatre: The Development of an Aesthetic*, trans. John Willett. New York: Hill and Wang.

Cixous, Hélène. 1981. "*The Laugh of the Medusa*." In *New French Feminisms*, ed. Elaine Marks and Isabelle de Courtrivon, 245–64. Amherst: University of Massachusetts Press. First published 1975, "*Le Rire de la Méduse*." *L' Arc* 61:39–54; 1976, "*The Laugh of the Medusa*," trans. Keith Cohen and Paula Cohen. *Signs* 1 (Summer): 875–99.

Churchill, Caryl. 1982. *Top Girls*. London: Methuen.

————. 1983. *Fen*. London: Methuen.

————. 1985a. *Objections to Sex and Violence*. In *Plays by Women*, vol. 4, ed. Michelene Wandor, 12–51. New York: Methuen.

————. 1985b. *Plays: One*. Includes *Owners, Traps, Vinegar Tom, Light Shining in Buckinghamshire, Cloud 9*. London: Methuen.

Churchill, Caryl, and Lan David. 1986. *A Mouthful of Birds*. London: Methuen.

Doane, Mary Ann. 1987. *The Desire to Desire: The Woman's Film of the 1940s*. Bloomington: Indiana University Press.

Dolan, Jill. 1987. "The Dynamics of Desire: Sexuality and Gender in Pornography and Performance." *Theatre Journal* 39, no. 2 (May 1987): 156–74.

Euripides. *The Bacchae*. *The Bacchae and Other Plays*. Trans. Philip Vellacott. 1967. Baltimore: Penguin, 181–228.

Féral, Josette. 1982. "Performance and Theatricality: The Subject Demystified." *Modern Drama* 25, no. 1 (March 1982): 170–81.

Foucault, Michel. 1979. *Discipline and Punish*, trans. Alan Sheridan. New York: Vintage.

————. 1980. *The History of Sexuality*, trans. Robert Hurley. New York: Vintage.

Goldman, Michael. 1975. *The Actor's Freedom*. New York: Viking.

Freud, Sigmund. 1961. *Civilization and Its Discontents*. *The Standard Edition of Complete Psychological Works of Sigmund Freud*. Vol. 21. London: The Hogarth Press. 64–145.

Irigaray, Luce. 1977. *This Sex Which Is Not One*, trans. Catherine Porter with Carolyn Burke. Ithaca: Cornell University Press.

Jones, Ann Rosalind. 1985. "Writing the Body: Toward an Understanding of *l' ecriture feminine*." In *Feminist Criticism and Social Change: Sex, Class and Race in Literature and Culture*, ed. Judith Newton and Deborah Rosenfelt, 86–101. London: Methuen.

Lacan, Jacques. 1977. *Ecrits: A Selection*, trans. Alan Sheridan. New York: Norton.

Laplanche, J., and Pontalis, J.-B. 1973. *The Language of Psycho-Analysis*, trans. Donald Nicholson-Smith. New York: Norton.

Lucretius. *On the Nature of Things*, Trans. H. Hannaford Brown. 1950. New Brunswick: Rutgers University Press.

Pavis, Patrice. 1982. *Languages of the Stage: Essays in the Semiology of the Theatre*. New York: Performing Arts Journal Publications.

Silverman, Kaja. 1983. *The Subject of Semiotics.* New York: Oxford University Press.

Wandor, Michelene. 1972. *The Body Politic: Writings from the Women's Liberation Movement in Britain 1969–1972.* London: Stage 1.

———. 1986. *Carry On, Understudies: Theatre and Sexual Politics.* London: Routledge and Kegan Paul.

Wittig, Monique. 1981. "One Is Not Born a Woman." *Feminist Issues,* Winter, 47–54.

SUE-ELLEN CASE

Toward a Butch-Femme Aesthetic

In the 1980s, feminist criticism has focused increasingly on the subject position: both in the explorations for the creation of a female subject position and the deconstruction of the inherited subject position that is marked with masculinist functions and history. Within this focus, the problematics of women inhabiting the traditional subject position have been sketched out, the possibilities of a new heterogeneous, heteronomous position have been explored, and a desire for a collective subject has been articulated. While this project is primarily a critical one, concerned with language and symbolic structures, philosophic assumptions, and psychoanalytic narratives, it also implicates the social issues of class, race, and sexuality. Teresa de Lauretis's article "The Technology of Gender" (in *Technologies of Gender*, 1987) reviews the recent excavations of the subject position in terms of ideology, noting that much of the work on the subject, derived from Foucault and Althusser, denies both agency and gender to the subject. In fact, many critics leveled a similar criticism against Foucault in a recent conference on postmodernism, noting that while his studies seem to unravel the web of ideology, they suggest no subject position outside the ideology, nor do they construct a subject who has the agency to change ideology ("Postmodernism," 1987). In other words, note de Lauretis and others, most of the work on the subject position has only revealed the way in which the subject is trapped within ideology and thus provides no programs for change.

For feminists, changing this condition must be a priority. The common appellation of this bound subject has been the "female subject," signifying a biological, sexual difference, inscribed by dominant cultural practices. De Lauretis names her subject (one capable of change and of changing conditions) the feminist subject, one who is "at the same time inside and outside the ideology of gender, and conscious of being so, conscious of that pull, that division, that doubled vision" (1987, 10). De Lauretis ascribes a sense of self-determination at the micropolitical level to the feminist subject. This feminist subject, unlike the female one, can be outside of ideology, can find self-determination, can change. This is an urgent goal for the feminist activist/ theorist. Near the conclusion of her article (true to the newer rules of composition), de Lauretis begins to develop her thesis: that the previous work on the female subject, assumes, but leaves unwritten, a heterosexual context for the subject and this is the cause for her continuing entrapment. Because she is still perceived in terms of men and not within the context of other women, the subject in heterosexuality cannot become capable of ideological change (1987, 17–18).

De Lauretis's conclusion is my starting place. Focusing on the feminist subject, endowed with the agency for political change, located among women, outside the ideology of sexual difference, and thus the social institution of heterosexuality, it would appear that the lesbian roles of butch and femme, as a dynamic duo, offer precisely the strong subject position the movement requires. Now, in order for the butch-femme roles to clearly emerge within this sociotheoretical project, several tasks must be accomplished: the lesbian subject of feminist theory would have to come out of the closet, the basic discourse or style of camp for the lesbian butch-femme positions would have to be clarified, and an understanding of the function of roles in the homosexual lifestyle would need to be developed, particularly in relation to the historical class and racial relations embedded in such a project. Finally, once these tasks have been completed, the performance practice, both on and off the stage, may be studied as that of a feminist subject, both inside and outside ideology, with the power to self-determine her role and her conditions on the micropolitical level. Within this schema, the butch-femme couple inhabit the subject position together—"you can't have one without the other," as the song says. The two roles never appear as . . . discrete. The combo butch-femme as subject is reminiscent of Monique Wittig's "j/e" or coupled self in her novel *The Lesbian Body*. These are not split subjects, suffering the torments of dominant ideology. They are coupled ones that do not impale themselves on the poles of sexual difference or metaphysical values, but constantly seduce the sign system, through flirtation and inconstancy into the light fondle of artifice, replacing the Lacanian slash with a lesbian bar.

However, before all of this *jouissance* can be enjoyed, it is first necessary to bring the lesbian subject out of the closet of feminist history. The initial step in that process is to trace historically how the lesbian has been assigned to the role of the skeleton in the closet of feminism; in this case, specifically the lesbian who relates to her cultural roots by identifying with traditional butch-femme role-playing. First, regard the feminist genuflection of the 1980s—

the catechism of "working-class-women-of-color" feminist theorists feel impelled to invoke at the outset of their research. What's wrong with this picture? It does not include the lesbian position. In fact, the isolation of the social dynamics of race and class successfully relegates sexual preference to an attendant position, so that even if the lesbian were to appear, she would be as a bridesmaid and never the bride. Several factors are responsible for this ghosting of the lesbian subject: the first is the growth of moralistic projects restricting the production of sexual fiction or fantasy through the antipornography crusade. This crusade has produced an alliance between those working on social feminist issues and right-wing homophobic, born-again men and women who also support censorship. This alliance in the electorate, which aids in producing enough votes for an ordinance, requires the closeting of lesbians for the so-called greater cause. Both Jill Dolan and Alice Echols develop this position in their respective articles.

Although the antipornography issue is an earmark of the moralistic 1980s, the homophobia it signals is merely an outgrowth of the typical interaction between feminism and lesbianism since the rise of the feminist movement in the early 1970s. Del Martin and Phyllis Lyon describe the rise of the initial so-called lesbian liberatory organization, the Daughters of Bilitis (DOB), in their influential early book, *Lesbian/Woman* (1972). They record the way in which the aims of such organizations were intertwined with those of the early feminist, or more precisely, women's movement. They proudly exhibit the way in which the DOB moved away from the earlier bar culture and its symbolic systems to a more dominant identification and one that would appease the feminist movement. DOB's goal was to erase butch-femme behavior, its dress codes, and lifestyle from the lesbian community and to change lesbians into lesbian feminists.

Here is the story of one poor victim who came to the DOB for help. Note how similar this narrative style is to the redemptive, corrective language of missionary projects: "Toni joined Daughters of Bilitis . . . at our insistence, and as a result of the group's example, its unspoken pressure, she toned down her dress. She was still very butch, but she wore women's slacks and blouses . . . one of DOB's goals was to teach the lesbian a mode of behavior and dress acceptable to society. . . . We knew too many lesbians whose activities were restricted because they wouldn't wear skirts. But Toni did not agree. 'You'll never get me in a dress,' she growled, banging her fist on the table." The description of Toni's behavior, her animal growling noise, portrays her as uncivilized, recalling earlier, colonial missionary projects. Toni is portrayed as similar to the inappropriately dressed savage whom the missionary clothes and saves. The authors continue: "But she became fast friends with a gay man, and over the months he helped her to feel comfortable with herself as a woman" (*Lesbian/Woman* 1972, 77). Here, in a lesbian narrative, the missionary position is finally given over to a man (even if gay) who helps the butch to feel like a woman. The contemporary lesbian-identified reader can only marvel at the conflation of gender identification in the terms of dominant, heterosexual culture with the adopted gender role-playing within the lesbian subculture.

If the butches are savages in this book, the femmes are lost heterosexuals who damage birthright lesbians by forcing them to play the butch roles. The authors assert that most femmes are divorced heterosexual women who know how to relate only to men and thus force their butches to play the man's role, which is conflated with that of a butch (*Lesbian/Woman* 1972, 79). Finally, the authors unveil the salvationary role of feminism in this process and its power to sever the newly constructed identity of the lesbian feminist from its traditional lesbian roots: "The minority of lesbians who still cling to the traditional male-female or husband-wife pattern in their partnerships are more than likely old-timers, gay bar habituées or working class women." This sentence successfully compounds ageism with a (homo)phobia of lesbian bar culture and a rejection of a working-class identification. The middle-class upward mobility of the lesbian feminist identification shifts the sense of community from one of working-class, often women-of-color lesbians in bars, to that of white upper-middle-class heterosexual women who predominated in the early women's movement. The book continues: "the old order changeth however" (here they even begin to adopt verb endings from the King James Bible) "as the women's liberation movement gains strength against this pattern of heterosexual marriages, the number of lesbians involved in butch-femme roles diminishes" (*Lesbian/Woman* 1972, 80).

However, this compulsory adaptation of lesbian feminist identification must be understood as a defensive posture, created by the homophobia that operated in the internal dynamics of the early movement, particularly within the so-called consciousness-raising groups. In her article with Cherrié Moraga on butch-femme relations, Amber Hollibaugh, a femme, described the feminist reception of lesbians this way: "the first discussion I ever heard of lesbianism among feminists was: 'We've been sex objects to men and where did it get us? And here when we're just learning how to be friends with other women, you got to go and sexualize it' . . . they made men out of every sexual dyke" (1983, 402). These kinds of experiences led Hollibaugh and Moraga to conclude: "In our involvement in a movement largely controlled by white middle-class women, we feel that the values of their culture . . . have been pushed down our throats . . . ," and even more specifically, in the 1980s, to pose these questions: "why is it that it is largely white middle-class women who form the visible leadership in the anti-porn movement? Why are women of color not particularly visible in this sex-related single issue movement?" (1983, 405).

When one surveys these beginnings of the alliance between the heterosexual feminist movement and lesbians, one is not surprised at the consequences for lesbians who adopted the missionary position under a movement that would lead to an antipornography crusade and its alliance with the Right. Perhaps too late, certain members of the lesbian community who survived the early years of feminism and continued to work in the grass-roots lesbian movement, such as Joan Nestle, began to perceive this problem. As Nestle, founder of the Lesbian Herstory Archives in New York, wrote: "We lesbians of the 1950s made a mistake in the 1970s: we allowed ourselves to be trivialized and reinterpreted by feminists who did not share our culture" (1981, 23). Nestle also notes the class prejudice in the rejection of butch-femme roles: "I wonder why there is such a consuming interest in the butch-fem lives of upper-class women, usually more literary figures, while real-life, working butch-fem women are seen as imitative and culturally backward . . . the reality of passing women, usually a working-class lesbian's method of survival, has provoked very little academic lesbian-feminist interest. Grassroots lesbian history research is changing this" (1981, 23).

So the lesbian butch-femme tradition went into the feminist closet. Yet the closet, or the bars, with their hothouse atmosphere have produced what, in combination with the butch-femme couple, may provide the liberation of the feminist subject — the discourse of camp. Proust described this accomplishment in his novel *The Captive*:

> The lie, the perfect lie, about people we know, about the relations we have had with them, about our motive for some action, formulated in totally different terms, the lie as to what we are, whom we love, what we feel in regard to those people who love us . . . — that lie is one of the few things in the world that can open windows for us on to what is new and unknown, that can awaken in us sleeping senses for the contemplation of the universes that otherwise we should never have known. (Proust, 213; in Sedgwick 1987)

The closet has given us camp — the style, the discourse, the *mise en scène* of butch-femme roles. In his history of the development of gay camp, Michael

Bronski describes the liberative work of late-nineteenth-century authors such as Oscar Wilde in creating the homosexual camp liberation from the rule of naturalism, or realism. Within his argument, Bronski describes naturalism and realism as strategies that tried to save fiction from the accusation of day-dream, imagination, or masturbation and to affix a utilitarian goal to literary production—that of teaching morals. In contrast, Bronski quotes the newspaper *Fag Rag* on the functioning of camp: "We've broken down the rules that are used for validating the difference between real/true and unreal/false. The controlling agents of the status quo may know the power of lies; dissident subcultures, however, are closer to knowing their value" (1984, 41). Camp both articulates the lives of homosexuals through the obtuse tone of irony and inscribes their oppression with the same device. Likewise, it eradicates the ruling powers of heterosexist realist modes.

Susan Sontag, in an avant-garde assimilation of camp, described it as a "certain mode of aestheticism . . . one way of seeing the world as an aesthetic phenomenon . . . not in terms of beauty, but in terms of the degree of artifice" (1966, 275). This artifice, as artifice, works to defeat the reign of realism as well as to situate the camp discourse within the category of what can be said (or seen). However, the fixed quality of Sontag's characteristic use of camp within the straight context of aestheticization has produced a homosexual strategy for avoiding such assimilation: what Esther Newton has described as its constantly changing, mobile quality, designed to alter the gay camp sensibility before it becomes a fad (1972, 105). Moreover, camp also protects homosexuals through a "first-strike wit" as *Fag Rag* asserts: "Wit and irony provide the only reasonable modus operandi in the American Literalist Terror of Straight Reality" (1984, 46).

Oscar Wilde brought this artifice, wit, irony, and the distancing of straight reality and its conventions to the stage. Later, Genet staged the malleable, multiple artifice of camp in *The Screens,* which elevates such displacement to an ontology. In his play, *The Blacks,* he used such wit, irony and artifice to deconstruct the notion of "black" and to stage the dynamics of racism. *The Blacks* displaced the camp critique from homophobia to racism, in which "black" stands in for "queer" and the campy queen of the bars is transformed into an "african queen." This displacement is part of the larger use of the closet and gay camp discourse to articulate other social realities. Eve Sedgwick attests to this displacement when she writes: "I want to argue that a lot of energy of attention and demarcation that has swirled around issues of homosexuality since the end of the nineteenth century . . . has been impelled by the distinctly indicative relation of homosexuality to wider mappings of secrecy and disclosure, and of the private and the public, that were and are critically problematical for the gender, sexual, and economic structures of the heterosexist culture at large. . . . 'the closet' and 'coming out' are now verging on all-purpose phrases for the potent crossing and recrossing of almost any politically-charged lines of representation. . . . The apparent floating-free from its gay origins of that phrase 'coming out of the closet' in recent usage might suggest that the trope of the closet is so close to the heart of some modern preoccupations that it could be . . . evacuated of its historical gay specificity. But I hypothesize that exactly the opposite is true." Thus, the camp success in ironizing and distancing the regime of realist terror mounted by heterosexist forces has become useful as a discourse and style for other marginal factions.

Camp style, gay-identified dressing and the articulation of the social realities of homosexuality have also become part of the straight, postmodern canon, as Herbert Blau articulated it in a special issue of *Salmagundi:* "becoming homosexual is part of the paraphilia of the postmodern, not only a new sexual politics but the reification of all politics, supersubtilized beyond the unnegotiable demands of the sixties, from which it is derived, into a more persuasive rhetoric of unsublimated desire" (1983, 233). Within this critical community, the perception of recognizable homosexuals can also inspire broader visions of the operation of social codes. Blau states: "there soon came pullulating toward me at high prancing amphetamined pitch something like the end of Empire or like the screaming remains of the return of the repressed — pearl-white, vinyl, in polo pants and scarf — an englistered and giggling outburst of resplendent queer . . . what was there to consent to and who could possibly legitimate that galloping specter I had seen, pure ideolect, whose plunging and lungless soundings were a full-throttled forecast of much weirder things to come?" (1983, 221–22). Initially, these borrowings seem benign and even inviting to the homosexual theorist. Contemporary theory seems to open the closet door to invite the queer to come out, transformed as a new, postmodern subject, or even to invite straights to come into the closet, out of the roar of dominant discourse. The danger incurred in moving gay politics into such heterosexual contexts is in only slowly discovering that the strategies and perspectives of homosexual realities and discourse may be locked inside a homophobic "concentration camp." Certain of these authors, such as Blau, even introduce homosexual characters and their subversions into arguments that conclude with explicit homophobia. Note Blau's remembrance of things past: "thinking I would enjoy it, I walked up Christopher Street last summer at the fag end of the depleted carnival of Gay Pride Day, with a disgust unexpected and almost uncontained by principle. . . . I'll usually fight for the right of each of us to have his own perversions, I may not, under the pressure of theory and despite the itchiness of my art, to try on yours and, what's worse, rather wish you wouldn't. Nor am I convinced that what you are doing isn't perverse in the most pejorative sense" (1983, 249). At least Blau, as in all of his writing, honestly and openly records his personal prejudice. The indirect or subtextual homophobia in this new assimilative discourse is more alluring and ultimately more powerful in erasing the social reality and the discursive inscriptions of gay, and more specifically, lesbian discourse.

Here, the sirens of sublation may be found in the critical maneuvers of heterosexual feminist critics who metaphorize butch-femme roles, transvestites and campy dressers into a "subject who masquerades," as they put it, or is "carnivalesque" or even, as some are so bold to say, who "cross-dresses." Even when these borrowings are nested in more benign contexts than Blau's, they evacuate the historical, butch-femme couples' sense of masquerade and cross-dressing the way a cigar-store Indian evacuates the historical dress and behavior of the Native American. As is often the case, illustrated by the cigar-store Indian, these symbols may only proliferate when the social reality has been successfully obliterated and the identity has become the private property of the dominant class. Such metaphors operate simply to display the breadth of the art collection, or style collection, of the straight author. Just as the French term *film noir* became the name for B-rate American films of the forties, these notions of masquerade and cross-dressing, standing in for the roles of working-class lesbians, have come back to us through French theory on the one hand and studies of the lives of upper-class lesbians who lived in Paris between the wars on the other. In this case, the referent of the term Left Bank is not a river, but a storehouse of critical capital.

Nevertheless, this confluence of an unresolved social, historical problem in the feminist movement and these recent theoretical strategies, re-assimilated by the lesbian critic, provide a ground that could resolve the project of constructing the feminist subject position. The butch-femme subject could inhabit that discursive position, empowering it for the production of future compositions. Having already grounded this argument within the historical situation of butch-femme couples, perhaps now it would be tolerable to describe the theoretical maneuver that could become the butch-femme subject position. Unfortunately, these strategies must emerge in the bodiless world of "spectatorial positions" or "subject positions," where transvestites wear no clothes and subjects tread only "itineraries of desire." In this terrain of discourse, or among theorized spectators in darkened movie houses with their gazes fixed on the dominant cinema screen, "the thrill is gone" as Nestle described it.

Peggy Shaw and Lois Weaver in *Split Britches Cabaret*. (Photo by Morgan Gwenweld.)

In the Greenwich Village bars, she could "spot a butch 50 feet away and still feel the thrill of her power" as she saw "the erotic signal of her hair at the nape of her neck, touching the shirt collar; how she held a cigarette; the symbolic pinky ring flashing as she waved her hand" (1981, 21–22). Within this theory, the erotics are gone, but certain maneuvers maintain what is generally referred to as "presence."

The origins of this theory may be found in a Freudian therapist's office, where an intellectual heterosexual woman, who had become frigid, had given way to rages, and, puzzled by her own coquettish behavior, told her story to Joan Riviere sometime around 1929. This case caused Riviere to publish her thoughts in her ground-breaking article entitled "Womanliness as a Masquerade" that later influenced several feminist critics such as Mary Russo and Mary Ann Doane and the French philosopher Jean Baudrillard. Riviere began to "read" this woman's behavior as the "wish for masculinity" which causes the woman to don "the mask of womanliness to avert anxiety and the retribution feared from men" (1929, 303). As Riviere saw it, for a woman to read an academic paper before a professional association was to exhibit in public her "possession of her father's penis, having castrated him" (1929, 305–6). In order to do recompense for this castration, which resided in her intellectual proficiency, she donned the mask of womanliness. Riviere notes: "The reader may now ask how I define womanliness or where I draw the line between genuine womanliness and the 'masquerade' . . . they are the same thing" (1929, 306). Thus began the theory that all womanliness is a masquerade worn by women to disguise the fact that they have taken their father's penis in their intellectual stride, so to speak. Rather than remaining the well-adjusted castrated woman, these intellectuals have taken the penis for their own and protect it with the mask of the castrated, or womanhood. However, Riviere notes a difference here between heterosexual women and lesbian ones — the heterosexual women don't claim possession openly, but through reaction-formations; whereas the homosexual women openly display their possession of the penis and count on the males' recognition of defeat (1929, 312). This is not to suggest that the lesbian's situation is not also fraught with anxiety and reaction-formations, but this difference in degree is an important one.

I suggest that this kind of masquerade is consciously played out in butch-femme roles, particularly as they were constituted in the 1940s and 1950s. If one reads them from within Riviere's theory, the butch is the lesbian woman who proudly displays the possession of the penis, while the femme takes on the compensatory masquerade of womanliness. The femme, however, foregrounds her masquerade by playing to a butch, another woman in a role; likewise, the butch exhibits her penis to a woman who is playing the role of compensatory castration. This raises the question of "penis, penis, who's got the penis," because there is no referent in sight; rather, the fictions of penis and castration become ironized and "camped up." Unlike Riviere's patient, these women play on the phallic economy rather than to it. Both women alter this masquerading subject's function by positioning it between women and thus foregrounding the myths of penis and castration in the Freudian economy. In the bar culture, these roles were always acknowledged as such. The bars were often abuzz with the discussion of who was or was not a butch or femme, and how good they were at the role (see Davis and Kennedy 1986). In other words, these penis-related posturings were always acknowledged as roles, not biological birthrights, nor any other essentialist poses. The lesbian roles are underscored as two optional functions for women in the phallocracy, while the heterosexual woman's role collapses them into one compensatory charade. From a theatrical point of view, the butch-femme roles take on the quality of something more like a character construction and have a more active quality than what Riviere calls a reaction-formation. Thus, these roles qua roles lend agency and self-determination to the historically passive subject, providing her with at least two options for gender identification and with the aid of camp, an irony that allows her perception to be constructed from outside ideology, with a gender role that makes her appear as if she is inside of it.

Meanwhile, other feminist critics have received this masquerade theory into a heterosexual context, retaining its passive imprint. In Mary Ann Doane's influential article entitled "Film and the Masquerade: Theorising the Female Spectator," Doane, unfortunately, resorts to a rather biologistic position in constructing the female spectator and theorizing out from the female body. From the standpoint of something more active in terms of representation such as de Lauretis's feminist subject or the notion of butch-femme, this location of critical strategies in biological realities seems revisionist. That point aside, Doane does devise a way for women to "appropriate the gaze for their own pleasure" (1982, 77) through the notion of the transvestite and the masquerade. As the former, the female subject would position herself as if she were a male viewer, assimilating all of the power and payoffs that spectatorial position offers. As the latter, she would, as Riviere earlier suggested, masquerade as a woman. She would "flaunt her femininity, produce herself as an excess of femininity—foreground the masquerade," and reveal "femininity itself . . . as a mask" (1982, 81). Thus, the masquerade would hold femininity at a distance, manufacturing "a lack in the form of a certain distance between oneself and one's image" (1982, 82). This strategy offers the female viewer a way to be the spectator of female roles while not remaining close to them, nor identifying with them, attaining the distance from them required to enter the psychoanalytic viewing space. The masquerade that Doane describes is exactly that practiced by the femme—she foregrounds cultural femininity. The difference is that Doane places this role in the spectator position, probably as an outgrowth of the passive object position required of women in the hetero-sexist social structures. Doane's vision of the active woman is as the active spectator. Within the butch-femme economy, the femme actively performs her masquerade as the subject of representation. She delivers a performance of the feminine masquerade rather than, as Doane suggests, continues in Riviere's reactive formation of masquerading compensatorily before the male-gaze-inscribed-dominant-cinema-screen. *Flaunting* has long been a camp verb and here Doane borrows it, along with the notion of "excess of femininity," so familiar to classical femmes and drag queens. Yet, by reinscribing it within a passive, spectatorial role, she gags and binds the traditional homosexual role players, whose gender play has nothing essential beneath it, replacing them with the passive spectatorial position that is, essentially, female.

Another feminist theorist, Mary Russo, has worked out a kind of female masquerade through the sense of the carnivalesque body derived from the work of Mikhail Bakhtin. In contrast to Doane, Russo moves on to a more active role for the masquerader, one of "making a spectacle of oneself." Russo is aware of the dangers of the essentialist body in discourse, while still maintaining some relationship between theory and real women. This seems a more hopeful critical terrain to the lesbian critic. In fact, Russo even includes a reference to historical instances of political resistance by men in drag (1985, 3). Yet in spite of her cautions, like Doane, Russo's category is once again the female subject, along with its biologically determined social resonances. Perhaps it is her reliance on the male author Bakhtin and the socialist resonances in his text (never too revealing about gender) that cause Russo to omit lesbian or gay strategies or experiences with the grotesque body. Instead, she is drawn to depictions of the pregnant body and finally Kristeva's sense of the maternal, even though she does note its limitations and problematic status within feminist thought (1985, 6). Finally, this swollen monument to reproduction, with all of its heterosexual privilege, once more stands alone in this performance area of the grotesque and carnivalesque. Though she does note the exclusion, in this practice, of the "the already marginalized" (6), once again, they do not appear. Moreover, Russo even cites Showalter's notion that feminist theory itself is a kind of "critical cross-dressing," while still suppressing the lesbian presence in the feminist community that made such a concept available to the straight theorists (1985, 8). Still true to the male, heterosexual models from which her argument derives, she identifies the master of *mise en scène* as Derrida. Even when damning his characterization of the feminist as raging bull and asking "what kind of drag is this," her referent is the feminist and not the bull . . . dyke (1985, 9). This argument marks an ironic point in history: once the feminist movement had obscured the original cross-dressed butch through the interdiction of "politically incorrect," it donned for itself the strategies and characteristics of the role-playing, safely theorized out of material reality and used to suppress the referent that produced it.

In spite of their heterosexist shortcomings, what, in these theories, can be employed to understand the construction of the butch-femme subject on the stage? First, how might they be constructed as characters? Perhaps the best example of some workings of this potential is in Split Britches' production of *Beauty and the Beast.*[1] The title itself connotes the butch-femme couple: Shaw as the butch becomes the Beast who actively pursues the femme, while Weaver as the excessive femme becomes Beauty. Within the dominant system of representation, Shaw, as butch Beast, portrays as bestial women who actively love other women. The portrayal is faithful to the historical situation of the butch role, as Nestle describes it: "None of the butch women I was with, and this included a passing woman, ever presented themselves to me as men; they did announce themselves as tabooed women who were willing to identify their passion for other women by wearing clothes that symbolized the taking of responsibility. Part of this responsibility was sexual expertise . . . this courage to feel comfortable with arousing another woman became a political act" (1981, 21). In other words, the butch, who represents by her clothing the desire for other women, becomes the beast—the marked taboo against lesbianism dressed up in the clothes of that desire. Beauty is the desired one and the one who aims her desirability at the butch.

This symbolism becomes explicit when Shaw and Weaver interrupt the Beauty/Beast narrative to deliver a duologue about the history of their own personal butch-femme roles. Weaver uses the trope of having wished she was Katharine Hepburn and casting another woman as Spencer Tracy, while Shaw relates that she thought she was James Dean. The identification with movie idols is part of the camp assimilation of dominant culture. It serves multiple purposes: (1) they do not identify these butch-femme roles with "real" people, or literal images of gender, but with fictionalized ones, thus underscoring the masquerade; (2) the history of their desire, or their search for a sexual partner becomes a series of masks, or identities that stand for sexual attraction in the culture, thus distancing them from the "play" of seduction as it is outlined by social mores; (3) the association with movies makes narrative fiction part of the strategy as well as characters. This final fiction as fiction allows Weaver and Shaw to slip easily from one narrative to another, to yet another, unbound by through-lines, plot structure, or a stable sense of character because they are fictional at their core in the camp style and through the butch-femme roles. The instability and alienation of character and plot is compounded with their own personal butch-femme play on the street, as a recognizable couple in the lower East Side scene, as well as within fugitive narratives on-stage, erasing the difference between theatre and real life, or actor and character, obliterating any kind of essentialist ontology behind the play. This allows them to create a play with scenes that move easily from the narrative of beauty and the beast, to the duologue on their butch-femme history, to a recitation from *Macbeth,* to a solo lip-synced to Perry Como. The butch-femme roles at the center of their ongoing personalities move masquerade to the base of performance and no narrative net can catch them or hold them, as they wriggle into a variety of characters and plots.

This exciting multiplicity of roles and narratives signals the potency of their agency. Somehow the actor overcomes any text, yet the actor herself is a fiction and her social self is one as well. Shaw makes a joke out of suturing to any particular role or narrative form when she dies, as the beast. Immediately after dying, she gets up to tell the audience not to believe in such cheap tricks. Dies. Tells the audience that Ronald Reagan pulled the same trick when he was shot — tells them that was not worth the suturing either. Dies. Asks for a Republican doctor. Dies. Then rises to seemingly close the production by kissing Weaver. Yet even this final butch-femme tableau is followed by a song to the audience that undercuts the performance itself.

Weaver's and Shaw's production of butch-femme role-playing in and out of a fairy tale positions the representation of the lesbian couple in a childhood narrative: the preadolescent proscription of perversity. Though they used *Beauty and the Beast* to stage butch-femme as outsiders, the quintessential childhood narrative that proscribes cross-dressing is *Little Red Riding Hood,* in which the real terror of the wolf is produced by his image in grandmother's clothing. The bed, the eating metaphor, and the cross-dressing by the wolf, provide a gridlock closure of any early thoughts of transgressing gender roles. Djuna Barnes wrote a version of this perspective in *Nightwood.* When Nora sees the transvestite doctor in his bed, wearing women's nightclothes, she remarks: "God, children know something they can't tell; they like Red Riding Hood and the wolf in bed!" Barnes goes on to explicate that sight of the cross-dressed one: "Is not the gown the natural raiment of extremity? . . . He dresses to lie beside himself, who is so constructed that love, for him, can only be something special. . . ." (1961, 78–80).[2] *Beauty and the Beast* also returns to a childhood tale of taboo and liberates the sexual preference and role-playing it is designed to repress, in this case, specifically the butch-femme promise. As some lesbians prescribed in the early movement: identify with the monsters!

What, then, is the action played between these two roles? It is what Jean Baudrillard terms *séduction* and it yields many of its social fruits. Baudrillard begins his argument in *De la séduction,* by asserting that seduction is never of the natural order, but always operates as a sign, or artifice (1979, 10). By extension, this suggests that butch-femme seduction is always located in semiosis. The kiss, as Shaw and Weaver demonstrate in their swooping image of

Lois Weaver, Peggy Shaw, and Deb Margolin appear in *Upwardly Mobile Home,* a Split Britches production. (Photo by Eva Weiss.)

it, positioned at its most clichéd niche at the end of the narrative, is always the high camp kiss. Again, Baudrillard: seduction doesn't "recuperate the autonomy of the body . . . truth . . . the sovereignty of this seduction is trans- sexual, not bisexual, destroying all sexual organization. . . ." (1979, 18). The point is not to conflict reality with another reality, but to abandon the notion of reality through roles and their seductive atmosphere and lightly manipulate appearances. Surely, this is the atmosphere of camp, permeating the *mise en scène* with "pure" artifice. In other words, a strategy of appearances replaces a claim to truth. Thus, butch-femme roles evade the notion of "the female body" as it predominates in feminist theory, dragging along its Freudian baggage and scopophilic transubstantiation. These roles are played in signs themselves and not in ontologies. Seduction, as a dramatic action, transforms all of these seeming realities into semiotic play. To use Baudrillard with Riviere, butch-femme roles offer a hypersimulation of woman as she is defined by the Freudian system and the phallocracy that institutes its social rule.[3]

Therefore, the female body, the male gaze, and the structures of realism are only sex toys for the butch-femme couple. From the perspective of camp, the claim these have to realism destroys seduction by repressing the resonances of vision and sound into its medium. This is an idea worked out by Baudrillard in his chapter on pornography, but I find it apt here. That is, that realism, with its visual organization of three dimensions, actually degrades the scene; it impoverishes the suggestiveness of the scene by its excess of means (1979, 49). This implies that as realism makes the spectator see things its way, it represses her own ability to free-associate within a situation and reduces the resonances of events to its own limited, technical dimensions. Thus, the seduction of the scene is repressed by the authoritarian claim to realistic representation. This difference is marked in the work of Weaver and Shaw in the ironized, imaginative theatrical space of their butch-femme role-playing. Contrast their freely moving, resonant narrative space to the realism of Marsha Norman, Beth Henley, Irene Fornes's *Mud,* or Sam Shepard's *A Lie of the Mind.* The violence released in the continual zooming-in on the family unit, and the heterosexist ideology linked with its stage partner, realism, is directed against women and their hint of seduction. In *A Lie of the Mind,* this becomes literally woman-battering. Beth's only associative space and access to transformative discourse is the result of nearly fatal blows to her head. One can see similar violent results in Norman's concerted moving of the heroine toward suicide in *'night, Mother* or Henley's obsession with suicide in *Crimes of the Heart* or the conclusive murder in Fornes's *Mud.* The closure of these realistic narratives chokes the women to death and strangles the play of symbols, or the possibility of seduction. In fact, for each of them, sexual play only assists their entrapment. One can see the butch Peggy Shaw rising to her feet after these realistic narrative deaths and telling us not to believe it. Cast the realism aside—its consequences for women are deadly.

In recuperating the space of seduction, the butch-femme couple can, through their own agency, move through a field of symbols, like tiptoeing through the two lips (as Irigaray would have us believe), playfully inhabiting the camp space of irony and wit, free from biological determinism, elitist essentialism, and the heterosexist cleavage of sexual difference. Surely, here is a couple the feminist subject might perceive as useful to join.

NOTES

A version of this article appears in the journal *Discourse* 11, no. 1, from the Center for Twentieth Century Studies, University of Wisconsin-Milwaukee.

1. There is no published version of this play. In fact, there is no satisfactory way to separate the spoken text from the action. The play is composed by three actors, Deborah Margolin along with Shaw and Weaver. Margolin, however, does not play within the lesbian dynamics, but represents a Jewish perspective. For further discussions of this group's work see Kate Davy, "Constructing the Spectator: Reception, Context, and Address in Lesbian Performance," *Performing Arts Journal* 10, no. 2 (1986): 43–52; Jill Dolan, "The Dynamics of Desire: Sexuality and Gender in Pornography and Performance," *Theatre Journal* 39, no. 2 (1987): 156–74; and Sue-Ellen Case, "From Split Subject to Split Britches," *Contemporary Women Playwrights,* ed. Enoch Brater (forthcoming).

2. My thanks to Carolyn Allen, who pointed out this passage in Barnes to me in discussing resonances of the fairy tale. In another context, it would be interesting to read the lesbian perspective on the male transvestite in these passages and the way he works in Barnes's narrative. "The Company of Wolves," a short story and later a screenplay by Angela Carter, begins to open out the sexual resonances, but retains the role of the monster within heterosexuality.

3. The term *hypersimulation* is borrowed from Baudrillard's notion of the simulacrum rather than his one of seduction. It is useful here to raise the ante on terms like artifice and to suggest, as Baudrillard does, its relation to the order of reproduction and late capitalism.

REFERENCES

Barnes, Djuna. 1961. *Nightwood.* New York: New Directions.

Baudrillard, Jean. 1979. *De la seduction.* Paris: Editions Galilee.

Blau, Herbert. 1983. "Disseminating Sodom." *Salmagundi* 58–59: 221–51.

Bronski, Michael. 1984. *Culture Clash: The Making of Gay Sensibility.* Boston: South End Press.

Davis, Madeline, and Kennedy, Elizabeth Lapovsky. 1986. "Oral History and the Study of Sexuality in the Lesbian Community: Buffalo, New York, 1940–1960." *Feminist Studies* 12, no. 1:7–26.

de Lauretis, Teresa. 1987. *Technologies of Gender.* Bloomington, Ind.: Indiana University Press.

Doane, Mary Ann. 1982. "Film and the Masquerade: Theorising the Female Spectator." *Screen* 23:74–87.

Dolan, Jill. 1987. "The Dynamics of Desire: Sexuality and Gender in Pornography and Performance." *Theatre Journal* 39, no. 2:156–74.

Echols, Alice. 1983. "The New Feminism of Yin and Yang." In *Powers of Desire: The Politics of Sexuality,* ed. Ann Snitow, Christine Stansell, and Sharon Thompson, 440–59. New York: Monthly Review Press.

Hollibaugh, Amber, and Moraga, Cherrié. 1983. "What We're Rollin' Around in Bed With: Sexual Silences in Feminism." In *Powers of Desire: The Politics of Sexuality,* ed. Ann Snitow, Christine Stansell, and Sharon Thompson, 395–405. New York: Monthly Review Press.

Martin, Del, and Lyon, Phyllis. 1972. *Lesbian/Woman.* New York: Bantam.

Nestle, Joan. 1981. "Butch-Fem Relationships: Sexual Courage in the 1950s." *Heresies* 12:21–24. All pagination here is from that publication. Reprinted in Joan Nestle. 1987. *A Restricted Country,* 100–109. Ithaca: Firebrand Books.

Newton, Esther. 1972. *Mother Camp: Female Impersonators in America.* Englewood Cliffs, N. J.: Prentice-Hall.

"Postmodernism: Text, Politics, Instruction." 1987. International Association for Philosophy and Literature. Lawrence, Kansas, April 30–May 2.

Riviere, Joan. 1929. "Womanliness as a Masquerade." *International Journal of Psycho-Analysis* 10:303–13.

Russo, Mary. 1985. "Female Grotesques: Carnival and Theory." Working Paper no. 1. Center for Twentieth Century Studies, Milwaukee. Page citations for this text. Reprinted in *Feminist Studies Critical Studies,* ed. Teresa de Lauretis. Bloomington: Indiana University Press, 1986.

Sedgwick, Eve. 1987. "The Epistemology of the Closet." Manuscript.

Sontag, Susan. 1966. *Against Interpretation.* New York: Farrar, Strauss & Giroux.

Wittig, Monique. *The Lesbian Body.* Trans. David LeVay. New York: William Morrow, 1975.

ROSEMARY CURB

Mirrors Moving beyond Frames: Sandra Shotlander's *Framework* and *Blind Salome*

> The Delphic oracle remembered herself as an originary source of time-consciousness and historical being — until Apollo killed her. The Delphic oracle, embodied as a female dragon, was slain by Apollo. . . . The oracle, robbed of her memories and bodily members, becomes the vehicle of Apollo's utterances. . . .
>
> As we reproduce, are forced to reproduce, the world shaped by men, the demise of the oracle at Delphi continues. *Reproductive remembering: men's attempt to impregnate women by force.* Just as God, man's absolute and reified idea of himself, once placed thoughts of the True, the Good, and the Beautiful in men, man attempts to implant his ideas in women. Women, subjected to forced insemination, become filled, saturated with the man-become-god. . . . We cannot produce ourselves. The horizons of our time and history are bare. Sterilized against our will, we are fragmented, dismembered.
>
> — Jeffner Allen, *Lesbian Philosophy: Explorations*

How can the feminist artist mirror the wholeness of the dismembered body? Where can the feminist scholar discover lost memory? If women are gagged, raped, forced to incubate the seed of male dominance generation after generation, can woman-conscious drama re-member the scattered fragments of a pre-Apollonian oracle?

In *Framework* (1983) and *Blind Salome* (1985) Sandra Shotlander portrays female characters tunneling into the timeless labyrinth in order to see beyond time and sight boundaries of patriarchal conditioning. They are re-membering their originary selves. Rather than engaging foes in external combat, the characters search within for a voice or a vision leading to self-discovery. The inner, almost mystical, truth they seek comes paradoxically by way of peripheral vision. The frame itself stretches into infinity and mirrors the characters.

For truth seekers and visionaries in Shotlander's plays, traditional frames of reference within the perceivable world recede. Even the horizon shimmers and blurs like a desert oasis or mirage pot of gold at the end of the rainbow. Shotlander shows a female Protean self-as-other mirrored in the vacillating frames of art and history. The frames vacillate as received knowledge fades into the sharper focus of inner reality. In *Women's Ways of Knowing: The Development of Self, Voice, and Mind,* Mary Field Belenky, Blythe McVicker Clinchy, Nancy Rule Goldberger, and Jill Mattuck Tarule describe this "constructed knowledge" which embraces contradictions and ambiguities as "integrating the voices" (1986, 133–37).

In *Framework* two Australian women coincidentally meet in a corner of the New York Metropolitan Museum of Art where Picasso's *Portrait of Gertrude Stein* faces O'Keeffe's *Black Iris.* However, the meeting and the subsequent relationship between the two women is represented as a memory flashback of one of them. Thus the action is simultaneously time past and time present for the audience.

Blind Salome likewise dramatizes fantasy and memory sequences embedded in present action. Four Australians (two women and two men) traveling together across Europe and, at the moment of action, staying in a pensione in Assisi, seek the subjective truth of their individual selves reflected in medieval art. They are studying the lives of St. Francis and St. Clare and recording their changing consciousness of self in relation to others in their journals, which they intend to share with each other. The male characters are blatantly searching for an *anima.* The women, however, are not searching for an *animus.* Rather they are deliberately shedding patriarchal values, modes of thought, and especially the misogynist encumbrances of modern psychoanalytic theories.

In both plays Shotlander uses past and present events simultaneously in order to demonstrate the present effects both of tradition and of one's own past. Furthermore, she uses the metaphor of external travel as a mirror for characters' interior search—from Australia to America in *Framework* and from Australia to Europe in *Blind Salome.* Most significantly, she has her female characters find a path to the center of self through some sort of eccentricity. Like Mary Daly's "Outsiders" (1978, 186), discussed below with *Framework,* Shotlander's characters paradoxically find focus not in the center of the frame, but at the periphery. Liberation, therefore, consists of stripping away facades, expanding the frame, peeling off the veils.

The set of *Framework* (*F*) consists of two large frames raised one step above the stage and angled to form a corner. When the dramatized scene is the Metropolitan Museum, O'Keeffe's *Black Iris* occupies the stage-left frame and Picasso's *Portrait of Gertrude Stein* occupies stage right. When the paintings are pushed back, the scene becomes Lee's apartment: the Stein frame becomes Lee's living room with chairs and table and the Iris frame becomes her bedroom. The set reflects the lives of women as Lee imagines them:

> I think we are trained for the sides of existence, for fixing dinner, nailing and jointing to hold ourselves together, but when it comes to the picture, we don't know what to do. I've been unscrewing the frame for some time now, wrenching it off. According to Stein it starts with an internal movement, not of people or light but inside the painting. (*She speaks in Stein's voice.*) Modern paintings have made a very definite effort to leave their frames. (*F,* 10)

Like the inconspicuous frame for a significant famous painting, women have been trained, as Lee describes, to be the border or scaffolding but never the centerpiece of history. Throughout *Framework* both women struggle to unscrew patriarchal frames and gender-assigned stereotypes.

The audience or reader perceives the drama through the framing consciousness of Lee Price, a middle-aged woman in the process of divorcing the husband she followed to America approximately a decade and a half before the events that the play dramatizes. Lee is experiencing a new sense of freedom to pursue her own interests. She is seeking the self she laid aside when she married. The drama captures Lee at several significant transitions: her separation and divorce from Tim, her sending her "fully American" daughter Sarah off to her first year at Sarah Lawrence College, and her facing her formerly abandoned lesbian sexuality and her homesickness for Australia in the person of Iris Blakely.

Nonchronologically *Framework* dramatizes the budding, blossoming, withering, and possibly reviving of a union between Lee and Iris. They meet, and, under the spell of life reflected in art, become emotionally entangled, share their private histories and secret art, and then part. Since Iris has no apparent research or business purpose for her travel, when her visa runs out, she returns to Australia. Lee and Iris keep in touch by letters and phone calls. About a year later Iris returns to Lee, and they end whatever relationship they had. Their union is better defined in its ending than its beginning or development. Iris returns to an earlier relationship with Penny in Australia. But later she writes to Lee that Penny has become no more than a friend; she urges Lee to come to Australia. Since the play ends, as it begins, with Lee's departure, what is dramatized seems rather a Chinese box of infinite regressions or memory traces—one branching off to another, creating a web of connections across time.

Framework opens as a posed still photograph: Lee and Iris looking at the Stein portrait. After a blackout, Lee appears alone, speaking as if she had stepped out of the photograph into a time after or beyond the events that she remembers/re-members: "Snap. A picture in the mind. Snap. A camera putting an incident into a frame" (*F,* 1). The final scene with Lee packing, moving through her New York apartment, remembering her losses, echoes the prologue: "Snap. A camera putting an incident into a frame. Snap. I am defined every day, but I am choosing my definitions" (*F,* 43). In jumbled achronological snips of overlapping and repeated recorded conversations, phone calls, letters, photos, the intense but fleeting passion that Lee shared with Iris unravels.

Scenes in the museum or in Lee's apartment shift from Lee's reflections on her past with Iris or with her husband Tim to present commentary on art and history. The paintings of Stein and the *Black Iris* witness and reflect all dramatized action. This technique reverses the specular process by making objects ordinarily seen be the seers of action played before them in their dispassionate omniscience. Anticipating "reunion" with Iris, Lee wonders if she can call what she and Iris had a "union" and what a union is. With the passion only a memory, Lee ponders the unflinching stasis of the art that drew them together. Unmoved by the ebb and flow of passion, unions, and reunions, the stolid thought-laden Stein and the fragile floating blossom do not blink as the women approach each other again and again like cinematic reruns.

Lee, the Americanized Australian transplant, aligns herself with Stein, affectionately parodies Stein's thought and style of speech, quotes gustily from *Everybody's Autobiography*. Like the immovable Stein, laden with ideas, she freely dispenses coffee, tea, wine, wisdom from a safe home base, where she records and files, collects and frames whatever beauty or knowledge passes through her life. The museum gallery itself seems an annex to her apartment, one more box among the many cubes that make up the city. Reflecting the portrait, Lee not only parodies the personality of Stein but also Picasso's cubist style.

For Lee, becoming Americanized has meant being cut down to fit a masculine cube and retaining only a dim memory of the expansiveness that she associates with the Australian landscape—a paradise lost in her memory. Like a good wife, a bird in a gilded cage, Lee followed her husband to America, leaving behind with some regret (but more relief) her Australian woman lover of three months. Even though Lee perceived herself transgressing the safe barriers of social propriety by abandoning herself to a clandestine woman lover, she played out a butch-femme charade in order to box in her transgression.

In America Lee lives in a box of an apartment in a freezing foreign city of heated boxes. She is urged to be grateful that her husband's money pays for the heat. In describing her struggle for independence to Iris, Lee acknowledges the confining role that her father and then husband played in her life:

> I knew fathers were there to control. I married one to control me. He never shouted, he just took possession. He made me completely dependent. . . . When Tim left I felt like a vacant possession. When I possess myself I'll be completely independent. (*F,* 14)

Lee has allowed male control to protect her from her terror of her own wildness, freedom, and sexuality.

Iris, on the other hand, is the dark, changing, mysterious, evanescently touchable flower. At their first meeting she tells Lee that her surname, *Blakely,* means "dweller by a black wood." For Lee she also represents the freshness of Australia: the clear light squeezing through the wattles. If Lee is the ebb, Iris is the flow. Lee is the bulky, rooted rock of Stein. Iris is the free-floating wanderer. Whereas Lee is intellectual and analytic, Iris is sensual and intuitive. Like the iris, which closes to light (intellectual analysis) or heat (Lee's impetuous passion), Iris opens only on her own terms of safety. For example, she redecorates Lee's bedroom, painting the walls a pale mauve and having a purplish-black doona cover made for the bed. Iris erotically rolls herself into the center of the doona and announces, "I'm curling into the flower" (*F,* 25). In other words, she literally gives herself to Lee as the dark, wet hidden center of the iris.

Lee's fascination with Iris and O'Keeffe's *Black Iris* recalls a past road not taken back in Australia. Unaware of what she was seeking, Lee tells Iris that she once traveled to New Mexico in search of O'Keeffe.

> I didn't find her but I found the desert. It's always the way, I look for something and find something else. Now I'm trying to find the thing I'm not looking for. (*F,* 8)

Apparently the American desert reminds Lee of Australia. Mystical search necessarily requires the simplicity of the desert in order to explore the inner landscapes of the soul. Although Iris never describes her purpose in traveling, it is only after she returns home to Australia and then returns to America and finally to Australia that she recognizes that her travels embody her intuitive search for self. Lee's departure for Australia at the end of the play likewise conjures up her pilgrimage to the American desert to find O'Keeffe.

Through travel, both global and interior, Lee and Iris seek and fear flashes of illumination that dazzle from the periphery. In her foreword to the play, Judith Rodriguez notes that Lee and Iris discover themselves through travel:

> All journeys risk finding more than their apparent goals. How many Australians have recognized crucial aspects of their lives, when set adrift, abroad, from the known securities and relationships that sometimes hide personal horizons. (*F*, n.p.)

Just as memories surface unexpectedly to illuminate present situations, travel abroad helps to discover home.

What finally do Lee and Iris mirror for each other? Both claim Stein as hero and praise Stein's eccentricity. In the women's initial discourse, "eccentric" becomes a code for the more dangerous word both wish to convey but neither is ready to say aloud: lesbian. Compare Mary Daly's description of the witches' sisterhood of "eccentricity":

> The women hunted as witches were (are) in a time/space that is not cocentric with androcracy. Hags are Self-centering, constituting the Society of Outsiders, defining gynocentric boundaries. This the dreaded option of Dreadful, Dreadless Crones, . . . (1978, 186)

From their first encounter, Iris and Lee exchange lesbian "Outsider" signals to transmit their mutual knowledge of lesbian history and culture. Lee's presumption of Iris's lesbian identity (the "uniform") leads her to break the museum protocol of silence and anonymity. Seeing O'Keeffe's *Black Iris,* Iris exclaims "Wow! It's fantastic!" Lee coolly responds, "It's a flower you know, according to O'Keeffe, not a vagina, that's just the way you're looking at it" (*F*, 2). Iris is embarrassed because she is caught off guard speaking aloud in public, because she doesn't know O'Keeffe's work, and because she *was* looking at it that way. Iris's response doubly transgresses an unstated propriety of representation. If the object of desire in a work of art is female, the gaze (representing power and possession) is male. As Ann Kaplan states, "the gaze is not necessarily male (literally), but to own and activate the gaze, given our language and the structure of the unconscious, is to be in the 'masculine' position" (1978, 30). Not only has Iris seen the flower as female genitalia, but she publicly proclaims both her spontaneous desire and simultaneous identification with it. The lesbian gaze combines the doubly transgressive pleasure of power with collaboration in one's own submissive objectification.

Lee, however, capitalizes on Iris's embarrassment to flirt with her. She describes O'Keeffe as "an old woman, who sits in the desert, wears black and paints bones." Iris exclaims, "An eccentric!" (*F*, 2) and adds the overt lesbian signal that what she likes about eccentricity is that it's not normal. Both women passionately praise O'Keeffe's original and female eye.

Iris admits that her travel is a quest for eccentricity—that is, a quest for peripheral vision (the view of the cultural outsider, the lesbian). Intuitively Iris knows that in order to re-member her authentic abnormal/normal self she must search for eccentricity. Marilyn Frye defines a lesbian as one who

> is disloyal to phallocratic reality. . . . The event of becoming a lesbian is a reorientation of attention in a kind of ontological conversion. It is characterized by a feeling of a world dissolving, and by a feeling of disengagement and re-engagement of one's power as a perceiver. (1983, 172)

Although Iris does not name her quest lesbian, she is seeking the unnamed unknown reality out of the frame of phallocentrism.

Iris describes her past before she began the quest for what might be called lesbian mysticism as rather flat: "Before I left, my eye could only see things as ordinary. I'd walk down the street—shops, faces, ordinary. I'd get out of bed, wash, brush my teeth, put on clothes and feel ordinary" (*F*, 3). Iris's discovery of O'Keeffe through Lee and Lee through O'Keeffe leads her on her eccentric spin. After telling Lee that O'Keeffe's paintings leave her breathless, she admits that she paints a little but never shows her paintings to anyone because she paints her dreams: "my own world, very female" (*F*, 8).

A climax of spontaneous lesbian recognition, Iris and Lee reel off a hilarious litany of Lesbian heroes noted for theatrical eccentricity (*F*, 18):

Iris. Have you read "Portrait of a Marriage"?
Lee. Vita Sackville West and Violet Keppel. Yes, fascinating. (*Pause*) And Vita and Virginia.
Iris. Yes, fascinating. (*Pause*) Have you read "Amazon of Letters"?
Lee. Natalie Barney. She delivered herself in a box of lilies.
Iris. That was Natalie and Renée.
Lee. And Natalie and Romaine.
Iris. And Natalie and Lilliane.

Lee. And Natalie and the Duchess.

Iris. And Natalie and the thirty-six other women.

Lee. And Radcliffe and Una.

Iris. And Collette and Missy.

Lee. And Djuna—

Iris. Barnes and Dolly—

Lee. Wilde.

Iris. And of course, Gertrude and Alice.

Lee. Of course.

Iris. And what about Carson McCullers and Annemarie.

Lee. And Kate and Sita.

Iris. And the ladies in that Welsh valley.

Lee. Llongollen?

Iris. Yes.

Lee. And what about H.D. and Bryher.

Iris. And what about me?

Lee. Yes.

Antiphonally boasting their mutual knowledge of lesbian history plays out an orgasmic verbal ritual that leaves them happily exhausted but deflated.

Lee notes Iris's lesbian "uniform": sneakers and sweatshirt. Iris protests that her clothes are practical and her identity. She refuses to acknowledge that they identify her as a lesbian. Ironically it is Iris who is appalled when Lee casually reveals that she had an affair with a woman just before leaving Australia. Is Iris jealous of a woman from Lee's past or shocked with the sudden revelation that her relationship with Iris is not her first lesbian experience? Iris focuses her outrage on the fact that Lee was impressed with a woman in a dinner suit, "a transvestite." In her quest for eccentricity, Iris is obsessed with authenticity. That Lee should have been "bowled over by a transvestite reading poetry" (*F,* 21) bothers Iris because she judges the woman inauthentic. Lee argues that the theatrical butch costuming gives the woman freedom to express her identity and to be romantic:

> She and her friends used to go to the first night of the opera in cloaks, tails, top hat, and cane. . . . Can't you see, the clothes were part of the charade she and her friends built around themselves? (*F,* 22)

When Iris returns to Australia the first time, Lee immerses herself in lesbian literature, reading her way through a whole women's bookshop. While the analytical Lee is spending their separation researching lesbian culture, Iris is drifting in search of the self spinning elusively on the edge of her vision. She withdraws from Lee as she has from Penny twice before. At first she accuses Lee of role-playing: "passive and active, you do everything for me, you look after me" (*F*, 39). However, Iris, in a frenzy of packing to return to Australia the first time, casts Lee in the role of care-taking wife or mother to gather up her mislaid sandshoes, books, passport (*F*, 30–31).

Iris also admits a typical lesbian dilemma: "I'm frightened of relationship. I let people so far and then retreat. I've learnt to be protective in trying to be strong" (*F*, 39). To proclaim lesbian identity often takes such strength that the tough cocoon surrounding the "out" lesbian makes her ironically so inaccessible to the approaches of love that she finds genuine intimacy terrifying. As an eccentric visionary, Iris chooses to be isolated. Having found her authentic lesbian identity mirrored in the intensely female art of O'Keeffe, Iris might be free to embrace the mirror that a loving relationship with another woman offers. Such embrace embodies a healthy narcissism and auto-eroticism capable of freeing her from the stunted sexual repression that Luce Irigaray describes (1985, 63).

Although it is the framework of Lee's memory that records and narrates the growth and transformation of Iris, Lee also learns that she grows through her losses. The loss of her illusions about male protection and control has enabled her to find her authentic independence. Her final word on stripping away the patriarchal crust quotes Stein on deserts, architecture, and religion: "Deserts can have looking, of course, but not seeing or painting" (*F*, 44). The play ends (as it begins) with Lee heaving herself Steinishly into action (departure for Australia) for which she takes full responsibility. Like the modern paintings, to which she has referred in one of her Stein impersonations, Lee is moving at last out of her frame. No longer will she be passive as a desert. She will assume the power of the one who looks and creates.

Blind Salome (*B*) dramatizes the complexity of relationships among four strong-willed characters, each on an individual quest of self-discovery. Bernice Wyham, an educated Australian in her late thirties, is confronting a personal crisis at a psychic and intellectual crossroads in her life. Her marriage to a slightly younger and dependent husband, Phillip, seems to have slumped both of them into such boredom that their relationship with each other is less significant than their separate searches for inner awareness. In fact, both Bernice and Phillip seek personal liberation through relationships with other traveling companions.

Bernice admits that she invited her older sister, Della, to join the party

Lenore Milner as Lee and Janet Andrewartha as Iris in the original
production of Sandra Shotlander's *Framework,* Melbourne,
Australia, 1983. (Photo by Pat Mitchell.)

as companion for Christopher Thornton, a psychiatrist in his sixties and devoted disciple of Della's late husband Zouche. As Chris explains to Bernice, Zouche (Zeus?) was more than a mentor: "He was like a father to me. . . . We were all brides of Zouche. It wouldn't have been easy being his wife" (B, 7). Not only does Chris have no desire to pursue Zouche's widow, but Della herself develops an intense aversion to Chris and an attachment to Phillip. Meanwhile Chris pursues Bernice, who prefers solitude to companionship with any of them. In addition to the four Australians, an almost silent character, whom the others call the Pale English Girl, appears intermittently, writes letters to Chris, but hardly interacts, except in a symbolic fashion, with the others.

As in *Framework,* art and history mirror the living characters, superimposing the past on the present. Chris contemplates what he calls "the Assisi problem" while examining Giotto's frescoes depicting dramatic moments in the lives of St. Francis and St. Clare. Scenes of dialogue are often introduced or interspersed with a brief *mise en scène,* which symbolically portrays the obsession or anxiety of one or several characters, most significantly at the beginning of the two acts.

For example, the play opens with a dramatization of the Giotto painting depicting St. Francis in the process of cutting off St. Clare's hair as preparation for receiving her vows, while a choir chants the *Magnificat* three times. As the scene fades, Chris himself is burning the long hair of St. Clare with his cigarette lighter. Enjoying this shamanistic moment of triumph, Chris announces, "I've created a relic full of ashes" (B, 1). On the contrary, he has reduced a relic to ashes. Later in conversation with Bernice it is clear that he identifies himself with Francis and Bernice with Clare. He tells her that he can see her wearing Franciscan brown. Although Chris readily psychoanalyzes the dreams and responses of the others in clinical terms, he fails to recognize the transparent wish-fulfillment evident in his own game of playing the lives of the saints. Cutting Clare/Bernice's hair as he accepts her submission gives Chris sexual and spiritual power over Bernice. Although Chris desires such power, he cannot ask for it directly until frustration finally prompts him to plead his suit without the symbolic trappings.

Another *mise en scène* portrays Chris's negative fantasy of being the head of John the Baptist presented on a platter for Salome/Bernice's pleasure. In this fantasy Della carries the beheading sword on a platter for her sister, and Phillip acts as acolyte to the two women. If he had any personal insight, Chris would instantly recognize his paranoid delusion. Like Lee's memory devices and recordings in *Framework,* these symbolic moments function dramatically as visual snapshots, conveying both denotative and connotative meanings. Barthes notes in his explanation of the polarization of structural functions of the image: "on the one hand there is a sort of paradigmatic condensation at the level of connotators (that is, broadly speaking, of the symbols), which are strong signs, scattered, 'reified'; on the other a syntagmatic 'flow' at the level of denotation" (1977, 51). Chris imagines himself simultaneously elevated and destroyed by women.

In her foreword to *Blind Salome* Susan Hawthorne notes:

> Sandra was searching for a way to comment on Jungian theories of the unconscious, and in particular the part played by the anima (represented, according to Jung, in her own life by fellow analyst and lover, Toni Wolf). Jung claims that every person has an essence of the opposite sex within. . . . Sandra . . . suggests that men may be chasing a hidden, ungraspable entity in seeking solace in women and in the idea of the "anima," but women have no such desire to seek out their animus. (*B,* n.p.)

Chris, echoing Jung, tries to convince Phillip that his fascination with the English girl reveals his search for his *anima.* Chris chortles paternalistically, "Uncharted territory, mystery, women's jouissance. Have fantasies, do you? . . . Finding your female side—anima. Feeling a bit at sea there, aren't you? Should write it down in your journal" (*B,* 10). Jung sees a man's wife not only as his *anima,* but also as a bolster against his own weakness:

> The persona, the ideal picture of a man as he should be, is inwardly compensated by feminine weakness, and as the individual outwardly plays the strong man, so he becomes inwardly a woman, i.e., the anima, for it is the anima that reacts to the persona. But because the inner world is dark and invisible to the extroverted consciousness, and because a man is all the less capable of conceiving his weakness the more he is identified with the persona, the persona's counterpart, the anima, remains completely in the dark and is at once projected, so that our hero comes under the heel of his wife's slipper. If this results in a considerable increase in her power, she will acquit herself none too well. She becomes inferior, thus providing her husband with the welcome proof that it is not he, the hero, who is inferior in private, but his wife. In return the wife can cherish the illusion, so attractive to many, that at least she has married a hero, unperturbed by her own uselessness. (1953, 193)

Chris has imbibed Jung's concept of the *anima* as the life blood of his own potency and feels himself persecuted by women who refuse to accept their role of reflecting his magnificence.

Luce Irigaray questions whether male psychoanalysts, such as Freud, who base their analysis of women's psychosis on the notion of "penis envy," simply cannot tolerate women not envying men what men perceive as the all-important physical representation of male power: "If women had desires other than 'penis-envy,' this would call into question the unity, the uniqueness, the simplicity of the mirror charged with sending man's image back to him" (1985, 51). Chris suffers from such panic, akin to a loss of male identity.

Initially Chris's likeliest female devotée is the English girl who addresses him as "Dear International Intellectual" because she found his name listed in a Cambridge Dictionary. She tells him that she is having difficulty coming to a consciousness of herself as a woman since all thought seems to be male-inscribed:

> I know we have gynaecology, but I notice that the diagrams in anatomy books are all the male figure. Men, it appears, have lungs, brains, stomachs, and hearts, while I am breasts, uterus, and ovaries. Is this lack of anatomy why men are said to be thinkers, activators, and rulers, while women are the breeders, feeders, and follow the leaders? (*B*, 16–17)

Chris smugly concurs that she is right in recognizing male superiority: Logos is male wisdom; Eros has been ascribed as female. Her role is to nurture men. The girl replies that she has been reading a call to women to arise like butterflies "to spin new myths of femaleness from the cocoon of the old husk of self. We should create ourselves" (*B*, 19). Chris responds with horror: "Those cries of liberation are nothing but the squawking of parrots, a defensive collective expression of women who are trying to be masculine" (*B*, 20). Chris's letters represent male anxiety in the face of women's potential liberation.

Just as Chris's journal serves as a mirror of his psyche, his Polaroid camera literally captures specular representation. He wields the camera like a weapon, ready to attack his off-guard companions with it. As they squirm watching the magic phantom sharpening into obscene exhibition of the hidden, evanescent representation of their psyches in the photograph, Chris gloats over his sadistic, predatory sexual conquest: "It's coming, it's coming, it's a beauty." When Chris leaves his Polaroid behind after his departure, his three disgruntled companions consider using it themselves for the remainder of their journey, but they choose simply to abandon the intrusive mechanical eye, which has captured them, not as they would like to perceive themselves, but as Chris prefers to "fix" them in his clinical judgment.

In a comparable moment of recognition in *Framework,* Lee asks Iris, "If we were in a painting right now and people had come to look at us, what would they see?" (*F,* 26). "Women waiting for absent men," replies Iris. In fact, the scene dramatizes the moment of most intense and blissful intimacy between the two women, when Iris gives Lee the purplish-black doona cover, wraps herself in it as the delicate center of the O'Keeffe painting, and cuddles Lee into the center of the doona with her. In both plays the women acknowledge how women have been misperceived.

While Chris is pursuing Bernice unsuccessfully, Della and Phillip carry on with apparent adulterous abandon. Both Della and Phillip are obsessively trailing the English girl, whom Chris has diagnosed as anorexic. At the end of the first act, Della and Phillip drive off for a picnic in the country on the way to search out and buy an art object Phillip has been seeking. They spend the night away from the pensione and return with what sounds like a slightly concocted story about hitting a pig on the road.

Intellectualizing the tense situation, Chris proclaims the mythological significance of sacred pigs:

> Oh, yes, sacred animal in some parts, to do with fertility and profane laughter. Gravid sows buried in pits to Demeter. . . . A whole herd of pigs fell into the chasm when Hades carried Persephone down to hell. . . . There was a pig Goddess gave birth to belly laughter, Baubo I think she was called, yes, Baubo, lifted her skirts to lift Demeter's spirits after the loss of Persephone. (*B,* 32)

According to Barbara G. Walker, the boar sacrifice associated with later celebration of the Eleusinian Mysteries was an early attempt to reassign creative power to males. The custom of driving pigs into pits in the rites of Demeter presupposed their sacred powers of regeneration (1983, 112–13). Chris further blurts out: "In myth it wasn't unusual for gods to rape goddesses, and then to marry them" (*B,* 32). Chris's ridiculous pedantry reconfirms his arrogance. His commentary also suggests that the sexual maneuvers among all the characters have ancient mythic meaning. Bernice and Della are entering a psychic rebirth akin to the Eleusinian rites.

What might seem a betrayal of sisterly loyalty draws Della and Bernice into a tighter bond. Bernice tells Della, "I've never felt it so necessary to take action and yet I'm paralysed. I can't ask either of you what happened that

night" (*B,* 37). Just as Lee and Iris in *Framework* travel away from Australia
in search of an elusive inner identity to be found in returning there either
geographically or in memory, so Bernice and Della must travel a long distance
from Australia and act out estranging flirtations with each other's men in order to recognize the primacy of the sister-bond. Not until Della and Phillip
have been flagrant in spending the night away together is Bernice forced to
confront her sister. However, before Bernice can communicate directly with
Della, she must finally banish Chris, who diminishes into a pest rather than
an opponent by the end of the play.

Throughout *Blind Salome* Sandra Shotlander plays with the first line of
The Magnificat prayer: "*Magnificat anima mea dominum.*" At the outset the line
accurately represents Chris's notion of what women are good for: to reflect
and magnify the lord, the male. According to Jung, every man defines himself
in relation to, as reflected by, in opposition to, and in triumph over his *anima.*
For Chris this symbolic concept justifies the capture of a real woman by every
man. Perceiving Bernice as his *anima,* Chris tries to get her to accept her role
as his reflector. For Chris women are mirrors for men, nurturers of the male
ego. Jeffner Allen's forced impregnation with the god-like male Logos, here
suggested, also implies the Lacanian "Name-of-the-Father" male ownership
of women's *jouissance.* Bernice exhibits what Jane Gallop refers to as "the feminist practice of unauthorization" (1982, 47). Bernice unwittingly parodies the
Latin in the opening scene by saying, "It's a magnificent day, soul stirring"
(*B,* 1). Far from being a reflector of male grandeur, Bernice identifies herself
with nature. Her soul reflects itself and magnifies nothing more than the
beauty of the day. She refuses to be a mirror for men.

Chris first attempts to seduce Bernice by comparing her to Bernini's
statue of St. Teresa in ecstasy. Coincidentally Jane Gallop notes that Stephen
Heath finds " . . . beneath Lacan's fancy talk of signifiers lurks a sexist prejudice tied to an ideology of representation" (1982, 50). She refers to Lacan's
statement: ". . . just as with Saint Teresa—you only have to go and look at
the Bernini statue in Rome to understand immediately that she's coming, no
doubt about it" (1982, 50). Similarly, Chris's comparison projects his own
desire on to Bernice. In comparing Bernice to Giotto's St. Clare, Chris is specifically asking her to be his reflector, perhaps Jung's "blind Salome" devoid
of understanding. Bernice responds in the name and voice of all the silenced
female saints:

> And what if, in the silence one day, she got up and sounds issued from
> her lips, halting at first and then getting louder, words coming from her

lips, mounting in the throat, a voice, shouting, shrill, the shriek of a nag across the centuries. Now you listen to me. I'm fed up, I'm fed up with this cloister. I don't want to be a virgin abbess, anymore. I don't want to hang around here, listening to people like you. I don't want you to go away feeling loved. You can go and lie down on a bed of twigs for a while. I'm going in search of my own holy grail, and it will be shined so well with "Brasso" by the kitchen maid who cherishes it, it will shine with an awful clarity, a clear shining light of the She-Who-Shines-For All. I'm going to clarify things a bit, a resurrection of the great mother for a start, the "Magna Mater" in her full glory, primitive and passionate. I'm fed up with your one and only God my soul must magnify. I'm going to reverberate in this silence. I'm going to perform a few unbridled movements. You and your tight controlled focus. I don't want your marble ecstasy. I'm about to leap waterfalls and straddle chasms. I'm going to dance, remove all the veils. I'm going to spread my thighs mountainous and sit on you. (*B,* 42)

Bernice then jumps on the astonished Chris, who cries out in terror for help, claiming that she has gone completely mad. At this moment Phillip walks in. Despite his intimacy with Della, Phillip is horrified to see his wife astride the wriggling Chris. She assures him, "This has nothing to do with sex, well gender, yes, sex no" (*B,* 43). In this moment of assertiveness, Bernice can finally ask Della and Phillip what happened. When they say that nothing happened (no sexual activity?), she can blast them with her new consciousness:

What do you mean, nothing happened? Why didn't you fall blindly in love, why didn't you fall so blindly in love that you could feel. Then we could struggle with this reality instead of eternal visions. (*B,* 43)

Bernice reviles the male visions that have imprisoned women too long. Like the characters in *Framework,* she discovers her center in a moment of eccentricity.

The image of women coming to consciousness, which the English girl mentions in her letter to Chris, is the butterfly coming out of the chrysalis. The *mise en scène,* which she performs as the prelude to the second act, is the gradual unfolding of herself from her shawl—opening and closing it, feeling her arms, hair, and body as if they were new discoveries.

As prologue to the last scene of the play, the English girl opens a bag containing makeup and slowly and deliberately in ritual fashion puts it on as a mask. During the ritual Bernice enters and sits opposite the girl and serves as her mirror. At one point Bernice reaches across the table and smooths the red paint around the girl's mouth. During a blackout following Bernice's outburst and assertion, the girl speaks:

> In the morning we put on the masks, draw on the skin of Woman. "But this is a mask, this isn't us," we say. At night when we lie down, tear and wrench as we might, it won't come off. We think it is ingrained, but after all it's only artifice—gunk! (*B*, 46)

Ironically the girl has seemed so pale and wraithlike to Phillip while he is pursuing her as his *anima* that she has faded in and out of visibility for him. With makeup, however, she becomes completely visible to him. The conventional mask that women wear to lure men reassures him. Whereas Phillip, like most men, is conditioned to see women masquerading conventional sexual lures as *anima*/mirror, the girl is only trying on the mask, not imprisoning herself in it.

After Chris's departure, Phillip's potency (his attractiveness to Della) diminishes. The ambivalence and struggle gripping the women earlier in the play also eases. No longer defined and confined by the male gaze, the women can determine their own fate by pulling the past into the present. Bernice relinquishes her roles as St. Clare in submission and St. Teresa in ecstasy, the female mystic spiritually pregnant with the Word of the male god.

The women have found the truth they sought through travel, through art, through history, at the newly liberated core of self. In order to reach that center each has had to perform some eccentricity, some act of disloyalty to patriarchal tradition and civilization. The English girl rejects the symbolic gender roles: male Logos and female Eros. Della chooses to support and bond with her sister in preference to her lover (in whatever sense). Bernice, the central quester, simply chooses self above all as her highest good. In small ways all three women emerge somewhat from the confining chrysalis of patriarchy.

In both *Framework* and *Blind Salome* Sandra Shotlander's female characters seek to shed the confining and blinding veils created by the male gaze that brands woman as "Other." Lee and Iris laugh at being perceived as "women waiting for absent men" (*F*, 26). If Della and Bernice are waiting in early scenes of *Blind Salome*, they have broken their bonds and flown on ahead by the end. Even the English girl is moving beyond a silent and passive receptivity to male authority. The newly conscious female visionary perceives herself as both seer and seen. But can she simultaneously be the subject and object of her own discourse? She must break through the male-defined mirror.

She cannot simply reverse the polarities, since the terms of the duality, male and female, are far from culturally and politically equal. Even the linguistic signs in English (female/male, woman/man) indicate her subordination. Julia Kristeva's analysis of the lonely gaping female mouth in Samuel Beckett's *Not I* (1980, 148–58) suggests absence of female intelligence reflecting itself.

Can the silenced Delphic oracle re-member her originary voice and vision? The lesbian artist, mystic, visionary activist awakens like the slumbering dragon to re-member herself. She refuses to reproduce the male Logos, refuses to be fragmented or minimized into a reflector/magnifier of male primacy. The Delphic dragon flashes forth transmitting signals in a new language. Shotlander's plays re-member the originary dragon.

NOTE
I appreciate the careful reading and suggestions from my writing support group at Rollins College under the direction of Twila Papay, Richard Scharine, and especially Sandra Shotlander herself.

REFERENCES
Allen, Jeffner. 1986. *Lesbian Philosophy: Explorations.* Palo Alto: Institute of Lesbian Studies.

Barthes, Roland. 1977. *Image-Music-Text,* trans. Stephen Heath. New York: Hill and Wang.

Belenky, Mary Field; Clinchy, Blythe McVicker; Goldberger, Nancy Rule; and Tarule, Jill Mattuck. 1986. *Women's Ways of Knowing: The Development of Self, Voice, and Mind.* New York: Basic Books.

Daly, Mary. 1978. *Gyn/Ecology: The Metaethics of Radical Feminism.* Boston: Beacon Press.

Frye, Marilyn. 1983. *The Politics of Reality: Essays in Feminist Theory.* Trumansburg, N.Y.: Crossing Press.

Gallop, Jane. 1982. *The Daughter's Seduction: Feminism and Psychoanalysis.* Ithaca: Cornell University Press.

Irigaray, Luce. 1985. *Speculum of the Other Woman,* trans. Gillian C. Gill. Ithaca: Cornell University Press.

Jung, Carl G. 1953. *Two Essays on Analytical Psychology.* New York: Pantheon.

Kaplan, E. Ann. 1983. *Women and Film: Both Sides of the Camera.* New York: Methuen.

Kristeva, Julia. 1980. *Desire in Language: A Semiotic Approach to Literature and Art.* New York: Columbia University Press.

Shotlander, Sandra. 1985. *Blind Salome.* Montmorency, Australia: Yackandandah Playscripts.

———. 1984. *Framework.* Montmorency, Australia: Yackandandah Playscripts.

Walker, Barbara G. 1983. *The Woman's Encyclopedia of Myths and Secrets.* New York: Harper and Row.

JILL DOLAN

Bending Gender to Fit the Canon: The Politics of Production

The insistent work of liberal feminists to make visible the once-hidden talent of women in theatre has been primarily responsible for the growing number of women playwrights working in the professional arena. But the mainstream critical response to plays written by women continues to reveal deepseated gender biases. By creating a different "horizon of expectations,"[1] these biases inform how male critics writing for influential daily newspapers or monthly magazines receive a play written by a woman, especially one that dramatizes concerns traditionally associated with women. Most mainstream critics are powerful enough to influence a production's success or failure in a given venue, and their response molds and to a certain extent predetermines the response of potential spectators for the play reviewed. Because it is such an important factor in the collective audience's interpretation of a play's meaning, mainstream criticism both shapes and reflects the ideological workings of the dominant culture whose concerns it represents.

The production history of Marsha Norman's 'night, Mother is an excellent case study of the gender-biased politics of reception, since it is one of the first plays written by a woman and addressing women's concerns to gain widespread attention, critical acclaim, and economic success. When 'night, Mother opened on Broadway in 1983, it provoked a media response polarized around gender differences.

On one hand, powerful male New York critics such as Frank Rich and Mel Gussow, writing for the New York Times, struggled to reconcile Norman's gender—and her female characters—with their desire to inscribe the play into the predominantly male canon of good American drama. On the other hand, the feminist press was split between claiming—or disclaiming—Norman as the vanguard of their own separate canon, or applauding her elevation into the dominant male realm.

Canon-formation and deconstruction is an issue currently debated in literary criticism as a result of the wider consideration of marginalized texts prompted by women's and black studies. The terms of the debate are governed by traditional critics—who jealously guard the historical canon as a necessary standard with which to compare any succeeding drama or literature—and by revisionist critics, who see the traditional canon and the literary history it enshrines as a project of a class of privileged, powerful, mostly white male subjects whose ideology it represents.[2]

Some feminist critics suggest that the inclusion of women's writing in the traditional canon is problematical, since female systems of signification are unavailable to men, who cannot read their signs and therefore dismiss their meanings.[3] Sue-Ellen Case takes a less biological than historical approach to the problem of women's place in the dramatic canon, using the example of Hrotsvit von Gandersheim. Case argues that the patriarchal biases of the cultural authorities caused them to deny a place in the canon for Hrotsvit as the first female playwright. By failing to allow her to set the precedent that canons intrinsically deem necessary, these cultural authorities left no standard of comparison within the canon for future women playwrights.

"The seemingly dramatic standards which select the playwrights in the canon are actually the same patriarchal biases which organize the economy and social organization of the culture at large," Case writes.[4] She adds that "exclusion from the canon of the greats suggests a failure on the part of the playwright to produce a dramatic experience which has important historical resonances."[5] The history of cultural authority and its charter to set transcendent literary and dramatic standards remains unimpugned by Hrotsvit's absence from the canon. Instead, the individual playwright is blamed for her inability to meet its criteria.

As the following analysis suggests, Marsha Norman took great pains to avoid Hrotsvit's alleged mistakes. Two questions are included within the parameters of my debate: If Marsha Norman's play is allowed into the traditional canon, will it establish a precedent for women playwrights to follow? Or, is *'night, Mother* read as a contender for membership in the canon because it so closely follows the male precedent the canon has already set?

The traditional dramatic canon that *'night, Mother* was measured against has certain explicit rules. First, a play must conform to the rule of universality by transcending the historical moment and speaking to a generic spectator. Also, as Janet Staiger, writing about canon-formation in cinema studies, points out, canons are formed to reinforce and reproduce "a hegemonic culture and economic structure."[6] For *'night, Mother* to be inserted into the canon, it should not substantially threaten its dramatic or ideological values. And, to support the canon's economic imperatives in the context of late capitalism and twentieth-century Broadway play production, it also had to generate institutional recognition that would make it viable as a profitmaking product.

After *'night, Mother* received the 1983 Pulitzer Prize for drama, it became a profitable success on Broadway, meeting the canon's requirements for institutional and economic recognition. But some New York critics, such as Howard Kissel at *Women's Wear Daily*, remained ambivalent about Norman and the canonization of her play. Their hesitations turned on the issue of universality. Since women's concerns are not seen as generic to theatre, in which the active dramatic agents and the spectators to whom they play have historically been men, some critics doubted that the play qualified for the canon. Others insisted that its strict adherence to Aristotelian principles made it imminently eligible.

In feminist circles, *'night, Mother*'s canonization as prototypical good American drama or as the vanguard of the new feminist drama was seriously debated. Since one of the aims of feminist literary and dramatic criticism is to deconstruct the male canon and its underlying ideology, including a woman's text in the dominant canon is a complicated gesture. A popular alternative for some feminists is to construct a counter-canon with feminist criteria for inclusion. The female version of the canon often rescues obscured women from literary or theatrical history, and replaces the generic male reader/spectator with a generic female. The universal qualities sought are those that might explain or describe what are considered prototypical female experiences.

But the female canon has its own ideological, critical, and aesthetic standards, however "playfully pluralistic."[7] While liberal feminists celebrated Norman's success in the dominant culture, and some cultural feminists wanted to canonize *'night, Mother* in a new, feminist "best of" list, many materialist feminists argued that any canon is by definition exclusionary, since it perpetuates only a particular ideological view. A materialist feminist perspective points out that both the dominant cultural and feminist dramatic canons tend to universalize and idealize subject positions.

The question to pose with regard to *'night, Mother*'s placement in any canon is how Norman's gender switch away from the theatre's usual male axis of categorization informed mainstream and feminist critical response. The canon-formation issue is crucial to this investigation because Norman's play was not presented as "women's theatre" in a 100-seat house in the West Village. The play moved through the prescribed hierarchy of regional theatre readings, workshops, and productions that culminate with a Broadway production. Broadway is the context from which plays become literature to canonize. The radical element of Norman's play was not that it was written by a woman about a mother/daughter relationship, but that it was performed in a space historically reserved for male playwrights to address father/son relationships.

A chronology of events in the play's production history will prove helpful to contextualize the assessment that will follow. *'night, Mother* was first produced at the American Repertory Theatre (ART) in Cambridge, Massachusetts, in December 1982. Robert Brustein, artistic director of ART and generally considered the "dean" of American theatre critics, was enthusiastic about the script and agreed to produce the play. After a successful and critically acclaimed run in Cambridge, the Broadway production opened March 31, 1983, to widely favorable reviews. Norman won the 1983 Pulitzer Prize for drama for *'night, Mother* on April 19, 1983. After 388 performances on Broadway (over a year's run), *'night, Mother* opened at the Cheryl Crawford Theatre of the Westside Arts Center, also in New York City, where it closed after 54 performances.

Certain features of this chronology are significant to the play's reception. Brustein's favorable disposition to Norman's work ensured its production at ART, where it was promoted as "an authentically American play but with the stark inevitability of Greek tragedy."[8] Even prior to its Broadway run, Brustein began *'night, Mother*'s comparison to the canon's Aristotelian criteria by emphasizing its adherence to the unities of time, space, and action. Under Brustein's leadership, the ART has become one of the most respected regional theatres in the country. The current trend in American theatre is to fill Broadway houses with productions that transfer from regional repertories. *'night, Mother*'s success in Cambridge, with Brustein's blessing, brought the play to Broadway advertised primarily on the strength of good reviews from the ART production.[9]

After Norman won the Pulitzer Prize, the press documents the effect of the national attention the honor conferred.[10] *Variety* exclaimed, "What a difference a Pulitzer makes."[11] The reporter noted that *'night, Mother* had doubled its $5,000 per day box office income and that advance sales were starting to build. The Pulitzer award had a favorable impact on the public's perception of the play and influenced spectators' expectations by validating and legitimizing the production.

Author's Intent

The unusual institutional approbation awarded Norman's play, in light of the historical lack of notice for women playwrights, makes it interesting to investigate from a feminist point of view the meanings Norman intended her work to communicate to spectators. While author's intent is a somewhat taboo factor in reception theory, which emphasizes the individualized exchange between culturally constituted readers and shifting texts, Norman's intentions with *'night, Mother* are somewhat illuminating. Norman did have a specific plan for the reception of her play. But her collaborators, in the process of reading and reconstructing her text as their production, imposed their own meanings. They created a performance text that diverged from the written text, and these new meanings ultimately influenced critics' and spectators' responses.

The dramaturgical process currently at work in American theatre impinges *a priori* on the issue of authorship. Since theatre is a collaborative art, the playwright's text is a schematic outline for other production elements. Often, the original script is cut, characters are changed or deleted, and dialogue is rewritten based on what the cast and director find will or will not "play." As Elizabeth Wray writes in *Performing Arts Journal,* the playwright is

> assigned a front row seat for watching layers of aesthetic preconceptions applied to her play by her director, designers, and producer. All too often, the finished product has little to do with her initial vision. She discovers too late that she has compromised her play away.[12]

The performance text presented each evening is an amalgamation of the director's, actors', and designers' interpretations of the playwright's text.

Play publishing houses usually option scripts after their initial productions have received enough attention to be appealing to regional or community theatre groups. The acting script published and sold to other producing organizations when they request rights to the play solidifies performance decisions incorporated up to the Broadway production. Indicated stage directions range from movements ("*Stands up, moves toward the phone*") to qualities of vocal delivery ("*Almost a whisper*") that are a faithful record of the Broadway presentation, which as a result becomes the standard by which all subsequent productions of the play will be modeled after, deviate from, or compared to.

In addition to the expectations generated by critical response to previous productions, the spectator's reading of the performance text has been influenced before she or he arrives at the theatre by the producers' marketing and advertising strategies, by published reviews, and by her or his own ideological perceptions and cultural heritage. These combined expectations and spectators' subsequent individualized readings of the play can work to obscure the playwright's original intent.

Yet as the hoary question of authorship resurfaces, Marsha Norman is considered responsible for the entire presentation of the play *'night, Mother.*

She, not director Tom Moore, receives the Pulitzer Prize and the press coverage. As Norman says wryly,

> Most [critics] can't tell the difference between the play and the production. They don't understand that the director is the author of the production. It is a myth that playwrights have total control. . . . Of course, ultimately you end up taking *full* responsibility for the production.[13]

This process of altering an author's text through a collaborative process, then attributing the final product to the playwright as "her" text becomes significant to the play's reception.

Although Hill and Wang published an edition of the play, the acting version distributed by Dramatists Play Service, Inc., is more important to consult for guidelines to how the play is to be presented and received. The text sold for production includes a property plot and list, a costume plot, and a scene design rendering that are not included in Hill and Wang's version. The detail of these lists is intended to carefully control the play's presentation and thereby affect its reception.

'night, Mother is a one-act, two-character play. Jessie Cates, a woman in her late thirties or early forties, tells her mother, Thelma, that she intends to commit suicide and proceeds to carry out her promise. Jessie insists she is telling Thelma in advance simply so the older woman will be prepared when it happens. Although Jessie wants her last evening with her mother to be calm and uneventful, a mirror-image of all their evenings together, the night becomes a probing exploration into the reasons for Jessie's choice.

Jessie has been caring for Thelma and intends to relinquish her household duties in proper form. As Jessie delivers her instructions, it becomes clear that her life with her mother is routine and mundane, and probably will not change significantly until they die. Their conversation also reveals that under the domestic veneer lies a "problem" of the sort that propels many American family dramas. In Norman's published text, epilepsy is blamed as the prime motivating factor for Jessie's ruined life—her failed marriage, her delinquent son, her inability to hold a job, and ultimately, her decision to commit suicide.

This is a simple outline of Norman's plot devices, onto which she layers carefully constructed character portraits. Norman's notes on the characters are significant in light of critics' response to *'night, Mother.* Jessie is:

> pale and vaguely unsteady, physically. It is only in the last year that Jessie has gained control of her mind and body, and tonight, she is determined to hold onto that control.[14]

Norman goes on to describe aspects of Jessie's personality, but gives no further information about Jessie's appearance. Norman continues:

> Thelma is Jessie's mother, in her late fifties or early sixties. She has begun to feel her age, and so takes it easy when she can . . . she speaks quickly and enjoys talking. . . . Her sturdiness is more a mental quality than a physical one, finally. She is chatty and nosy and this is *her* house. (P. 5, emphasis in original)

Throughout the text, Norman assigns wry observations to Thelma. Her perspective is characteristically one of resignation, but she sees her condition as universally human, rather than personal. "Things happen," Thelma says. "You do what you can about them and you see what happens next" (p. 39). Jessie, on the other hand, is unremittingly personal. Her justification for suicide is "I'm just not having a very good time and I don't have any reason to think it'll get anything but worse" (p. 7).

At the Actors Theatre of Louisville, Norman had worked previously with both Anne Pitoniak, who would play Thelma, and Kathy Bates, who would play Jessie. In fact, while she was writing the play, Norman invited Pitoniak and Bates to her Manhattan apartment to read an unfinished version. In some sense, the play's casting must have influenced even the initial construction of Norman's script.

Although the actresses expected to be replaced by well-known performers when the play moved from ART to Broadway, both were retained. According to media interviews, Norman exerted a great deal of effort to ensure that less well-known performers would play the roles, so that spectators would not be distracted from her play's meaning by their expectations and knowledge of more familiar performers.[15]

Once the play hit the regional theatre circuit, however, the policy of casting unknown performers was for the most part discarded. Thelma, as opposed to Jessie, is generally cast with a star performer. For instance, Mercedes McCambridge played the role at the Arkansas Rep, and Sylvia Sidney played it at the Pittsburgh Public Theatre. Star-casting, as Norman feared, could substantially alter the play's reception.

In the acting edition of *'night, Mother,* Norman sets out very particular instructions about the play's presentation in the author's note that precedes the script:

> The time is the present, with the action beginning about 8:15. Clocks onstage in the kitchen and on a table in the living room should run

throughout the performance and be visible to the audience. There will be no intermission. The play takes place in a relatively new house built way out on a country road . . . under no circumstances should the set and its dressing make a judgement about the intelligence or taste of Jessie and Thelma. It should simply indicate that they are very specific real people who happen to live in a particular part of the country. Heavy accents, which would further distance the audience from Jessie and Thelma are also wrong. (Pp. 6–7)

Norman wants to avoid provoking a condescending response to Jessie and Thelma, although her desire that the set not comment on the women's intelligence or taste seems to anticipate such a response. She is misguided in thinking that the set for her play—or its entire presentation—can be detached from ideological readings, but her aim was the kind of transcendent universality that would seem to obscure these readings. Norman intends to keep audience identification primary by deleting any sense of regionalism. A note at the end of the property plot in the acting edition corroborates her approach: "All food, cleaning supply, refrigerator, and candy props should be national brands which do not indicate any specific area in the country" (p. 62).

Norman was striving for a reception of her play that would validate its aim toward universal meanings and transcendence, and that would inch it toward acceptance into the male realm of historically lasting drama. The Pulitzer Prize was not enough to secure this fate for her play. Beth Henley, with whom Norman was linked for a time in popular press reviews, won the Pulitzer Prize in 1981 for her comedy *Crimes of the Heart*. Henley, at twenty-nine years of age, was the first woman to win the Pulitzer for drama in twenty-three years. The difference between *'night, Mother*'s reach for qualification as tragedy and *Crimes*'s categorization as comedy helps to explain why critics grappled with canonizing Norman's play, and not Henley's.

Crimes of the Heart was generally received as a regional play—it was flavored with Southern dialect, ambiance, and eccentricities, and was not reviewed as making a universal statement. *Crimes* was a comedy people could laugh at (i.e., distance themselves from). Comedy usually resolves its problems in a conventional manner such as the reinscription of its protagonists and antagonists in the culturally sanctioned order of society or family.

The comparison between the two plays is worth noting, however, because of the similar circumstances of their productions and the similarity of the themes they address, albeit in different styles. Suicide, for example, is a recurring theme in *Crimes of the Heart*. The MaGrath sisters' mother has killed herself, and when Babe feels desperate over her dilemma, she, too, attempts first to hang herself, then to gas herself in the family oven. But where Norman paints Jessie's suicide as an acceptable response to a pointless life, Henley gives her situations a comic turn that points out the absurdity of the whole enterprise. Mrs. MaGrath has hung not only herself, but the family cat as well; Babe can't find a rope strong enough to break her neck, and she bangs her head on an oven rack when she attempts to kill herself with gas. Meg MaGrath pulls Babe away from the oven and exclaims, "We've just got to learn how to get through these real bad days here. I mean, it's getting to be a thing in our family."[16]

Norman makes suicide a tragic act of heroism, but Henley discounts it as neither heroic nor an appropriate response to depression or anxiety. Norman's play presents the family as an inadequate life-supporting mechanism; Henley offers the reintegration of the MaGrath family as her play's happy ending. In both plays, the families are women-centered, yet for various reasons, one can argue whether or not either play is definitively feminist. Neither *'night, Mother* nor *Crimes of the Heart*, however, was meant to be received as a feminist alternative to mainstream drama.

Both *'night, Mother* and *Crimes of the Heart* were released as films in 1986. *'night, Mother* was promoted on the strength of the play's notices three years before, although Sissy Spacek as Jessie and Anne Bancroft as Thelma were featured prominently in the advertisements. *Crimes*'s advertisements ran a tag line that played up its absurdist comedy and featured a family-like portrait of the star performers Diane Keaton, Jessica Lange, and Sissy Spacek. No mention was made of its history as a play. *'night, Mother* failed at film box offices, while *Crimes* was very successful, gaining two Academy Award nominations.

Advertising good literature, it seems, does not necessarily guarantee economic success. Almost as Norman intended, her play and her film were contextualized as "art," and both had to struggle for the laurels that confer success within that realm. Although it dealt with similar issues, *Crimes of the Heart*, as a comedy, was always clear about its value as entertainment, and both the play and the film were highly successful in those terms.

Kitchen Drama versus Domestic Drama: The Mainstream Critical Response

Once *'night, Mother* was in production, press documentation makes it obvious that Norman's collaborators began to contradict her stated intent toward universal meanings, particularly with regard to the characters. For instance, despite Norman's insistence that the set not comment on the characters' intelligence or taste, designer Heidi Landesman had a very particular response to Thelma and Jessie, which she chose to reflect in her set for the Broadway production. Landesman explains how other theatre groups might design the play:

> The environment has to be unbelievably depressing, but in such a way that the audience sees it, but Thelma and Jessie don't. . . . Also, it should only become depressing over time to people watching it. . . . [Landesman tinted the set with] "yucko" colors with nothing bright to relieve the eye. . . . The other trick was to show how kitschy and bad their taste was, and how poor their cultural environment was, without making it comic. I used lots of trashy pieces, but all of them were very familiar, things you might find in Woolworth's. . . . And nothing popped out as being overwhelmingly hideous.[17]

Landesman's choices were clearly at odds with Norman's intent and would eventually affect the critical response to *'night, Mother.*

Although New York critics are notorious for overlooking design achievements, most of the reviewers at least mentioned Landesman's set, a production element that differed substantially from Norman's conception of the play. *Variety* said, "The lower-middle-class living room and kitchen are Polaroid accurate."[18] Norman's script never mentions the Cates's class status. If anything, given her aim at universality, Norman would probably prefer a general middle-class ambiance.

Howard Kissel, in *Women's Wear Daily,* came closest to characterizing Norman's intended nondescription by calling the set one of those "characterless boxes carved out by giant cookie cutters after WWII." John Beaufort, in the *Christian Science Monitor,* gave the set the "Good Housekeeping Seal of Approval," an implicitly condescending reference to what are traditionally considered women's values.[19]

Each of these publications, of course, is geared toward the interests and ideology of its particular constituency and, as a result, take somewhat different perspectives on the productions they review. *Variety* is the mouthpiece of the entertainment industry; *Women's Wear Daily* is centered in the garment industry; the *Christian Science Monitor's* ideology is explicitly clarified through its denominational affiliation. The *New York Times* remains the arbiter of sophisticated, cultured, monied tastes and values.

Frank Rich, in the *New York Times,* tried to place Norman in the context of American values that would stake a claim for the play's transcendent appeal. In an article about the visual arts' influence on set design, Rich noted the stylistic similarities to painter Edward Hopper in *'night, Mother*'s set design.[20] Landesman created a false proscenium arch with black borders that narrowed the stage opening and somewhat forced the spectator's perspective into the living room/kitchen set. Rich wrote that the set is "framed in black to give us Hopper's perspective of looking through a window at night."[21]

Rich also pointed out that both the publicity poster and the *Playbill* cover used for *'night, Mother*'s program quote Hopper's *Solitude*. The painting is of a long country road, drawn in perspective, with a solitary house among trees along its side. *'night, Mother*'s *Playbill* cover is a photograph shot from the same perspective as the painting: a country road surrounded by trees, which partially hide a bungalow-style house. The perspective's vanishing point sends the viewer's eye through the trees to a bright spot on the horizon where the sun, it appears, would be setting. The scene is domestic, but also lonely: The *Playbill* cover evokes a feeling of suburban isolation similar to Hopper's solitary, rural scene. This allusion to a key figure in American art helped Rich to contextualize *'night, Mother* as serious, transcendent drama.

Within this domestic scene, the male reviewers' responses to Jessie and Thelma are significant in relation to their ambivalence about the gender subtext and their comparison of the play to canonical standards. Thelma Cates is variously called the "fuddled mother," "scatterbrained but decent," "not too bright," a "fussy, silly woman with a frumpy wardrobe and an insatiable sweet tooth," and a "lonely flibbertigibbet of a vacant mother."[22] Robert Asahina, in the quarterly literary journal the *Hudson Review,* wrote sarcastically and condescendingly,

> Thelma is not so quietly deranged . . . prattling on inanely about hot chocolate, knitting, television and a host of lowbrow concerns with which Norman has burdened her in order to let the audience know that this is a drama about Real People.[23]

Robert Brustein, on the other hand, championing the play as an authentic American drama, calls Thelma "salty, shrewd, good natured" and sees her as an affirmative life force.[24] Brustein is alone among the male critics in this positive view of Thelma. Feminist writer Trudy Scott takes Brustein's view even farther by focusing her review on Thelma as the play's dramatic agent:

> Jessie dispassionately lists her reasons for not wanting to live, revealing herself as an emotionally dead character. Thus, the compelling and pro-

pelling viewpoint of the drama falls to Thelma. . . . the remainder of
'night, Mother charts the progress of Thelma's dilemma.[25]

Scott frames her discussion of the play within the mother/daughter conflict, and she privileges the mother's perspective:

> Norman's portrayal of a woman's capacity to give, to sustain, to fight
> for a child's life and, ultimately, to accept the voluntary withdrawal of
> that life is painful and precise. . . . Rarely do playwrights attempt serious explorations of the experiences of older women.[26]

Most critics tend to see Thelma's desperate attempts to keep her daughter alive
as "absurd suggestions,"[27] and place Jessie's choice at the center of the dramatic
action.

In a clear example of reception filtered through gender biases, the male
critics' responses to Jessie were based almost uniformly on her physical appearance onstage, which substantially altered their reception of the play. They
collapsed performer Kathy Bates's appearance into the character's and proceeded
to construct their own list of reasons for why Jessie decided to commit suicide. First among these, according to critics, is her weight. Although the fatal,
tragic flaw in Norman's text is epilepsy, the production's received flaw, which
provides the cause of Jessie's ultimate demise, is fat.

Typically, John Simon, in *New York* magazine, was most blatant in his
word choice. He called Jessie "fat, unattractive, and epileptic." Other reviewers
followed in kind, describing Jessie—although they were responding to Bates's
performance and her body—as an "overweight young woman with sallow skin,"
"a good looking, though overweight woman, sloppily dressed," "pudgy and
plain," "heavy set, slow moving and morose," and "overweight and homely."[28]
The male critics unanimously saw Jessie as a loser. She has lost her husband;
her son is a juvenile delinquent; she is epileptic, and groggy with self-hatred.
Her salient characteristic in performance, however, is not her personal history,
but her weight. Even a woman writing in *Ms.* magazine condemned Jessie
as "dumpy from over-eating."[29] These critics correlated what they saw onstage
to the play's motivating action so emphatically that Jessie's appearance became
more significant than Norman's actual dramatic device.

Jessie's appearance is never mentioned in Norman's script. In fact, the dialogue seems to indicate that if anything, Jessie is thin. Thelma tells her daughter, "You never liked eating at all, did you? Any of it. What have you been living on all these years, toothpaste?" (p. 36). Norman had Kathy Bates in mind for the role of Jessie while she was writing, but there is no evidence that weight was a factor when Norman constructed the character nor that she wanted to cast Bates because of her body size. If she had been thinking in terms of Bates's weight, Norman probably would have deleted Thelma's reference to Jessie's ability to live on toothpaste.

Jessie's weight is not an issue in Norman's play as written, but eating as a ritual exchange in the shared history between mother and daughter is prevalent in the script. As Lynda Hart has pointed out, Jessie's desire for nourishment is now spent. She can no longer find the right food; even the elaborate preparation of hot chocolate in *'night, Mother* is useless, since Jessie has lost her taste for the treat. Hart says that "Jessie's lack of appetite denies the whole mother/daughter history" of love as nurturance.[30] Based on this feminist textual analysis of Norman's script, it is even more ironic that Jessie is condemned in performance for gluttony.

A character's appearance is used frequently in dramatic literature as a psychological barometer. Richard III's evil, for instance, is presented in direct relation to his misshapen appearance and, of course, Cyrano's nose is a prime example of appearance molding character. But these physical qualities are intrinsic to the dramatic text, a predetermined element in the play's reception. My point here is to indicate that spectators' expectations of a character's appearance must correlate with the performer's appearance, or other inferences are drawn based on culturally dictated readings of the body they see in space.[31]

This gender bias in relation to character and performers' appearance has a direct bearing on a play's categorization as tragedy or melodrama.[32] Writing on the dominant press reception to Norman's play, dramaturg Collette Brooks noticed that critics frequently compared *'night, Mother* to plays prototypical of American tragedy, such as *Death of a Salesman*. Brooks agreed that "For all intents and purposes, *'night, Mother* was written in 1949 by Arthur Miller,"[33] and dismissed Norman's play from a feminist perspective because of its similarity to the male standard. Other critics felt compelled to grapple with the play's difference from the canon.

As critics hold marginalized texts like *'night, Mother* beside canonized texts like *Death of a Salesman,* the history of literary selection is thrown into relief against an ideological background of cultural power. Discussing recent feminist critiques of literary canon-formation, Christine Froula observes, "The critique of patriarchal/canonical authority assumes that literary authority is a mode of social authority and that literary value is inseparable from ideology."[34] From a revisionist perspective, cultural authorities have determined the canon's selection and then mystified its terms, so that this reified body of work seems to have always been in place. The invisibility of both its constructors and the origins of its construction render the canon peculiarly (but purposefully) remote from question or attack.

Barbara Herrnstein Smith emphasizes that the canon was originally formed according to standards of value and evaluation that have since been mystified and obscured, leaving their by-product—the traditional canon—as an apparently empirical measurement against which all ensuing literary work is compared. But, as Smith points out, "All value is radically contingent, being neither an inherent property of objects nor an arbitrary projection of subjects, but, rather, the product of the dynamics of an economic system."[35] The mystification of the literary economic (or cultural) system in which canon-formation works obscures what Smith calls the "personal economy"—a subject's needs, interests, and resources—on which the larger system is based. Cultural authority and power constructs the ideal reader and critic from a group of similar subjects, for whom the canon meets its personal contingencies of value. The value systems of other, less powerful or authoritative subjects are then characterized as "pathological."[36]

The cultural power invested in a canon allows it to perpetuate the dictums of the ideology it represents. Annette Kolodny points out that canonization projects and protects the construction of the canon:

> The fact of canonization puts any work beyond questions of establishing its merit and, instead, invites students to offer only increasingly more ingenious readings and interpretations, the purpose of which is to validate the greatness already imputed by canonization.[37]

How, then, is a woman's novel or play to be compared to this self-perpetuating list of male novels and plays, which expands its ranks only for those works that already resemble its historical members?

'night, Mother does bear a distinct resemblance to *Death of a Salesman,* Miller's classic American domestic drama, which won the Pulitzer in 1949. In some ways, both Jessie Cates and Willy Loman have been denied the promises of the mythic American Dream and both resort to suicide as a final effort to shape their lives. Willy Loman, however, is a father, and his death leaves at least a financial legacy to his wife and sons. Jessie's death leaves no similar legacy to her mother and in effect wipes out even the heritage of regeneration Thelma might have left at her own death.

Death of a Salesman was revived on Broadway almost exactly a year after *'night, Mother* opened. From a body image perspective, it is interesting to note how critics responded to the physical appearance of the male performers in the virtuosic Willy Loman role. Lee J. Cobb set the standard in the original 1949 performance. Cobb was a big man, but reviewers do not refer to him as overweight or unattractive. Instead, they recall his massive size as a mark of authority.

Douglas Watts remembered Cobb's Willy as a "large, lumbering victim." Comparing Dustin Hoffman to Cobb in the 1984 revival, Frank Rich noted, "Mr. Hoffman's Willy is a total break with the mountainous Lee J. Cobb image. He's a trim, immaculately outfitted go-getter in a three-piece suit." Edwin Wilson, in the *Wall Street Journal,* wrote,

> Most Willy's . . . have been large in stature. . . . Seeing a smaller man like Mr. Hoffman in the part, one realizes the values that come from size. Willy's wife and young sons look up to him, and this is easier to understand in a larger man. . . .[38]

Since Hoffman could not gain authority from his size, the conception of the character was changed to accommodate the actor, and Loman garnered his authority elsewhere. In Miller's play, the actor and the character are not locked into a transcendent, absolute correlation. Writer John Beaufort noted that "Mr. Miller reportedly has restored the word 'shrimp' and certain other allusions that designated Willy's stature. The changed emphasis creates an unmistakably new perspective."[39] In the *Salesman* revival, the character was collapsed into the appearance of the male star. In *'night, Mother,* the performer's appearance was collapsed into the reception of the character. Since the culture is not as prescriptive about how men should look in certain social or performance roles, Willy Loman cannot be considered a failure because he is short or heavyset. The man matters more than the body. This is the opposite of the reception to Kathy Bates in the role of Jessie.

For *'night, Mother* to be a tragedy according to the dominant culture's criteria, Jessie should have been played by a performer with the body size and appearance of Farrah Fawcett. The death by choice of an unsuccessful, homely, overweight woman is considered melodrama because its implications do not resonate enough to be considered tragedy by the generic male spectator.

The analogy to *Death of a Salesman* is also apt in terms of *'night, Mother*'s genre categorization. Paul Lauter, writing on the evolution of literary standards, notes that canons were originally formed to keep high art separate from the popular culture of the lower classes. Lauter says, "The literary canon is, in short, a means by which culture validates social power."[40] Like canons, genre categories are also expedient ways of ranking drama or literature according to what is actually a social hierarchy.

Arthur Miller's plays are generally classified as domestic drama, in that they deal with family issues in which father/son relationships are privileged. *'night, Mother* can also be categorized as domestic drama, but the classification assumes different connotations when the writer is a woman and the mother/daughter conflict is foregrounded. Reviewers' responses walked a fine line between wanting to applaud *'night, Mother* for its "moral inquiry" and trivializing its "domestic cliché."[41] In the change from male writer to female and father/son focus to mother/daugher, domestic drama is reduced to kitchen drama, which is considered specific rather than universal, and melodramatic rather than tragic.

Domesticity and family assume different meanings when received in the context of plays by women. While Miller can write about the family and be canonized, Norman's attempt to tackle similar issues is seen as evidence of the preoccupations of her gender class. Howard Kissel, for example, dismissed the play by comparing it to other "shockers" like *Sorry, Wrong Number.*[42] *Sorry, Wrong Number* is about a bedridden woman who overhears her own murder being plotted and tries to get someone to believe her story before the murder finally takes place. The comparison is somewhat revealing, since it indicates that Kissel categorized the play in a genre known for female hysteria and paranoia. Another reviewer deprecated *'night, Mother* as a "suspense melodrama."[43]

David Richards called *'night, Mother* "resolutely domestic" and compared it to *K2,* Patrick Meyers' two-(male)-character play in which a pair of climbers are trapped on a mountainside.[44] Meyers uses a situation of entrapment to allow his characters wide-ranging philosophical speculation. Norman's characters are trapped in the quotidian detail of home and hearth. Jessie and Thelma's preoccupations are philosophical and existential, but because their debate rages in the context of a home and because they are women, their reception is qualitatively different.

Defined as the ability to speak to the generic spectator, universality is the criterion critics applied when deciding whether *'night, Mother* deserved a place in the canon's legions. As Staiger notes,

> Claims for universality are disguises for achieving uniformity, for suppressing through the power of canonic discourse optional value systems.

Such a cultural "consensus" fears an asserted "barbarism" and a collapse into the grotesque and monstrous, because it recognizes the potential loss of its hegemony. It is a politics of power.[45]

Under the rubric of universality, critics determined whether or not *'night, Mother* had the potential to subvert the cultural hegemony of the male canon. If the play could be perceived as universal by the generic male spectator, the threat of what was seen as its particularized female perspective could be neutralized. Some critics decided that *'night, Mother* failed this test, while others argued either that it passed or that the play did not attempt universality.

Variety, the industry barometer of economic success, called *'night, Mother* a "non–box office subject" that

> lacks universal application. . . . There's pity but no terror, no purgative release for the audience. The heroine's action, as the author no doubt intended, remains a private, isolated instance of human failure. The audience isn't a partner.[46]

Norman's play fails to be universal because it does not quite meet the criteria of Aristotle's *Poetics,* and does not address or relieve the fears of the spectators to whom *Variety* would have it speak. The *Daily News* reviewer wrote that

> the troubling aspect of the play is that Jessie is not a truly tragic figure. Her self containment as she busily sets things in order about the house suggests one dedicated to her awful purpose, true, but also suggests a congenitally deranged woman.[47]

By suggesting Jessie's problems are hereditary and therefore individual, Watts denied the play's universal appeal. The *Newsday* reviewer approved of what he perceived as Norman's limits in *'night, Mother*: "There is no awkward stretch for imagery or universality . . . [the play] doesn't develop to reveal a deeper truth."[48] Ironically, considering Norman's stated intent, this critic applauds her for avoiding universality.

Robert Brustein, however, Norman's initial champion, insisted that *'night, Mother* did pass the universality test. He returned to Aristotle to justify his belief in the play, writing that *'night, Mother* is "*chastely* classical [emphasis mine] in its observance of the unities," particularly time, which is measured synchronously onstage and in the audience. Brustein said this helps explain the enduring strength and validity of the *Poetics.* . . . Nothing reinforces one's faith in the power and importance of the theatre more than the emergence of an authentic, universal playwright—not a woman playwright, mind you, not a regional playwright, not an ethnic playwright, but one who speaks to the concerns and experiences of all humankind.[49]

Clearly, Brustein perceives Norman as an authentic, universal playwright.

Women Playwrights and the Feminist Canon

Brustein attempted to obscure Norman's gender under an Aristotelian mantle of respectability. Other writers refused to accept her as generic and made her gender an issue. Some way had to be found to contextualize the playwright that would avoid threatening the male dramatic bastion. Critic Robert Asahina, who disliked the play and wondered at the Pulitzer award, wrote, "I suppose the logic was to honor the playwright, not the play."[50]

This emphasis on the person over the play appears in feminist criticism as well as in mainstream contexts. In the politically disparate feminist press, two documents regarding *'night, Mother* and Marsha Norman are pertinent: an interview with Norman in *Ms.* magazine and two opposing reviews in *Women & Performance Journal.*

Trudy Scott's positive review of *'night, Mother,* quoted earlier, ran directly before my own negative review in the same issue. My review is, in a sense, a response to the mainstream press reception to Norman's play, and stands as a critique of the context into which it tried to insert Norman and her work. I saw the play as co-opted into a scheme of male dramatic and ideological values, and noted that women are getting the Pulitzer Prize for plays that

> depict women killing themselves or living totally immobilized in their backwoods, suburban homes. . . . It's ironic; or is it? When so-called feminist plays like *'night, Mother* and *Crimes of the Heart* are cheerfully honored by the . . . coveted prize, there's a not-so-subtle message underlying the Pulitzer awards. It's a form of anti-feminist backlash.[51]

My response was colored by a mistrust of the institutional approval Norman's play received. The review went on to question whether the play is at all feminist:

The premise alone defies feminist categorizing: If feminist plays are defined as those that show women in the painful, difficult process of becoming full human beings, how can a play in which suicide is assumed from the first moments be a thorough consideration of women?[52]

I privileged the daughter's dilemma, with which I felt it was impossible to empathize, and saw the mother as a one-note character with objectives that are exercises in futility. In a surge of cultural feminism, I failed to find a universal application for the play, although my implied spectators were women. By shifting the axis of categorization for universality to women, my review implied that Norman's play does indeed fit the requirements of the male canon and does not belong in a canon of any kind of feminist plays.

I now think that *'night, Mother* is typical of liberal and cultural feminist drama that is, as Case remarks, "animated by the absent male."[53] All the intimacies shared by Jessie and Thelma somehow relate to the father, son, and brother, whose impact on the narrative is integral to every revelation and action the two women undertake. Like most traditional American dramas, *'night, Mother*'s focus on individual suffering and the play's unwillingness to discuss Jessie's dilemma in terms of a wider social context make it weak as a political statement and inadequate from a materialist feminist perspective.

The lack of further feminist press response available on *'night, Mother* is partly because Broadway prices generally keep these productions inaccessible to those outside a comfortable income bracket and therefore might not be of interest to many feminist press readers. (The play opened at ticket prices of $27.50 top on weeknights, and $29 on weekends.)

In addition, the feminist press has been slow to develop a feminist critique of performance. When they do cover theatre by women, feminist reviewers seem caught between applauding the woman's efforts and critiquing the work against a standard that is yet to be defined in the balance between ideology and art. Since the feminist canon is nascent at best, particularly in theatre, the feminist press tends to shy from the work and to concentrate instead on the woman. *Ms.* magazine's feature on Norman is a good example.

Ms. magazine's editorial viewpoint generally subscribes to liberal feminist ideology in that it frequently features women who are successful by the dominant culture's standards. When it strays from its liberal feminist stance, the magazine leans toward a cultural feminist critique, highlighting women's essentially female attributes. Both tendencies are apparent in the Norman interview.

The *Ms.* profile "Playwright Marsha Norman: An Optimist Writes About

Suicide, Confinement, and Despair" stresses Norman's feminine abilities. She is a good listener ("I listen better than any other thing") and she has an intuitive knack for "speaking the generally unspoken."[54] The interviewer is careful to keep Norman accessible to the readership; she is compared to literary women like Tillie Olsen and Toni Morrison, who are credited with "giving voice to those who generally go unheard."[55]

The interview clarifies that although Norman sees herself as a role model for young women, she is careful to distance herself from feminism as a movement ("I don't join or show up at meetings").[56] Yet Norman clearly knows that because her story about a mother and daughter has garnered a great deal of attention on Broadway, it is a victory for herself and for other women. She admits, "The theatre says, Who lives today? Whose stories matter?"[57] The interview foregrounds mother/daughter relationships. Norman speaks at length about the daughter's need for autonomy from the mother and stresses that their relationship is material for drama as much as the more familiar father/son relationship.

The *Ms.* feature, however, generally places Norman outside the theatre context. She is inscribed as a woman first and as a playwright only secondarily. Even the graphic layout of the article helps support the writer's contextualization of Norman, and would undoubtedly influence the reader's reception. The photograph of Norman that runs on the first page of the feature is dark and arty. Her face is placed against a black background, outside of any specific locale or setting.[58] The feature includes no mention of either women's theatre or other women playwrights. It ends as a picture of a woman capitalizing on her ability to listen, to relate to others, and to translate women's unique experience.

This position is the basis of cultural feminism, in that it valorizes, rather than deconstructs, sexual difference. Mel Gussow picks up on these cultural feminist ideals and persistently ties Norman to the context of her domestic environment in his *New York Times Sunday Magazine* cover story. In contrast to the *Ms.* article, however, he also scrutinizes Norman's position in theatre in relation to the male-dominated canon of good drama. Gussow places her at the "crest of a wave of adventurous young women playwrights — a proliferation that is the most encouraging and auspicious aspect of the current American theatre."[59]

Again, the supporting graphic material that surrounds Gussow's text offers clues to his perspective. Norman is featured on the cover of the magazine section. The photo is a full body shot, in which Norman, with her arms folded across her chest, stands to the right of a few rows of empty theatre seats in what is obviously a plush Broadway house. Norman looks serious and businesslike; she is not smiling.

On the first page of Gussow's story, a photo of Norman is placed above the headline, "Women Playwrights: New Voices in the Theatre." The photo displays Norman in her work environment. Her word processor is to the left with a cup of coffee beside it, and a telephone is obvious in the background. In the foreground of the photo, below the word processor, is Norman's knitting. She faces front, unsmiling, with her hands resting on the table top positioned like hands in dishwashing advertisements. Her fingers are long and feminine, and her wedding ring is on her left hand.

The remainder of the article is illustrated with photos that generalize this contextualization to the other women mentioned. The playwrights are pictured either alone, out of any context, or in empty theatre auditoriums. Production photographs are relegated to domestic space—Pitoniak and Bates in the kitchen, the cast of *Crimes of the Heart* in the kitchen celebrating a birthday, and the three characters of Tina Howe's *Painting Churches* in the family home. Although many of the women Gussow proceeds to mention have written nondomestic plays, the kitchen and hearth are what the *Times* chooses to highlight.

While it is obvious that Gussow would like to elevate Norman's play into the canon of good American drama, he is frustrated by the problem of her gender, which he foregrounds throughout the article. Unintentionally or not, Gussow undermines Norman's stature by insistently highlighting her feminine domesticity:

> Shortly before *'night, Mother* opened on Broadway, after spending a long evening making script revisions with her director, Tom Moore, she returned to her Manhattan apartment and typed the changes into her computer. It was 2:30 in the morning by the time she was satisfied with the result, and as the printer clattered out a clean copy of the play, Miss Norman sat back and took up her knitting, adding inches to her new red sweater. The juxtaposition of the technological and the homespun is a quintessential picture of this artist at work.[60]

Although Norman has become successful in what Gussow defines as a man's world, she has not lost her femininity; she still knits, and her values remain homespun. Technology is her tool, but her knitting needles, clattering along with the printer, are equally representative of her new voice.

Gussow feels *'night, Mother* is qualified for inscription into the male canon, since "the audience has shared a catharsis of grief and pain" and the play is as "tough-minded as it is sensitive."[61] Norman qualifies for male privilege, but she continues to be feminine—sensitive and emotional. Norman and her sisterhood of young women playwrights are marked by their difference from men when aspiring to the same dramatic ends.

Gussow quotes Jon Jory, producing director at the Actors Theatre of Louisville—where Norman's work first caught public attention—who says, "The characters in [women's] plays very often seem more emotionally affecting to the audience than characters men have been writing about . . . women are creating characters you can love."[62] Gussow's portrayal of Norman continues along this theme.

Unlike the *Ms.* article, which foregrounded Norman's intuitive female abilities, Gussow links her to female places and spheres, emphasizing her home life with her husband and family. He describes her as an upper-middle-class, cultured intellectual:

> She and her husband, Dann Byck Jr., often play Schubert in their living room in private piano-clarinet duets. . . . Sitting at her dining room table surrounded by the objects of her life . . . a conversation with her roams freely from Kierkegaard to Aristotle, from Flaubert to Doris Lessing.[63]

The roaming conversation, however, is always personal: "She speaks about her fears."

Not surprisingly, Norman's appearance is much more important to Gussow's feature than to the *Ms.* interview. He writes that her "dark view of life comes not from a Samuel Beckett, but from an affable, determined, and *petite* [emphasis mine] young woman who looks more like a graduate student than a serious playwright wrestling with profound emotions."[64] Space can be made for her in the male canon of mountainous men, since she will never be tall enough to tower over the old figures. Norman herself admits, "I am convinced that the fact that I am five foot four is a real factor in the way I see the world. . . . Eighty percent of the people on the planet are taller than I am. . . . I am wandering around in this land of giants."[65]

The size analogy is clear throughout Gussow's article. The women he discusses in addition to Norman are described as a small but growing minority, climbing up the beanstalk of traditional American drama. Lumping them together solely by gender, he likens playwrights who are essentially dissimilar when analyzed according to ideological concerns and theatrical style. Norman is rendered the prototype of his group profile, and Broadway theatre and Pulitzer prizes are the standard-bearers to which he assumes all women playwrights aspire.

By failing to acknowledge that some women playwrights do write from a more polemical, feminist ideological stance than Marsha Norman, and that some write to challenge the form and content of the dramatic canon, Gussow neatly sidesteps any reference to the history of feminist theatre or to the issue of a two-gender audience. Norman aids and abets him by remarking, "Now we can write plays and not have people put them in a little box labelled 'women's theatre.'"[66]

Feminist theatre women were invited to respond to Gussow's interpretation of the gender issue in a special section of *Performing Arts Journal (PAJ)*. The women writing in *PAJ* unanimously reproached Gussow for inserting Norman and others like her at the head of what he described as a homogeneous, new phenomenon. Collette Brooks, former associate artistic director of Interart Theatre, noted that the writers Gussow featured "all share certain socio-economic affinities . . . through pieces such as his, the *Times* sustains reputations it largely served to create in the first place."[67] In its position of power to mold spectator response and delineate a horizon of expectations for theatre-goers, the *Times* creates stars of its own choosing, who serve the paper's—and its readers'—ideological interests. Brooks went on to say:

> By canonizing these works, effectively suppressing alternative visions, we are at once crippling an art form and leaving our psychic landscape strewn with testaments to the extraordinary limitations that this culture has placed upon human possibility.[68]

In his rush to add a woman to the male list of good American drama, Gussow missed the possibility of a shift in the gender of the spectator that will fundamentally disrupt the construction of the canon. Norman's play can be considered for canonical membership because Norman is still writing for male spectators under the guise of universality. Staiger writes,

> If a [play] is claimed to be universal, what the proponents of such a possibility are implying is that such a [play] speaks in the same way to everyone. Not only does this claim wipe out historical, cultural, and social difference, but it denies sexual difference, treating all individuals as uniformly constituted.[69]

By conferring the mantle of universality on Marsha Norman, and giving her the microphone as the new voice of American theatre, Gussow denied the sexual difference of both playwrights and spectators. Director Roberta Sklar wrote in the *PAJ* response, "Historically, the audience has been called upon to receive the theatre within the generic category of Man. Now we are called upon to receive it within the term Woman, as the gender sensibility of the audience is being re-defined."[70]

Sklar's cultural feminist assertion is debatable, in that a new, feminist canon constructed for female spectators presents the same danger of universalizing for exclusionary subject positions as the generic category of "Man" has done throughout theatre history. Fitting a woman's play into any canon—male or female—implies that it is acquiescent to the ideology perpetuated by that canon. Canons, by implication, exclude not only worthy plays but worthy spectators on the basis of their ideological perspectives. In feminist critical analysis, the gender of the spectator is being reconsidered and reassigned, but the reinstallation of another monolithic subject position from which to view performance should be avoided. A useful byproduct of the deconstruction of traditional canons will be the dismembering of the generic spectator whom the dramatic canons once addressed.

Wresting authority away from the powerful, controlling voices in cultural discourse is an ongoing project in feminist criticism. Christine Froula succinctly summarizes the feminist critique of canon-formation:

> We can, through strategies of rereading that expose the deeper structures of authority, and through interplay with texts of a different stamp, pursue a kind of collective psychoanalysis, transforming "bogeys" that hide invisible power into investments both visible and alterable. In doing so, we approach traditional texts not as the mystifying (and self-limiting) "best" that has been thought and said in the world, but as a *visible* past against which we can . . . imagine a different future.[71]

Studying texts like Marsha Norman's *'night, Mother* against the context of traditional texts forces an awareness of the ideological nature of cultural discourse. As women playwrights continue to assert their voices in the traditional male forum, gender will remain an issue with which to reckon.

NOTES

1. The "horizon of expectations" is a term borrowed from reception theory. See Robert Holub, *Reception Theory: A Critical Introduction* (New York: Methuen, 1984), particularly 42–44.

2. See Robert von Hallberg, ed., *Canons* (Chicago: University of Chicago Press, 1984); Annette Kolodny, "Dancing Through the Minefield: Some Observations on the Theory, Practice and Politics of a Feminist Literary Criticism," *Feminist Studies*

6, no. 1 (Spring 1980); and Paul Lauter, "Race and Gender in the Shaping of the American Literary Canon: A Case Study from the Twenties," in *Feminist Criticism and Social Change,* ed. Judith Newton and Deborah Rosenfelt (London, New York: Methuen, 1985) for current discussions of the politics of canon formation.

3. See Kolodny for a thorough discussion of female significations in literature and their implications for gender-based interpretation.

4. Sue-Ellen Case, "Reviewing Hrotsvit," *Theatre Journal* 35, no. 4 (December 1983): 534.

5. Ibid.

6. Janet Staiger, "The Politics of Film Canons," *Cinema Journal* 24, no. 3 (Spring 1985): 2.

7. Kolodny, 19.

8. ART promotional piece, housed at the Lincoln Center Library for the Performing Arts, Billy Rose Theatre Collection.

9. Promotional piece for the Broadway production, housed at the Lincoln Center Library for the Performing Arts, Billy Rose Theatre Collection.

10. This was also the year Alice Walker won the Pulitzer for her novel *The Color Purple,* which made it seem as though feminists were finally carrying off mainstream prizes. But in retrospect, it is clear that Norman's play did not threaten the dominant culture, and that Walker's book struck some sort of nerve that three years later was translated into Steven Spielberg's racist, sexist, comic, and certainly not radical film version.

11. *Variety,* April 22, 1983, 2.

12. Elizabeth Wray, in Gayle Austin, ed., "The Woman Playwright Issue," *Performing Arts Journal* 21, 7, no. 3 (1983): 92.

13. Kathleen Betsko and Rachel Koenig, eds., *Interviews with Contemporary Women Playwrights* (New York: Beech Tree Books, 1987), 324.

14. Marsha Norman, *'night, Mother,* Acting Edition (New York: Dramatists Plays Service, Inc., 1983), 4. All other references appear in the text.

15. See Mel Gussow, "Women Playwrights: New Voices in the Theater," *New York Times Sunday Magazine,* May 1, 1983, 22.

16. Beth Henley, *Crimes of the Heart* (New York: Penguin Books, 1982), 120.

17. Susan Lieberman, "'night, Mother," *Theatre Crafts* 19, no. 5 (May 1985): 22, 46.

18. Humm., *Variety,* April 6, 1983, 82.

19. Howard Kissel, *Women's Wear Daily,* April 1, 1983, 15; John Beaufort, *Christian Science Monitor,* April 22, 1983, 11.

20. Frank Rich, *New York Times,* July 28, 1983.

21. Ibid. When the production moved to the smaller off-Broadway house, another reviewer mentioned that it "allows for more of a sense of audience voyeurism than the wider Broadway stage" (Jack Gilhooley, *Stage,* June 1984, 29). *'night, Mother* falls squarely in the tradition of fourth-wall realism.

22. Jack Gilhooley, *Stage,* June 1984, 29; Humm., *Variety;* David Richards, *Washington Post,* May 15, 1983; Douglas Watts, *New York Daily News,* April 1, 1983, 3.

23. Robert Asahina, *Hudson Review* 37, no. 1 (Spring 1984): 101.

24. Robert Brustein, *New Republic,* May 2, 1983.

25. Trudy Scott, *Women & Performance Journal* 1, no. 1 (1983): 78.

26. Ibid. As a former editor of *Women & Performance Journal,* I have information about the reviewing context that would not be available to the average reader. Trudy Scott is a white woman in her early fifties who was married and has children and grandchildren. These facts are only relevant to the extent that not many professional theatre critics share Scott's social background, which made her perspective unique. The point, of course, is that not all readers and spectators share the prominent reviewers' white, middle-class, heterosexual male background either, but because their perspectives are widely accessible and bear the power of print, they are cloaked in the universal guise.

27. Richard Gilman, *Nation,* May 7, 1983, 586.

28. John Simon, *New York,* April 11, 1983, 56–57; Walter Kerr, *New York Times,* March 10, 1983; Kissel, *Women's Wear Daily;* Brendan Gill, *New Yorker,* April 11, 1983, 10; Sy Syna, *News World,* April 1, 1983; Gilman, *Nation;* Asahina, *Hudson Review.*

29. Elizabeth Stone, "Playwright Marsha Norman," *Ms.,* July 1983, 56.

30. Lynda Hart, "Doing Time: Hunger for Power in Marsha Norman's Plays," *Southern Quarterly* 25, no. 3 (Spring 1987): 76.

31. See Kate Davy, "Buying and Selling a Look," *Parachute* (Spring 1986) for a relevant discussion of performers' influence on women's body size and the influence of performers' body size on spectator response.

By way of comparison, although Jessie was condemned for her weight, the epilepsy factor got a much more positive press response. Although in Norman's script, Jessie blames her epilepsy for her failure to secure or hold a job, Bruce Chadwick reported in the *Daily News* (February 14, 1984, 49) that organized groups of doctors were going to see *'night, Mother* for insight on how to treat their epileptic patients.

32. See E. Ann Kaplan, "Theories of Melodrama: A Feminist Perspective," *Women & Performance Journal* 1, no. 1 (1983) for a discussion of melodrama and female film spectatorship that has implications for the gender-biases of genre categories.

33. Collette Brooks, "The Woman Playwright Issue," 89.

34. Christine Froula, "When Eve Reads Milton: Undoing the Canonical Economy," in *Canons,* 164.

35. Barbara Herrnstein Smith, "Contingencies of Value," in *Canons,* 15.

36. She writes that canon validation "commonly takes the form of privileging absolutely—that is 'standard'-izing—the particular contingencies that govern the preferences of the members of the group and discounting or . . . pathologizing all other contingencies" (22).

37. Kolodny, 8.

38. Frank Rich, *New York Times,* March 30, 1984; Edwin Wilson, *Wall Street Journal,* April 4, 1984; Douglas Watts, *New York Daily News,* March 30, 1984.

39. John Beaufort, *Christian Science Monitor,* March 30, 1984.

40. Lauter, 18.

41. Gilman, *Nation.*

42. Kissel, *Women's Wear Daily.*

43. Syna, *News World.*

44. Richards, *Washington Post.*

45. Staiger, 10.

46. Humm., *Variety.*

47. Watts, *New York Daily News,* April 1, 1983.

48. Alan Wallach, *Newsday,* April 1, 1983.

49. Brustein, *New Republic.*

50. Asahina, *Hudson Review.*

51. Jill Dolan, "*'night, Mother,*" *Women & Performance Journal* 1, no. 1 (1983): 79.

52. Ibid.

53. Sue-Ellen Case, "The Personal Is Not the Political," *Art and Cinema* 1, no. 3 (Fall 1987): 4.

54. Stone, 56.

55. Stone, 57.

56. Stone, 58.

57. Ibid.

58. Erving Goffman, in *Gender Advertisements* (New York: Harper and Row, 1976), analyzes the content of advertising displays to study how women are imaged. He finds that while women are frequently displayed out of context, against blank backgrounds, men are always placed in contexts and are usually active within them.

59. Gussow, *New York Times Sunday Magazine,* 22.

60. Gussow, 31.

61. Gussow, 22.

62. Gussow, 30.

63. Gussow, 31. Norman and Byck are now divorced.

64. Gussow, 22.

65. Gussow, 40.

66. Ibid.

67. Brooks, 88.

68. Brooks, 90.

69. Staiger, 16.

70. Roberta Sklar, "The Woman Playwright Issue," 101.

71. Froula, 171, her emphasis.

Contributors

STEPHANIE ARNOLD is associate professor of theatre at Lewis and Clark College in Portland, Oregon, where she teaches performance and dramatic literature. Her writing focuses on West Coast women working in feminist and ethnic theatre.

GAYLE AUSTIN is director of the Southeast Playwrights Project (formerly the Atlanta New Play Project) and literary manager of the Horizon Theatre Company. She was previously coordinator and literary manager for The Women's Project in New York City and has taught at both Hunter College and the University of South Carolina-Spartanburg.

NANCY BACKES has taught English at the University of Wisconsin-Milwaukee, where she is in the process of completing her Ph.D. Backes has published fiction, as well as articles on the American theatre, and the early careers of American modernists, and currently works in grants administration at the University of Wisconsin-Parkside, where she also writes and edits the faculty publication.

JAN BRESLAUER is a lecturer in communication at the University of California, San Diego, where she is currently supervising the Feminist Theatre Workshop. She is currently completing her doctoral dissertation on "Drama of Testimony" while writing film and theatre criticism for *Theatre* and numerous West Coast publications.

SUSAN CARLSON is an associate professor of English at Iowa State University, where she teaches drama. She has published a book on Henry James's plays and articles on Caryl Churchill, Trevor Griffiths, British women's theatre groups, *As You Like It,* and Doris Lessing.

SUE-ELLEN CASE is associate professor in the School of Drama at the University of Washington. She is the author of *Feminism and Theatre* in addition to numerous articles and is editor of *Theatre Journal.*

ROSEMARY CURB is associate professor of English at Rollins College, Winter Park, Florida. She has published a number of articles on Afro-American and Feminist Drama and is co-editor, with Nancy Manahan, of *Lesbian Nuns: Breaking Silence.*

MARY K. DESHAZER is associate professor of women's studies and English and coordinator of the Women's Studies Program at Wake Forest University. She is the author of *Inspiring Women: Reimagining the Muse,* as well as essays on modern women's poetry, sexism and language, and feminist pedagogy.

ELIN DIAMOND teaches in the English Department at Rutgers University. The author of *Pinter's Comic Play*, she has a book in press on feminist and dramatic theory, focusing on women playwrights.

JILL DOLAN is an assistant professor in the Department of Theatre and Drama at the University of Wisconsin, Madison. She is the author of *The Feminist Spectator as Critic*. She is co-editor, with Brooks McNamara, of *The Drama Review: 30 Years of Writing on the Avant-Garde*. Dolan has published feminist performance criticism and theory in *Theatre Journal, Drama Review, Journal of Popular Culture*, and *Art & Cinema*, among other publications.

YOLANDA BROYLES GONZÁLEZ is associate professor of German studies and of Chicano studies at the University of California at Santa Barbara. Her cross-cultural work includes *The German Response to Latin American Literature*. Her current research interests are oral tradition and popular culture, as well as Turkish women in the Federal Republic of Germany.

JONNIE GUERRA is associate professor of English at Mount Vernon College. She is the author of articles on Emily Dickinson and serves on the board of directors of the Emily Dickinson Society.

LYNDA HART is assistant professor of English at the University of Pennsylvania. Her teaching and research interests are modern/contemporary drama and feminism and theatre. She is the author of *Sam Shepard's Metaphorical Stages*, as well as a number of articles on contemporary drama.

ANITA PLATH HELLE is assistant professor of English and Women's Studies at Iowa State University. Her published essays concern the problem of language and identity in autobiographical representations by twentieth-century women writers.

HELENE KEYSSAR is professor of communication at the University of California, San Diego. She is the author of *Feminist Theatre, The Curtain and the Veil: Strategies in Black Drama, New Roots for the Nation: The Films of Robert Altman*, and co-author of *Right in Her Soul: The Life of Anna Louise Strong* and *Remembering War: A U.S.-Soviet Dialogue*. Keyssar has directed numerous works for theatre and, since 1983, has been producing interactive television programs with the Soviet Union.

VIVIAN M. PATRAKA is associate professor of English at Bowling Green State University, where she teaches drama and women's studies. She is co-editor of *Feminist Re-Visions: What Has Been and What Might Be* and co-author of *Sam Shepard*. Patraka is a contributing editor to *Women and Performance: A Journal of Feminist Theory*, and president of the Women and Theatre Program of ATHE.

JANELLE REINELT is professor of theatre arts at California State University, Sacramento, and the book review editor for *Theatre Journal*. Her work has appeared in *Modern Drama, Yale/Theatre, Women and Performance, West Coast Plays, Theatre Journal,* and the *Brecht Yearbook.*

JENNY S. SPENCER teaches at the University of Massachusetts at Amherst. She has published articles on the work of contemporary British playwright Edward Bond and on Marsha Norman. Her current research is on British socialist theatre.

MARGARET B. WILKERSON is professor of theatre and chair of the Department of Afro-American Studies at the University of California at Berkeley. She is a member of the Executive Council of the American Society for Theatre Research and editor of *9 Plays by Black Women.*